Ethical Economy

Studies in Economic Ethics and Philosophy

Volume 73

Ethical Economy describes the theory of the ethical preconditions of the economy and of business as well as the theory of the ethical foundations of economic systems. It analyzes the impact of rules, virtues, and goods or values on economic action and management. *Ethical Economy* understands ethics as a means to increase trust and to reduce transaction costs. It forms a foundational theory for business ethics and business culture. The Series *Ethical Economy. Studies in Economic Ethics and Philosophy* is devoted to the investigation of interdisciplinary issues concerning economics, management, ethics, and philosophy. These issues fall in the categories of economic ethics, business ethics, management theory, economic culture, and economic philosophy, the latter including the epistemology and ontology of economics. Economic culture comprises cultural and hermeneutic studies of the economy. One goal of the series is to extend the discussion of the philosophical, ethical, and cultural foundations of economics and economic systems. The series is intended to serve as an international forum for scholarly publications, such as monographs, conference proceedings, and collections of essays. Primary emphasis is placed on originality, clarity, and interdisciplinary synthesis of elements from economics, management theory, ethics, and philosophy.

The book series has been accepted into SCOPUS (March 2019) and will be visible on the Scopus website within a few months.

Aziza Karbekova
Editor

Ethics of the AI Economy: A System View from the Positions of the Theory of Stakeholders

Springer

Editor
Aziza Karbekova
Department of Economics, Accounting and Finance
Jalal-Abad State University named after B. Osmonov
Manas, Kyrgyzstan

ISSN 2211-2707 ISSN 2211-2723 (electronic)
Ethical Economy
ISBN 978-3-032-23422-3 ISBN 978-3-032-23423-0 (eBook)
https://doi.org/10.1007/978-3-032-23423-0

This Springer imprint is published by the registered company Springer Nature Switzerland AG
The registered company address is: Gewerbestrasse 11, 6330 Cham, Switzerland

Introduction

Ethical Approach to Developing the AI Economy for the Systemic Consideration of Stakeholder Interests

The AI economy represents a new model of economic activity, built on advanced automation technologies and characterized by widespread use of smart communications—both human–machine (e.g., neural networks, chatbots, voice assistants), machine-to-machine (i.e., based on the Internet of Things), and AI-mediated human communication (e.g., voice-to-text input, automatic translation, and automated text proofreading for errors and typos).

The undeniable and significant advantages of the AI economy include unprecedented acceleration of communication, substantial reduction of transaction costs, revolutionary increases in labor productivity, and enhanced transparency, accountability, predictability, and manageability of economic processes. Simultaneously, all stakeholders (households and B2C users of digital technologies, B2B consumers, AI developers, B2G users and government regulators, and various partners, investors, and civil society organizations) face specific challenges and pursue their own interests within the AI economy.

The core issue lies in the fact that current approaches to AI economic development pay insufficient attention to the ethical dimensions of smart automation, leaving stakeholder concerns especially acute, insufficiently addressed, and unresolved. Although some efforts have been made in academic literature to discuss the ethical aspects of the AI economy, these attempts remain fragmented, and the accumulated knowledge in the field is scattered and unsystematized. As a result, there is lingering uncertainty about the exact nature of the ethical challenges posed by the AI economy and how they can be comprehensively mitigated.

This book aims to fill that gap by systematizing the ethical dimensions of the AI economy, thereby presenting an integrated ethical framework for AI-driven economic activity that thoroughly accounts for stakeholder interests. The content unfolds across four sections, each offering a distinct perspective on the ethics of the AI economy.

The first part focuses on cyber threats arising from the use of neural networks, presenting them as ethical challenges within the AI economy. It explores issues of ethical innovation governance and improving quality of life in the context of AI. A dedicated chapter develops an ethical model for organizing smart city systems that balances the interests of all stakeholders. This part is especially valuable for the book's topic because it addresses cyber fraud, cyber extremism, and cybercrime as threats to the AI economy's security and proposes forward-looking solutions to these issues.

The second part addresses the ethical aspects of social adaptation and human communication in the AI economy to support its sustainable development. It formulates methodological principles for analyzing public opinion in the information society, explains the transformation of human identity under the influence of AI, and explores innovations in intercultural communication in the context of widespread smart technologies. This part contributes to the book's topic by systematically analyzing the social consequences of AI economic development and outlining a path for their comprehensive optimization in support of social adaptation and humanization of the AI economy.

The third part examines the ethics of machine learning in the AI economy through the lens of stakeholder theory. Its chapters delve into the challenges and contradictions of integrating AI systems into education and explore the dialectic between artificial and natural intelligence within the framework of digital civilization. This part is essential for the book's development of its core topic because it defines the limits of AI technologies and explores scientific, methodological, and practical strategies to expand those limits through flexible, high-performance machine learning systems with user-friendly interfaces.

The concluding fourth part outlines the ethical boundaries of smart automation in the state regulation of the AI economy. This part includes chapters that explain the role of AI in the development and implementation of public socio-economic policy, present AI technologies as a catalyst for sustainable economic development, explore the relationship between the growth of the AI economy and the state of the environment, and raise the issue of making AI more environmentally responsible.

What makes this part particularly notable is its in-depth examination of how the efficiency of government institutions can be enhanced through the smart automation of e-government systems in the context of the AI economy. The importance of this part to the book's topic lies in its presentation of a scientific vision for the balanced development of the AI economy—one that simultaneously strengthens technological leadership and supports social stability.

At the heart of the book's scientific innovation is the development of a new ethical approach to the advancement of the AI economy, the key advantage of which lies in its systemic consideration of stakeholder interests achieved for the first time. The originality of this new approach is that it considers and addresses a wide range of socio-economic contradictions and conflicts that arise and intensify with the development of the AI economy. This is accomplished through the identification of the ethical root causes of such contradictions and conflicts. The deeper perspective on the AI economy offered by this approach enables a clearer understanding of the logic and patterns governing its development.

This book stands out in the existing body of scientific literature because it simultaneously addresses both cyber threats and the ethics of the artificial intelligence economy. The boundary between these two domains lies along the perimeter of the legal framework governing cyber-social systems within the AI economy. Cyber threats constitute offenses subject to legal liability. Although the fight against such threats varies from country to country, there exists a global practice of ensuring cybersecurity.

On the other hand, the ethics of the AI economy belongs to the realm of soft law: its violations do not entail legal consequences for business entities but trigger market-based responses. These responses manifest as declining stakeholder loyalty, reduced investment appeal, falling sales and profits, loss of market position, brain drain, increased difficulty in attracting financial resources, and eventual financial shortages. They may also lead to the displacement of entrepreneurial structures from advantageous supply and distribution chains within the AI economy. This divergence makes it impossible to apply a unified toolkit for managing the risks associated with both cyber threats and ethical issues in the AI economy.

Unlike cyber threats, which have been studied in considerable detail, the ethics of the AI economy remains a relatively unexplored and still-forming area of research. The systematic study of both cyber threats and AI economy ethics presented in this book provides a comprehensive and multifaceted explanation of the risks inherent in this economy from the perspectives of various stakeholders. It also offers an integrated economic and legal framework for managing these risks. To promote more ethical business practices in the AI economy, the book proposes methodological approaches and practical solutions distinct from those used to combat cyber threats, focusing specifically on the domain of ethics.

The book makes a theoretical contribution to the body of scholarly literature on ethical economics by reinterpreting the essence of the AI economy from an ethical standpoint. The scientific and practical insights presented in the book have real-world relevance because they form a methodological foundation and propose promising applied solutions for countercyclical regulation of the AI economy, paving the way for its long-term sustainable development. The book's innovative proposals also offer opportunities to improve the planning and forecasting of the AI economy's trajectory through a more comprehensive consideration of its ethical dimensions.

The primary target audience for this book is scholars engaged in studying economic ethics. For them, the book offers a comprehensive review of the ethical components of the AI economy through the lens of stakeholder theory, identifies the most pressing shortcomings in the spread of smart automation, characterizes national models for ethical compliance in the AI economy, and proposes effective mechanisms for its humanization and environmental adaptation.

The secondary, non-academic audience includes representatives of the AI economy's business community, who will find numerous international case studies of "smart" automation, along with their detailed analysis from the standpoint of economic ethics. For them, the book also offers practical recommendations for more ethical uses of AI. Moreover, the book is intended for institutions engaged in regulating the AI economy, whose representatives may find value in the scientific methodologies and applied proposals for improving public governance of AI technology dissemination, through enhanced oversight of the ethical standards upheld by society and the business sector.

Jalal-Abad State University Named After B. Osmonov
Jalal-Abad, Kyrgyzstan
Aziza B. Karbekova

Contents

Cyber Threats from the Use of Neural Networks as Ethical Challenges of the AI Economy

Ethical Model of Organisation of the Smart City System in the AI Economy with Complex Consideration of Interested Parties' Views

Rustam R. Rashidov, Elena G. Popkova, Saida G. Makhkamova, Valentina A. Rudenko, and Yulia A. Evdoshkina

Abstract The organisation of a smart city system is aimed at achieving the UN Sustainable Development Goals at the local level. This process became a response to quick socioeconomic and environmental challenges faced by cities in the age of digitalisation (including the dissemination of artificial intelligence), global crises, and other factors. Management of the transition to smart cities is ensured with the help of the tools of artificial intelligence, which allows accelerating it and raising its effectiveness, but which also might lead to the emergence of ethical problems. In the course of the study of the aspects of the organisation of the smart city system in the AI economy, we revealed two ethical models that are peculiar to this process.

This paper aimed to identify the options of ethical models of organisation of the smart city system in the AI economy with comprehensive consideration of stakeholders' interests. To achieve this aim, we used the methods of systematisation, comparison, and induction. The scientific novelty of the research consists in determining and assessing the specifics of the ethical models of organisation of the smart city system in the AI economy in the context of consideration of all stakeholder's interests.

R. R. Rashidov
Alfraganus University, Tashkent, Uzbekistan

E. G. Popkova (✉)
Armenian State University of Economics, Yerevan, Armenia

S. G. Makhkamova
Tashkent State University of Economics, Tashkent, Uzbekistan
e-mail: s.makhkamova@tsue.uz

V. A. Rudenko · Y. A. Evdoshkina
Volgodonsk Engineering and Technical Institute (branch) of National Nuclear Research University MEPhI, Volgodonsk, Russia
e-mail: VARudenko@mephi.ru; YAEvdoshkina@mephi.ru

A. Karbekova (ed.), *Ethics of the AI Economy: A System View from the Positions of the Theory of Stakeholders*, Ethical Economy 73,
https://doi.org/10.1007/978-3-032-23423-0_1

Keywords Ethical model • Smart city system • AI economy • Stakeholder's interests • Confidentiality • Digital Readiness • Infrastructure

JEL Codes O18 • P25 • Q56 • Q57 • J24

1 Introduction

The creation of a system of smart cities falls under SDG 11. The policy of local communities and local authorities determines the basis of this process. The AI economy ensures its implementation with the help of various tools, which contribute to the achievement of the best results for the sustainable development of cities.

The policy of organisation of the system of smart cities is necessary for solving problems and challenges that emerge due to various socioeconomic, energy, and environmental factors. The growth of the urban population leads to pressure on the local system of healthcare, labour market, infrastructural support (housing and utilities sector, IT sector, etc.), and resources (energy, food, and natural) (Ryan and Gregory 2019). An increase in urban population is observed in many developing countries, where citizens, seeking to improve their well-being, move from rural communities to cities or leave cities that do not have proper conditions for quality life activities. In this case, cities and territories where population decreases are not oriented, in most cases, towards practices that help retain the population. Also, city management might not take into account the interests of all stakeholders.

The issue of taking into account the interests of all stakeholders is the top-priority aspect during the evaluation of the effectiveness of the organisation of the smart city system in the AI economy. A special place in the system of interests of various parties belongs to ethical aspects, which are connected with community participants' view of limits, norms, and scales of digitalisation, openness and transparency of data. In this case, the top-priority role in the management of the organisation of smart cities belongs to sociocultural factors of all interested parties (population, business environment, developers and sellers of digital intellectual technologies, services, and local authorities).

Since the topic of creating the smart city system given possible ethical aspects is relevant to modern science and urban management, the study of ethical models of smart city systems is very important.

The goal of this paper was to establish the forms of ethical models of organisation of the smart city system in the AI economy with comprehensive consideration of stakeholders' interests.

2 Methodology

For this research, we utilised a range of methods and took into account the positions of scholars and analysts who study the ethical problems of the organisation of smart city systems and opportunities to overcome them.

The method of systematisation allowed revealing the main components of the studied systems of smart cities. The comparative method enabled us to compare the characteristics of the ethical models of organisation of the smart city system in the AI economy with a focus on the interests of all stakeholders. The method of induction was used to collect data on the consideration of ethical issues given the interests of stakeholders connected with the directions of organising the systems of smart cities.

At the current stage of integration of the AI economy into the management of territories, there is no sufficient theoretical and methodological apparatus which would present a range of options for the organisation of smart cities that would include a focus on the main ethical problems appearing during neglect of stakeholders' interests.

Ryan and Gregory (2019) presented an analysis of the ethical aspects of implementing AI into the system of smart cities and dwelt on the examples of implementing intellectual information systems in Hamburg, Copenhagen, Helsinki, and Amsterdam. The value of this research consists in revealing the key ethical problems of this process, which include possession of data, transparency, and consent.

Sanchez et al. (2024) distinguished a range of ethical problems faced by local authorities during the creation of smart city systems with the help of AI tools. These problems include disinformation, possible violations of confidentiality, accountability, transparency, and bias

Hartley and Aldag (2024) analysed theoretical features and the philosophy of the creation of the smart city system and considered the results of its implementation by the example of Singapore, which demonstrates quick growth in this sphere.

Bondarenko et al. (2021) and Shevchenko (2024) elaborated on the issues of smart city and smart hotels. The problem of socio-ethical marketing in the marketplaces' activities was studied by Osadchaya (2025). Kim (2025) disclosed the advantages of the organisation of the smart city system through the example of Singapore, noting a high level of technological infrastructure, which contributes to the growth of the economy and quality of life of citizens with a high level of readiness for digital transformations. According to the author, this system also has ethical problems, concerned with the large-scale replacement of human capital with intellectual tools.

Ajaj et al. (2024) presented an analysis of factors influencing the improvement of smart city systems, on the example of Abu Dhabi. Oyadeyi and Oyadeyi (2025) described the main advantages of smart city systems by the example of Copenhagen, Oslo, and Zurich. The authors elaborated on the specifics of policy in this sphere, which are the basis for effectiveness and could be adapted by local authorities, which seek to meet the interests of all stakeholders.

Ergasheva et al. (2023) considered the level of correspondence of the processes of robotization to the principles and goals of sustainable development. The relevance of this research lies in determining the connection between these components, which are studied at the national and local levels.

3 Results

We considered the main types of organisation of the smart city system and established their ethical models which determine the consideration of stakeholders' interests.

To reveal the types of organisation of the system of smart cities and establish their ethical models (Table 1), we compiled a list of smart cities (leaders) based on the annual report by the International Institute for Management Development (2025). We analysed ten leading cities presented in this report.

Let us analyse the main features of the ethical models of the organisation of the leading smart cities.

Lausanne (Switzerland) demonstrated a certain deterioration in the rankings of smart cities due to the following:

- Reduction of security against the background of the high level of tracking contracts and movements of citizens. The latter was an advantage during the COVID-19 pandemic but turned out to be less effective since 2023. Accordingly, measures used for monitoring of contacts and movements of citizens do not meet the citizens' expectations;
- Focus on transparency, openness, and a high level of socio-technological infrastructure is dominating compared to insufficiently effective regulation of traffic, given the relatively small population (140,000 in 2023) and the housing problem (absence of new affordable accommodation) (The Great Wine Capitals 2023).

Thus, we can describe the ethical model of the organisation of the smart city system as developing. The above ethical проблемы (noted by 70% of the city population) are being solved; the spatial and technological organisation of city management is high.

Singapore faces the influence of the ethical problems of its citizens' treating the local authorities' policy in the context of ensuring the quality of life (Hartley and Aldag 2024). Despite the large ambitions of Singapore's authorities in the creation of technological and spatial support, there are ethical aspects that lead to the reduction of support for these initiatives. This is caused by insufficient satisfaction of citizens' needs in the context of transparent control over the authorities' activities and assessment of the execution of the authorities' promises (Kim 2025). Dissatisfaction with insufficient transparency and accountability of the government in the sphere of organisation of the smart city system adds up to failure to keep promises to preserve jobs that were subject to automatization with the help of AI. The use of intellectual services in waste management, transport, and energy spheres led to high dismissal

Table 1 Types of organisation of the system of smart cities and their ethical models

Smart city	Position in the rankings	Spatial and technological characteristics of the smart city type	Ethical model
Lausanne (Switzerland)	2025—10th 2024—7th	High spatial and technological organisation	Developing, ethical problems with the organisation (safety, traffic, affordability of accommodation)
Singapore	2025—9th 2024—5th	Very high spatial and technological organisation	Developing, ethical problems with the organisation (support of the labour market under the influence of implementation of AI, confidentiality)
Canberra (Australia)	2025—8th 2024—3rd	Very high spatial and good technological organisation	Developing, ethical problems with the organisation (accommodation, technological infrastructure)
Copenhagen (Denmark)	2025—7th 2024—6th	Very high spatial and high technological organisation	Developing, ethical problems with the organisation (housing infrastructure)
London (UK)	2025—6th 2024—7th	Very high spatial and very high technological organisation	Developing, ethical problems with the organisation (accountability of organisations that deal with CCTV and face recognition, security, and confidentiality)
Abu Dhabi (UAE)	2025—5th 2024—10th	Good spatial and technological organisation	Developing, ethical problems with the organisation (accountability of organisations that store citizens' personal data, transparency of local authorities' activities)
Dubai (UAE)	2025—4th 2024—12th	Good spatial and technological organisation	Developing, ethical problems that include accountability of organisations that store citizens' personal data, informing citizens about the advantages of the smart city, and technological accessibility
Geneva (Switzerland)	2025—3rd 2024—4th	Very high spatial and technological organisation	The model of well-balanced consideration of ethical aspects in smart city management
Oslo (Norway)	2025—2nd 2024—2nd	Very high spatial and technological organisation	The model of well-balanced consideration of ethical aspects in smart city management
Zurich (Switzerland)	2025—1st 2024—1st	Very high spatial and technological organisation	The model of well-balanced consideration of ethical aspects in smart city management

Source: Prepared by the authors based on (International Institute for Management Development 2025; Puttkamer 2023; The Great Wine Capitals 2023; Hartley and Aldag 2024; Kim 2025; Thrive Project 2022; Skelton 2021; Ajaj et al. 2024; GO-Globe 2023; City of Geneva 2025; Slette 2024)

rates in these sectors and the impossibility for employees to find jobs that would conform to the ones they had before the large-scale integration of AI.

Canberra (Australia) is among the top 10 smart cities in the world. The change in its ranking was caused by a range of ethical aspects of the organisation of technological and housing infrastructure (Thrive Project 2022). We may note the advantages of the system of smart city organisation: high level of the management of green transformations of transport infrastructure (88.6% of all city transport are eco-friendly); effective management of the reduction of greenhouse gas emissions, ensured mainly due to ecologization of the city's transport infrastructure and decrease in the use of fossil fuels; support of accessibility and eco-friendliness of consumed energy (in 2022, 44% of energy used by the city accounted for renewable sources (wind and solar)); very high level of green spaces (353 sq. m per capita) (Thrive Project 2022).

However, this system of smart city organisation has several ethical problems, which include insufficient attention to citizens' interests; these are, in particular, affordability of accommodation and insufficient level of technological infrastructure.

Copenhagen (Denmark) also has certain ethical problems in the context of smart city organization in the AI economy. The important advantages of the smart city model used by Copenhagen include the focus on ecologization of the energy and transport sector (digital monitoring of lighting, eco-friendly transport, energy saving due to intellectual services); economic growth (including local authorities' support of start-ups); improvement of the city's ecosystem through innovative intellectual projects (Puttkamer 2023).

London (UK) is working on an improvement in meeting the citizens' interests in confidentiality protection during the use of AI in CCTV, city services of face recognition, etc. The Emerging Technology Charter is aimed at constant improvement of the ethical norms of using AI in city administration (Skelton 2021). Ethical problems caused by the development and use of AI are being solved due to the capabilities of civilian control in this sphere.

Due to initiatives of the local authorities, Abu Dhabi (UAE) was able to achieve significant progress in the realisation of the smart city project. Advantages that led to the growth of the city's ranking are as follows: growth of the level of the city's ecosystem sustainability, ensured by the use of AI in the management of energy consumption, and transition to renewable energy; enhancement of transport networks and effectiveness of transfers (installation of AI-based digital sensors that allow for effective tracking and control of city transport); improvement of security measures, involving digital intellectual technologies (CCTV and face recognition systems), which led to a decrease in the crime rate in the city (Thalpe 2025). Despite the quick growth of the indicators of the organisation of the smart city system, Abu Dhabi's population has doubts about the accountability of city authorities, which have confidential data on citizens and their businesses, obtained thanks to the use of AI. According to Ajaj et al. (2024), the city administration lacks transparency in the sphere of organisation of the smart city system.

Dubai (UAE) is peculiar for the growth of its smart city system's effectiveness. The main results in this sphere are as follows: an increase in environmental sustainability due to the use of intellectual methods of infrastructure and economy management (reduction of CO_2 emissions, reduction of energy consumption, and ensuring access to clean water); creation of opportunities for improvement of citizens' economic well-being, due to new jobs in city infrastructure (GO-Globe 2023). The advantages of integrating AI in city management are accompanied by ethical problems. Among these we should note insufficient awareness of the citizens about the capabilities of the smart city (citizens without a high level of digital readiness); digital inequality (it is possible to create interactive projects of digital literacy support); and issues of protection of data collected by city services.

Geneva (Switzerland) demonstrates the improvement of the organisation of the smart city system. Since 2016, local authorities, community, and business environment have been adopting and implementing the provisions of the Comprehensive Plan & Decision-Making Guide, which involves the integration of AI technologies in support of citizens' healthy lifestyle, improvement of the real estate market, improvement of the sustainability of land use model, and prevention of environmental problems (this includes measures presented in the Climate Smart Communities), (City of Geneva 2025).

Oslo (Norway) has high indicators of the organisation of smart city systems, especially in 2024–2025. Oslo has a comprehensive consideration of the interests of all stakeholders and seeks the achievement of high sustainability. The level of waste management and construction control (the use of eco-friendly materials), as well as the management of renewable energy and social sphere (capabilities of labour resources in the local labour), education, healthcare system, economic sphere (creation of conditions for retention of talented employees, implementation of projects that ensure the growth of GDP), and improvement of the city ecosystem (growth of green spaces), and security management, are all in line with ethical norms (Slette 2024). This approach to the organisation of the smart city system builds up city residents' trust in local authorities.

Similar to Oslo, Zurich (Switzerland) implements an effective policy of organising the smart city system, which does not violate ethical norms and takes into account the views of all interested parties. The most notable implications of such policy are the eco-friendliness of public transport, the energy efficiency of public spaces and city buildings, and the focus on green energy and a high level of ecologization in waste processing (Oyadeyi and Oyadeyi 2025). The policy of local authorities in the integration of AI can be described as supporting but not opposing social traditions.

4 Discussion

In this paper, we revealed and characterised the types of ethical models of the organisation of smart city systems in the AI economy given the comprehensive consideration of stakeholders' interests. We revealed a model of well-balanced consideration of ethical aspects in smart city management and the developing model, which is peculiar for certain ethical problems with organisation.

The first model has vivid advantages and is seen in developed economies, oriented towards well-balanced socioeconomic, technological, and environmental development. Adaptation of the experience of countries using this model could be used by countries with a high level of partnership at the level of local authorities, communities, and businesses. Within parity relationships, decisions on the limits of integration of AI are made; these limits must not violate the interests of all stakeholders of the city community.

The second model, which is also seen in cities that are among the leaders in the rankings of smart city development, demonstrates that many cities are at the stage of implementation of AI in city management. The focus on consideration of the interests of all stakeholders might be sometimes moved to the background, but perspectives of resolving ethical problems that emerge in the management are very good.

5 Conclusions

Summing up this research, it is necessary to note the importance of accounting for the ethical aspects and needs of all interested parties, which are inherent in the organisation of the smart city system in the AI economy. The possibilities of preventing conflicts caused by violation of ethical norms involve the cooperation of all interested parties. The absence of high activity in the local community cannot be considered a reason for local authorities to ignore these norms during the integration of AI tools into city services and processes.

Ethical problems could be prevented through citizens' and business environment's active participation in the discussion of the creation of smart city's digital intellectual services, involvement of local businesses and residents with the corresponding projects, and constant informing of residents and businesses about the possibility to file complaints and provide recommendations in this regard.

Perspectives of the development of smart cities depend on further transformations of the AI economy, including the emergence of tools adapted to the city management system. Approaches to their successful adoption in the context of compliance with ethical norms can be determined today. Expert communities and local authorities can form frameworks for discussing intellectual integration into the system of city management with the participation of all interested parties.

References

Ajaj, R., M. K. Buniya, I. Y. Wuni, and O. S. Yosif. 2024. A case study on the barriers towards achieving sustainable smart city for Abu Dhabi. *IET Smart Cities* 6:112–128. https://doi.org/10.1049/smc2.12077.

Bondarenko, V. A., V. A. Larionov, and T. S. Romanishina. 2021. A study of demand for implementing "smart hotels" in the "smart city" concept: A focus on the consumer. *Practical Marketing* 2 (288): 42–48. https://doi.org/10.24412/2071-3762-2021-2288-42-48.

City of Geneva. 2025. *City of Geneva city council pledges to become a climate smart community*. https://www.cityofgenevany.gov/314/Sustainability-in-Geneva (Accessed 14.04.2025).

Ergasheva, S. T., N. A. Khaydarova, T. N. Litvinova, and T. Y. Cherepukhin. 2023. ESG management of robotized business in support of green economy development in Russia and Central Asia (2023). *Environmental Footprints and Eco-Design of Products and Processes, Part* F1766:13–21. https://doi.org/10.1007/978-3-031-46525-3_2.

GO-Globe. 2023. *Future of smart cities in the UAE: Innovation and sustainability*. https://www.go-globe.com/the-future-of-smart-cities-in-the-uae/ (Accessed 14.04.2025).

Hartley, K., and A. Aldag. 2024. Public trust and support for government technology: Survey insights about Singapore's smart city policies. *Cities* 154:105368. https://doi.org/10.1016/j.cities.2024.105368.

International Institute for Management Development. 2025. *Smart City Index. What makes a city the most livable, in 2025?* https://www.imd.org/smart-city-observatory/home/ (Accessed 14.04.2025).

Kim, J. V. 2025. Technological determinism in smart cities: AI's role in urban transformation and workforce disruption in Singapore. *IGEE Proceedings* 2 (1): 20–30. https://doi.org/10.69841/igee.2025.008.

Osadchaya, S. M. 2025. Violation of the principles of socio-ethical marketing in the activities of marketplaces. *Practical Marketing* 1 (331): 48–52. https://doi.org/10.24412/2071-3762-2025-1331-48-52.

Oyadeyi, O. A., and O. O. Oyadeyi. 2025. Towards inclusive and sustainable strategies in smart cities: A comparative analysis of Zurich, Oslo, and Copenhagen. *Research in Globalization* 10:100271. https://doi.org/10.1016/j.resglo.2025.100271.

Puttkamer, L. 2023. *City Portrait: Smart City Copenhagen*. https://www.beesmart.city/en/smart-city-blog/copenhagen (Accessed 14.04.2025).

Ryan, Mark, and Anya Gregory. 2019. Ethics of using smart city AI and Big Data: The case of four large European cities. *The ORBIT Journal* 2 (2): 1–36. https://doi.org/10.29297/orbit.v2i2.110.

Sanchez, T. W., M. Brenman, and X. Ye. 2024. The ethical concerns of artificial intelligence in urban planning. *Journal of the American Planning Association* 91 (2): 294–307. https://doi.org/10.1080/01944363.2024.2355305.

Shevchenko, D. A. 2024. Smart city: An overview of mechanisms and tools. *Practical Marketing* 10 (328): 45–48. https://doi.org/10.24412/2071 3762 2024-10328-45-48

Skelton, S. K. 2021. *London publishes guidelines for ethical use of smart city tech*. https://www.computerweekly.com/news/252507107/London-publishes-guidelines-for-ethical-use-of-smart-city-tech/ (Accessed 14.04.2025).

Slette, S. B. 2024. *Oslo excels in smart city index*. https://www.storebrand.com/sam/dk/asset-management/insights/solutions-spotlight-blog/solutions-spotlight-folder/oslo-excels-in-smart-city-index (Accessed 14.04.2025).

Thalpe, W. 2025. *The impact of Abu Dhabi' smart city initiatives on urban living*. https://www.linkedin.com/pulse/impact-abu-dhabi-smart-city-initiatives urban living-wathsala-thalpe-kwqxc/ (Accessed 14.04.2025).

The Great Wine Capitals. 2023. *Lausanne in the top 5 of the most "intelligent" cities*. https://www.greatwinecapitals.com/wine-stories/lausanne-in-the-top-5-of-the-most-intelligent-cities/ (Accessed 14.04.2025).

Thrive Project. 2022. *Canberra, the world's most sustainable city*. https://thrivabilitymatters.org/most sustainable-city-canberras-example/ (Accessed 14.04.2025).

Ethical Approach to Innovations Management in the AI Economy with Balanced Compliance with Stakeholders' Interests

Gulnora G. Jamalova, Dilobar M. Mavlyanova, Elena G. Popkova, and Natalia V. Przhedetskaya

Abstract This paper elaborates on the ethical aspects of innovations management in the context of the AI economy and possibilities of ensuring balanced compliance with stakeholders' interests, analyses the structure of the AI economy as an economic and socio-technological system in which technological core interacts with the elements of macro-environment, reveals the dualistic nature of AI as a driver and result of innovative processes which ensures large-scale transformation of the traditional system of innovations management, and characterises institutional, economic, and technological mechanisms of agreement of stakeholders' interests, which form potential for effective implementation of ethical norms during the development and use of innovations based on AI.

The methodological framework of this research is formed by the system approach, which combines the foundations of innovative management, neo-institutionalism, digital transition, and theories of open innovations and stakeholders. The information framework of the research is formed by scientific and export publications, standards, and provisions of the regulation of the ethical use of AI. The methodology is presented by the system approach, analysis, comparison, observation, generalisation, and the graphical method.

The main value of the paper consists in determining the mechanisms of ensuring the ethical approach to innovations management in the conditions of the AI economy, which allow achieving the balance of stakeholders' interests. The provided provisions are based on understanding ethical issues of the use of AI not from the

G. G. Jamalova · D. M. Mavlyanova
Tashkent State University of Economics, Tashkent, Uzbekistan
e-mail: g.jamalova@tsue.uz

E. G. Popkova (✉)
Armenian State University of Economics, Yerevan, Armenia

N. V. Przhedetskaya
Rostov State University of Economics, Rostov-on-Don, Russia

A. Karbekova (ed.), *Ethics of the AI Economy: A System View from the Positions of the Theory of Stakeholders*, Ethical Economy 73,
https://doi.org/10.1007/978-3-032-23423-0_2

positions of restrictions of innovative development but from the position of internal resources, which forms additional potential for raising the value of innovations.

Keywords Artificial intelligence • Ethical management • Innovations • Digital economy • AI economy • Balance of interests • Stakeholders • Ethical challenges • Technological development

JEL Codes D83 • L86 • M14 • M15 • O32 • O33 • Q01 • Q55 • Q56

1 Introduction

Artificial intelligence is becoming increasingly important in the global economy and public processes. It transforms approaches to production, management, and communications, and offers effective support of many sectors of business in the conditions of technological transition. According to Goldman Sachs, generative AI could lead to an increase in world GDP of 7% over the next ten years, growth of labour efficiency by 1.5%, and create the basis for automatization for approximately 300 million jobs around the world (Goldman Sachs 2023). McKinsey & Company assesses AI's influence on the economy even more optimistically. According to them, this technology will allow creating $ 2.6–4.4 trillion in value-added annually, automatization will influence 60–70% of work time spent by employees for current tasks, and an increase in productivity will reach 0.1–0.6% per year (McKinsey and Company 2023).

In the conditions of growth of not only technological but also the economic and social influence of AI on public processes, there emerge acute issues of regulating the development of this technology, which covers ethical aspects. International humanitarian organisations, in particular, UNESCO, suggest general recommendations on ethical provisions of the development and use of AI. They offer the main principles of ethical management of AI, which cover respect for the rights and dignity of humans, justice and inclusion, transparency, accountability, human control and oversight, as well as environmental sustainability. The recommendations also include a call for multiparty management of this process, which includes the involvement of all stakeholders (government, business sector, educational and scientific establishments, and civil society) with the preparation of common demands for the policy of AI development, as well as demand for global coordination of efforts to ensure the ethical use of technologies (UNESCO 2022).

Against this background, some scholars draw attention to establishing the most critical ethical problems, which can potentially threaten the just sustainable development of mankind. Here the focus is on AI's ability to increase power and inequality based on algorithmic discrimination (Crawford 2022); the closed character of decisions in algorithmic systems of AI, which ruins trust in technologies and demands regulatory oversight (Pasquale 2015); exploitation of big data by technological giants to manipulate human behaviour and create an economic model that disrupts privacy, autonomy, and democratic processes (Zuboff 2019), and other ethical problems of using AI. These issues and problems determine the relevance of this research and the use of the ethical approach to innovations management in the conditions of the AI economy, which is achieved due to balanced adherence to the interests of stakeholders.

2 Methodology

The AI economy is manifested as a new paradigm of economic development, which is based on an interdisciplinary combination of the ideas of innovative development, neo-institutionalism, and digital transition. It is set on J. Schumpeter's view as a result of "disruptive" innovations, which change the structure of the market, transform business models, and are the main source of economic growth (Cockburn et al. 2018; Schumpeter 1942). In the context of studying the ethical approach to innovations management and consideration of stakeholders' interests, this study covers the concept of responsible innovations (which take into account social acceptability, ethics, and public value of innovations) and the Stakeholder theory (identification and classification of stakeholders in realising ethical norms in innovations management in the sphere of AI). Certain aspects of the work are disclosed through the theory of open innovations, the concept of the triple innovative spiral, and the theory of institutional design, which allow expanding the horizon of studying the AI economy and innovations management.

The methodological framework of the research is formed by general scientific methods, supplemented by individual tools of scientific cognition based on the combination of qualitative and quantitative methods. The main issues of the paper are viewed through the lens of the system approach, which allows combining different approaches and concepts and viewing processes and phenomena in their interconnection. Theoretical and methodological provisions of this work are viewed with the use of the systemic scientific review. Additional research methods include comparative analysis of international policies on regulation of ethical aspects of innovations management in the AI economy, analysis of the regulatory and legal sphere of the studied problem, and the methods of comparison and generalisation.

The theoretical and methodological basis of the research is formed by scholarly works and expert documents devoted to various aspects of the formation of the AI economy and ethical challenges connected with the use of AI during innovations management. The potential of the AI economy is viewed through the lens of general-purpose technologies, which can radically transform economic processes and business models (Trajtenberg 2018). Attention is drawn to the dualistic nature of AI as a subject and object of innovation (Cockburn et al. 2018). The conceptual structure of the AI economy is disclosed through studies that track the correlation between the implementation of AI technologies and economic growth (Makridis and Mishra 2022; Rao et al. 2024) and the influence of change management on the achievement of sustainability principles in the sector of the AI economy (Popkova et al. 2024).

Ethical challenges of AI development are studied from the position of a range of socio-ethical problems, such as non-transparency of algorithmic systems of AI (Pasquale 2015), asymmetry of authority in the conditions of development of these technologies (Crawford 2022), misuse of access to them (Zuboff 2019), and change in the structure of markets through domination of technological platforms (Varian 2018). As a response to these challenges, certain approaches to ensuring the ethical management of AI, including the concept of ethically agreed design (IEEE 2019), a regulatory framework based on the risk-oriented approach (European Commission 2021), and ethical principles of good society based on AI (Floridi et al. 2018) are viewed.

The influence of AI on innovations management is viewed through the lens of the concept of open innovations (Chesbrough 2003), the triple spiral model (Etzkowitz and Leydesdorff 2000), and analysis of the change in the decision-making economy (Agrawal et al. 2019). Simultaneously, the provisions of technical approaches to responsible AI (Arrieta et al. 2020) and innovations management in the context of support of competitiveness (Tadevosyan 2023) are disclosed.

The objective of this research is to develop conceptual foundations of the development of the ethical approach to innovations management in the conditions of the AI economy, which ensures balanced compliance with the interests of different groups of stakeholders. Achievement of this objective envisages the following tasks: studying the structure and specifics of the AI economy, analysing the transformation influence of AI on the processes of innovations management, systematising the main ethical challenges connected with the implementation of AI technologies in the context of innovations management, studying current approaches to the formation of ethical frameworks of the use of AI, and offering the mechanisms of agreeing stakeholders' interests during innovations management in the conditions of the AI economy.

3 Results

At the modern stage of economic development, traditional business models and socioeconomic relationships are subject to serious transformations, which are connected with large-scale implementation of innovations taking place almost in all spheres of human activities. Since the early twenty-first century, digital technologies have become a driver of technological development. Big Data, the Internet of Things, cloud technologies, AI, 3D printing, blockchain, and other digital technologies perform the main role in most everyday and economic processes. However, one of the key technologies offering disruptive changes and performing the most multi-aspect pressure on the economy is AI. From the position of the theory of General-purpose technologies (GPTs), AI is a universal technology that can influence all spheres of production and consumption. It has the potential for large-scale structural changes and the formation of long-term waves of economic growth (Trajtenberg 2018).

The concept of the AI economy comes from the idea of general penetration and dissemination of the influence of this technology, which is reflected in productiveness, labour market, structure of the economy, form of interaction between economic agents, etc. In this context, the structure of economic relationships is based on stable technological foundations, which interact with important elements of the macro-level (Fig. 1.)

Thus, technological core, consisting of machine learning, natural language recognition, computer vision, and generative AI, ensures the key operational effects, which require the corresponding reflection among such components of macro-environment as Big Data (data centres, data market, and data economy), human capital (digital literacy and AI-based education), digital platforms and services (AI-as-a-Service, automatization based on AI), and infrastructure and regulatory support (institutional provisions, ethical norms, and legal regulation). In aggregate, this structure of the AI economy forms an economic socio-technological system, within which each interaction between the elements has a significant impact on other components.

According to the specifics of such a system, its basis is determined by innovations. However, unlike the traditional economy, innovations in the AI economy not only create new products, services, or technologies—they can also transform the main mechanisms of functioning of business and market systems. Thus, AI has a dualistic nature: it is a result and driver of the innovative process at the same time (Cockburn et al. 2018). These trends transform the paradigm of innovations

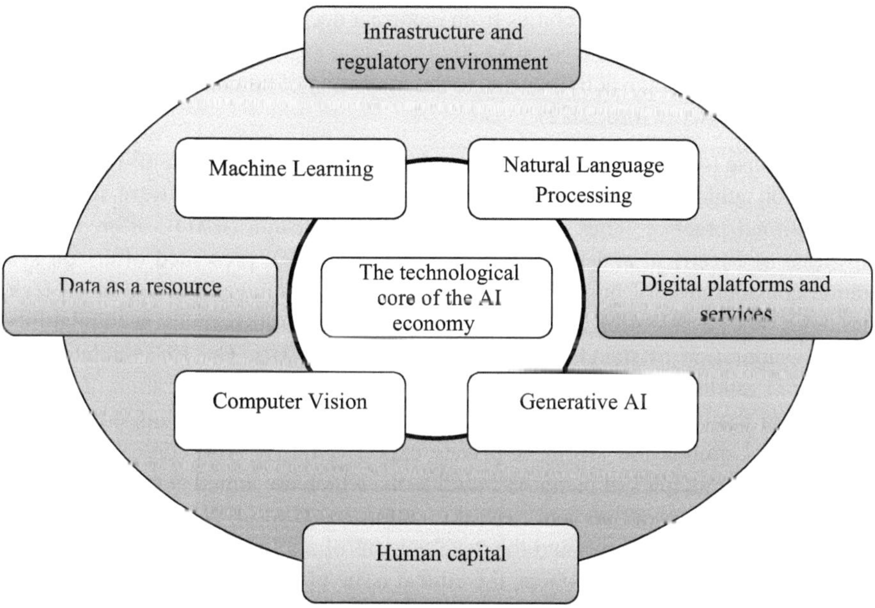

Fig. 1 Structure of the digital economy. Source: Developed by the authors based on (Makridis and Mishra 2022; Rao et al. 2024; Varian 2018)

management. In this context, AI contributes to the transformation of internal processes of innovative management to the models of open innovations (Chesbrough 2003), at which the idea of triple innovative spiral (interaction between universities, business, and government) is actualised (Etzkowitz and Leydesdorff 2000), and mechanisms of innovations management are transformed through implementing the tools of automatization in the spheres of strategic planning, forecasting, and generation of hypotheses and Big Data analytics (Haefner et al. 2021). All these changes, caused by AI, accelerate the cycle of development and implementation of innovations. New products and technologies appear in the market faster, and their penetration in public processes is characterised by larger scale and depth.

Simultaneously with the significant positive impact of AI on the innovative process, its technological specifics, connected with autonomy and use during decision-making, cause more concerns from the position of the ethical component. The main ethical issues on the use of AI in innovations management are concerned with the following aspects:

- Transparency of AI algorithm due to the inability to explain its actions and choices in different conditions (Pasquale 2015; UNESCO 2022);
- Discrimination, which reflects algorithmic criteria or reservations regarding the assessment of alternative variants with the help of AI (Crawford 2022; Zuboff 2019);
- Confidentiality and data security, which form a range of challenges for consent and transparency of usage and restriction of access to personal and confidential information (Zuboff 2019);
- The responsibility which comes from incorrect decisions made by systems based on AI (Crawford 2022; UNESCO 2022);
- Autonomy of human activities due to the limitation of human influence in certain AI systems (Crawford 2022).

As a response to these reservations, several important official and semi-official provisions on ethical innovation management, connected with AI, were formed in international practice. Thus, the Ethically Aligned Design (EAD), offered by the Institute of Electrical and Electronics Engineers (IEEE), presented offers on systemic consideration of human values during the development and use of AI technologies. The key attention was paid to human-centrism, transparency, accountability, and consideration of stakeholders' interests (IEEE 2019). The EU regulatory act (Artificial Intelligence Act) determines parameters for the classification of AI systems from the position of their influence on security, discrimination, control, etc. (European Commission 2021). A private expert initiative AI4People formed five main ethical principles of using AI-based tools, which are aimed at ensuring utility, justice, damage prevention, and control of autonomy (Floridi et al. 2018).

Based on these activities and the development of a joint position of global institutions, experts, and practitioners, the ethical issue of using AI in the conditions of the AI economy ceased to be a reservation for innovations. On the contrary, provisions on the management of ethical risks of this technology allowed turning the ethical approach to innovations management into a certain internal resource, which guarantees adherence to general human values in the considered sphere, raises the level of trust in innovators and their solutions and ensures support from state and global regulators.

Active prepared actions in the context of the development and implementation of ethical norms regarding digital transformation and innovations management based on AI allowed forming a stable concept for coordinating and balancing the interests of many stakeholders, including governmental and inter-governmental bodies, technological companies and developers, individual and corporate users of innovations, society on the whole, public sector, etc. However, the achievement of rational proportions in consideration of all stakeholders' interests in innovations management in the conditions of the AI economy requires the development and use of certain mechanisms that can correctly identify, group, and agree on these interests.

Methods that should be applied for the resolution of the given problem may have different natures and conceptual bases. They could be founded on institutional mechanisms, such as ethical committees, regulatory "sandboxes", advisory bodies, etc. (Batool et al. 2025), use economic levers of agreeing the interests through fiscal or compensation tools, public-private partnership, or other measures (Agrawal et al. 2019), use technological approaches to correction of the interests of different economic agents through technological standards of the audit of AI algorithms, tools of digital education or explanatory AI (Arrieta et al. 2020).

Thus, ensuring the ethical approach to innovations management in the conditions of the digital economy has sufficient potential for achieving the balance of stakeholders' interests, which allows for the distribution of influence between different groups of stakeholders, consideration of the complexity of socioeconomic and technological relationships, and support of ethical norms during the use of technical innovations based on AI.

4 Discussion

The issue of ethical norms and principles in the management of innovations that use AI as the basis of scientific and analytical processes is among the relevant and actively discussed problems in modern scholarly literature. The main aspect of the discussion is concerned with the treatment of the role of AI in scientific research and solutions. On the one hand, AI is defined as a tool that offers larger opportunities in the sphere of generation and processing of information, and, on the other hand—as a factor of risk connected with violation of privacy, interference with the sphere of human competence and responsibility, etc. Despite the large progress in the development of approaches and norms aimed at regulation of certain aspects of ethical problems during the use of AI in innovations management, reservations regarding AI remain scientific and practical problems which require further discussion and resolution.

Another aspect of the studied problem is balanced compliance with stakeholders' interests, which emerge in the process of managing innovations based on

AI. This issue requires the development of a separate methodological basis and systemic scientific work aimed at the identification of the list of stakeholders, determination of their interests and their agreement, establishment of agreement and disagreement of interests, and description of the mechanism of formation of these interests and determination of the means of influencing them. This research has a large scientific value and could be a topic for further research, and its result could be the development of a comprehensive model of balancing stakeholders' interests on the use of the ethical approach to innovations management in the conditions of the AI economy.

The AI economy also requires further research connected with methodological substantiation of its essence and nature, more detailed consideration of its specifics and structure, as well as interaction of elements, and assessment of the perspectives of its development and characteristics of the related risks. An additional topic of discussion around the AI economy is the evaluation of the potential influence of the wide application of ethical norms to the use of AI technologies in the sphere of innovations management at all stages of their life cycle.

5 Conclusion

The modern global economy is in the process of large technological transformations, based on the active dissemination of digital technologies, among which the main role belongs to AI. In this context, AI is viewed as a universal technology that has the potential to influence all spheres of economic and public life. This view allows differentiating the AI economy as a complex socioeconomic and technological system, the basis of which is formed by a technological core consisting of the technologies of machine learning, computer vision, language recognition, and generative programmes which interact with Big Data, human capital, digital platforms, and regulatory infrastructure as the elements of macro-environment. AI has a dualistic nature, being a driver and a result of innovations at the same time. This leads to its ability to transform the models of innovations management, which is manifested through the shift of internal organisational innovative processes to the models of open innovations and acceleration of the cycle of development and implementation of innovations.

Together with the positive influence of AI on innovative processes, its use is connected with a range of ethical risks and problems. They are primarily concerned with problems with transparency of AI algorithms, risks of discrimination set in its algorithms, issues of data confidentiality and security, and responsibility for decisions and preservation of humans' autonomy in socio-technological systems. Reacting to these challenges, the world expert community developed provisions and recommendations to ensure the ethical management of AI-based innovations. These actions allowed turning ethical aspects of the use of AI from systemic reservations to potential opportunities and factors of support of the corresponding norms and requirements.

The formed conceptual basis of the ethical approach to innovations management in the conditions of the AI economy can be a basis for agreeing the interests of stakeholders, which include government bodies, scholars, developers, technological companies, consumers of innovations, and the public. The main mechanisms that can ensure such an agreement of interests are institutional, economic, and technological ones. They allow correcting behaviour and demands of economic agents, influencing their behaviour in the context of the search for common interests and achievement of consensus regarding innovations management in the digital economy.

References

Agrawal, A., J. Gans, and A. Goldfarb. 2019. *Prediction machines: The simple economics of artificial intelligence*, 272. Harvard Business Review Press.

Arrieta, A. B., N. Díaz-Rodríguez, J. Del Ser, A. Bennetot, S. Tabik, A. Barbado, S. Garcia, S. Gil-Lopez, D. Molina, R. Benjamins, R. Chatila, and F. Herrera. 2020. Explainable Artificial Intelligence (XAI): Concepts, taxonomies, opportunities and challenges toward responsible AI. *Information Fusion* 58:82–115. https://doi.org/10.1016/j.inffus.2019.12.012.

Batool, A., D. Zowghi, and M. Bano. 2025. AI governance: A systematic literature review. *AI and Ethics* 1 (1): 1–15. https://doi.org/10.1007/s43681-024-00653-w.

Chesbrough, H. 2003. *Open innovation: The new imperative for creating and profiting from technology*. Harvard Business School Press. https://www.researchgate.net/publication/235700923_Open_Innovation_The_New_Imperative_for_Creating_and_Profiting_From_Technology (Accessed 14.04.2025).

Cockburn, I. M., R. Henderson, and S. Stern. 2018. The impact of artificial intelligence on innovation. In *The economics of artificial intelligence: An agenda*, 115–146. University of Chicago Press. https://doi.org/10.3386/w24449.

Crawford, K. 2022. Atlas of AI. Power, politics, and the planetary costs of artificial intelligence. *Perspectives on Science and Christian Faith* 74:61–62. https://doi.org/10.56315/PSCF3-22Crawford.

Etzkowitz, H., and L. Leydesdorff. 2000. The dynamics of innovation: From national systems and «Mode 2» to a Triple Helix of university–industry–government relations. *Research Policy* 29 (2): 109–123. https://doi.org/10.1016/S0048-7333(99)00055-4.

European Commission. 2021. Proposal for a Regulation laying down harmonised rules on artificial intelligence. *Digital Strategy*. https://digital-strategy.ec.europa.eu/en/library/proposal-regulation-laying-down-harmonised-rules-artificial-intelligence (Accessed 13.04.2025).

Floridi, L., J. Cowls, M. Beltrametti, R. Chatila, P. Chazerand, V. Dignum, C. Lütge, R. Madelin, U. Pagallo, F. Rossi, B. Schafer, P. Valcke, and E. Vayena. 2018. AI4People – An ethical framework for a good AI society: Opportunities, risks, principles, and recommendations. *Minds and Machines* 28 (4): 689–707. https://doi.org/10.1007/s11023-018-9482-5.

Goldman Sachs. 2023. *Generative AI could raise global GDP by 7%*. https://www.goldmansachs.com/insights/articles/generative-ai-could-raise-global-gdp-by-7-percent (Accessed 15.04.2025).

Haefner, N., J. Wincent, V. Parida, and O. Gassmann. 2021. Artificial intelligence and innovation management: A review, framework, and research agenda. *Technological Forecasting and Social Change* 162:120392. https://doi.org/10.1016/j.techfore.2020.120392.

IEEE. 2019. Ethically aligned design: A vision for prioritizing human well-being with autonomous and intelligent systems (Version 2). *IEEE global initiative on ethics of autonomous and intelligent systems*. https://standards.ieee.org/wp-content/uploads/import/documents/other/ead_v2.pdf (Accessed 13.04.2025).

Makridis, C., and S. Mishra. 2022. Artificial intelligence as a service, economic growth, and well-being. *Journal of Service Research* 25:109467052211202. https://doi.org/10.1177/10946705221120218.

McKinsey & Company. 2023. *The economic potential of generative AI: The next productivity frontier*. https://www.mckinsey.com/capabilities/mckinsey-digital/our-insights/the-economic-potential-of-generative-AI-the-next-productivity-frontier#introduction (Accessed 14.04.2025).

Pasquale, F. 2015. *The black box society: The secret algorithms that control money and information*. Harvard University Press. http://www.jstor.org/stable/j.ctt13x0hch (Accessed 15.04.2025).

Popkova, E. G., S. T. Ergasheva, N. K. Savelyeva, and M. A. Troyanskaya. 2024. Change management for the sustainable development of the agrarian economy of artificial intelligence. *Global Journal of Flexible Systems Management* 25:79–90. https://doi.org/10.1007/s40171-024-00383-2.

Rao, B., C. Lipizzi, and M. Mansouri. 2024. Anatomy of an AI economy. In *2024 IEEE International Symposium on Systems Engineering (ISSE)*, 1–8. IEEE. https://doi.org/10.1109/ISSE63315.2024.10741091.

Schumpeter, J. A. 1942. *Capitalism, socialism and democracy*, 381. New York: Harper and Brothers.

Tadevosyan, R. 2023. Innovations and international competitiveness: Countrylevel evidence. *Economics and Sociology* 16 (3): 248–260. https://doi.org/10.14254/2071-789X.2023/16-3/13.

Trajtenberg, M. 2018. *AI as the next GPT: A political-economy perspective*. National bureau of economic research working paper no. 24245. https://doi.org/10.3386/w24245

UNESCO. 2022. *Recommendation on the ethics of artificial intelligence*. https://www.unesco.org/en/articles/recommendation-ethics-artificial-intelligence (Accessed 13.04.2025).

Varian, H. 2018. *Artificial intelligence, economics, and industrial organization* (NBER Working Paper No. 24839). National Bureau of Economic Research https://www.nber.org/papers/w24839 (Accessed 14.04.2025).

Zuboff, S. (2019). *The age of surveillance capitalism: The fight for a human future at the new frontier of power*. PublicAffairs. https://www.hbs.edu/faculty/Pages/item.aspx?num=56791 (Accessed 13.04.2025).

Quality of Life as an Ethical Criterion of the Development of the AI Economy from the Position of the Theory of Stakeholders

Salamat U. Astanova, Dono A. Sativaldiyeva, Elena G. Popkova, Konstantin V. Vodenko, and Platon A. Lifanov

Abstract The development of artificial intelligence (AI) has a large effect on social protection, providing new opportunities and requiring attention to ethical, confidential, and economic aspects. Successful adaptation to this can ensure the improvement of the quality of life and social protection of people. The quick development of digital technologies and AI introduced serious changes in many spheres of life, including healthcare, education, and business. AI can change different industries in different ways. However, it must be used responsibly and in compliance with ethical criteria. Such spheres as healthcare, education, smart cities, etc. are directly connected with the development of AI and can improve the quality of life. Modern technologies transform the traditional ideas of business models, and the generally accepted logic of production processes and managerial decision-making is changed. In some cases, implementation of large projects in certain cases is impossible without the application of AI technologies.

Quality of life is an evolving category, which receives new content depending on society's ideals, the historical period, and approach to its definition. AI can improve people's lives and the quality of life in many ways. The ethics of AI can be viewed as a set of principles determining the way AI must work. These principles are usually oriented towards safety, justice, and humanistic values, protection of consumer

S. U. Astanova
Osh Technological University Named After M.M. Adyshev, Osh, Kyrgyzstan

D. A. Sativaldiyeva
Tashkent State University of Economics, Tashkent, Uzbekistan

E. G. Popkova (✉)
Armenian State University of Economics, Yerevan, Armenia

K. V. Vodenko
Platov South-Russian State Polytechnic University (NPI), Novocherkassk, Russia

P. A. Lifanov
Platov South-Russian State Polytechnic University (NPI), Novocherkassk, Russia

Volgograd State Agricultural University, Volgograd, Russia

A. Karbekova (ed.), *Ethics of the AI Economy: A System View from the Positions of the Theory of Stakeholders*, Ethical Economy 73,
https://doi.org/10.1007/978-3-032-23423-0_3

rights, and prevention of possible abuses in the sphere of information technologies. Ethics of AI is understanding the interaction between AI systems and the world and creating inclusive, safe, confidential, and responsible technologies.

Keywords Artificial intelligence · AI economy · Stakeholders · Quality of life · Ethics · Technologies · Automatization

JEL Codes O14 · O32 · O33 · M14 · L15

1 Introduction

The quality of life could be defined as a reflection of the level of psychology and living of humans; human development and urbanization reflect a level of the quality of life. The quality of life could be treated as the economic, social, and technological well-being of humans (Essoussi 2019). The quality of life could be also treated as a complex and integral notion, which determines and evaluates objective and subjective characteristics of all spheres of life activities of humans, namely economic, social, psychological, political, and cultural, including education, and spiritual.

Artificial intelligence has a large potential and helps people in everyday life. Its usage helps in many tasks, saves time, and improves the quality of life. Apart from economic advantages, artificial intelligence contributes to the improvement of the quality of life. For example, in medicine, artificial intelligence can help in the early detection of diseases, optimisation of treatment, and personalization of medical services. AI algorithms are used in the analysis of medical images, which allows doctors to make quicker and more precise diagnoses. Artificial intelligence has become a part of everyday life, manifested in voice assistants, recommendation systems, and smart devices, which make our lives simpler. AI systems can adapt to the individual needs of users, offering personalized experiences in different spheres, from entertainment to purchases.

AI ethics is seen as a set of principles that stakeholders (from engineers to government officials) apply for the development and responsible use of AI technology. This leads to a safe, humane, and eco-friendly approach to artificial intelligence. AI ethics can be treated as a part of technology ethics, which is focused on systems with artificial intelligence. It comprises the moral behaviour of people during the development and use of AI, as well as the behaviour of machines in machine ethics. Since AI technologies continue to develop, organisations work on ethical codes of AI, to use the leading experience in this sphere.

Artificial intelligence has a large technological effect on economic development, gradually replacing robotization and automatization. In this status, artificial intelligence allows for the best opportunities for the growth of productivity and an increase in the quality of life. However, its application may lead to the growth of inequality between economic development of certain countries and an increase in contradictions between the capabilities of technological giants and the potential of small and medium business (Lukichyov and Chekmarev 2022).

The goal of this research was to study the quality of life as a part of ethical principles in the development of the economy of artificial intelligence from the position of the stakeholder theory.

2 Materials and Methods

Transformations that take place in the world under the influence of globalisation and the digitalisation of public processes inevitably lead to further improvement, implementation, and use of AI technologies in economic processes. Companies and countries that will show timely reaction to new challenges and will be able to cope with the task of the wide usage of the methods and tools of artificial intelligence in their activities will be able to guarantee the leading positions in the general civilisation development.

The issues of the quality of life, artificial intelligence, the AI economy, and stakeholders were studied in many scholarly works. Let us mention some of them, which were considered for this research.

Österle (2022) stated that it is necessary to have a strong understanding of the quality of life to be able to explain the patterns of human behaviour and their influence on well-being. According to the scholar, there is a need for a discipline of Life Engineering to elaborate on the concepts of traditional ethics and philosophy in the interconnection with technical, economic, and social development.

Gruetzemacher and Whittlestone (2022) studied the existing literature sources with a focus on the transformative potential of artificial intelligence in connection with the effects of historical technologies. The scholars strived towards helping researchers and decision-makers to understand potential future applications of artificial intelligence and elaborate on resources and tools for this.

Figueiredo (2024) dwelt on the overlapping of artificial intelligence and the stakeholder theory and the possibilities of enhancement of stakeholder management with the help of artificial intelligence. According to the scholar, AI can improve the effectiveness of stakeholder management through improved data analysis, predictive insights, and customised engagement tactics.

Qin et al. (2024) considered the intersection of artificial intelligence and economic development to understand the comprehensive and multidisciplinary character of the study on the use of artificial intelligence in economic development. The scholars provided the theoretical basis for understanding the vast potential of artificial intelligence in the economy.

Savzikhanova et al. (2023) elaborated on the impact of big data and the economy of artificial intelligence on the quality of life in developed countries and studied the directions of intellectualization in the main sectors of the economy and society in the USA, Germany, Ireland, and Canada. The authors demonstrated the connection between the development of intellectualization in big data and the AI economy and the quality of life of the population and described the perspectives of further development of these phenomena.

Essoussi (2019) considered the influence of AI robots and the development of industrial intelligence on the existing and new problems of the quality of life and states that artificial intelligence has more cons than pros.

Holmes et al. (2023) dwelt on the prospects of key stakeholders on the ethics of artificial intelligence in connection with remote higher education and described many ethical issues in connection with data, algorithms, and education.

3 Results

Artificial intelligence is the approach that allows computers and software to think similarly to the human mind. This is achieved through the study of the regularities of the functioning of the brain and analysis of cognitive processes. As a result, intellectual systems and solutions are created.

Artificial Intelligence could be defined as an interdisciplinary branch of computer science, which includes smart machines that can deal with complex tasks, including tasks that need human intelligence. AI expands human capabilities, for it allows the processing and analysis of large arrays of data. With correct data, AI allows for the assessment of the information obtained and the receipt of conclusions or the formation of economic forecasts. AI has become an important factor in economic growth, influencing different spheres due to its innovative capabilities. Due to the automatization of processes, data analytics, and machine learning, AI facilitates an increase in labour productivity and a decrease in costs. For example, the use of robotized systems in production allows reducing labour costs and decreasing the number of errors, thus improving the quality of products. In the service sphere, AI improves customer services through chatbots, which, in turn, increases customer satisfaction and stimulates demand.

There is also the issue of AI ethics. The principles of AI ethics are important for protecting people from dangerous effects and potential misuse of power by those who have AI technology. Governments, businesses, and other stakeholders must cooperate to use the opportunities and deal with complex ethical challenges presented by AI (Ferretti 2025).

AI is widely used also in healthcare. AI systems can help in diagnosing diseases, and analysis of medical images, medicines, and personalized medicine. For example, AI algorithms can detect cancer at early stages with a high level of precision, which allows improving the treatment. The main advantages of AI are the growth of effectiveness and precision of the execution of tasks, automatization of routine processes, and reduction of costs. AI can process large arrays of data quicker and with higher accuracy, compared to humans, which allows for better decisions and increased productivity in different sectors.

AI ethics are moral rules that companies use for fair and responsible development and application of artificial intelligence. However, there is no unified and generally acknowledged set of principles of AI ethics. The most common principles of AI ethics include human well-being and dignity, dealing with bias and discrimination, transparency, protection of data privacy, diversity, improvement of digital skills, etc. (SAP 2024).

Given the modern global challenges and trends, the role of artificial intelligence in the economy grows, for it influences its different spheres and contributes to its effectiveness. The specific directions of using AI in the economy include automatization of processes, analysis of large arrays of data, personalization of services, forecasting of market trends, and other important aspects. Understanding these aspects is very important for the assessment of the aggregate effect of AI on the economy. AI technologies raise effectiveness and facilitate the implementation of innovations and the development of new products. This emphasises the importance of understanding and introducing AI to ensure competitiveness and sustainable development of economic processes in modern conditions.

The quality of life could be defined as the complex characteristics of satisfaction of material and cultural needs of humans and conditions of life activities, free development of the individual and society on the whole. These characteristics include the indicators of comfort and safety of living, stability of the living environment, accessibility of education and culture, effectiveness of the healthcare system, etc.

The top ten countries by the quality of life are shown in Table 1.

According to Stanford University Human-Centered Artificial Intelligence (2024), the global AI leaders are the US, China, the UK, India, the UAE, France, South Korea, Germany, Japan, and Singapore.

To assess the quality of life, quantitative, qualitative, and integral indicators are used. Quantitative indicators include GNP or GNP per capita, level of consumption

Table 1 Quality of life index by country 2025

	Country	Quality of life index
1.	Luxembourg	220.1
2.	Netherlands	211.3
3.	Denmark	209.9
4.	Oman	208.9
5.	Switzerland	205.0
6.	Finland	203.8
7.	Iceland	202.0
8.	Norway	195.0
9.	Qatar	193.3
10.	Sweden	193.2

Source: Numbeo (2025)

of different material goods and services, level of employment, etc. Qualitative indicators of the quality of life include working, living, and other conditions. Integral indicators of the quality of life characterise the combination of its partial characteristics and criteria, both quantitative and qualitative.

Quality of life is a notion used for assessing and measuring the level of satisfaction, health, comfort, and general well-being of people or the ratio of these aspects in the context of a certain individual, group of people, or settlement. It reflects the level of the person's satisfaction with life. The term "quality of life" covers a lot of different factors, such as health, economic well-being, social relations, education, entertainment, environment, accommodation conditions, safety, etc.

The impact of artificial intelligence on the quality of life is seen in that AI can create new jobs in such spheres as software development and robotics; raise productiveness, automatize routine tasks and allowing people to focus on more creative and strategic tasks; automatize tasks that are dangerous or boring.

It is expedient to consider the quality of life as the criterion of ethics in the development of the AI economy given the stakeholder theory.

Stakeholder theory addresses business ethics and values during the management of stakeholders involved in a certain project. Stakeholder theory is used in many important fields: corporate social responsibility, strategic management, project management, and business ethics. Proactive and systemic involvement and interaction of the company with stakeholders can facilitate the company's functioning and form the potential for the maximum integration of the company's development strategy with the social and business environments and form a systemic and dynamic business model of the company.

An important feature of the modern development of the stakeholder theory is the provisions of its direct connection with the formation of a socially responsible company. Constant consideration of the different interests of stakeholders, the satisfaction of which influences the company's future, leads to an increase in the business's responsibility before society on the whole and stakeholders as its representatives.

According to the stakeholder theory, organisations and corporations must act for the benefit of these stakeholders, which will lead to long-term success. Thus, the theory of stakeholders helps identify the key differences between interested groups, spheres of potential conflicts, and ways to neutralise them and develop adequate measures aimed at more effective management. On the whole, the theory and practice of stakeholders are promising in the sense of systemic involvement of new participants in the management processes and pragmatic focus on the resolution of problems.

Returning to artificial intelligence, its specific features are very diverse. It can be used in different spheres. The main sectors of application of AI are as follows: automatization—AI allows performing routine tasks and optimising work processes without human participation; data analysis—processing of large arrays of data and detection of hidden connections; decision making; forecasting; image recognition—with the help of computer vision and signals processing; interaction with humans—through natural language, voice assistants, etc. In everyday life, AI covers a wide range of applications, e.g., prevention of fraud, systems of home automatization; recommendations and purchases; machine learning in routine activities; analysis of health and fitness, etc.

4 Discussion

At present, human life depends on machines a lot; however, intelligent machines produced by artificial intelligence cannot remove or replace the natural human role. It is expected that future societies will leave most of their activities to smart machines. These activities may include information processing, decision-making, motor vehicle traffic, firefighting, traffic regulation, etc. (Essoussi 2019).

Artificial intelligence changes the world, opening new horizons to business, science, and society. However, the development of this technology is accompanied by multiple ethical challenges, such as bias of algorithms, danger to privacy, and risks of irresponsible use. The ethical approach to the development of AI becomes the key factor in its safe implementation and usage. Ethics of AI is the key aspect of its implementation, which influences consumers' trust and stable development of society. A responsible approach to the development of AI allows avoiding many challenges and ensures its safe and effective usage.

Thanks to AI technology, computers and machines can learn and adapt to data, make decisions, and perform complex tasks without human participation. Being able to gather, analyse, and use data, artificial intelligence can improve effectiveness and productiveness in different sectors. AI can help solve global problems, such as medical diagnostics, fighting climate change, and improvement of the quality of education. Responsible use of this technology will ensure its positive effect on society.

Artificial intelligence provides many opportunities for the development of technologies and society on the whole. However, its application is connected with a range of ethical problems, which require careful consideration and resolution. AI plays an important role in the management of different aspects of society's life. It is used in medicine for diagnostics, in education for personalisation of education, in the economy for analysis of market trends, etc. AI can also improve the quality of life. The notion of the quality of life is one of the most complex notions for the study of society's characteristics. This notion reflects all aspects of society's life, which are directly influenced by economic, social, political, and ideological laws of public development. The quality of life is characterised by the level of satisfaction of human needs, predetermined by the corresponding norms, customs, and traditions, as well as the level of personal demands.

5 Conclusions

Artificial intelligence is a modern term that describes machines performing cognitive processes that are similar to human processes. These processes include, among others, learning, understanding, thinking, and interactions. Artificial intelligence can have different forms, such as technical infrastructure, part of the production process, or product of the final consumer.

The potential of AI to improve the quality of life is practically unlimited. Special attention in this sphere must be given to ethical aspects and issues of safety, which will ensure the responsible use of AI. The growing integration of AI into the economy opens new opportunities for the improvement of the quality of life, creation of jobs, and sustainable development.

AI ethics is a set of guiding principles used by interested parties to guarantee the responsible development and use of AI technology. This means the application of a safe, human-centred, and environmentally-friendly approach to AI. Effective management of AI ethics benefits all stakeholders. The concept of stakeholders is very popular nowadays. Effective interaction with stakeholders ensures flexibility and stability of the company and facilitates the determination of new opportunities for territories' development. Ethical AI has an important role in the development and implementation of technologies. It can ensure justice, transparency, confidentiality, and human-centeredness for the favourable development of society. Future development of AI may bring greater integration of this technology into our lives. One of the directions is the development of more complex and autonomous systems, which will allow AI to solve more complex tasks and reduce the need for human control. Another promising direction is the development of ethical standards and regulatory frameworks to ensure the safe and responsible application of AI.

Artificial intelligence has a large effect on everyday life, raising effectiveness, convenience, and safety in different spheres. Still, its development leads to new challenges, which require attention and solutions. Understanding these aspects and active support in the development of AI technologies will ensure their harmonious integration into society, facilitating progress and growth of the quality of life. Artificial intelligence is one of the most important technological sectors of the world economy. It will become an inseparable part of the technologies of the future and will provide new opportunities in many spheres of human activities.

References

Essoussi, H. 2019. Implications of artificial intelligence on quality of life (a prospective study of the advanced technological reality and the vague human future). *International Journal of Inspiration & Resilience Economy* 3 (1): 1–7. https://doi.org/10.5923/j.ijire.20190301.01.

Ferretti, T. 2025. *The ethics and politics of artificial intelligence*. https://www.lse.ac.uk/study-at-lse/online-learning/insights/the-ethics-and-politics-of-artificial-intelligence (Accessed 01.04.2025).

Figueiredo, J. M. P. C. 2024. *The impact of artificial intelligence on the stakeholder theory: A bibliometric review analysis*. PQDT-Global.
Gruetzemacher, R., and J. Whittlestone. 2022. The transformative potential of artificial intelligence. *Futures* 135 (2022): 102884. https://doi.org/10.1016/j.futures.2021.102884.
Holmes, W., F. Iniesto, S. Anastopoulou, and J. G. Boticario. 2023. Stakeholder perspectives on the ethics of AI in distance-based higher education. *The International Review of Research in Open and Distributed Learning* 24 (2): 96–117. https://doi.org/10.19173/irrodl.v24i2.6089.
Lukichyov, P. M., and O. P. Chekmarev. 2022. Economics of artificial intelligence and the principal-agent concept. *Russian Journal of Innovation Economics* 12 (2): 1069–1082. https://doi.org/10.18334/vinec.12.2.114514.
Numbeo. 2025. *Quality of life index by country 2025*. https://www.numbeo.com/quality-of-life/rankings_by_country.jsp?title=2025&displayColumn=0 (Accessed 01.04.2025).
Österle, H. 2022. Ethics or quality of life? In *Perspectives on digital humanism*, ed. H. Werthner, E. Prem, E. A. Lee, and C. Ghezzi. Cham: Springer. https://doi.org/10.1007/978-3-030-86144-5_35.
Qin, Y., Z. Xu, X. Wang, et al. 2024. Artificial intelligence and economic development: An evolutionary investigation and systematic review. *Journal of the Knowledge Economy* 15:1736–1770. https://doi.org/10.1007/s13132-023-01183-2.
SAP. 2024. *What is AI ethics?* https://www.sap.com/resources/what-is-ai-ethics (Accessed 01.04.2025)
Savzikhanova, S. E., Z. A. Gasanova, N. M. Fomenko, T. I. Isabekova, and N. E. Eminova. 2023. Quality of life in the Big Data and AI economy: Modern experience and future perspectives. In *Challenges of the modern economy. Advances in science, technology & innovation*, ed. Y. G. Buchaev, A. S. Abdulkadyrov, J. V. Ragulina, A. A. Khachaturyan, and E. G. Popkova. Cham: Springer. https://doi.org/10.1007/978-3-031-29364-1_81.
Stanford University Human-Centered Artificial Intelligence. 2024. *Global AI power rankings: Stanford HAI tool ranks 36 countries in AI*. https://hai.stanford.edu/news/global-ai-power--rankings-stanford-hai-tool-ranks-36-countries-in-ai (Accessed 01.04.2025).

Ethics of Digital Personnel Management in the AI Economy with Systemic Consideration of Interested Parties' Views

Gulnora K. Ibragimova, Elena G. Popkova, Konstantin V. Vodenko, and Platon A. Lifanov

Abstract The processes of transition to the AI economy are connected with many implications for society, government, and government bodies. HR policy in the conditions of intellectualization involves digital personnel management. Large-scale dissemination of AI tools and digital services based on them leads to the emergence of new rules and conditions of work for digital personnel. This might lead to a possible violation of management ethics. In this research, we show that different subjects of the business environment can set various requirements for digital personnel. These requirements may negatively influence the ethics of digital personnel management, creating threats to the quality and efficiency of labour.

We consider AI tools used for digital personnel management at the level of digital labour platforms and companies that use the work of digital personnel in offices. The analysis shows that digital labour platforms are more attractive for digital personnel compared to companies that are oriented towards digital personnel's work in offices from an ethical point of view. The goal of this research was to systematise the specifics of ethics of digital personnel management depending on the tools of the AI economy with systemic consideration of the interested parties' views. The novel aspect of this research lies in establishing the features of the development of the AI economy in digital personnel management in various conditions of employment.

G. K. Ibragimova
Tashkent State University of Economics, Tashkent, Uzbekistan
e-mail: g.ibragimova@tsue.uz

E. G. Popkova (✉)
Armenian State University of Economics, Yerevan, Armenia

K. V. Vodenko
Platov South-Russian State Polytechnic University (NPI), Novocherkassk, Russia

P. A. Lifanov
Platov South-Russian State Polytechnic University (NPI), Novocherkassk, Russia

Volgograd State Agricultural University, Volgograd, Russia

A. Karbekova (ed.), *Ethics of the AI Economy: A System View from the Positions of the Theory of Stakeholders*, Ethical Economy 73,
https://doi.org/10.1007/978-3-032-23423-0_4

Keywords Digital personnel management · AI economy · Digitalization · Intellectualization · Ethics · Employment · Employers · Interested parties

JEL Codes E24 · F66 · J08 · J22 · J23 · J24 · O32 · O33

1 Introduction

The transition of the economy from the age of digitalization to intellectualization brings new opportunities and perspectives, as well as challenges for companies, human resources, and sectors. The AI economy envisages the emergence of advantages in the management of the main processes which create additional value of products through saving on traditional processes, which are transferred for execution to intellectual tools. Human resources management (from selecting, training, and management of coaching to the improvement of professional and digital resilience, management of the main processes of the work of employees and groups of employees, and assessment of productivity) in the conditions of the AI economy involves many advantages that can ensure technological and economic growth. However, it also entails a range of vivid and clear threats, which are connected with such aspects as ethics of digital personnel management, non-compliance with which can, in certain cases, lead to promising personnel being unable to work at companies with unacceptable management methods. Also, failures in processes could be caused by companies' HR policies involving the unilateral consideration of the views of owners and managers but neglecting the expectations of all interested parties (digital personnel, specialists, scholars studying the given problem, representatives of public organisations, and society). These failures could lead to the termination of production or logistics processes, which may lead to loss of image and further bankruptcy. This is applied especially to large corporations, which capitalization depends on all events that are known to the public.

The objective of this research was to systematise the specifics of the ethics of digital personnel management depending on the tools of the AI economy with systemic consideration of the interested parties' views. Achievement of this goal involved the following tasks: revealing the main tools of the AI economy that are used by the business environment during digital personnel management and assessing the ethics of digital personnel management in the conditions of the use of these tools of the AI economy depending on the focus on the systemic consideration of interested parties' views.

2 Materials and Methods

In this paper, we used methods allowing us to reveal and analyse the influence of the tools of the AI economy on the ethics of digital personnel management. Their choice was predetermined by the focus on the need for maximum disclosure of the topic of this research. A systemic approach was utilised to reveal the main components of the mechanism of transition to the AI economy in digital personnel management. The subject analysis was aimed at assessing the consideration of views of all interested parties in the process of intellectual management of digital personnel. Content analysis was used to reveal the key features of the ethics of digital personnel management in the conditions of the AI economy in the context of ensuring systemic consideration of the views of all interested parties.

The extant scientific works devoted to the issues of digital personnel management in the AI economy could be classified in the following directions. Oladeji Olaniyi et al. (2024) dwelt on the problems of transition of HR policy of most companies, due to insufficient readiness of personnel, for professional activities with the use of innovative intellectual technologies. However, provisions of this work did not assess ethical problems as the key ones in ensuring the effectiveness of digital personnel management.

Cruz and Gameiro (2023) analysed the issues of the formation of socioeconomic relations during the interaction of digital intermediary platforms, customers, and performers (digital personnel). According to the authors, such relations become a new economic paradigm and require more thorough attention. The authors also note the importance of the government's participation in this interaction, for it is the subject capable of ensuring guarantees of social and economic protection of citizens who function in the role of digital personnel.

Weritz (2022) presented a range of important provisions for the organisation of a digital workplace at large innovative companies given the requirements for digital personnel. The research was performed by the example of large service corporations. Baumgartner et al. (2021) considered digital personnel as a digital workforce, which is different from traditional personnel due to a range of advantages connected with high digital and professional readiness for transformations.

Maxyutova et al. (2022) presented an analysis of socioeconomic factors of regulating the labour market in Kyrgyzstan and Kazakhstan. The authors elaborated on the problem of the negative impact on equality due to the large scale implementation of technologies (including intellectual) and the growth of personnel cuts due to their replacement with technologies.

Andrieux et al. (2024) considered the advantages of implementing AI tools in personnel management at companies and noted the importance of considering ethical problems connected with intellectualization. This research is valuable to the development of a roadmap for personnel management with the help of AI. Rodgers et al. (2023), Purohit and Banerjee (2025), and Langer and Konig (2023) presented a justification of an approach to managing ethical issues of using AI in personnel management.

Despite the existence of the works devoted to the considered topic, there exists a need for complex systematisation of the features of digital personnel management in the AI economy with systemic consideration of the interested parties' views.

3 Results

Before embarking on the tasks of this research, it is necessary to dwell on the nature of the phenomenon of digital personnel. This term is rather debatable at the current stage of development of science.

Cruz and Gameiro (2023) define digital personnel as a workforce functioning remotely with the help of digital technologies (including digital platforms). According to the scholars, digital personnel are personnel without a full-time job but receiving tasks at digital platforms. Even though within functioning at digital platforms, digital personnel have large freedom of choice, they are still within certain management. This is formed according to requirements set by customers or the digital platform itself.

Weritz (2022) defines digital personnel as companies' labour resources whose work could be remote or office-based; it is connected with digitalization and is characterised as a digital workplace. The authors note that the following requirements are set for digital personnel: knowledge and skills in the sphere of web development and big databases analysis; skills in command management (also remotely), which is ensured by the skills in digital and traditional communication; skills and experience in personal growth; readiness and ability for transformations in work, training, and communications; digital literacy and possession of professional knowledge given the integration of ICT. Baumgartner et al. (2021) state that digital personnel are the most valuable strategic resource for the digitalization and intellectualization of companies.

We think that both categories of digital personnel are influenced by interested parties and, accordingly, may face ethical problems.

Let us dwell on the modern tools of the AI economy, which are used in digital personnel management. The specifics of the ethics of the management of digital personnel, who choose digital tasks or receive orders at digital service platforms, should be considered. The world's leading digital service platforms for remote employment are analysed (Table 1). We reveal the type of AI tools, which are used in digital personnel management in the context of these digital platforms' functioning based on the analysis of the materials of these platforms' websites.

Let us further dwell on the use of AI in digital personnel management in different companies. In 2023, the leading bank holding Morgan Stanley (USA) implemented a digital service AI @ Morgan Stanley Assistant, which ensures the training and support of employees during the use of digital information from various sources. In the beginning, this initiative faced serious opportunism from the management of structural departments, teams, and employees. In the process of adaptation, it was seen that this service became better in many respects, compared to personnel of the

Table 1 Characteristics of the ethics of management and tools of the AI economy that are used in the interaction with digital personnel at digital labour platforms

	Digital platform of employment and its specifics	AI tools, Ethics of management
1	Dynamite Jobs—registered in the USA, works at the global level (USA, Canada, South America, Europe). Remote offices in each country of operation. Goal—supporting companies to outsource work to private performers.	Complex verification of the business image of the employer company is used to protect the rights and interests of job applicants (digital personnel). Requirements for employers: observation of agreements on the volume of work and payment; absence of additional tasks, which are not agreed upon, in the work; absence of the requirements for the work in the office. Requirements for job applicants: professional experience and skills in digital work. AI tools: analysis of big databases used for questionnaires and applications processing, machine learning to find similarities in indicators: offer-demand. Ethics of digital personnel management: no AI tools that violate privacy, moral values, and interests of job applicants. Systemic consideration of the views of all interested parties: high for all parties.
2	Working Nomads—registered in the USA, with offices in the UK, Spain, Singapore, Portugal, the Phillippines, New Zealand, the Netherlands, Mexico, Japan, Ireland, Germany, France, and Colombia. Goal: supporting the employment of digital personnel of the digital nomad category, including creating and guaranteeing their socioeconomic and legal support in the country of their residence and work.	Requirements for digital personnel who seek employment at the digital platform as digital nomads: positive references (recommendations) from previous jobs; absence of a criminal record; high professionalism, work experience. Requirements for employers: observation of agreements on the volume of work and payment; absence of additional tasks, which are not agreed upon, in the work; absence of the requirements for the work in the office. AI tools: analysis of big databases, machine learning. Ethics of digital personnel management: no AI tools that violate privacy, moral values, and interests of job applicants. Systemic consideration of the views of all interested parties: high for all parties.

(continued)

Table 1 (continued)

	Digital platform of employment and its specifics	AI tools, Ethics of management
3	Remotive—digital platform of employment with the main office in the USA. Provides work for digital employees in the USA, South America, Canada, the EU, and countries of Asia. Goal: the entire range of support for job applicants, and control over employers in the process of employment.	Complex verification of employers (image, economic sustainability, and work ethics. AI Career Coach digital service is used for the creation of CVs; and the provision of advice for behaviour during interviews to achieve better results. Ethics of digital personnel management: observed in the part of the protection of labour resources from imposing tasks and functions that are not envisaged by the agreement, interfering with the view of personal and professional potential, and imposing the behaviour model during interviews with employers. Systemic consideration of the views of all interested parties: high for all parties, with priority support of digital personnel
4	Pangian—digital platform of employment (USA). This digital platform is presented in 150 countries of the world. Goal: Provide employment for talented digital personnel (including those with small or no experience but with knowledge and skills in the digital environment).	Requirements for employer companies: business image, social and economic sustainability, compliance with terms of working with digital personnel stipulated by the agreement. Requirements for job applicants: professional experience (however, personnel with insufficient or no experience could be hired), skills in digital work, and communication skills. AI tools: analysis of big databases, machine learning; using AI service for creating CVs and compiling recommendations for acquisition of new skills and knowledge. Ethics of digital personnel management: protection of digital personnel from non-contractual obligations. Systemic consideration of the views of all interested parties: high for all parties.

(continued)

Table 1 (continued)

	Digital platform of employment and its specifics	AI tools, Ethics of management
5	Crossover—digital platform of employment (USA). It functions in most countries in Europe, North and South America, Asia, and Africa. Goal: meeting demand and providing offers in the market of digital labour in the sphere of high technologies.	Requirements for employer companies: high image and level of R&D; compliance with requirements on the management of digital personnel, stimulated by the agreement. Requirements for job applicants: high level of education in the professional sphere: high digital readiness; work experience; achievements in the professional sphere: readiness for full-time remote employment. AI tools: analysis of big databases; machine learning (used in chatbots); computer vision (used during video conferences); AI service for compilation of CVs. Ethics of digital personnel management: observed in the part of digital personnel protection from non contractual obligations; might be violated during the use of AI for the creation of CVs and the use of computer vision during videoconferences (observation of behaviour, reactions, speech, and manners). Systemic consideration of the views of all interested parties: rather high for all parties focus on high-tech companies of the Silicon Valley in the USA.

Source: Compiled by the authors based on Elphick (2025)

holding This includes knowledge, communication skills, and creativity. As of now, the service is used in the sphere of financial consulting. It can analyse 100,000 documents instantaneously, which is due to the powerful software used as its basis (Estrada 2023). Despite the frequent announcements from the holding's management that AI is to supplement labour resources and is not aimed at replacing them, March 2025 saw the dismissal of 2000 employees (TIMESOFINDIA.COM 2025). This measure could be explained by the growth of AI integration and the expansion of automatization on its basis. Personnel cuts do not stimulate the professional growth of human resources, since they are not confident in the perspectives of their employment. In this case, the use of AI in digital personnel management, in the sector of digital financial banking, is aimed at training the digital service to perform various tasks and functions without human participation.

The international network of companies PwC (with the main office in the UK), which functions in the sphere of management consulting and audit, integrated AI services similar to those used by Morgan Stanley. The analysis revealed that the application of these services led to trends of personnel cuts, like in the case of Morgan Stanley. AI services turn out to be more productive, which leads to their large-scale integration and them replacing less effective labour resources. According to Coghlan (2024), PwC planned personnel cuts of 5% in company offices around the world. This indicator is not final, since representatives of the IMF published a statement that, in the short-term, integration of AI might lead to the dismissal of approximately 40% of labour resources. This would lead to the growth of inequality and deterioration of the indicators of sustainable development of the economy and society. Though PwC announced that it would compensate for the negative effect of personnel cuts for the labour market, by hiring digital personnel in other spheres, dismissed employees cannot find the required vacancies in the banking sector. Similar to Morgan Stanley, employees of PwC face serious ethical problems, for they work in the conditions of the use of new digital services (e.g., video recording), to which they do not always give their consent, and their opinion in this matter is neglected; the same is true for the use of AI, which does not take into account certain socio-psychological characteristics.

4 Discussion

In this paper, we studied the specifics of using AI tools in digital personnel management within the digital platforms of employment and at companies and assessed the level of systemic consideration of the views of all interested parties in the context of this process.

It is worth noting that the ethics of digital personnel management in the AI economy, by the example of digital employment platforms, could be assessed as rather high. Tools of artificial intelligence, used in their activities, are similar, on the whole, across all considered platforms. However, certain AI tools and services lead to the emergence of ethical problems. This is observed in the following aspects:

- Computer vision, used for video recording of the behaviour of job applicants. This service provides digital labour platforms with data on the personal features of individuals looking for jobs. Despite this service being aimed at the maximum effectiveness of employment, it creates issues of moral and ethical character, which leads to the reluctance of many talented applicants to look for a job on such digital platforms;
- Service of compiling CVs and preparations of references and recommendations on communication with the employer, which is based on machine learning and analysis of big databases. These service negatively influence the individuality of candiates. As a result, digital platforms that use this complex primarily support the interests of employees, who are a source of income to them.

In high-tech companies with full-time office employees, ethics of digital personnel management in the context of the AI economy face more challenges, compared to the example of digital labour platforms. The reason is that decisions on the transition to artificial intelligence are made by owners and managers who are oriented towards the protection of their interests, to support the competition of business and growth of revenues.

Given the above, we believe that digital labour platforms are a more attractive option for digital personnel in the conditions of quick digitalization and intellectualization. One of the reasons for this is that creation of favourable conditions of work for digital personnel is the main direction of activities of these platforms.

5 Conclusion

The modern trends of the AI economy are connected with diverse approaches to digital personnel management. A specific feature of digital labour platforms in the processes of digital personnel management is protecting interests and meeting expectations of all interested parties (digital platform, job applicants, employer companies/or companies that outsource different tasks) and additional focus on support of digital personnel or hiring companies. The parity of relationships is retained, and digital labour platforms are oriented towards digital personnel as the main source of their prospective development. Ethical norms are complied with in the case of digital labour platforms.

As for the management of digital personnel in leading high-tech companies in the conditions of the AI economy, certain ethical problems may arise. They are caused by the focus not on systemic consideration of views of interested parties but on the interests of owners and/or management.

The modern problems of integrating artificial intelligence into the management of digital personnel must be solved with the help of the government. Even though most countries with a market economy regulate relationships without government's interference, it still might be needed. At the current stage, the labour market is unstable and subject to deterioration, which is caused by the growth of intellectualization of economy with the use of AI. Social inequality, being the result of these tranformations, will become a threat for individual countries and at the global level.

References

Andrieux, P., R. D. Johnson, J. Sarabadani, and C. V. Slyke. 2024. Ethical considerations of generative AI-enabled human resource management. *Organizational Dynamics* 53:1. https://doi.org/10.1016/j.orgdyn.2024.101032.

Baumgartner, C., F. Hartl, and T. Hess. 2021. New workplace, new mindset: Empirical case studies on the interplay between digital workplace and organizational culture. In *International conference on Wirtschaftsinformatik*, 91–107. Cham: Springer. https://doi.org/10.1007/978-3-030-86800-0_7.

Coghlan, J. 2024. *1 in 4 CEOs expect to sack staff due to AI this year—PwC survey*. https://hunstonpartners.com/1-in-4-ceos-expect-to-sack-staff-due-to-ai-this-year-pwc-survey/ (Accessed 12.04.2025).

Cruz, S. A., and A. Gameiro. 2023. Digital work platform: Understanding platforms, workers, clients in a service relation. *Frontiers in Sociology* 7:1075808. https://doi.org/10.3389/fsoc.2022.1075808.

Elphick, M. B. 2025. *The top 9 remote work platforms for 2025*. https://www.crossover.com/resources/the-top-9-remote-work-platforms-for-2025 (Accessed 12.04.2025).

Estrada, S. 2023. *Morgan Stanley debuts a new tool for employees: An AI assistant to answer common investing and personal finance queries*. https://finance.yahoo.com/news/morgan-stanley-debuts-tool-employees-110502479.html (Accessed 12.04.2025).

Langer, M., and C. J. Konig. 2023. Introducing a multi-stakeholder perspective on opacity, transparency and strategies to reduce opacity in algorithm-based human resource management. *Human Resource Management Review* 33 (1): https://doi.org/10.1016/j.hrmr.2021.100881.

Maxyutova, A., S. Kaliyeva, R. Rakhmetova, M. Meldakhanova, and G. Khajiyeva. 2022. Socio-economic factors in labour market regulation. *Migration Letters* 19 (5): 561–570. https://doi.org/10.33182/ml.v19i6.2375.

Oladeji Olaniyi, Oluwaseun, F. A. Ezeugwa, C. G. Okatta, A. Arigbabu, and P. C. Joeneke. 2024. Digital workforce assessing the interplay and impact of AI, automation, and employment policies. *Archives of Current Research International* 24 (5): 124–139. https://doi.org/10.9734/acri/2024/v24i5690.

Purohit, R., and T. Banerjee. 2025. Artificial intelligence-based organizational decision-making in recruitment practice. *Human Systems Management* 44 (1): 173–186. https://doi.org/10.3233/HSM-240044.

Rodgers, W., J. M. Murray, A. Stefanidis, W. Y. Degbey, and S. Y. Tarba. 2023. An artificial intelligence algorithmic approach to ethical decision-making in human resource management processes. *Human Resource Management Review* 33:1. https://doi.org/10.1016/j.hrmr.2022.100925.

TIMESOFINDIA.COM. 2025. *Morgan Stanley to cut 2000 jobs; as AI and Automation come to investment banking*. https://timesofindia.indiatimes.com/technology/tech-news/morgan-stanley-to-cut-2000-jobs-as-ai-and-automation-come-to-investment-banking/articleshow/119309931.cms (Accessed 12.04.2025).

Weritz, P. 2022. Hey leaders, it's time to train the workforce: Critical skills in the digital workplace. *Administrative Sciences* 12 (3): 94. https://doi.org/10.3390/admsci12030094.

Cyber Fraud as a Threat to Economic Security

Ivan A. Chusov, Oxana V. Kravtsova, Sergey A. Dmitrienko, Natalya M. Gazaryan, and Dmitry V. Kalashnikov

Abstract The research focuses on cyber fraud in the world as a serious threat to the economic security of individuals and countries. In an era of digitalization, where processes of data exchange and storage are increasingly moving online, criminals are continually devising new methods to exploit vulnerabilities in network infrastructures, affecting individuals and organizations. In recent years, there has been a significant rise in instances of cyber fraud, from phishing attacks that now incorporate artificial intelligence, enabling fraudsters to launch more adaptive and personalized schemes, to complex breaches of banking systems. The authors present statistics on cyber threats and the financial losses incurred by individuals and businesses, highlighting the pressing need to address this issue. They argue for developing and implementing effective economic measures, including comprehensive strategies that combine regulation with incentives for businesses and individuals, to help prevent such crimes.

Keywords Cyber fraud • Economic security • Economic threat • International cooperation • Economics

JEL Codes O10 • K39 • Z13

1 Introduction

Cyber fraud as a threat to economic security is one of the most pressing issues in today's society. With each passing year, the number of cyber fraud crimes is increasing, underscoring the need to study this problem and seek effective measures to address it.

I. A. Chusov (✉) · O. V. Kravtsova · S. A. Dmitrienko · N. M. Gazaryan · D. V. Kalashnikov
Volgograd Cooperative Institute (Branch) of the Russian University of Cooperation, Volgograd, Russia
e-mail: s.a.dmitrenko@ruc.su; ngazaryah@ruc.su; d.v.kalashnikov@ruc.su

A. Karbekova (ed.), *Ethics of the AI Economy: A System View from the Positions of the Theory of Stakeholders*, Ethical Economy 73,
https://doi.org/10.1007/978-3-032-23423-0_5

2 Materials and Methods

One of the reasons cyber fraud has become such a significant threat is the global interconnectivity of economies. An attack on one company or financial institution can have local consequences and trigger a domino effect impacting international markets.

Governments worldwide are actively developing legislative initiatives to combat cybercrime, yet even the strictest regulatory measures often prove insufficient. This is due to the rapidly evolving nature of these threats: criminals adapt with astonishing speed, sometimes outpacing the cybersecurity software and protective measures employed by companies.

According to the United Nations, financial losses from cyber fraud in East and Southeast Asia in 2023 were estimated at $18–$37 billion (UNODC 2024).

The primary cause of these losses was schemes orchestrated by transnational criminal groups in Southeast Asia. The Philippines, Vietnam, Malaysia, Singapore, and Thailand face serious cyber threats and a surge in fraud cases involving digital technologies. The number of deepfake-related incidents increased by 1530% from 2022 to 2023. Weak cybersecurity infrastructure, a lack of regulatory frameworks, and burgeoning digital economies contribute to this vulnerability.

China serves as a prime target and a base for cybercrime. The country's rapid digital transformation has led to a rise in threats, including phishing, hacks, and fraud targeting citizens and businesses.

In Japan, threats in the corporate sector are on the rise, with many organizations experiencing compromised business communications and ransomware attacks.

Certain areas in Myanmar, such as KK Park, have become hotspots for digital technology crimes. These criminal centers serve as bases for various illicit online activities that are difficult to track and suppress due to their isolated and fortified locations.

Throughout the region, illegal online casinos and high-risk cryptocurrency services are emerging as key components of organized crime infrastructure, providing cover for financial crimes and the spread of fraudulent schemes.

Data stolen using info stealers, disseminated through these channels, contain information obtained from users across various countries, including Russia. Criminal groups leverage this data to launch attacks worldwide.

In March 2024, in the province of Nakhon Si Thammarat (Thailand), more than 70 individuals were detained on suspicion of fraud aimed at deceiving citizens of China, Russia, and Thailand.

The United Nations recommends that governments improve monitoring and legislative regulation, including enhanced measures to combat money laundering, improved control over cryptocurrency transactions, and the licensing of virtual assets.

Between 2020 and 2023, Russia has witnessed a steady rise in cyber fraud, affecting all major digital sectors—from banking operations and online purchases to innovative blockchain technologies (Koimshidi and Sarkisyan 2023).

Notably, the emergence of sophisticated phishing techniques that incorporate artificial intelligence has enabled fraudsters to create more adaptive and personalized attacks. Vishing has also advanced significantly, now incorporating deepfake technologies into its arsenal, opening new horizons for deception.

The growing popularity of cryptocurrencies and NFTs has created a new domain for fraud, where cybercriminals exploit the general public's limited understanding of blockchain technologies for their gain.

The number of incidents and the overall financial damage from cyberattacks increase each year, underscoring the need for active collaboration between the government, businesses, and society in cybersecurity to ensure a higher level of protection for the financial and personal data of Russian citizens (Table 1).

In 2024, there is an intensification of old and new cyber fraud schemes (Fig. 1).

The current situation in cyber fraud in Russia in 2024 is as follows (Fig. 2).

Cybercrime poses a serious threat to the economic security of any nation. It continues to grow in scale and complexity. With the rapid digitization of the economy, businesses and government agencies are becoming increasingly reliant on

Table 1 Table of cyber fraud in Russia in 2020–2023

Year	Type of fraud	Description	Number of cases	Damage (in billions of rubles)
2020	Phishing	Sending fake emails and websites to collect personal data	5000	3.5
2020	Vishing	Telephone calls to defraud and steal financial data	3200	4.0
2020	Pyramid schemes	Promise of high returns when investing in dubious projects	2500	6.1
2021	Phishing	Increase in phishing using social networks and messengers	8200	5.2
2021	Vishing	Increased number of frauds using fake technical services	4500	5.5
2021	Counterfeit online stores	Creating fake sites to sell non-existent products	3800	3.9
2022	Phishing	New methods of spoofing bank websites and authorization pages	10,000	7.4
2022	Vishing	Using Deepfake technologies to deceive and collect data	6100	6.7
2022	Cryptocurrency scams	Use of fake ICOs and crypto exchanges for embezzlement	5200	8.0
2023	Phishing	Using AI to create more convincing and layered scam attacks	12,500	9.8
2023	Vishing	Targeted attacks on senior and vulnerable citizens	7000	7.2
2023	NFT scam	Using NFT to launder money and sell invisible assets	4000	6.5

Source: Developed by the authors

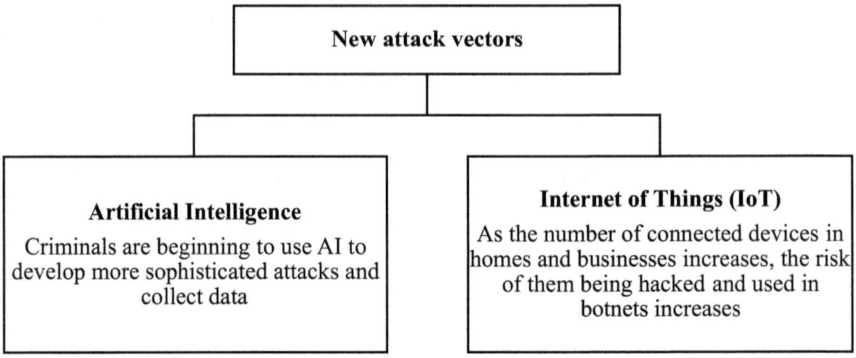

Fig. 1 New attack vectors. Source: Developed by the authors

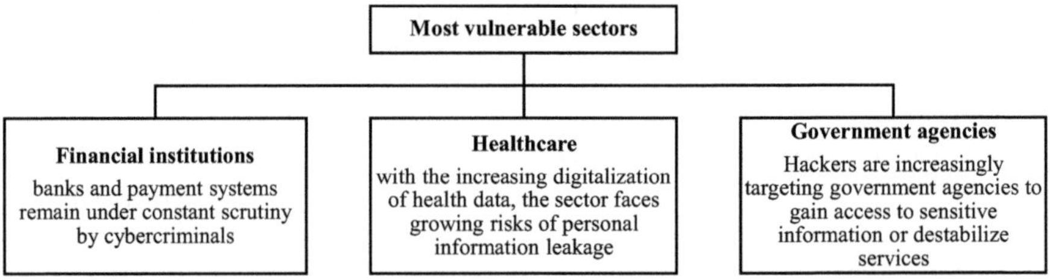

Fig. 2 Most vulnerable sectors. Source: Developed by the authors

technology. This dependence leaves them vulnerable to various cyber threats, from data theft to sophisticated attacks (e.g., ransomware and supply chain breaches).

The first alarming fact is that cybercriminals can inflict significant financial damage. Hackers can infiltrate banking networks, steal funds, and block access to critical financial data, undermining not only financial institutions but also public trust in the entire banking system.

Targeted attacks on industrial facilities and infrastructure present a considerable threat to the national economy. Meanwhile, espionage and sabotage in sectors such as energy, transportation, and other key industries can cause substantial financial losses and disrupt the operation of vital systems.

The risk posed by the leakage of confidential information is equally significant; vast amounts of data stored by companies and government agencies can be exploited for blackmail, fraud, or even political interference. The authors believe that data breaches can erode competitive advantages on the international stage and damage reputations, potentially leading to financial losses.

It is also important to note that small and medium-sized enterprises suffer from cybercrime because their limited resources for protection often leave their systems exposed and ill-prepared to counter cyber threats, resulting in serious financial setbacks.

Countermeasures against cybercrime are diverse, encompassing technical and organizational methods. Advanced technologies provide many tools to defend against malicious attacks, while education and increased awareness help prevent potential threats.

Key strategies are as follows:

1. Developing and implementing advanced cybersecurity systems that incorporate intrusion detection and prevention systems (IDS/IPS), firewalls, and antivirus software;
2. Isolating and segmenting networks and dividing the network into subnets limit access to confidential information and reduce the risk of malware spreading, ensuring that attackers cannot access the most sensitive company data even if a breach occurs;
3. Training employees; staff may inadvertently cause data leaks or virus infections due to carelessness or a lack of knowledge. Regular training sessions and awareness campaigns help foster cybersecurity literacy and enable personnel to recognize threats such as phishing and social engineering;
4. Collaborating with law enforcement agencies—joint efforts with the police, intelligence services, and other governmental bodies help track and curb the activities of cybercriminals both domestically and internationally. Systemic information sharing about new threats and vulnerabilities between commercial and governmental organizations promotes the swift adoption of new defensive measures;
5. Establishing a robust legal framework for cybersecurity—effective regulation will set stringent standards for data protection and impose penalties for cybercrimes, thereby deterring potential wrongdoers;
6. Creating international agreements and treaties that form a global security network and enhance accountability for violations in this sector.

3 Results

The authors chose to focus on measures that require the development and implementation of effective economic-level countermeasures. These measures involve creating comprehensive strategies that combine regulation with incentives for businesses and individuals to help prevent such offenses:

1. Strengthening economic oversight and monitoring financial flows. Collaborating with financial regulators, government bodies should establish and implement mechanisms that enable real-time tracking of suspicious transactions. Advanced technologies (e.g., artificial intelligence and machine learning) can significantly aid in automating data processing and expediting the detection and prevention of fraudulent schemes;
2. Encouraging companies to invest in cybersecurity—for instance, through tax breaks and subsidies. Such economic incentives can motivate businesses to allocate more resources toward protecting their information systems. Government initiatives that support the development of security technologies and stimulate

research projects in this field will help create effective solutions to counter cyber threats;

3. Developing cyber risk insurance systems is a crucial step in the economic fight against cybercrime. These insurance products can substantially reduce companies' financial losses during attacks. Moreover, having insurance coverage may compel organizations to enhance their security measures to lower insurance premiums;
4. Fostering international cooperation in this area, including the exchange of information on cyber threats and joint efforts to bolster economic cybersecurity.

4 Conclusion

In conclusion, as the digital economy becomes the central pillar of global interaction, protecting against cybercrime is crucial for ensuring the economic security of individual nations and the global system. Only comprehensive and coordinated measures can effectively counter this threat and pave the way for a stable and secure digital economy of the future.

References

Koimshidi, G. F., and A. Z. Sarkisyan. 2023. Analysis and forecast of the dynamics of it fraud in the Russian Federation For 2023. *Bulletin of the Moscow University of the Ministry of Internal Affairs of Russia* 2:89–101. https://doi.org/10.24412/2073-0454-2023-2-89-101.

UNODC. 2024, October. Transnational organized crime and the convergence of cyber-enabled fraud, underground banking and technological innovation in Southeast Asia: A shifting threat landscape. *Technical Policy Brief*. Bangkok, Thailand: UNODC. Retrieved from https://www.unodc.org/roseap/uploads/documents/Publications/2024/TOC_Convergence_Report_2024.pdf (Accessed 10 November 2024).

Applying a Neural Network Algorithm to Detect ChatGPT-Generated Text Within Management Document Repositories as a Tool to Enhance the Efficiency of Decision Support Systems

Sergey V. Bolotnikov, Yaroslav V. Nikulin, Lyubov V. Borodacheva, and Lev A. Ivanyan

Abstract The research aims to evaluate the accurate percentage at which humans can identify text generated by a neural network system (e.g., ChatGPT) within a collection of textual documents used for managerial decision-making. Additionally, the research aims to propose an assessment algorithm that enhances the quality of document recognition, suitable for integration into decision support system frameworks, justify the role of the implemented control (assessment) operation in the process of preparing and executing managerial decisions, and review potential approaches for automating the proposed assessment. The research methodology involves case study analysis examining instances of digital tools used for detecting generated text, document analysis, content analysis employing Osgood's dependency analysis method, a sociological scientific-practical field experiment, and semantic and syntactic text analysis. Based on experimental data, this research quantitatively measures the actual proportion of managerial documents generated by neural networks during human visual document recognition. Conclusions are drawn regarding the feasibility of using generated documents in the managerial decision-making process. The authors developed a three-tiered assessment algorithm for managerial documents, utilizing quantitative frequency methods (content analysis) and the construction of a C. Osgood matrix, suitable for application in the development and support systems of managerial decision-making at operational and strategic levels.

Keywords Text data set • Management decisions • Management documents • Generative networks • ChatGPT • Model collapse • Assessment • Identification of generated text • Decision support systems • Algorithmic approach

---

S. V. Bolotnikov (✉) · Y. V. Nikulin · L. V. Borodacheva · L. A. Ivanyan
Moscow Polytechnic University, Moscow, Russia

A. Karbekova (ed.), *Ethics of the AI Economy: A System View from the Positions of the Theory of Stakeholders*, Ethical Economy 73,
https://doi.org/10.1007/978-3-032-23423-0_6

JEL Codes C81 • C12 • C13 • C44 • C45 • C87 • D02 • D82 • D83 • D85 • J21 • J23 • J24 • M15

1 Introduction

The current period is marked by a significant increase in the application of neural network technologies in the management and operational activities of organizations (Justino et al. 2024). Artificial intelligence technologies are used for content generation and monitoring and analyzing the environment in which economic agents operate (Justino et al. 2024; Kalla et al. 2023).

For instance, neural network technologies can be utilized for big data analysis within analytical departments, including in Decision Support Systems (DSS) and OLAP (OnLine Analytical Processing) systems (Kalla et al. 2023; Rashidi et al. 2023).

Decision support systems are largely based on the extensive processing of information from numerous individual information sources (Bellini et al. 2024). This approach is legitimate when a significant portion (at least 96%) of the information is generated by human actors (within their professional activities), enabling the formation of successful managerial decisions at the strategic level (Kraus et al. 2020; Wu et al. 2024). However, the current trend is an increasing use of neural network tools for text generation (e.g., the ChatGPT algorithm and its equivalents), which leads to a significant rise in generated texts across various secondary sources (Akram 2023). The ease and simplicity of using text-based neural networks for users result in the widespread abandonment of independently written texts in management practices (Kraus et al. 2020; Yu 2023).

As a result, generated texts are used in big data analytics and are employed by decision support systems (DSS) to formulate managerial decisions (Akram 2023). This situation (applicable to graphical and text-based neural networks) leads to the emergence of the so-called "model collapse" effect, where AI systems degrade because they are trained on data generated by AI. Training on a substantial volume of generated data leads to a decrease in the accuracy of neural network systems and their overall quality (Dohmatob et al. 2024). Considering that DSS are often used in making strategic decisions, algorithm errors and the presence of generated managerial documents in circulation lead to an unacceptable increase in managerial business risks when making decisions (Justino et al. 2024).

In summary, based on the review of information sources, the following problems can be identified:

1. The significant increase in the volume of generated text within the overall textual data used by DSS leads to the "model collapse" effect and results in increased business risks when making strategic decisions;

2. Combating this effect forces DSS experts and analysts to expend a large amount of time and resources on data cleaning and filtering;
3. The necessity for specialized removal of AI-generated content is increasing (potentially discarding up to 90% of all data initially collected for model training in the future), leading to a critical decline in document generation quality;
4. Currently, technologies for recognizing text generated by models like ChatGPT and separating it from human-generated content are underdeveloped, which could be utilized by AI developers and DSS users.

These issues define the objectives of this research.

2 Materials and Methods

General issues concerning the application of neural network technologies to support strategic managerial decisions are explored by M. d. R. T. F. Justino et al. in the research titled "The Role of Artificial Neural Networks (ANNs) in Supporting Strategic Management Decisions" (Justino et al. 2024). However, the full scope of neural network applications at the strategic level is not fully characterized.

The implementation of neural network systems for business analytics and operational management (operation analysis) is addressed in the research titled "Deep Learning in Business Analytics and Operations Research: Models, Applications, and Managerial Implications" by M. Kraus, S. Feuerriegel, and A. Oztekin (Kraus et al. 2020). This research does not consider the issues of misinformation within data sets used for analysis.

An example of applying AI-based technologies for labor market assessment is the operation of a neural network system that supports strategic decision making in developing educational programs. The fundamental model of this system is described by S. V. Bolotnikov, L. V. Borodacheva, Ya. V. Nikulin, and M. A. Lastovsky (Bolotnikov et al. 2025). This research examines the mechanism of neural network analysis of a heterogeneous array of managerial documents.

The role of generative neural networks like ChatGPT in various aspects of data research is detailed by D. Kalla et al. in the research "Study and Analysis of ChatGPT and Its Impact on Different Fields of Study" (Kalla et al. 2023), though it does not address the technology for filtering out irrelevant information.

The integration of neural network tools with management information systems is discussed by B. Wu et al. in the research titled "Integration of Computer Networks and Artificial Neural Networks for an AI-Based Network Operator." However, information on the use of AI in intelligent Decision Support Systems (DSS) is fragmented (Wu et al. 2024).

Basic definitions of the "model collapse" problem in generative neural networks are provided by E. Dohmatob, Y. Feng, and J. Kempe (Dohmatob et al. 2024). Nevertheless, there is no detailed analysis concerning specific neural network services.

A comprehensive characterization of the "model collapse" mechanism is offered by E. Zhang et al. in the research titled "All-around Neural Collapse for Imbalanced Classification" (Zhang et al. 2024). The authors conclude that the quality of generative networks inevitably deteriorates when trained on generated text.

The issue of detecting and segregating generated texts within the overall array of textual managerial documents is examined by A. Akram. However, there is no emphasis on generative networks like ChatGPT (Akram 2023).

An evaluation of tools capable of identifying generated texts within data sets is conducted by V. Bellini et al. in the research titled "Between Human and AI: Assessing the Reliability of AI Text Detection Tools" (Bellini et al. 2024). However, the application of these tools is explored within a narrowly defined professional segment.

Case studies on the recognition of documents created by humans and those generated by neural networks are detailed by H. H. Rashidi et al. (Rashidi et al. 2023). Empirical observations highlight instances of false source identification of texts.

The legitimacy of using AI-generated texts in scientific research and education is explored in Yu H.'s article, "Reflection on Whether ChatGPT Should Be Banned by Academia from the Perspective of Education and Teaching" (Yu 2023). The conclusions regarding the usefulness of neural networks are ambiguous.

The research hypothesis is that existing visual methods for humans to evaluate managerial documents do not reliably identify the presence of AI-generated text. Implementing an algorithm to verify whether a text document is generated by neural networks like ChatGPT will increase the proportion of relevant text within the dataset, thereby reducing processing time in the formulation of managerial decisions.

The research objectives are as follows:

1. To experimentally assess the accurate percentage of irrelevant (AI-generated by systems such as ChatGPT) text within the dataset of documents used for managerial decision-making;
2. To propose an algorithmic solution for the verification (assessment) of managerial text documents by potential DSS experts, enabling the detection of AI-generated text through either manual or automated checks.

The research tasks are as follows:

1. To conduct a sociological scientific-practical field experiment to determine the percentage of AI-generated text within the provided set of managerial documents;
2. To evaluate the level of understanding among consumers of managerial documents generated by neural networks and their readiness to further utilize these documents in supporting decision-making;
3. To propose an algorithmic solution that ensures the segregation of managerial documents by experts or decision-makers through visual inspection or the use of digital tools.

3 Results

To achieve the research objectives and test the hypotheses, the authors conducted a sociological scientific-practical experiment. The subjects of the experiment were 111 first- to fourth-year students from Moscow Polytechnic University, studying in the fields of “Management,” “Business Process Management,” and “Information Technology for Business Management.” The overall logic of the experiment involved asking participants to identify the presence of text generated by a neural network within a textual document used for managerial decision-making. The focus of the experiment was the participants’ ability to recognize AI-generated text and their willingness to use such texts in management.

The experiment aims to determine the extent to which participants could detect AI-generated text in a managerial document. The experiment is classified as a sociological scientific-practical linear type.

The main control characteristic was the identification of text generated by neural networks within the managerial decision document. Neutral factors in the experiment included participants’ evaluative opinions on the relevance of AI-generated documents used for managerial decisions. When forming the experimental group, factors such as gender, academic performance, and field of study were not considered. The selection for group inclusion was determined randomly using a random number generator.

The experimental group was prohibited from using software methods to detect neural networks, including the “Antiplagiarism” system and algorithms and methods for identifying the use of neural networks. Each group member relied solely on their own experience and judgment.

The experiment was conducted using a specially developed program (web application) based on HTML, CSS, PHP, and MySQL technologies. During the experiment, participants were presented with a text document generated by a neural network, specifically the GPT-o language model. Participants were not informed about how the text was generated. The text was a formulated managerial decision, specifically an order from the general director. Relying on their experience and knowledge, participants were tasked with determining whether the managerial document contained AI-generated text. To achieve this, participants were asked questions and provided with a response scale ranging from complete agreement to complete disagreement, with five steps on the scale. Participants were identified by their age, as well as the date and time of the testing (survey). Responses in the form of numerical data were entered into the experiment’s database. The experiment was conducted under double-blind conditions. The selection of texts and group members was performed using a random number generator.

Question No. 1 in the survey: “Rate the clarity of the above text.” The results were distributed as follows (Fig. 1): over 69% of participants responded that the text was completely clear to them; 25.2% indicated that the text was rather clear. Notably, no participants reported the text as partially or completely unclear, indicating that

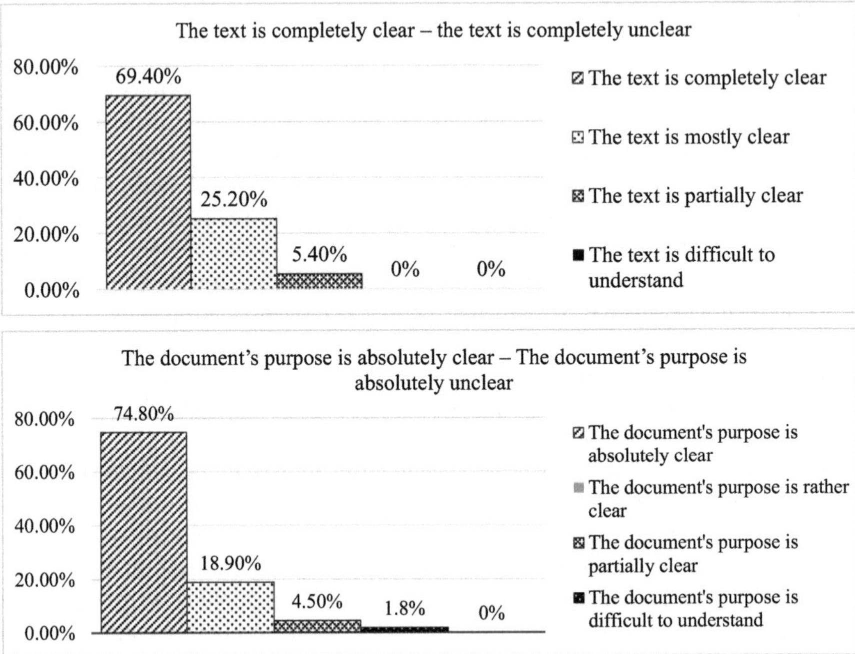

Fig. 1 The results of the experiment to determine the degree of human recognition of generated texts (question 1: "Evaluate the text's comprehensibility"; question 2: "Evaluate the belonging of the text to the documents characterizing the managerial decision"). Source: Developed by the authors

the neural network was capable of producing a highly comprehensible managerial decision text.

Question No. 2: "Assess whether the document belongs to documents characterizing a managerial decision." This question aimed to determine the respondents' understanding of the document's purpose. According to the answers, over 74% of respondents stated that the purpose of the text was absolutely clear to them (Fig. 1).

The subsequent question No. 3 addressed the text's structure. The results showed that over 69% of respondents rated the text as highly structured.

The primary research question was Question No. 4: "Assess the likelihood of neural network involvement in the creation of this document" (Fig. 2). Responses to this question were not entirely conclusive. Thus, 18% of respondents indicated that the text was entirely generated by a neural network, 33.3% stated that the use of generated text was highly probable, 26.1% believed that there were sections of AI-generated text within the document, 15.3% felt that the use of generated text was unlikely, and 7.2% were certain that the text was written by a human.

Question 5 addressed the possibility of using the document in a managerial decision (Fig. 2). According to the answers provided, 41.4% of respondents indicated that the document can be used without restrictions, 28.8% stated that it can be used

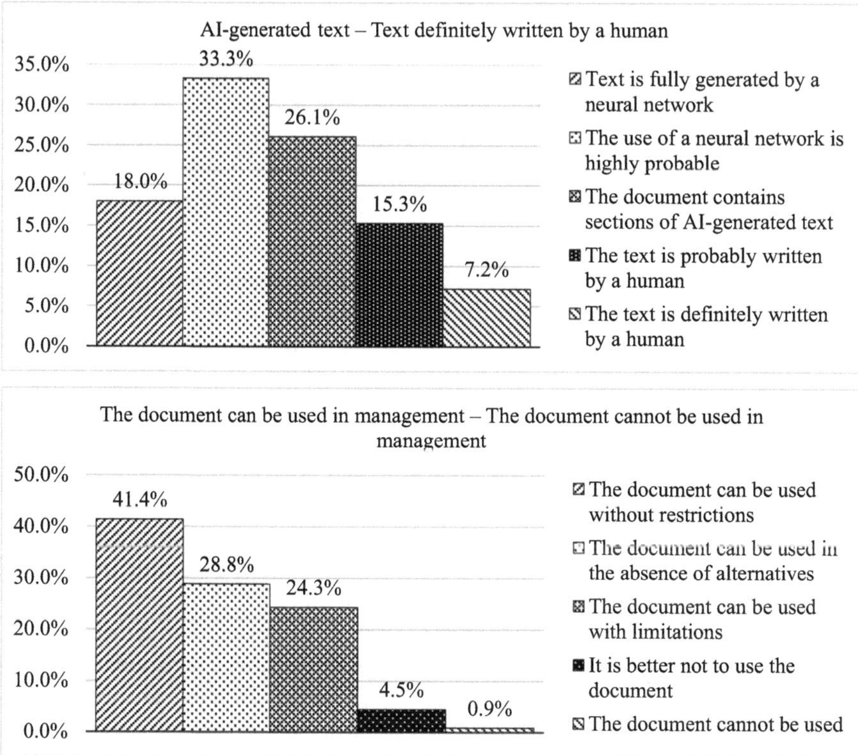

Fig. 2 The results of the experiment to determine the degree of human recognition of generated texts (question 4: "Assess the probability of using a neural network to compose this document"; question 5. "Assess the possibility of using this document to form a management decision"). Source: Developed by the authors

in the absence of alternatives, 24.3% felt it can be used with limitations, and less than 4% believed it is better not to use the document.

Thus, individuals currently find it difficult to determine the use of neural networks in the text of a managerial decision. However, the structure, purpose, and clarity of documents generated by neural networks are understandable to humans. This demonstrates that generated texts can be utilized in the managerial decision-making process; there is no objective means for an individual employee to promptly identify the source of document creation.

This fact poses significant managerial risks due to the presence of factual errors and formatting violations in generated documents. The inability to separate AI-generated documents from those created by humans significantly increases the likelihood that such documents will enter databases used for training generative networks, thereby reducing the accuracy of document preparation and provoking an increase in errors, potentially leading to a model collapse. Managerial decisions that incorporate generated documents will carry an elevated risk.

Potential solutions are as follows. The confirmation of the impossibility for individuals to accurately segregate managerial documents without specialized tools necessitates the introduction of a three-tiered filter and an additional control (verification) operation for handling incoming managerial documentation, following the sequence: data collection—data processing and structuring—assessment (evaluation) for AI-generated documents—data analysis—data exchange.

The following conceptual approaches are proposed for evaluating documents for generated text:

1. Expert approach: By assessing a collection of documents generated by neural networks, it is possible to identify the most frequently occurring (consistent) phrases characteristic of generated text. Based on this, a checklist for a visual-expressive inspection of incoming managerial documents can be developed. Additionally, a control operation is implemented that blocks the use of a document unless it passes the generated text check. Documents that fail verification should be sent for additional fact-checking and assessment of their formatting accuracy;
2. Approach based on advanced anti-plagiarism software: It is proposed to make plagiarism checks a mandatory operation when handling incoming documents, ensuring 100% control of the document flow at entry;
3. Statistical approach: It is suggested to use the frequency method (content analysis) for evaluating managerial documents. Based on stable, characteristic semantic units of generated text, it is possible to apply the dependency analysis methodology for calculating the co-occurrence of various elements in C. Osgood's text. Forming a matrix of possible and actual co-occurrences of semantic units will allow the identification of dependencies within the text. If the actual co-occurrence rate of semantic units is lower than the probabilistic rate, this can be considered a marker that the text was generated.

These solutions can be implemented in a coordinated manner. The following algorithm for assessing managerial documents is proposed within the framework of supporting the development and decision-making processes:

1. Incoming documentation that supports managerial decisions is categorized by level, depending on the information consumer: operational, tactical, or strategic;
2. For managerial documents at the operational and tactical levels, two control operations are implemented: verification using existing anti-plagiarism software tools and expert evaluation by an employee (information consumer) based on a visual express-check checklist;
3. Documents that pass the controls are utilized within the DSS (Decision Support System). Documents that do not pass the controls are sent for additional fact-checking and verification of the correctness of their formatting;
4. For managerial documents at the strategic management level, steps 1–4 are executed, followed by an additional phase of statistical evaluation using C. Osgood's matrix;

5. Strategic decision documents that have passed at least three control operations are permitted within the strategic decision support system;
6. Strategic decision documents that fail to pass even one control operation are sent for additional fact-checking and verification of the correctness of their formatting.

A possible development path for this algorithmic approach involves modeling it using widely adopted business process description notations, as well as digitizing the assessment process based on existing information technologies.

4 Conclusion

1. The analysis of literature sources reveals the existence of the "model collapse" problem, characterized by a sharp decline in text generation quality due to the increasing volume of AI-generated documents in the training datasets of neural networks like ChatGPT;
2. Additionally, there is a likely rise in business risks and costs associated with verifying incoming managerial information when economic entities develop managerial decisions at operational and strategic levels;
3. The factors outlined in points 1 and 2 negatively impact the overall quality of functioning of decision support systems;
4. The degree to which humans can recognize AI-generated text in managerial documents was determined through a sociological scientific-practical experiment. The experiment results showed the following:
   - None of the participants reported the text as partially or completely unclear, indicating that the neural network is capable of producing highly comprehensible managerial decision texts;
   - Over 74% of respondents stated that the purpose of the managerial document was absolutely clear to them, and more than 69% rated the text as highly structured;
   - Only 18% of respondents unequivocally identified the text presented in the experiment as AI-generated;
   - Overall, 51% of the experiment participants indicated a high likelihood that the text was generated by a neural network, suggesting a significant probability of identification errors when working with managerial documents.
5. To address the problem identified in this research, a three-tiered assessment algorithm for incoming managerial documents is proposed, which includes software evaluation based on existing anti-plagiarism tools, expert evaluation using a developed visual express check checklist, and statistical evaluation based on the dependency analysis methodology for calculating the co-occurrence of various elements in the text according to C. Osgood's method.

6. This algorithm can be further enhanced and expanded through the application of modern information technologies, thereby improving the overall quality of decision support systems.

References

Akram, A. 2023. *An empirical study of AI-generated text detection tools*. https://doi.org/10.48550/arXiv.2310.01423.

Bellini, V., F. Semeraro, J. Montomoli, M. Cascella, and E. Bignami. 2024. Between human and AI: Assessing the reliability of AI text detection tools. *Current Medical Research and Opinion* 40 (3): 353–358. https://doi.org/10.1080/03007995.2024.2310086.

Bolotnikov, S. V., L. V. Borodacheva, Y. V. Nikulin, and M. A. Lastovsky. 2025. The Application of Neural Network Systems for Data Mining in Assessing Demanded Competencies for the Development of New Educational Programs. In *Big Data and Artificial Intelligence for Decision-Making in the Smart Economy*, edited by A.B. Karbekova, L. Žák, and I. Milenković, 643–657. Studies in Big Data, vol. 168. Cham: Springer, https://doi.org/10.1007/978-3-031-78686-0_43.

Dohmatob, E., Feng, Y., Subramonian, A., & Kempe, J. 2024. *Strong model collapse*. https://doi.org/10.48550/arXiv.2410.04840.

Justino, M. D. R. T. F., J. Texeira-Quirós, A. J. Gonçalves, M. G. Antunes, and P. R. Mucharreira. 2024. The role of Artificial Neural Networks (ANNs) in supporting strategic management decisions. *Journal of Risk and Financial Management* 17 (4): 164. https://doi.org/10.3390/jrfm17040164.

Kalla, D., N. Smith, F. Samaah, and S. Kuraku. 2023. Study and analysis of chat GPT and its impact on different fields of study. *International Journal of Innovative Science and Research Technology* 8 (3): 827–833. https://doi.org/10.5281/zenodo.7767675.

Kraus, M., S. Feuerriegel, and A. Oztekin. 2020. Deep learning in business analytics and operations research: Models, applications and managerial implications. *European Journal of Operational Research* 281 (3): 628–641. https://doi.org/10.1016/j.ejor.2019.09.018.

Rashidi, H. H., B. D. Fennell, S. Albahra, B. Hu, and T. Gorbett. 2023. The ChatGPT conundrum: Human-generated scientific manuscripts misidentified as AI creations by AI text detection tool. *Journal of Pathology Informatics* 14:100342. https://doi.org/10.1016/j.jpi.2023.100342.

Wu, B., J. Xu, Y. Zhang, B. Liu, Y. Gong, and J. Huang. 2024. Integration of computer networks and artificial neural networks for an AI-based network operator. *Applied and Computational Engineering* 64:114–119. https://doi.org/10.54254/2755-2721/64/20241370.

Yu, H. 2023. Reflection on whether Chat GPT should be banned by academia from the perspective of education and teaching. *Frontiers in Psychology* 14:1181712. https://doi.org/10.3389/fpsyg.2023.1181712.

Zhang, E., Li, C., Geng, C., & Chen, S. 2024. *All-around neural collapse for imbalanced classification*. https://doi.org/10.48550/arXiv.2408.07253.

On the Problem of Combating Cyberterrorism and Cyber-Extremism Through the Use of Profiling Technologies and Artificial Intelligence Algorithms

Aleksey P. Popov, Marina A. Akimenko, Inna A. Pavlenko, and Elena G. Berberova

Abstract The research examines the pressing issue of combating cyberterrorism and cyber-extremism amid the digital transformation of society. The authors emphasize the growing threat of cyberattacks employed by terrorist and extremist groups to destabilize society, spread destructive ideologies, and organize criminal activities. The use of profiling technologies and artificial intelligence (AI) algorithms is proposed as an effective tool to counter these threats. Profiling, based on the analysis of behavior, communication patterns, and digital traces, enables the early detection of potential perpetrators. In turn, AI algorithms can process vast amounts of data, identify anomalies, and predict possible cyberattacks. The research analyzes advanced machine learning methods, such as neural networks and text data analysis, which can be used for the automatic detection of extremist content and suspicious online activity. Special attention is given to the legal aspects of employing these technologies, including issues related to personal data protection and the prevention of abuse. The authors stress the need for a balance between ensuring security and upholding human rights. In conclusion, the authors provide recommendations for integrating profiling and AI technologies into cybersecurity systems, which will enhance the effectiveness of the fight against cyberterrorism and cyber-extremism while minimizing risks to society. The research is of interest to cybersecurity professionals, law enforcement agencies, and researchers engaged in digital transformation and AI.

Keywords Crime • Cyberterrorism • Cyber-extremism • Technologies • Artificial intelligence • Profiling

JEL Codes K4 • K41 • K410

A. P. Popov · M. A. Akimenko (✉)
Pyatigorsk State University, Pyatigorsk, Russia

I. A. Pavlenko · E. G. Berberova
Rostov State University of Economics, Rostov-on-Don, Russia

A. Karbekova (ed.), *Ethics of the AI Economy: A System View from the Positions of the Theory of Stakeholders*, Ethical Economy 73,
https://doi.org/10.1007/978-3-032-23423-0_7

1 Introduction

Today's life is almost universally dependent on digital technologies, a situation that manifests a dual nature. On the one hand, it opens up new avenues for development. On the other hand, it creates serious challenges in the realm of information security. One of the most pressing and dangerous phenomena in cyberspace is cyberterrorism and cyber-extremism. These forms of criminal activity pose threats on a national level, also threatening the safety of individuals, their privacy, and their property. Cyberattacks targeting critical infrastructure, the dissemination of extremist content, manipulation of public opinion, and the recruitment of citizens (especially youth) into various extremist and terrorist organizations are becoming increasingly sophisticated and widespread.

Amid rapid technological advancement, traditional methods of countering cyber threats often prove insufficient. This calls for new approaches based on advanced technologies such as non-technical or non-verbal profiling and artificial intelligence (AI) algorithms. Profiling enables the analysis of users' online behavioral patterns to detect suspicious activities. AI algorithms can process enormous volumes of data, uncover hidden patterns, and predict potential threats.

The research aims to explore the potential of employing profiling technologies and AI to combat cyberterrorism and cyber-extremism. The research examines contemporary methods for detecting and preventing cyber threats and considers the ethical and legal aspects of utilizing these technologies. The relevance of the research topic is underscored by the urgent need to develop effective mechanisms for protecting cyberspace in the face of the growing complexity and scale of cyberattacks.

2 Methodology

To address the challenge of combating cyberterrorism and cyber-extremism using profiling technologies and AI algorithms, this research employs a comprehensive methodological approach based on the following framework:

- Analysis of theoretical foundations and contemporary research. In the initial stage, existing scholarly work on cyberterrorism, cyber-extremism, and the application of profiling and AI in cybersecurity is systemically reviewed. Literature analysis, comparative studies, and data synthesis are employed to identify key trends, challenges, and gaps in current approaches;
- Data collection and processing. Data related to cyberattacks, extremist content, and online user behavior is gathered to develop and test AI algorithms. Methods such as web scraping, open-source intelligence (OSINT) analysis, and database research on cyber threats are utilized, with particular emphasis on ensuring data representativeness and anonymity;

- Development of profiling models. Based on the collected data, the authors created profiling models to identify suspicious behavioral patterns. Machine learning techniques, including clustering, classification, and time-series analysis, are used to detect anomalies and predict potential threats;
- Implementation of AI algorithms. AI algorithms, including neural networks, deep learning methods, and natural language processing (NLP), are developed and tested to automate the detection and prevention of cyber threats. These algorithms are designed to analyze textual, graphical, and network traffic data to identify extremist content and coordinate cyberattack responses;
- Testing and performance evaluation. The developed models and algorithms are tested on real-world data using metrics such as accuracy, recall, F1 score, and other performance indicators. A comparative analysis is conducted to assess the effectiveness of the proposed methods against traditional cybersecurity approaches;
- Ethical and legal analysis. Ethical and legal aspects of using profiling and AI technologies are incorporated into the methodology. Expert evaluations and analyses of regulatory frameworks are employed to develop recommendations for balancing security needs with the protection of human rights;
- Formulation of conclusions and recommendations. In the final stage, research findings are synthesized, and practical recommendations are formulated for government bodies, law enforcement agencies, and cybersecurity companies.

Thus, the research methodology combines theoretical analysis with practical development and testing of technologies and considers ethical and legal factors, offering a comprehensive approach to combating cyberterrorism and cyber-extremism.

3 Results

The development of today's society is inconceivable without various information technologies. Simultaneously, the application of these technologies exhibits a dual nature. On the one hand, there are numerous positive, cross-border aspects related to the development and widespread integration of information technologies, including the opportunities offered by the Internet.

This process has become ubiquitous and evolved according to its own unique patterns, collectively known as digitalization. Moreover, with each passing year, digitalization is expanding its reach across an increasing number of entities and sectors while acquiring cumulative significance.

In recent years, digitalization has actively permeated various sectors of the economy, becoming a key factor in enhancing business efficiency, improving the quality of public services, and expanding opportunities for citizens. Moreover, it has also become indispensable for all government structures. The Russian Federation is actively developing digital services to simplify interactions between citizens, government agencies, and businesses. According to the Ministry of Digital Development, by early 2024, more than 90% of public services were provided electronically via the Gosuslugi portal. This has significantly reduced the burden on government offices and accelerated the process of obtaining documents and permits (Sovcombank 2024).

The Gosuslugi platform now boasts over 90 million users, demonstrating a high level of citizen engagement in digital interactions with the state. One of the key innovations of 2024 was the introduction of electronic medical records, which allow patients to store and manage their health information online. This not only simplifies access to medical data but also expedites the process of seeking medical care. In parallel with the advancement of government services, digital platforms for business are gaining popularity. In 2024, there was a noticeable increase in the number of small and medium-sized enterprises actively utilizing digital tools for business management. Platforms such as "My Business" and "1C: Enterprise" assist entrepreneurs in automating accounting processes, managing sales, and interacting with clients online (IaaSSaaSPaaS 2024).

However, alongside the positive trends mentioned above, there are also negative aspects. Abuses on various Internet platforms and the active use of popular websites and services to commit illegal activities are becoming increasingly common. Current realities indicate that cybercrime continues to grow, even exponentially, thereby posing a serious threat to the security and stability of the digital realm (Akimenko and Ovcharenko 2022).

Nowadays, cybercrime stands as one of the world's most pressing issues, given its enormous latent potential and transboundary nature. It now affects businesses, state companies, and corporations, as well as entire nations and individual citizens. Alongside the positive trends in information technology development observed in 2024, the year has also been significant for the world of cybersecurity, marked by numerous cyberattacks, data breaches, the emergence of new threat groups, and the discovery of zero-day vulnerabilities.

Reports of breaches in the IT infrastructure of various organizations (governmental and business), along with constant cyberattacks, targeted hacker actions, the detection of new malware, cyber-espionage, and the ever-present threat of phishing, have become part of our everyday reality. Experts in information security believe that cybercriminal activity continues to escalate each year; 2024 is no exception. They are confident that this trend will persist in the near future and that the level of cyber threats will not diminish. According to law enforcement data, in the first seven months of 2024, the damage from IT crimes in Russia amounted to 91 billion rubles. In the entirety of 2023, this figure reached 157 billion rubles. These figures are based on citizen reports received by the authorities. Furthermore, official statistics indicate that between 2020 and 2023, the number of IT crimes increased by 27%, from 510,000 to 677,000 registered cases (Weimann 2012).

Alongside active and passive criminal activities of an economic nature, one of the leading forms of cybercrime is the manifestation of various types of cyberterrorism and cyber-extremism. The relevance of this issue grows with the expansion of digital technologies and the increasing volume of data. In this context, AI, enhanced by the integration of non-verbal scanning techniques, becomes a crucial tool in investigating cybercrimes (Akimenko and Ovcharenko 2022).

Being a relevant security threat, cyberterrorism involves using computer technologies to commit acts of violence, intimidation, or destabilization. Unlike classical terrorism (Popov et al. 2014), cyberterrorism employs digital tools and network resources to execute its criminal schemes. In investigations of such crimes, non-verbal scanning serves as a valuable supplement to analytical methods by helping identify potential threats and establish connections among various elements associated with cyberterrorism.

Cyberterrorism poses a serious threat, inflicting potential economic damage and endangering lives and public safety. In an era of rapidly advancing technologies, traditional countermeasures prove increasingly inadequate. Many organizations, especially small and medium-sized enterprises, lack the human and financial resources needed to ensure robust cybersecurity.

Moreover, global experience shows that cyberterrorism is often the cumulative, criminologically driven result of another unlawful phenomenon in today's reality—cyber-extremism of various forms (IaaSSaaSPaaS 2024). Cyber-extremism represents a significant threat to national security and public order. It involves using internet technologies to disseminate extremist ideas, recruit new members, and organize terrorist actions. In this light, AI technologies become an essential instrument in countering cyber-extremism. Let us consider the key areas where AI can be beneficial in this fight.

In the authors' view, AI has already emerged as a powerful tool for preventing, detecting, and responding to cyberterrorist and cyber-extremist threats. This research examines the primary areas of AI application in the fight against cyberterrorism, along with its advantages and challenges.

The authors believe that implementing algorithms in the form of criminal profiles for cyber-extremists and cyber terrorists, developed by experts in criminal profiling or non-verbal scanning, will prove highly effective. Since non-verbal scanning involves technologies that analyze non-verbal signals and human behavior, incorporating these algorithms into various AI systems will enable the scanning of online content for extremist ideas and propaganda. Such systems can analyze posts on social networks, forums, and other public platforms, quickly identifying inappropriate content.

AI systems can analyze user behavior and online interactions to predict the likelihood of radicalization. This involves studying communication patterns and participation in discussions. AI can help identify groups at risk of radicalization, enabling targeted preventive measures, such as educational programs and public awareness campaigns. By employing big data analytics, AI can track changes in public sentiment and detect potential surges in extremist activity or interest in violent ideologies.

AI systems can analyze user behavior and online interactions to predict the likelihood of radicalization. This includes examining communication patterns and participation in discussions. AI can help identify groups at risk of radicalization, enabling targeted preventive measures (e.g., educational programs and public awareness campaigns). By employing big data analytics, AI can monitor shifts in public sentiment, detecting potential surges in extremist activity or interest in violent ideologies.

AI algorithms can examine interactions on social media to identify networks associated with cyber-extremism and detect attempts to organize unlawful activities. The use of chatbots on social media platforms, which automatically respond to extremist content by warning users and countering its spread, may also help reduce the proliferation of extremist ideas.

AI systems can fact-check and identify misinformation, aiding in the fight against propaganda, fake news, and fabricated reports, the so-called "injections" of false information about tragedies or alleged social "evils" by state or municipal bodies that are often exploited in the context of cyber-extremism.

Despite the advantages mentioned, the application of AI, integrated with non-verbal scanning techniques or criminological profiling, to combat cyberterrorism and cyber-extremism may raise concerns regarding human rights violations and the protection of privacy. Therefore, alongside the development of AI algorithms based on data and criminal profiling models, creating a legal framework for using AI in this field is a priority.

AI offers many possibilities, including countering contemporary criminal phenomena such as cyber-extremism by detecting extremist content (Weimann 2012), performing predictive analytics, monitoring social media, and automating response tasks. Nevertheless, it is essential to consider ethical and legal aspects to ensure respect for human rights when employing these technologies. Effectively combating cyber-extremism requires a comprehensive approach that integrates technology, law enforcement, and community engagement, as cyber-extremism often begets cyberterrorism.

Countering cyberterrorism faces numerous challenges (Weimann 2012) that call for a multifaceted and integrated strategy. The application of technologies and criminal profiling algorithms, combined with the capabilities of artificial intelligence, can be highly productive, given that AI is itself a product of the digital environment—just as cyber-extremism and cyberterrorism are.

As noted earlier, the primary problem lies in the gap in legislation regarding the use of AI. Experience shows that for the effective and ethical implementation of AI algorithms designed to combat cyber-extremism and cyberterrorism, the current legal framework often falls short in addressing today's realities. Currently, cybersecurity and data protection laws frequently fail to consider the specific nature, current capabilities, and unique features of AI, creating legal gaps that complicate the regulation of AI in information analysis and processing.

Furthermore, data protection regulations contain certain deficiencies and imperfections, thereby failing to provide adequate data security. In the authors' view, there is a social necessity for legislative regulation of products developed by AI algorithms to counter cyber-extremism and cyberterrorism. The existing legal vacuum on this issue gives rise to additional problems in the practical application of AI. In cases of error or abuse by AI systems, it is currently unclear who would bear legal responsibility: the developers, the operators, or the owners of the systems. This creates legal gaps that could be exploited to evade accountability.

Moreover, since AI is an informational product, it is not entirely clear who will be liable when AI algorithms make mistakes in identifying a perpetrator based on criminal profiling methods. Questions remain regarding the legal consequences of such errors and who ultimately bears responsibility for these mistakes, whether individuals or legal entities. Alternatively, such failures in AI performance should be considered anomalies—essentially, errors under criminal law resulting in unintentional harm. According to the authors, this notion of anomalies in AI performance should be enshrined in the general part of the criminal code.

4 Conclusion

The challenge of countering cyberterrorism and cyber-extremism remains one of the most pressing issues in today's digital society. On the one hand, technological development opens up new avenues for communication and information exchange. On the other hand, it creates a fertile ground for the spread of destructive ideas and the commission of cybercrimes. In this context, applying profiling technologies and AI algorithms appears to be a promising avenue for combating these threats.

Profiling enables the identification of potentially dangerous individuals by analyzing their digital behavior, which facilitates the early detection of threats. AI algorithms, in turn, automate the analysis of vast amounts of data, significantly enhancing the effectiveness of law enforcement and security agencies. The combined use of these technologies allows not only rapid response to cyberattacks that have already occurred but also the prediction of potential incidents, preventing them at the preparatory stage.

However, implementing such technologies is accompanied by several challenges, including issues of personal data protection, respect for citizens' rights and freedoms, and the risk of misuse of monitoring tools. To minimize these risks, clear legal frameworks and ethical standards governing the use of profiling and AI for security purposes must be developed.

In conclusion, profiling and AI technologies hold significant potential for countering cyberterrorism and cyber-extremism. However, their successful application requires a comprehensive approach that encompasses technical and legal, organizational, and ethical aspects. Only by doing so can a balance be achieved between ensuring security and protecting fundamental human rights in the digital age.

This research indicates that cyberterrorism and cyber-extremism represent serious threats to the information security of the state, society, and individual citizens. Traditional methods of combating these phenomena are often insufficient in the face of rapidly advancing technologies and increasingly complex cybercrime (Akimenko and Tsukanova 2024). In light of this, the use of profiling technologies and AI algorithms will allow for the effective identification of potential threat sources at an early stage and the analysis of online user behavior. In the authors' view, this will make it possible to predict and prevent the recruitment of new members into extremist and terrorist organizations and the widespread dissemination of extremist content.

Furthermore, the application of AI will streamline these processes and increase the rate of detection of such unlawful activities because AI can process large volumes of data and identify patterns and anomalies, which makes it an indispensable tool in the fight against cyberterrorism and extremism. However, this process is complex and labor-intensive, which creates a social need to address several issues within the legal framework. Particularly, the use of profiling technologies and AI necessitates thorough consideration of matters related to personal data protection and the prevention of abuse.

Based on this research, the authors have reached the following conclusions and formulated several legal and organizational proposals to enhance the prevention and counteraction of cyberterrorism and cyber-extremism in their various forms. First and foremost, there is a social imperative to develop and implement legislative acts regulating the use of profiling technologies and AI in countering cyberterrorism and extremism while ensuring the protection of citizens' rights and freedoms. Additionally, to effectively combat these crimes, specialized units could be established within the Ministry of Internal Affairs and security agencies. Such units might include a Cyber Threat Analysis Center, a Cyber Profiling Department, a Digital Forensics Laboratory, and others. For example, a Cyber Profiling Department could specialize in creating profiles of cyber terrorists and extremists using profiling technologies. Its activities would involve analyzing online behavioral patterns to detect suspicious activity, with its algorithms developed in close cooperation with psychologists and behavioral analysis experts. Additionally, there is a social need to create a Digital Forensics Laboratory that would collect and analyze digital evidence using AI, develop methods and algorithms for data recovery and digital trace analysis, and support law enforcement agencies in investigating cybercrimes. These specialized units would enhance the effectiveness of the fight against cyberterrorism and cyber-extremism and ensure the security of the digital space in the face of contemporary technological challenges.

References

Akimenko, M. A., and I. A. Ovcharenko. 2022. On the problem of the using of forensic profiling in the investigation and disclosure of cybercrimes. *Eurasian Advocacy* 1 (56): 82–85. https://doi.org/10.52068/2304-9839_2022_56_1_82.

Akimenko, M. A., and O. V. Tsukanova. 2024. On some criminological signs of cyberterrorism and cyberextremism in modern conditions. In *University readings – 2024: Proceedings of the all-Russian conference with international participation*, 117–121. Pyatigorsk, Russia: Pyatigorsk State University.

IaaSSaaSPaaS. 2024, September 5. *Almost 100 billion rubles have been lost by Russians this year already due to cybercrime.* Retrieved from https://iaassaaspaas.ru/it-bezopasnost/uzhe-pochti-100-milliardov-rubley-poteryali-rossiyane-v-etom-godu-iz-za-kiberprestupnosti (Accessed 28 March 2025).

Popov, A. P., M. P. Kireev, and A. A. Popov. 2014. Historical sources of understanding of terrorism. *Gaps In Russian Legislation* 1:89–92.
Sovcombank. 2024, September 4. *The damage from IT crimes in 2024 amounted to 99 billion rubles.* Retrieved from https://journal.sovcombank.ru/news/uscherb-ot-it-prestuplenii-v-2024-godu-sostavil-99-mlrd-rublei (Accessed 28 March 2025).
Weimann, G. 2012. Lone wolves in cyberspace. *Journal of Terrorism Research* 3 (2): 75–90.

Cybercrime in the Digital Age: Global Trends and Emerging Threats

Anna A. Pakhlyan

Abstract The advent of digital systems and the development of online and mobile technologies have made cybercrime a common phenomenon. Cybercrime is an emerging transnational crime. Its complex nature is due to its occurrence in the borderless cyberspace domain and the increasing involvement of organized criminal groups. The research focuses on identifying global trends of emerging cybercrime and identifying the primary target regions and countries affected by cybercrime attacks. The analysis of the UNODC database on cyber-related fraud revealed the leading directions in cybercrime cases. According to available data, Europe is the leader, with 86–95% of global cybercrime cases concentrated there. At the level of individual countries, cybercrime is most widespread in Germany, Spain, and Italy. The Americas account for 4–13% of global cybercrime cases, Asia for 1–7%, and Africa for less than 1%. However, underreporting and gaps in many countries' data distort the true picture. The research clarifies the geographical distribution of cybercrime's prevalence, which is essential to making the fight against it more targeted and purposeful.

Keywords Cybercrime • Cyberattacks • Cyber-related fraud • World Cybercrime Index (WCI)

JEL Codes A120 • K420 • K490 • O330

1 Introduction

The impact of the Internet on criminal opportunities appears at the following three levels:

A. A. Pakhlyan (✉)
Armenian State University of Economics, Yerevan, Armenia

A. Karbekova (ed.), *Ethics of the AI Economy: A System View from the Positions of the Theory of Stakeholders*, Ethical Economy 73,
https://doi.org/10.1007/978-3-032-23423-0_8

- It has created broader opportunities for traditional crimes that already exist in the physical or "real" world, such as forgery, fraud, and stalking;
- The Internet has provided new opportunities for traditional crimes, such as hacking, viruses, large-scale fraud, and others;
- The Internet has led to new opportunities for new types of crimes, such as spam, intellectual property theft, and electronic auction fraud (Jahankhani et al. 2014).

Cybercrime is a significant global challenge, estimated to cost hundreds of billions to trillions of dollars. Global cybercrime damage costs were predicted to grow by 15% per year, reaching $10.5 trillion annually by 2025, up from $3 trillion in 2015 (Morgan 2022).

Globally, an estimated 595.8 million adults have encountered cybercrime at least once, with approximately 463 million individuals from eight countries (Australia, France, Germany, India, Japan, New Zealand, the UK, and the USA) reporting victimization in 2022 (Gen and The Harris Poll 2023).

Some studies "suggested that the investment in cybersecurity can significantly contribute to building a sustainable economy, promoting safe practices in the digital environment, and creating new job opportunities" (Benaichouba et al. 2024).

Halkiopoulos et al. applied the Capacity Value-Based Pricing (CVBP) model to illicit cybercrime services, revealing the professionalization of cybercrime and the growing market for illegal services. It highlights the need for advanced AI methods to convert qualitative data into quantitative insights, aiding stakeholders in understanding the financial dynamics of cybercrime (Halkiopoulos et al. 2024).

The global distribution of cybercrime offenders and the relative level of "cyber criminality" within each country remain significant challenges. While the geography of cybercrime attacks can be mapped through cyber fraud victims, identifying the origins of cybercriminal activity is far more complex due to these offenses' clandestine and anonymous nature because cybercriminals actively conceal their identities.

To address this gap, researchers from the Department of Sociology of the University of Oxford have developed the first-ever World Cybercrime Index (WCI), which systemically ranks the most significant sources of cybercrime at the national level. This index provides a comprehensive assessment of the global geographic distribution of cybercriminal activity. The WCI was developed through collaboration between the University of Oxford and UNSW Canberra, marking a significant advancement in cybercrime research and policy development (Bruce et al. 2024).

Although most current efforts to mitigate cybercrime threats primarily focus on technical measures, some of the latest studies consider cybercrime as a social phenomenon and construct a theoretical framework that integrates the social, economic, political, technological, and cybersecurity factors that influence cybercrime. The findings indicate a strong link between socioeconomic development and cybercrime, with the nature and extent of that relationship varying across different income levels (Chen et al. 2023).

Another research highlights the importance of cybersecurity in combating cybercrime and protecting digital systems. It emphasizes the role of artificial intelligence (AI) in creating defenses against cyberattacks and stresses the importance of specialized groups in cyber defense. Furthermore, it highlights the need for companies to adopt tailored defenses against cyberattacks and to educate their employees about cybersecurity threats (Mijwil et al. 2023).

International cooperation and coordination are essential in addressing cybercrime effectively (Silva and Cavalcanti 2016). Cybercriminal activities often transcend national borders and require collaboration among countries to investigate, prosecute, and prevent them. Several key conventions and treaties play a significant role in addressing and combating cybercrime. The most important ones are the Council of Europe Convention on Cybercrime (Budapest Convention), the United Nations Convention against Transnational Organized Crime (UNTOC), and the African Union Convention on Cyber Security and Personal Data Protection (Malabo Convention) (Fahmy 2024).

However, regardless of the growing interest in cybercrime, its rapid growth and changing nature make a comprehensive study of the issue in professional circles relevant.

2 Methodology

This research used the UNODC database to determine the prevalence of cybercrime in countries worldwide. The database is generated through two leading indicators. The first one is the **UNODC data on cyber-related fraud**, reflecting the total number of reported incidents of fraud committed using digital means. This dataset provides an absolute count of cyber-related fraud cases recorded in a country or region. The second indicator is **the cyber-related fraud rate per 100,000 people. It is** calculated by dividing the total number of cyber-related fraud cases by the population of the given country and multiplying by 100,000. This metric allows for meaningful comparisons between countries or regions regardless of their population size, making it useful for trend analysis and cross-national assessments.

The WCI serves as a global metric of cyber criminality based on five types of cybercrime (technical products/services, attacks and extortion, data/identity theft, scams, and cashing out/money laundering). The raw data for the *WCI* was collected through an online survey of world-leading experts in cybercrime intelligence, investigations, and attribution.

The PESTLE analysis addressed the **macro-environmental factors** influencing cybercrime and cybersecurity on a global scale. PESTLE analysis helps understand the external factors that shape the rise of cybercrime and influence cybersecurity policies, providing a structured framework for assessing risks, challenges, and opportunities in combating cyber threats globally.

3 Results

Digital technologies have invaded everyday life and transformed contemporary business relationships, bringing new threats and challenges. The volume of cybercrime is growing at an incredible speed; its forms and mechanisms are continuously improving.

New technologies are giving rise to new types of crimes while expanding the possibilities for traditional criminal activity. Many widespread cybercrimes are manifestations of traditional crimes that existed before the emergence of the term "cyber" (Pakhlyan 2024, 2025a).

According to 2022 data (Pakhlyan 2025b; Petrosyan 2024b), about 39% of Internet users worldwide have experienced a cybercrime at least once in some way. Moreover, these indicators vary significantly among countries. The global average level of cybercrime victims among Internet users was exceeded in India (68%), the USA (49%), and Australia (40%). The proportion of Internet users who have experienced cybercrime is lower than the global average in New Zealand (38%), France (33%), the UK (33%), Germany (30%), and Japan (21%) (Petrosyan 2024b). Notably, all selected countries, except India (where information technology development is at a reasonably high level), are developed. This circumstance gives reason to assume that cybercrime tends to spread, especially in economically and technologically advanced countries.

According to data published by the World Bank, global GDP in 2023 amounted to $106.17 trillion (World Bank n.d.). Financial losses caused by cybercrime in the same year were estimated at $8.15 trillion (Petrosyan 2024a), which is equivalent to 7.7% of the global GDP generated jointly by 217 countries of the world. In other words, the global GDP in 2023 is only 13 times greater than the worldwide financial losses caused by cybercrime. The accurate scale of cybercrime becomes more understandable when we compare it with the GDP generated in individual countries. Thus, only two countries—the USA (with a GDP of $27.7 trillion) and China (GDP equal to $17.8 trillion)—produce more GDP than is extorted through cybercrime worldwide. The GDPs of Germany ($4.5 trillion), Japan ($4.2 trillion), and India ($3.6 trillion), which comprise the top five countries in the world in terms of GDP produced (World Bank n.d.), are about half as low as the financial losses caused by cybercrime worldwide (Petrosyan 2024a). By the end of 2023, these losses will reach $10.29 trillion, with projected continued growth to reach $15.63 trillion (Pakhlyan 2025b; Petrosyan 2024b).

The indicators of the "Corruption and Economic Crime" section of the United Nations Office on Drugs and Crime (UNODC) database (United Nations Office on Drugs and Crime (UNODC) n.d.) also include the category of "cyber-related fraud" (Table 1). UNODC's data on cyber fraud by region show that Europe is the most frequently targeted region for cyber fraud, and Africa is the least frequently targeted region. Data are not available for Oceania, which includes New Zealand and Australia. Cyberfraud statistics are also not available for South Asia and Central Asia.

Table 1 Cyber fraud statistics by region

Region/Subregion	Cyber-related Fraud Counts									
	2013	2014	2015	2016	2017	2018	2019	2020	2021	2022
AFRICA	–	–	–	187	–	–	–	35	–	222
Northern Africa	–	–	–	–	–	–	–	35	–	222
Sub-Saharan Africa	–	–	–	187	–	–	–	–	–	–
AMERICAS	15,878	17,525	24,510	24,291	19,983	38,777	45,357	102,034	65,370	72,158
Northern America	6914	8368	9315	12,471	14,788	18,294	25,084	35,305	42,260	41,340
Latin America and the Caribbean	8964	9157	15,195	11,820	5195	20,483	20,273	66,729	23,110	30,818
ASIA	23,174	19,378	4708	6324	5101	5828	7952	13,123	18,782	36,034
Central Asia	–	–	–	–	–	–	–	–	–	–
Eastern Asia	292	376	361	948	581	742	371	579	524	622
South-Eastern Asia	672	2118	4207	4320	4419	4928	7580	12,242	18,258	34,748
Southern Asia	–	–	–	–	–	–	–	–	–	–
Western Asia	22,210	16,884	140	1056	101	158	1	302	–	664
EUROPE	307,577	317,328	361,543	467,341	505,131	625,336	570,291	693,379	685,247	719,661
Eastern Europe	17,950	25,375	40,197	39,284	39,231	45,392	69,783	79,478	83,391	97,787
Northern Europe	69,809	78,179	104,013	128,278	134,604	173,238	4459	11,997	12,913	16,244
Southern Europe	29,325	23,836	27,576	106,573	143,140	199,551	272,209	357,149	326,539	343,633
Western Europe	133,493	189,938	189,757	193,206	188,156	207,155	223,840	244,755	262,404	261,997
OCEANIA	–	–	–	–	–	–	–	–	–	–
Total	346,629	354,231	390,761	498,143	530,215	669,941	623,600	808,571	769,399	828,075

Source: Calculated and compiled by the author based on (United Nations Office on Drugs and Crime (UNODC) n.d.)

According to the UNODC data, the vast majority of cyber frauds in 2013–2022 (85.8–95.3%) were concentrated in Europe. America accounted for 3.8–12.6% of cyber frauds (an incomprehensibly low figure given the high level of IT development in the USA). Asia accounted for 0.9–6.7%. Africa's share ranged from 0.004–0.027%. Thus, in 2022, 86.9% (719,661 cases) of cybercrime incidents recorded by UNODC occurred in Europe, 8.7% (72,158 cases) occurred in the Americas, 4.4% (36,034 cases) in Asia, and almost 0.027% (222 cases) in Africa (Table 1) (Pakhlyan 2025a; United Nations Office on Drugs and Crime (UNODC) n.d.).

Although the UNODC has been collecting cybercrime statistics since 2013, statistics are still unavailable for many countries (Table 1). Thus, the suspiciously low rate of cyber fraud trends in the Americas compared to other regions is because the North American region is represented exclusively by Canada, with no statistical data for the USA, which is supposed to be at the forefront in terms of the prevalence of cybercrime.

During 2021 and 2022, Canada recorded 40,260 and 41,340 cyber-fraud cases, respectively, exceeding the combined total for all 21 Latin American and Caribbean nations. Within that region, Costa Rica and Peru were the hardest hit. In 2022, Costa Rica registered 12,690 cases (41.2% of the regional total), and Peru reported 11,970 cases (38.8%).

Among the Asian subregions, the indicators for Eastern and Western Asia are low. Data for Central Asia are unavailable. Thus, Southeast Asia has been "lucky" to be affected by cyber fraud, represented by Singapore (24,605 cases in 2022) and Thailand (10,143 cases in 2022), which together account for 96.4% of Asia.

A strange trend has been observed in the statistical data concerning Asia. Thus, in 2013–2014, the number of cybercrime cases registered in the region significantly exceeded the indicators of the following period. Furthermore, this was recorded exclusively thanks to Western Asia. In Asia, the 23,174 cases recorded in 2013 were not surpassed until 2022, when the region saw 36,034 cybercrime incidents. A deeper, country-level analysis shows that Turkey accounted for most of these cases. In 2013, Turkey registered 20,175 cybercrime incidents—90.8% of all cases in West Asia and 87.1% of those across Asia. The following year, Turkey reported 16,854 cases, comprising 99.8% of West Asia's total (the remaining 0.2%, or 35 cases, occurred in Armenia) and 87% of Asia's overall figure. Notably, the unfounded decline in cybercrime in Asia in the following period is due to Turkey no longer providing data since 2015. Such circumstances indeed distort the accurate statistical picture.

In Europe, which is in the lead according to UNODC data, the "center of gravity" of cyber fraud is Germany, where 243,358 cases were registered in 2022, which is equivalent to 92.9% of cyber fraud cases in the Western Europe region and 36.4% in all of Europe. Next is the Southern Europe sub-region, where Italy and Spain are at the forefront of cybercrime, accounting for around 93% of cyber fraud cases registered in Southern Europe in 2022. Spain recorded 233,932 cyber fraud cases in 2022, equivalent to 32.5% of the total cases registered in Europe. Italy's figures are modest. In 2022, the country was the target of 101,698 cyber fraud cases, accounting for 14.1% of such cases in Europe.

The objective reason for the low prevalence of cybercrime in Africa is the lack of data for most countries. North Africa is represented (Table 1) only by indicators for Algeria and Morocco (data for Egypt, Libya, Sudan, and Tunisia are unavailable). Sub-Saharan Africa is represented only by indicators for Senegal and Uganda (another five dozen African countries in the sub-region are excluded from the UNODC database). However, even with more countries included, cybercrime in Africa would presumably still be low because the region is not at the forefront of digital technology and payment system adoption. The Asian and European regions are also not fully represented.

The absolute Cyber-related fraud counts show the distribution of countries that are the main targets of cybercrime on a global scale. In contrast, the relative cyber-related fraud rate per 100,000 people indicates countries where the impact of cyber-crime is most visible and targeted based on their size and population.

The global picture of the prevalence of cyber-related fraud indicators changes somewhat when cybercrime incidents are considered in terms of population size (Pakhlyan 2025a; United Nations Office on Drugs and Crime (UNODC) n.d.). The difference between cyber-related fraud and the cyber-related fraud rate per 100,000 people is most pronounced in Liechtenstein. Thus, being a dwarf state and a small economy, Liechtenstein is not included in the top ten countries with significant cybercrime cases on a global scale in absolute terms. However, when viewed per 100,000 population, the country appears in the leading positions (Liechtenstein was in fifth place with 160 cases of Cyber-related Fraud rate per 100,000 population in 2020; it was in the first place with 432.9 cases in 2021; it was in the second place with 467.9 cases in 2022). Simultaneously, the absolute indicators of recorded cybercrime cases were 62 cases in 2020, 169 cases in 2021, and 184 cases in 2022. According to the Worldometer, Liechtenstein's population was 39,870 people in 2024, ranking 188th out of 195 countries in the world (Worldometer n.d.), which is at least 2.5 times smaller than 100,000.

Spain, Germany, Italy, Canada, Singapore, Austria, Costa Rica, the UK, and Poland are simultaneously among the top ten countries in both indicators. These countries are the main targets of cybercrime on a global scale and face the most significant impact.

The WCI is a pioneering initiative designed to rank countries systemically based on their cybercrime threat level. Its primary objective is to provide a comprehensive, data-driven assessment of the global distribution of cybercriminal activity, addressing the longstanding challenge of tracing offenders due to the illicit and anonymous nature of their operations. Unlike technical tracking methods, which are often ineffective due to the obfuscation tactics employed by cybercriminals, the WCI leverages expert-driven insights to map key hubs of cybercrime (University of Oxford 2024).

The WCI findings reveal that cybercriminal activity is concentrated in relatively few countries. Some of those countries consistently ranked among the top ten in each category of cybercrime, highlighting their significant role in the global cyber-crime landscape. China, Russia, Ukraine, the USA, Romania, and Nigeria are among them (United Nations Office on Drugs and Crime (UNODC) n.d.; University of Oxford 2024). Russia emerged as the leading global cybercrime hub, ranking first overall. Russian cybercriminals are regarded as the most technically skilled and professional, with their operations exerting the most significant impact worldwide (Council of Europe 2001). The analysis of data (United Nations Office on Drugs and Crime (UNODC) n.d.; University of Oxford 2024) shows a discrepancy between the top ten countries ranked by the WCI and those in the UNODC cyber-related crime database (only the UK appears in all lists), which can be attributed to several key methodological and conceptual differences:

- Differences in data sources, collection methods, and crime categorization: WCI relies on expert assessments from cybersecurity professionals, investigators, and analysts who rank countries based on cybercrime impact, professionalism, and technical skills; UNODC cyber-related crime database compiles cybercrime incidents rather than the origins of cybercriminal networks, officially reported by the governments, law enforcement agencies, and international organizations. Besides, the WCI focuses on five categories of cybercrime, emphasizing technical sophistication, financial crimes, and organized cybercriminal networks, which may not align with the UNODC database and include a broad range of cyber-related offenses;
- Targeting Offender and Victim Countries: The WCI ranks nations where cybercriminals are active and operating, identifying the most significant source countries of cybercrime. The UNODC database concentrates on victim countries, emphasizing those experiencing high levels of reported cybercrime;
- Underreporting issues: Countries with **more substantial cybersecurity infrastructure and reporting mechanisms** (e.g., Western nations) may appear more frequently in the **UNODC database** due to higher cybercrime detection rates. In contrast, countries with **weaker enforcement or limited reporting structures** may be underrepresented.

A PESTLE analysis was conducted to assess the **macro-environmental factors** influencing cybercrime and cybersecurity on a global scale. The PESTLE toolkit covers political, economic, social, technological, environmental, and legal aspects (Table 2) shaping cyber threats and cybersecurity strategies worldwide.

4 Conclusion

The level of development in the region certainly affects the prevalence of cybercrime because it implies the involvement of "players" with intellectual potential and professional skills. However, countries that use relatively weak defense measures in the online domain, particularly those that have not made serious progress in the IT sector, can also become targets of cyberattacks.

While the geography of cybercrime attacks can be mapped, identifying the actors and origins of cybercriminal activity is far more complex due to these offenses' anonymous nature.

Table 2 PESTLE analysis of the cybercrime global trends

PESTLE analysis		
P	Political factors	1. Cybersecurity policies & regulations 2. International cooperation 3. State-sponsored cybercrime 4. Cybersecurity funding
E	Economic factors	1. Growth of the cybersecurity industry 2. Rising cost of cybercrime 3. Impact on businesses & economies 4. Cryptocurrency & money laundering
S	Social factors	1. Digitalization & remote work 2. Low public awareness 3. Cybersecurity training demand 4. Rise of cybercrime-as-a-service (CaaS) 5. Dark web expansion
T	Technological factors	1. Internet of Things (IoT) vulnerabilities 2. AI & machine learning in cybercrime 3. Blockchain & cybersecurity 4. Cloud security challenges
L	Legal factors	1. Data protection regulations 2. Emerging AI & cybercrime laws 3. Corporate liability for cybersecurity
E	Environmental factors	1. Energy consumption of cyberinfrastructure 2. Climate-related cyber threats 3. E-waste & data security risks

Source: Compiled by the author

The PESTLE analysis highlighted the complex and evolving landscape of cybercrime in the digital age. Governments, businesses, and individuals must adapt to emerging threats while balancing political, economic, social, technological, legal, and environmental challenges.

Political factors play a crucial role in shaping the global cybersecurity landscape. Governments worldwide are implementing stricter data protection laws to enhance digital security and privacy. Cybercriminal activities often transcend national borders and require international cooperation and collaboration among countries. Several key conventions and treaties play a significant role in addressing and combating cybercrime. The most important ones are the Council of Europe Convention on Cybercrime (Budapest Convention, 78 parties and 17 observer countries (Council of Europe 2001)), the United Nations Convention against Transnational Organized Crime (UNTOC), with 147 signatories and 192 parties (United Nations 2000), and the African Union Convention on Cyber Security and Personal Data Protection (Malabo Convention).

International cooperation efforts seek to standardize cybercrime legislation and improve cross-border enforcement. However, significant regulatory gaps persist, as the absence of global coordination hinders effective law enforcement against cybercriminal activities. Additionally, state-sponsored cybercrime has emerged as a geopolitical tool, with cyberattacks increasingly used for political interference and cyber warfare. In response to these growing threats, national governments are allocating more significant financial resources to cybersecurity initiatives, strengthening their digital defense capabilities.

The economic impact of cybercrime is profound, with global costs projected to reach $15.63 trillion annually by 2029 (Petrosyan 2024a). This growing threat has driven significant expansion in the cybersecurity industry as businesses increasingly invest in advanced security software, ethical hacking, and AI-driven protection systems. However, the rise of Ransomware-as-a-Service (RaaS) has made cyber extortion more accessible, enabling criminals to purchase and deploy ransomware attacks with minimal expertise. Cryptocurrencies facilitate anonymous financial transactions, making them a preferred tool for laundering and illicit activities. Cyberattacks and data breaches impose substantial economic burdens on businesses, leading to regulatory fines, legal liabilities, and costly recovery efforts, ultimately disrupting economies worldwide.

The forced digitalization of society and the expansion of remote work have accelerated cybersecurity risks as individuals and businesses rely on remote access systems that often lack robust security measures. Low public awareness of cyber threats leaves many users vulnerable to phishing attacks, identity theft, and other cybercrimes. Simultaneously, the rise of Cybercrime-as-a-Service (CaaS) has made cyberattacks more accessible, as criminal networks provide unique hacking tools for financial gain. Meanwhile, the dark web continues to expand, serving as a marketplace for stolen data, hacking tools, and illicit services, further complicating global efforts to combat cybercrime.

Cybercriminals are increasingly exploiting artificial intelligence (AI) and machine learning. The growing number of connected devices provides multiple entry points for cyberattacks, so the rapid expansion of the Internet of Things (IoT) has further amplified security risks. Blockchain technology appears as a dual challenge. Blockchain technologies are being used to enhance cybersecurity through secure transactions and, at the same time, facilitate cybercrime, such as cryptojacking. Meanwhile, the widespread adoption of cloud computing has introduced new security challenges.

Legal frameworks play a crucial role in shaping cybersecurity policies and enforcement. However, cross-border cybercrime remains challenging, as differences in national legal systems hinder international cooperation and prosecution efforts. Additionally, as artificial intelligence becomes more integrated into cybercrime tactics, governments are introducing regulations to address emerging threats.

The growing reliance on cyber ecosystems and infrastructure creates significant environmental challenges, particularly in energy consumption. Data centers and cryptocurrency mining operations require substantial power, contributing to high carbon emissions and sustainability concerns. Additionally, the improper disposal of electronic waste (e-waste) presents serious data security risks, as discarded devices may still contain sensitive information, making them targets for cybercriminals. Addressing these issues requires sustainable IT practices, improved energy efficiency, and secure e-waste management.

These conclusions and recommendations provide a comprehensive roadmap for policymakers, industry leaders, and global stakeholders to effectively address and mitigate the multifaceted challenges posed by cybercrime in the digital age.

Data Availability
Data on the share of Internet users who have ever experienced cybercrime in 2022 in selected countries, as well as the estimated cost of cybercrime worldwide in 2018–2029 that support the study's findings, are available at https://figshare.com/ with the identifier https://doi.org/10.6084/m9.figshare.28719098. Data on cybercrime trends worldwide are available with the identifier https://doi.org/10.6084/m9.figshare.28821638.v1.

References

Benaichouba, R., M. Brahmi, and L. Adala. 2024. Economic of cyber-security and society databases: Protecting the digital ecosystem from cyber-attacks. *International Journal of Professional Business Review* 9 (7): e04803. https://doi.org/10.26668/businessreview/2024.v9i7.4803.

Bruce, M., J. Lusthaus, R. Kashyap, N. Phair, and F. Varese. 2024. Mapping the global geography of cybercrime with the World Cybercrime Index. *PLoS One* 19 (4): e0297312. https://doi.org/10.1371/journal.pone.0297312.

Chen, S., M. Hao, F. Ding, D. Jiang, J. Dong, S. Zhang, et al. 2023. Exploring the global geography of cybercrime and its driving forces. *Humanities and Social Sciences Communications* 10:71. https://doi.org/10.1057/s41599-023-01560-x.

Council of Europe. 2001. *Convention on Cybercrime (Budapest Convention ETS No. 185) and its Protocols (signed November 23,* 2001*)*. Budapest, Hungary: Council of Europe. Retrieved from https://www.coe.int/en/web/cybercrime/the-budapest-convention (Accessed 1 March 2025).

Fahmy, W. 2024. The cybercrime acts and the electronic transaction in international law. *Economics, Law and Policy* 7 (1): 18–41. https://doi.org/10.22158/elp.v7n1p18.

Gen and The Harris Poll. 2023, February. *2023 Norton Cyber Safety Insights Report: Global Results.* Retrieved from https://www.gendigital.com/media/qcymrc1i/2023-ncsir-us-global-report_final.pdf (Accessed 1 March 2025).

Halkiopoulos, C., A. Papadopoulos, Y. C. Stamatiou, L. Theodorakopoulos, and V. Vlachos. 2024. A digital service for citizens: Multi-parameter optimization model for cost-benefit analysis of cybercrime and cyberdefense. *Emerging Science Journal* 8 (4): 1320–1344. https://doi.org/10.28991/ESJ-2024-08-04-06.

Jahankhani, H., A. Al-Nemrat, and A. Hosseinian-Far. 2014. Cybercrime classification and characteristics. In *Cyber crime and cyber terrorism investigator's handbook*, ed. B. Akhgar, A. Staniforth, and F. Bosco, 1st ed., 149–164. Waltham, MA: Syngress. https://doi.org/10.1016/B978-0-12-800743-3.00012-8

Mijwil, M. M., M. Aljanabi, and ChatGPT. 2023. Towards artificial intelligence-based cybersecurity: The practices and ChatGPT generated ways to combat cybercrime. *Iraqi Journal for Computer Science and Mathematics* 4 (1): 8. https://doi.org/10.52866/ijcsm.2023.01.01.0019.

Morgan, S. 2022. *2022 Official Cybercrime Report*. Northport, NY: Cybersecurity Ventures, eSentire. Retrieved from https://s3.ca-central-1.amazonaws.com/esentire-dot-com-assets/assets/resourcefiles/2022-Official-Cybercrime-Report.pdf (Accessed 1 March 2025).

Pakhlyan, A. 2024. "Criminogenic" IT progress: Global trends in cybercrime. *Amberd Bulletin* 4 (29): 71–78. https://doi.org/10.52174/2579-2989_2024.4-71.

Pakhlyan, A. 2025a. *Cybercrime trends worldwide: A statistical snapshot by region and nation.* figshare. Figure. https://doi.org/10.6084/m9.figshare.28821638.v1.

Pakhlyan, A. 2025b. *The cost and victims of cybercrime worldwide.* figshare. Figure. https://doi.org/10.6084/m9.figshare.28719098.

Petrosyan, A. 2024a, July 30. Annual cost of cybercrime worldwide 2018–2029. *Statista.* Retrieved from https://www.statista.com/forecasts/1280009/cost-cybercrime-worldwide (Accessed 1 March 2025).

Petrosyan, A. 2024b, August 5. Cybercrime encounter rate in selected countries 2022. *Statista.* Retrieved from https://www.statista.com/statistics/194133/cybercrime-rate-in-selected-countries/ (Accessed 1 March 2025).

Silva, K. B. D., and H. G. D. L. Cavalcanti. 2016. Criminality in the information age: Definitions on complex criminality. *Revista de Direito, Governança e Novas Tecnologias* 2 (2): 75–93. https://doi.org/10.26668/IndexLawJournals/2526-0049/2016.v2i2.1488.

United Nations. 2000. *United Nations Convention against Transnational Organized Crime.* (was adopted by resolution A/RES/55/25 of November 15, 2000 at the fifty-fifth session of the General Assembly of the United Nations). *New York, NY:* United Nations. Retrieved from https://treaties.un.org/pages/ViewDetails.aspx?src=TREATY&mtdsg_no=XVIII-12&chapter=18&clang=_en (Accessed 1 March 2025).

United Nations Office on Drugs and Crime (UNODC). n.d. *Corruption & economic crime database, fraud: Cyber-related (Cy).* Retrieved from https://dataunodc.un.org/dp-crime-corruption-offences (Accessed 1 March 2025).

University of Oxford. 2024, April 10. *World-first "Cybercrime Index" ranks countries by cybercrime threat level.* Retrieved from https://www.ox.ac.uk/news/2024-04-10-world-first-cybercrime-index-ranks-countries-cybercrime-threat-level (Accessed 1 March 2025).

World Bank. n.d. *GDP (current US$).* Retrieved from https://data.worldbank.org/indicator/NY.GDP.MKTP.CD (Accessed 1 March 2025).

Worldometer. n.d. *Countries of the world.* Retrieved from https://www.worldometers.info/geography/countries-of-the-world/ (Accessed 1 March 2025).

Features of Armenia's Digitalization Strategy Implementation in the Context of the Government's Digital Transformation

Khoren Mkhitaryan, Anna Sanamyan, Mariam Mnatsakanyan, and Erika Kirakosyan

Abstract On February 11, 2021, guided by Article 146 of the Constitution of the Republic of Armenia, the Government of the Republic of Armenia implemented Resolution "On approval of the digitalization strategy of Armenia, the Strategy Action Plan, and Result Indicators" (No. 183-L). This was a key and decisive step in regulating and managing the digitalization process. The digitalization strategy of the Republic of Armenia is based on three main directions: government, economy, and society. The research conducted by the authors concerns three main dimensions of digital transformation in the public administration system: key issues in the formation of digital government, threats and obstacles arising in the almost complete absence of cybersecurity, and the improvement of the digitalization of internal public administration systems to significantly reduce and completely eliminate unnecessary bureaucratic red tape, eliminate potential sources of corruption risks, form and continuously develop an optimal system for controlling digitalization processes, and increase the efficiency of certain existing digital systems. Ultimately, the mission of Armenia's digitalization strategy is to ensure the necessary conditions for effective and tripartite cooperation through the improvement of the digitalization processes of the three-layer chain of government-economy-society. Based on the conclusions made in the research, the authors provided several recommendations in the field of digital transformation of public administration.

Keywords Digital transformation • Cybersecurity • E-government • Information technology • E-governance • Digital government

JEL Codes H10 • H11 • H19

K. Mkhitaryan (✉) · A. Sanamyan · M. Mnatsakanyan · E. Kirakosyan
Armenian State University of Economics, Yerevan, Armenia

A. Karbekova (ed.), *Ethics of the AI Economy: A System View from the Positions of the Theory of Stakeholders*, Ethical Economy 73,
https://doi.org/10.1007/978-3-032-23423-0_9

1 Introduction

Under today's market dynamics, economic digitalization has become a central priority in the strategic development plans of almost every country worldwide. The processes of digital transformation of the economy and society provide broad opportunities in terms of further improving public administration, business, and entrepreneurship, as well as social processes. The digital transformation of the economy and society is becoming a driving force for improving public administration (Bessonova and Battalov 2020). In recent years, governments worldwide have accelerated the digital transformation of their economies. They see it as a means to boost the efficiency of public administration and an urgent necessity in response to rapidly evolving challenges, emerging threats, and unforeseen force-majeure risks. At the current stage of the state's economic development, the processes of digital transformation of the government, economy, and society have acquired particular importance due to the crucial role and significance of the latter in terms of the subsequent development of the above-mentioned sectors. Moreover, unlike traditional, non-digital economies, the driving force behind the digital transformation of government, economic, and social processes is the intensive use of innovations and new creations in the development of all branches and sectors of the economy (Karimov et al. 2021).

The digital transformation of public administration is considered a priority in Armenia's digitalization strategy. In recent years, the government has significantly restructured, adjusting the number and responsibilities of its sectoral and functional ministries. However, change management within public administration has progressed slowly, constrained by a rigid, mechanistic organizational model inherited from the bureaucratic era. Although several tangible results were achieved thanks to the implemented functional reforms (i.e., the introduction and implementation of some -e-government principles), the effectiveness of the state administration system remains insufficient. To form a competitive state in the contemporary international arena, it is necessary to improve the implemented economic policy and the activities of the state administration apparatus, reduce cases of unnecessary state regulation and intervention, etc. Additionally, the priority goals of the implementation of the Armenia Digital Strategy Action Plan adopted in 2021 are the diversification and improvement of the quality of services provided to the public by the government, increasing the efficiency of financial and economic activities of branch and functional bodies of state administration, and, most importantly, ensuring accessibility to official information as an important result of increasing the level of public trust (Government of the Republic of Armenia 2021).

2 Methodology

The success of achieving the goals of scientific research is largely determined by the methods used during the research work. The authors applied system, situational, and comparative analysis.

The research involves the collection and analysis of data, which serves to establish the relevance of this research and define its purpose.

At the stage of situational analysis, the authors defined opportunities and issues and assessed the current state and direction of the subject and object of the research.

The methodological basis of this research is based on using secondary information collection tools. The theoretical, informational, and methodological foundation for gathering secondary data drew on core technological theories and the work of Armenian and international scholars on various aspects of digitalization and digital transformation –their components, economic impact, and regulatory needs. Additionally, reports and publications from state bodies (whether directly or indirectly involved in sector regulation) served as key information sources.

To conduct a comprehensive and effective analysis, after collecting secondary information, the authors carried out its qualitative and quantitative analysis using a certain methodological toolkit with wide applicability. Using the quantitative method, the authors analyzed the state of cybersecurity, after which qualitative assessments characterizing the situation were given based on the results obtained.

3 Results

Scientific and technological progress continued its confident race in the twenty-first century. Technological innovations began to acquire their irreplaceable role and significance in public administration and broad sectors of society as a result of the further development of the Internet (Saritha et al. 2021). The introduction of an electronic system in public administration allows state departments and territorial and local self government bodies to significantly optimize all processes and simplify the relationship between the state, citizens, and businesses. The use of information and network technologies in public administration bodies began in the world after the creation of global networks in the 1990s (West 2005). The consistent application of these technologies automatically leads to the development of electronic and digital processes, primarily in the field of public administration.

Electronic document management and the concept of electronic government first appeared in 1998 in the monograph "The World of E-Government" by the famous professor at the University of Berkeley, George G. Curtin (Curtin et al. 2003).

There are quite a few studies on introducing electronic government in the Republic of Armenia. This shows that this area has not yet been fully studied.

While e-government is generally presented as e-democracy and the development of e-governance, it is important to recognize that issues related to access to information are identified with access to global markets (Sharifi and Zarei 2004). In the context of electronic and functional reforms in public administration, it is important to accurately understand the key role and significance of digital democracy, primarily in the field of participatory governance (Jaeger 2004).

E-governance involves automating and then digitalizing governmental, administrative, and social processes to drive digital transformation and boost public-sector

Table 1 Differences between electronic and digital government

Characteristics	Electronic Government	Digital Government
Main function	Automation of online services	Complete management transformation
Technologies used	ICT4D, websites, and electronic documents	Artificial intelligence, blockchain, cloud technologies, databases, and analytics
Working examples	Armenian State Electronic Governance Platform (E-gov.am); Online tax obligations platform (E-Tax); Electronic passports and ID cards; Online notary services platform MOJ e-Notary; Electronic health care (e-Health); Digital school education management system: dasaran.am; National Electronic Library of Armenia (e-Library.am); data.gov.am—government open data platform; Opendata.am—an information resource for civil society and business.	One-stop-shop integration of government services; Application of artificial intelligence for public administration decision-making; Citizen-centric platforms that offer personalized services.
Citizen engagement	Direct use of online services	Direct citizen involvement in data-driven policymaking as an important attribute of participatory governance

Source: Compiled by the authors

efficiency. At its core is the elimination of bureaucratic paperwork. Digital government builds on this by using data, artificial intelligence, cloud technologies, and blockchain to strategically and functionally transform governance, integrating state services into a true "one-stop shop" and applying AI to key decision-making (McLoughlin and Wilson 2013).

Table 1 presents the essential differences between electronic and digital government.

To increase the effectiveness of the implementation of Armenia's digital strategy, consistently implement relevant measures, and coordinate and oversee digitalization processes, the "Digital Armenia" Foundation was established in 2017 by the decision of the Government of the Republic of Armenia (Government of the Republic of Armenia 2017).

On February 27, 2025, the Government of Armenia adopted several decisions to promote digital transformation in various sectors. Such measures include forging international cooperation agreements, enhancing territorial governance, and launching various other initiatives. However, it is important to acknowledge that these digital-transformation efforts have not yet yielded the desired results. The implementation of the digitalization strategy in Armenia is extremely low. This primary concerns the low level of cybersecurity. The draft law "On cybersecurity," introduced in 2021 to protect vital information systems and critical infrastructures, has languished in draft form for four years. As a result, the country's cybersecurity remains low and unstable. This is evidenced by Armenia's low 90th position among 193 countries (International Telecommunication Union (ITU) 2021), falling behind Turkey, Azerbaijan, Egypt, Tanzania, Bangladesh, Kenya, and others. At that time, Turkey was 11th among the countries in the region, Azerbaijan was 40th, Iran was 54th, and Georgia was 55th. It should always be remembered that Armenia is the target of cyberattacks by Turkish and Azerbaijani hacker groups, whose activities are becoming increasingly active.

Additionally, the National Cybersecurity Center, whose formation deadline was set for September 2021, was never established. The Ministry of High-Tech Industry, which was required to develop cybersecurity exercises and organizational measures against cyberattacks in accordance with Armenia's digitalization strategy, also bears a large share of the blame for this. Additionally, the Ministry of High-Tech Industry is required to develop measures, a schedule, and responsible executors for implementing digital transformations in individual sectors of the economy and public administration.

Today, a wide range of Internet-connected devices is being rapidly deployed across government, public, and social sectors. According to Statista, the number of connected devices is expected to exceed 25 billion by 2030 (Fig. 1).

From this perspective, developing and implementing cybersecurity mechanisms and having a cyber-safe society have become an imperative and prerequisite for ensuring state security.

The digitalization of the Republic of Armenia's internal state-administration systems is implemented through the following functional areas:

- Digitalization of document circulation;
- Digital project management and task development;
- Automation of key processes of internal state administration systems;
- Ensuring data receipt, collection, storage, and transmission;

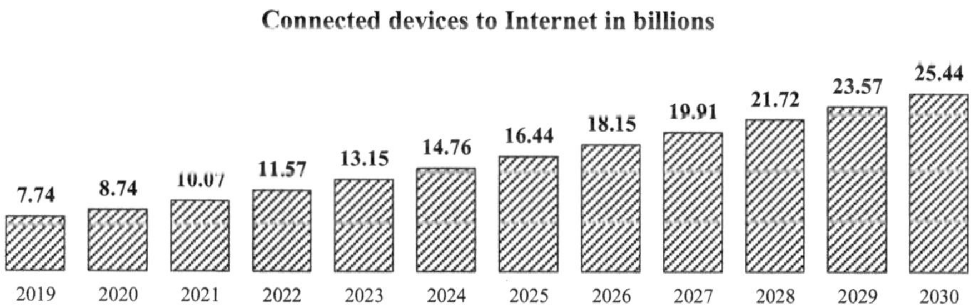

Fig. 1 The number of devices connected to the Internet. Source: Compiled by the authors based on Statista (Statista 2024)

- Financial flow management;
- Implementation of ongoing control and monitoring.

The process of creating fully digital, structured documents (JSON, XML) continues, albeit at an extremely slow pace.

Innovative programs, data-driven decisions, and active citizen engagement are important on Armenia's path to becoming a digital government.

4 Conclusions and Recommendations

Although the implementation of the digitalization strategy of the Republic of Armenia has moved somewhat from a dead end in recent years, there are several serious problems that hinder its effective development. Let us highlight the most significant of them:

1. Lack of organization and integration

The implementation of the digitalization strategy in Armenia is extremely low, the main reason being the lack of coordination and integration of relevant state structures. The Ministry of High-Tech Industry of the Republic of Armenia should assume responsibility for implementing the digitalization strategy, defining a roadmap, guidelines, and a schedule for creating a complete digital system of state services. Ensuring the integration of state departments in terms of increasing the efficiency of implementing the digitization strategy is also an important guarantee of success.

2. Cybersecurity threats and challenges

The main cyber threats in the Republic of Armenia are as follows:

- The presence of attacks on the state system, particularly DDoS (Distributed Denial of Service) attacks on the websites and information systems of state institutions from neighboring countries and their hacker groups, data leaks from state websites, and hybrid cyberattacks of war;
- The leakage of citizens' personal data. This refers to phishing attacks, which are aimed at stealing personal data, hacking individuals' e-mails, and obtaining access to bank accounts;
- Cyber threats directed at the financial and banking system, particularly cases of cyber fraud, through which citizens lose their financial resources through deception;
- The presence of propaganda and disinformation attacks using Deepfake technologies;
- Finally, attacks on the business environment, which include (Ransomware) attacks to encrypt company data and demand ransom, as well as the theft of intellectual property.

The main challenges of cybersecurity in the Republic of Armenia include the following:

- The slow and inconsistent implementation of cybersecurity in state and public administration, as well as in all social sectors and dimensions;
- The lack of personnel and professionals, primarily specialized cybersecurity experts;
- Ineffective fight against cybersecurity and a complete absence of specialized cyber police;
- Low level of cyber literacy. Many individuals and legal entities are unaware of cybersecurity rules, because of which they become easy targets.

3. Insufficient level of access to digital services

Significant regional disparities persist in Armenia: outside the capital, especially in rural communities, digital literacy remains low; high-speed Internet is largely unavailable.

4. The imperfection of the legislative framework

There are numerous legislative gaps in the areas of digital identity, data protection, and the practical application of artificial intelligence.

5. The problem of citizen trust

There is a lack of trust in the use of digital tools among some segments of society due to the insufficient level of digital literacy.

To effectively implement the digitalization strategy in Armenia, a comprehensive approach is necessary, including technological, legislative, legal, organizational, and social components. In the author's opinion, the following practical recommendations can contribute to successfully implementing the digitalization strategy.

1. Development of technological infrastructure

- Fast and universal internet access. It is necessary to provide high-quality Internet in all regions of the country, especially in rural communities (using fiber-optic networks, 5G, and satellite Internet technologies);
- Integration of state ICT4D systems;
- Modernization of state digital infrastructure;
- Modernization of servers and data storage centers (data centers);
- Involvement of artificial intelligence and big data technologies in public and state administration.

2. Development of operational measures to establish cybersecurity

- Consistent implementation of cybersecurity strategy. It is necessary to develop organizational measures to quickly respond to hacker attacks and develop specific actions to combat them;
- The creation of a new professional structure, the cyber police, to increase the effectiveness of the fight against cybercrime;

- Protection of personal data of individuals and legal entities;
- Organizing cybersecurity training courses for the public and private sectors.

3. Implementation of legislative and regulatory reforms

- Comprehensive legislation on digital governance. It is necessary to ensure regulation of digital signatures, electronic documents, artificial intelligence, and blockchain;
- Support for the digital economy. It is recommended to provide tax incentives for digital businesses, encouraging e-commerce and financial technologies (FinTech).
- Ensuring access to non-confidential data on official state websites.

4. Improving the quality of digital services

- Introduction of the "One-Stop-Shop" principle. It is necessary to create a single digital official platform to ensure accessibility to online public and state services by individuals and legal entities;
- AI and chatbots in state services. It is recommended to introduce AI-based consulting systems in state institutions that will help citizens obtain information and services;
- Development of electronic health systems. It is important to expand the "Armed" system to include electronic medical cards and telemedicine services.

5. Development of comprehensive measures and procedures to increase digital literacy

- Improving digital skills training and development activities. It is recommended to develop seminars, consultations, and training courses for the government and the public for the consistent implementation of digital processes;
- Developing digital training and artificial intelligence courses in schools and universities;
- Support for the digital transformation of businesses. It is necessary to digitalize educational programs for SMEs on e-commerce, CRM systems, and digital marketing.

6. Further intensification of innovation in digital transformation processes

- Development and implementation of national and private programs to promote small and medium-sized enterprises. The authors recommend creating an "Artificial Intelligence Institute" to encourage local companies to invest in the AI sector. Moreover, it is necessary to provide digital startups with financing mechanisms.
- Developing e-commerce and FinTech. It is necessary to facilitate e-commerce and accelerate the processing of digital payments. Expanding the use of blockchain technologies in the financial sector is also important;
- Smart city projects. It is necessary to implement smart transportation, smart lighting, and digital ecological monitoring systems in Yerevan and other major cities.

The simultaneous implementation of these steps will ensure the sustainable development of the Armenian digital government, improve the quality of service to citizens, and make Armenia one of the leaders in the digital economy in the region.

References

Bessonova, E., and R. Battalov. 2020. Digitalization as a tool for innovative economic development. *Economic Annals-XXI* 186 (11–12): 66–74. https://doi.org/10.21003/ea.V186-08.

Curtin, G. G., M. Sommer, and V. Vis-Sommer. 2003. *The World of E-Government*. 1st ed. New York, NY: Routledge.

Government of the Republic of Armenia. 2017. *Resolution "On establishing the Digital Armenia Foundation and approving its charter"* (August 3, 2017 No. 926-N). Yerevan, Armenia.

Government of the Republic of Armenia. 2021. *Resolution "On approval of the digitalization strategy of Armenia, the Strategy action plan, and result indicators"* (February 11, 2021, No. 183-L). Yerevan, Armenia.

International Telecommunication Union (ITU). 2021. *Global Cybersecurity Index 2020: Measuring commitment to cybersecurity*. Geneva, Switzerland: ITU. https://www.itu.int/dms_pub/itu-d/opb/str/D-STR-GCI.01-2021-PDF-E.pdf (Accessed 1 March 2025).

Jaeger, P. T. 2004. Beyond Section 508: The spectrum of legal requirements for accessible e-government Web sites in the United States. *Journal of Government Information* 30 (4): 518–533. https://doi.org/10.1016/j.jgi.2004.09.010.

Karimov, N. G., S. Sh. Saydullayev, and R. A. Parpieva. 2021. Digital transformation of the economy as a new challenge to economic security. In *Proceedings of ICFNDS '21: The 5th international conference on future networks and distributed systems*, 348–355. New York, NY: Association for Computing Machinery. https://doi.org/10.1145/3508072.3508129.

McLoughlin, I., and R. Wilson. 2013. *Digital government at work: A social informatics perspective*. Oxford, UK: Oxford University Press. https://doi.org/10.1093/acprof:oso/9780199557721.001.0001.

Saritha, K., M. Kurni, K. Madhavi, and D. Nagadevi. 2021. Integration of artificial intelligence and the internet of things with blockchain technology. In *Proceedings of the 2nd international conference on computational and bioengineering*, ed. S. Jyothi, D. M. Mamatha, Y. D. Zhang, and K. S. Raju, 449–457. Singapore: Springer. https://doi.org/10.1007/978-981-16-1941-0_45.

Sharifi, H., and B. Zarei. 2004. An adaptive approach for implementing e-government in I.R. Iran. *Journal of Government Information* 30 (5–6): 600–619. https://doi.org/10.1016/j.jgi.2004.10.005.

Statista. 2024. *Number of Internet of Things (IoT) connected devices worldwide from 2019 to 2033, by use case*. Retrieved from https://www.statista.com/statistics/1194701/iot-connected-devices-use-case/ (Accessed 1 March 2025)

West, D. M. 2005. *Digital government: Technology and public sector performance*. Princeton, NJ: Princeton University Press. Retrieved from https://www.jstor.org/stable/j.ctt7rqzx (Accessed 1 March 2025).

Ethical Aspects of Social Adaptation and Human Communication in the AI Economy for Its Sustainable Development

Robust Clustering Algorithms in Solving the Problem of Predicting the Behavior of Russian Language Learners

Iren Yu. Gats, Irina N. Dobrotina, Olga M. Aleksandrova, and Egor D. Vuychik

Abstract The research aims to theoretically substantiate the application of robust clustering algorithms to enhance the effectiveness of teaching methodologies for the Russian language. The authors explore the potential use of mathematical algorithms for predicting student behavior. The problem of forecasting learning activity related to the mastery of linguistic material necessitates the use of analytical tools capable of identifying differences among learners. This approach creates opportunities for designing individualized educational trajectories that consider the cognitive and behavioral characteristics of schoolchildren, which vary depending on the dominance of the right or left hemisphere of the brain. The methodological foundation of this research comprises fundamental research on hemispheric asymmetry and higher mental functions, as well as machine learning theory. The primary research method involves robust clustering algorithms, which allow for more accurate classification of students based on data analysis, including academic performance, task completion time, and common grammatical errors. Methods based on Mahalanobis distance facilitate the selection of individualized Russian language learning trajectories that align with specific didactic tasks set by the teacher. The research opens new perspectives in Russian language teaching methodologies by integrating mathematical modeling to improve the quality of philological education and adapt to the contemporary demands of the digital society. The research is original in that it establishes a connection between the cognitive approach in Russian language teaching methodologies and the application of robust clustering algorithms for predicting student behavior.

I. Y. Gats (✉)
Federal State University of Education, Moscow, Russia
e-mail: iju.gats@gupros.ru

I. N. Dobrotina · O. M. Aleksandrova
The Federal State Budget Scientific Institution «Institute of Content and Teaching Methods», Moscow, Russia

E. D. Vuychik
Moscow Pedagogical State University, Moscow, Russia

A. Karbekova (ed.), *Ethics of the AI Economy: A System View from the Positions of the Theory of Stakeholders*, Ethical Economy 73,
https://doi.org/10.1007/978-3-032-23423-0_10

Keywords Digital transformation • Artificial intelligence • Robust clustering • Language training • Individual approach

JEL Codes C60 • C61 • I20 • I2I • I24 • I28

1 Introduction

The understanding and prediction of the educational and linguistic actions of students are critical for improving the quality of philological general education. Students' responses to theoretical, theoretical-practical, and practical teaching methods, as well as to analytical-synthetic or synthetic types of exercises, allow educators to adapt linguo-didactic materials to meet the needs of specific student groups or individual learners. In the context of the active integration of digital tools, the implementation of a personalized approach to education has become one of the central tasks of contemporary methodology for teaching the Russian language. During a session of the Council for the Implementation of State Policy in the Support of the Russian Language and the Languages of the Peoples of Russia, it was emphasized that education should be tailored to individuals born into the digital society, who are proficient in linguistic, communicative, and ethical norms (Presidential Executive Office of Russian Federation 2024). Predicting the behavior of students in Russian language lessons, grounded in the theory of communicative activity-based learning, particularly in the development of cognitive features, has become a significant aspect of this process. This approach allows for the formation of individualized educational trajectories for each student. The scientific justification for this thesis can be found in the foundational works of A. N. Leontiev (1983), A. R. Luria (1973, 2020), and L. S. Vygotsky (2024). A. N. Leontiev highlights that the speech function relies on hemispheric integration, where the left hemisphere is responsible for constructing speech programs; the right hemisphere ensures their emotional and intentional execution (Leontiev 1983, pp. 83–84). Consequently, linguistic skills are formed not merely through the mechanical memorization of rules but also through their perception of real-life contexts that require analytical and synthetic approaches. The hemispheric asymmetry of the brain, which governs differences in information processing, significantly influences the perception and retention of educational material (Leontiev 1983, p. 86). For instance, students with a dominant left hemisphere are more adept at mastering grammatical patterns and analytical structures. Those with a dominant right hemisphere exhibit an enhanced ability to perceive metaphors and contextual meanings. A. R. Luria, one of the founders of neuropsychology, demonstrated that the left hemisphere predominantly handles the analytical processing of speech signals and grammatical and syntactic analysis (Luria 1973, 2020). It is fundamentally important for the perception, comprehension, and production of speech, structuring linguistic information, and processing logical connections between words and sentences. In contrast, the right hemisphere governs intonation, emotional coloring of speech, and contextual information processing, which aids in perceiving the broader meaning of a text and its emotional nuances (Luria 1973, 2020). Based on these distinctions, predicting educational and linguistic actions becomes crucial for high-quality linguistic education. Contemporary researchers, such as A. D. Deikina (2015), S. S. Frolkova (2022), D. S. Kvashnina (2023), V. Yu. Makarova (2021), T. A. Ostrikova (Ostrikova and Chuchva 2023), and A. A. Pronina (2024), emphasize that understanding each student's unique characteristics, their responses to different Russian language teaching methods, and their overall level of linguistic preparedness is crucial. These factors decisively influence the mastery of the norms of the Russian literary language, the acquisition of comprehensive knowledge about the language system, and the development of a strong grammatical structure in adolescent speech.

In the context of integrating artificial intelligence into education, predicting student behavior through robust clustering methods reveals patterns in grouping students with diverse learning needs. This allows Russian language teachers to anticipate potential challenges in advance and propose individualized solutions for learning. Predicting student behavior with consideration of hemispheric asymmetry and the application of robust clustering methods becomes a significant methodological foundation for designing personalized educational trajectories. This approach facilitates effective knowledge acquisition, sustains students' interest in studying the Russian language, and creates conditions for the conscious mastery of native language norms. This research substantiates the relationship between the implementation of a cognitive approach in teaching Russian and the application of a mathematical model based on the Mahalanobis distance (Mahalanobis 2018) for the development of linguo-didactic materials.

The search for sources in the Web of Science, Scopus, and RSCI databases connected to the application of robust algorithms for predicting classroom behavior in Russian language lessons revealed that the problem remains understudied. The introduction of robust clustering algorithms for predicting linguistic and educational actions requires an examination of modern active learning practices. Using content analysis, the authors selected sources with the key terms "cognitive approach" and "robust algorithms". Among the 57 sources identified by these keywords, significant results were highlighted from educational studies conducted by A. D. Deikina (2015), C. Denaro (Denaro et al. 2022), F. F. Dudyrev (Dudyrev and Maksimenkova 2020), I. M. Lerner (Lerner et al. 2023), P. G. Matukhin (2024), and M. A. Sivak and V. S. Timofeev (2021). The research by I. M. Lerner and co-authors applies cluster analysis to distinguish groups with varying educational needs, adapting electronic learning environments to learners' characteristics (Lerner et al., 2023, p. 5). Their results underscore the importance of an individualized approach, achievable through robust clustering algorithms that enable accurate differentiation of learners based on behavioral traits. The reliability of the obtained data is supported by the Cattell multifactorial testing method and cluster analysis. Using this approach, researchers identified student groups with diverse educational needs. The findings revealed significant variability in psychological characteristics, such as leadership tendencies, stress tolerance, social skills, and motivation. Based on these profiles, recommendations were made to improve the effectiveness of adaptive electronic learning environments. The study by C. Denaro highlights the efficacy of cluster analysis in assessing educational strategies (Denaro et al. 2022). Specifically, the authors identified groups of educators with different levels of engagement in active learning, making it possible to develop targeted recommendations to enhance teacher involvement and adopt active teaching methods. The relevance of such approaches is supported by the article "Simulators and Trainers in Professional Education" (Dudyrev and Maksimenkova 2020), which demonstrates the potential of simulation modeling in developing professional skills and strengthening educational platforms. Simulation modeling also supports the concept of a safe environment for practice and experimentation, making simulation technologies a crucial component of implementing adaptive strategies. This idea is proved by quantitative calculation methods in the article "Technology for the formation and application of simulation modeling in the educational process" (Suyumov et al. 2024). An interesting contribution comes from the work of P. G. Matukhin, which proposes an inverse frontal questioning methodology for training teachers of Russian using ChatGPT-4. This research underscores the importance of digital literacy and a critical approach to artificial intelligence technologies (Matukhin 2024). Educators developed more precise prompts for the neural network and adapted its responses to personalized learning. This research body highlights the potential of robust algorithms, simulation technologies, and cluster analysis in advancing educational methodologies and fostering adaptive strategies tailored to the diverse needs of learners and educators alike.

Based on a general theoretical analysis of the sources, a scientific hypothesis was formulated suggesting that the combination of clustering methods and artificial intelligence in the educational process opens up prospects for developing robust algorithms capable of predicting and accounting for the individual characteristics of learners. This is particularly relevant in the context of the digital transformation of education.

2 Materials and Methods

To reformulate the pedagogical phenomenon associated with implementing an individualized approach, the authors attempted to mathematize the issue of teaching school students with functional brain asymmetry. To ensure reliability, the authors employed mathematical modeling. The first stage of modeling involved data collection and laboratory verification, conducted under the conditions of daily Russian language lessons for students of the online school "Navyk" (Korolyov, Russian language teacher V. S. Sukhov) during the first semester of 2024. A total of 24 seventh-grade students (12 years old) participated in the experimental study. The students completed analytical-synthetic and synthetic tasks on morphological analysis of adverbs. The data were systematized in a convenient format, with characteristics identified that influence the individual mastery of linguistic and educational

Table 1 Characteristics of students for clustering learning material

Student	Achievement (grade, test score 1–10)	Time to complete the grammar task (in minutes)	Number of grammatical and orthographic errors	Teaching method Russian language	Hemispheric asymmetry
N1	8	15	2	speech pattern modification	left (cognitive-linguistic strategy)
N2	6	22	4	statement construction	right (communicative-speech strategy)
N	x_n	y_n	z_n	m_n	

Source: Compiled by the authors

material on the topic "Adverb as a Part of Speech: Its Meaning and Function in a Sentence" (Table 1).

The results of the first stage of the experimental study served as the foundation for creating a mathematical model with a didactic focus, allowing for a detailed examination of the cognitive and educational characteristics of students. In the second stage, by applying robust clustering algorithms, clusters of students were identified based on similar characteristics, such as academic performance, task completion time, number of errors, and other factors. During this stage of experimental laboratory work, the authors utilized the mathematical model with a didactic focus. We assumed that the greater the specificity (data on students, including their cognitive abilities, learning preferences, test results, time spent on tasks, and typical errors), the more valuable the results obtained. The level of robustness is a crucial characteristic of the machine learning system when addressing the task of predicting the behavior of learners studying Russian. The higher this parameter, the greater the likelihood of identifying the true cluster center when calculating aggregating functions (Shibzukhov 2018). In turn, clustering helps group data on verbal and non-verbal communicative acts (oral and written responses) of students into distinct clusters. The application of robust clustering algorithms, combined with the subsequent calculation of average aggregating functions, allows for the identification of the most prominent representatives of groups within the primary data sample. In the next stage, this will enhance the accuracy of the language teacher's selection of methods for teaching Russian.

3 Results

The principle of clustering using robust algorithms for solving the task of predicting student behavior in Russian language lessons is as follows. A set of measurements regarding the characteristics of students' verbal and non-verbal communicative acts (responses) is given as $X = \{x_1, \ldots, x_n\}$, $n \in \mathbf{Z}, n > 1$. The sets of verbal communicative acts $V = \{v_1, \ldots, v_k\}$, $k \in \mathbf{Z},\ 1 < k \leq n$, paraverbal communicative acts $P = \{p_1, \ldots, p_l\}$, $l \in \mathbf{Z},\ 1 < l \leq n$, and non-verbal communicative acts $G = \{g_1, \ldots, g_m\}$, $m \in \mathbf{Z},\ 1 < m \leq n$ belong to the set X. The sum of the elements in the sets V, P, and G equals the number of elements in X, (i.e., $n = k + l + m$). Within the set, X exists a subset of deviation values $O = \{o_1, \ldots, o_i\}$, $m \in \mathbf{Z},\ 1 \leq i \ll n$. The elements of the set O may belong to either the set V, the set C, or part of the elements in O may belong to the set of verbal communicative acts; another part belongs to the sets of non-verbal and paraverbal communicative acts. The set O is a subset of the set X. The stages of implementing the robust clustering algorithm are as follows:

- Perform classical clustering of all points in the set X;
- Identify anomalies within the set O;
- Work with the group of objects classified as "anomalies" (reduce the impact of anomalies on the main data sample and remove anomalies from the main data sample);
- Perform clustering of the objects in the set X, considering the work completed in stage three.

AI researchers propose using specific approaches to implement the second stage of the robust clustering algorithm described above: PACKD (Prototype-Aware Contrastive Knowledge Distillation) (Gu et al. 2023), ReConPatch (Contrastive Patch Representation Learning) (Hyun et al. 2024), FR-PatchCore (Feature-Level Registration PatchCore) (Jiang et al. 2024), DiffGAD (Diffusion-based Graph Anomaly Detector) (Li et al. 2024), KBJNet (Kinematic Bi-Joint Temporal Convolutional Network Attention for Anomaly Detection) (Mulia et al. 2024), ABIForest (Attention-Based Isolation Forest) (Utkin et al. 2022), and OptIForest (Optimal Isolation Forest) (Xiang et al. 2023). In this research, the authors applied a method based on the Mahalanobis distance metric (Mahalanobis 2018). Through this method, the similarity of measurements within the set X is assessed. On this basis, objects classified as "anomalies" are identified. The following formula of the mentioned metric is used to calculate the similarity between objects:

$$D_M(y) = \sqrt{(y - \mu)^T * S^{-1} * (y - \mu)}, \tag{1}$$

where $y = (y_1, y_2, y_3, \ldots, y_N)^T$ – multidimensional vector, $\mu = (\mu_1, \mu_2, \mu_3, \ldots, \mu_N)^T$ – set of mean values, and S – covariance matrix. The developed anomaly detection algorithm is incorporated into the clustering algorithm in the following manner:

- Compute the Mahalanobis metric for each value from the sets of verbal and non-verbal communicative acts of students;
- Calculate the average of all indicators found at the first stage $Average\_D_M(y)$;
- Calculate the dispersion coefficient $Var(D_M(y))$ of all values found at the first stage;

- Enter the variable r, which determines the degree to which the element belongs to the "anomaly" class;
- Calculate the threshold value $threshold = r * Var(D_M(y))$, which allows defining a boundary value, beyond which the element will be assigned an "anomaly" class identifier;
- Meet the condition "if $D_M(y) > threshold$" and assign the processed element the class identifier "anomaly"; the detection of outliers in the primary data sample will be implemented.

By successfully identifying the deviation values of the set O, it is possible to provide robust clustering of the measurements of the presented data sample with greater accuracy. The prediction algorithm comprises three sequential steps: the implementation of robust clustering, the computation of aggregation functions, and the calculation of final identifiers that define the behavior of learners of the Russian language. The predictive model for the behavior of students learning the Russian language consists of three components: input values, output values, and a transformation algorithm. The input values include data on verbal (V), non-verbal (G), and paraverbal (P) communicative acts, as well as their combinations. The output values are identifiers $B = \{b_1, \ldots, b_t\}$, $t \in \mathbf{Z}$, which determine specific behaviors of the learners.

The thesis on the creation of adaptive educational materials that consider the interests and knowledge of school students becomes even more relevant when considering the specifics of hemispheric brain dominance. The difference in the functioning of the right and left hemispheres affects the way a student perceives and processes information and, therefore, their success in learning. Hemispheric asymmetry of the brain determines a predisposition to analytical thinking (left-hemispheric type) or intuitive, image-based perception (right-hemispheric type). Let us outline how this can affect the adaptation of educational materials for the Russian language. The dominance of the left hemisphere of the brain manifests in adolescents' inclination toward logical thinking. These students generally appreciate order and consistency, demonstrate a strong grasp of the formal grammatical features of linguistic units, and handle cognitive-linguistic tasks more effectively, particularly those requiring text analysis, various types of linguistic analysis, and the development of plans. After studying grammatical rules, they tend to make fewer grammatical errors. For these learners, language teaching material is adapted based on the following principles:

- Clear structuring of the presentation and sequential presentation of lexical and grammatical material and step-by-step breakdown of educational and linguistic tasks;
- Support with algorithms and unambiguous instructions;
- Interpretation of the text based on different types of language analysis: syntactic analysis of sentences and word combinations, making schemes of sentences, determining the particle affiliation, lexical meaning of the word, establishing the features of the word form;
- Regularity of checking lexical and grammatical knowledge with clear criteria of evaluation;

- The use of the text as a basis for the analysis of the lexical and grammatical knowledge of the text.

The preferences of students with a right-hemispheric dominance are in the area of communicative-speech strategy with respect to language acquisition. Such individuals frequently exhibit a robust imagination, a proclivity for creativity, and an acute emotional perception of educational information. Such students are more readily assigned tasks related to the interpretation of texts, the selection of pictorial and expressive means to reveal the topic, and the creation of their own oral or written statements on a given topic. To cater to the needs of these students, the linguodidactic material is adapted based on the following principles:

- Tasks for composing texts, statements, and dialogues are given preference, requiring a rich vocabulary and the use of metaphors and comparisons;
- Tasks aimed at analyzing literary works and searching for subtext are offered;
- Multimedia resources are used more widely;
- Students are encouraged to write on free topics, without strict limits and restrictions for the manifestation of their individuality and creativity.

The following assignments will be appropriate in a variety of learning situations:

- Explain the phenomenon of language:
  - How can the specific marker of the past tense verb form, the suffix -*l*-, be explained?
  - What caused the emergence of the category of animacy in the Russian language?
  - Why are short adjectives not declined?
- In a written assignment, one student wrote: "The vast expanses of our country are boundless and necessary." What did the student mean by the word *"necessary"*? What is the nature of the error?

While preparing for the lesson, the Russian language teacher analyzes students' mistakes. As a rule, grammatical or spelling errors are linked to hemispheric specificity. For instance, left-hemispheric students may make errors in grammar and punctuation while easily handling logical tasks. Right-hemispheric students exhibit creativity but may struggle with adhering to spelling and punctuation rules and may introduce structural inconsistencies in their texts. The task for the teacher is to identify the type of hemispheric activity based on the nature of the errors. After conducting diagnostics, the teacher will need to develop individualized recommendations for selecting teaching methods, types of tasks, and forms of assessment. Predicting student behavior helps identify those who experience difficulties with specific aspects of the language system, such as grammar or vocabulary. If the teacher knows that certain types of tasks cause students stress or confusion, they can adjust the evaluation approach to make it more transparent and supportive. Robust clustering algorithms provide assistance to the teacher. In mathematical terms, the tasks solved by the students are elements of a set $E = \{e_1, \ldots, e_s\}$, $s \in \mathbf{Z}$, $s > 1$. In turn, they are subdivided according to hemispheric specificity into left-hemispheric ones

$Q = \{q_1, \ldots, q_f\}$, $f \in \mathbf{Z}$, $1 < f < s$ and right-hemispheric $W = \{w_1, \ldots, w_u\}$, $s \in \mathbf{Z}$, $1 < and < s$, with $s = f + u$, the sets Q, W are subsets of the set E E. If the pupil has completed more tasks from the set Q, then they have a left-hemispheric type of thinking of the binary set $H = \{\text{left} - \text{hemispheric}, \text{right} - \text{hemispheric}\}$; otherwise—the second identifier of the set H. If the student performs equally well on the Q and W tasks, additional testing is conducted based on the amount of time the student performs each type of task. The faster the learner decides within the framework of equivalent in complexity class tasks Q and W, the closer the coefficient $h \in \mathbf{R}$, $0 \leq h \leq 1$ to one of the values of the set H. If $h > 0.5$, the student predominantly exhibits right-hemispheric thinking; if $h < 0.5$, left-hemispheric thinking; if $h = 0.5$, additional testing is recommended for a more precise determination. The selection of these methods facilitated a study to substantiate robust clustering algorithms in the methodology of teaching the Russian language.

4 Conclusion

The research objective was achieved because the authors demonstrated the potential of robust clustering algorithms in the context of teaching methodology for the Russian language. First, the authors expanded the existing understanding that mathematics provides tools to enhance the accuracy of pedagogical measurements. Second, the authors confirmed that mathematical modeling can design individualized educational trajectories and support the teacher's effective methodological work. Third, robust clustering algorithms open new opportunities to develop linguoactive materials that account for the cognitive and behavioral characteristics of students. Analysis based on robust statistical methods, such as Mahalanobis distance, enables the identification of student groups with varying educational needs and improves the accuracy of student classification. The integration of robust algorithms into the methodology of teaching the Russian language strengthens the position of philological education in meeting the demands of modern digital society.

References

Deikina, A. D. 2015. Cognitive-semantic approach in teaching Russian language: Meta-semantics. In *Current issues of teaching Russian (native) language: Interregional conference (Part 1)*, ed. O. A. Skryabina, 188–191. Ryazan: Yesenin Ryazan State University.

Denaro, K., P. Kranzfelder, M. T. Owens, B. Sato, A. L. Zuckerman, R. A. Hardesty, et al. 2022. Predicting implementation of active learning by tenure-track teaching faculty using robust cluster analysis. *International Journal of STEM Education* 9:49. https://doi.org/10.1186/s40594-022-00365-9.

Dudyrev, F. F., and O. V. Maksimenkova. 2020. Training simulators in vocational education: Pedagogical and technological aspects. *Voprosy obrazovaniya [Educational Studies]* 3:255–276. https://doi.org/10.17323/1814-9545-2020-3-255-276.

Frolkova, S. S. 2022. Cognitive approach as an effective way of presenting material in Russian lessons. *Science and School* 5:244–250. https://doi.org/10.31862/1819-463X-2022-5-244-250.

Gu, Z., T. Yang, and L. Ma. 2023. Prototype-aware contrastive knowledge distillation for few-shot anomaly detection. In *Proceedings of BMVC 2023: 34th British machine vision conference*, 259–263. Durham: Durham University. Retrieved from https://papers.bmvc2023.org/0259.pdf (Accessed 01 November 2024).

Hyun, J., S. Kim, G. Jeon, S. H. Kim, K. Bae, and B. J. Kang. 2024. ReConPatch: Contrastive patch representation learning for industrial anomaly detection. In *Proceedings of WACV 2024: IEEE/CVF winter conference on applications of computer vision*, 2041–2050. Waikoloa, HI, IEEE. https://doi.org/10.1109/WACV57701.2024.00205.

Jiang, Z., Y. Zhang, Y. Wang, J. Li, and X. Gao. 2024. FR-PatchCore: An industrial anomaly detection method for improving generalization. *Sensors* 24 (5): 1368. https://doi.org/10.3390/s24051368.

Kvashnina, D. S. 2023. Comparative cognitive tasks as a means of forming a scientific linguistic world-picture in Russian language lessons in the 6th form. *Russian Language at School* 84 (6): 21–31. https://doi.org/10.30515/0131-6141-2023-84-6-21-31.

Leontiev, A. N. 1983. *Selected psychological works, in 2 volumes* (Vol. 2 by eds. V. V. Davydov, V. P. Zinchenko, A. A. Leontiev, A. V. Petrovsky). Moscow, USSR: Pedagogy.

Lerner, I. M., F. Y. Baikov, E. A. Karelina, S. G. Grigoriev, A. S. Sychev, and S. S. Dymkova. 2023. Developing typical profiles of generation Z students to improve the quality of the educational process. *Informatics and Education* 38 (6): 5–13. https://doi.org/10.32517/0234-0453-2023-38-6-5-13.

Li, J., Y. Gao, J. Lu, J. Fang, C. Wen, H. Lin, … X. Wang. 2024. DiffGAD: A diffusion-based unsupervised graph anomaly detector. *arXiv*. 10.48550/arXiv.2410.06549.

Luria, A. R. 1973. *Fundamentals of neuropsychology*. Moscow, USSR: Moscow University Press.

Luria, A. R. 2020. *Higher cortical functions of man*. St. Petersburg: Peter.

Mahalanobis, P. C. 2018. On the generalized distance in statistics [Reprint (1936)]. *Sankhya A* 80 (Suppl 1): 1–7. https://doi.org/10.1007/s13171-019-00164-5.

Makarova, V. Yu. 2021. Cognitive approach in teaching Russian language (On the example of working with poetic text). *World of the Russian Word* 2:88–97. https://doi.org/10.24412/1811-1629-2021-2-88-97.

Matukhin, P. G. 2024. Inverse frontal survey of the artificial intelligence system as a technique of Russian as a foreign language teachers training on the ChatGPT-4 queries and usage. In *Language as a factor of integration of educational systems and cultures: Proceedings of the XVI International Scientific and Practical Conference dedicated to the 10th anniversary of the Institute of Intercultural Communication and International Relations*, ed. M. A. Droga and A. A. Makhova, 47–55. Belgorod, Russia: Epicenter.

Mulia, M. A., M. B. Bahy, M. Z. F. N. Siswantoro, N. R. D. Riyanto, N. R. Sudianjaya, and A. M. Shiddiqi. 2024. KBJNet: Kinematic Bi-Joint temporal convolutional network attention for anomaly detection in multivariate time series data. *Data Science Journal* 23 (1): 10. https://doi.org/10.5334/dsj-2024-010.

Ostrikova, T. A., and L. M. Chuchva. 2023. Types and kinds of etymological exercises in Russian vocabulary. *Russian Language at School* 84 (1): 7–16. https://doi.org/10.30515/0131-6141-2023-84-1-7-16.

Presidential Executive Office of Russian Federation. 2024 November 5. *Meeting of the Presidential Council for State Policy on promoting the Russian language and languages of the peoples of the Russian Federation*. Retrieved from http://www.kremlin.ru/events/president/transcripts/75495 (Accessed 10 November 2024)

Pronina, A. A. 2024. Formation of orthographic literacy of students on the basis of cognitive-communicative approach. *Nauka i kultura Rossii [Science and Culture of Russia]* 1:130–134.

Shibzukhov, Z. M. 2018. Principle of empirical risk minimization and averaging aggregating functions. *Progress in Science and Technology. Contemporary Mathematics and its Applications. Thematic Surveys* 154:123–137.

Sivak, M. A., and V. S. Timofeev. 2021. Tuning of robust neural networks to solve the classification problem. *Proceedings of TUSUR University by Tomsk State University of Control Systems and Radioelectronics* 3 (24): 26–32. https://doi.org/10.21293/1818-0442-2021-24-3-26-32.

Suyumov, Ju., M. Lutfillayev, D. Yuldosheva, M. Xasanova, and A. Polvonov. 2024. Technology for the formation and application of simulation modeling in the educational process. *E3S Web of Conferences* 508:04008. https://doi.org/10.1051/e3sconf/202450804008.

Utkin, L., A. Ageev, A. Konstantinov, and V. Muliukha. 2022. Improved Anomaly detection by using the attention-based isolation forest. *Algorithms* 16 (1): 19. https://doi.org/10.3390/a16010019.

Vygotsky, L. S. 2024. *History of development of higher mental functions*. Moscow: Yurait Publishing House.

Xiang, H., X. Zhang, H. Hu, L. Qi, W. Dou, M. Dras, et al. 2023. Optiforest: Optimal isolation forest for anomaly detection. In *Proceedings of IJCAI-23: 32nd international joint conference on artificial intelligence*, 2379–2387. Macao: IJCAI. Retrieved from https://www.ijcai.org/proceedings/2023/0264.pdf (Accessed 01 November 2024).

Advanced Applications of LLMs in Marketing During the Purchase Stage

Evgeny V. Mishchenko

Abstract This research investigates the advanced application of Large Language Models (LLMs) in marketing strategies during the purchase stage, focusing on their effects on consumer behavior and marketing outcomes. Drawing on the Theory of Planned Behavior and Relational Marketing concepts, the research explores how LLM-powered virtual shopping assistants, dynamic social proof, and hyper-personalized interactions influence conversion rates, average order values, and customer satisfaction. A mixed-methods design integrates quantitative analysis (Structural Equation Modeling) with qualitative thematic insights from interviews and focus groups. Results show that LLM applications enhance consumer trust, streamline decision-making, and significantly improve purchase-related metrics. Ethical challenges (e.g., GDPR compliance and bias mitigation) are carefully addressed to ensure responsible and transparent AI usage. The findings suggest that LLM-driven personalization and real-time engagement represent critical levers for improving purchase-stage experiences and fostering sustainable customer loyalty. This research is of significant theoretical and practical importance, offering actionable recommendations for marketers while highlighting future research directions, including cross-cultural evaluations and the ethical dimensions of AI adoption in marketing contexts. Overall, LLMs are shown to be transformative tools for elevating marketing performance and reshaping digital consumer journeys at the point of purchase.

Keywords Consumer behavior • Large language models • Marketing strategies • Purchase stage • Virtual shopping assistants • Personalization • Relational marketing

JEL Codes D12 • M31 • M3

E. V. Mishchenko (✉)
Russian-Armenian University, Yerevan, Armenia

E-Commerce & Digital Marketing Association, Garden City, ID, USA
e-mail: em@ecdma.org

A. Karbekova (ed.), *Ethics of the AI Economy: A System View from the Positions of the Theory of Stakeholders*, Ethical Economy 73,
https://doi.org/10.1007/978-3-032-23423-0_11

1 Introduction

In the last decade, marketing has rapidly evolved due to advances in artificial intelligence (AI), which enable increasingly personalized consumer experiences, particularly at the critical purchase stage where buyer decisions converge (Radford et al. 2018; Weidinger et al. 2021). The most significant breakthroughs are Large Language Models (LLMs), sophisticated systems that process and generate human-like language (Brants et al. 2007; Vaswani et al. 2017). LLMs empower virtual shopping assistants, real-time social proof mechanisms, and hyper-personalization –tools that can enhance consumer trust, streamline decision-making, and boost overall satisfaction (Blokdyk 2018; Buttle and Maklan 2019; Fink 2020).

From a theoretical perspective, the Theory of Planned Behavior emphasizes the roles of attitudes, subjective norms, and perceived behavioral control in shaping purchase intentions (Ajzen 2020). Relational Marketing underscores that sustainable customer loyalty is forged through trustworthy and context-sensitive interactions (Araújo et al. 2022). By aligning LLM-driven initiatives with these theoretical constructs, marketers can more effectively foster consumer engagement and drive higher conversion rates.

Moreover, research by Court et al. (2009) demonstrates that consumer decision journeys are not strictly linear but involve multiple touchpoints—an insight that LLM-powered personalization can effectively exploit. Kumar and Reinartz (2012) further emphasize that integrated customer relationship management (CRM) tools, enhanced by LLMs, can solidify loyalty by meeting evolving consumer expectations.

This research investigates how LLMs affect consumer behavior and marketing performance during the purchase phase, drawing on quantitative and qualitative data. It explores whether AI-powered assistants, tailored messaging, and dynamic social proof bolster trust and positively impact key metrics such as conversion rates and average order values. The next section outlines the mixed-methods approach used to collect and analyze data, offering a roadmap for understanding LLMs' transformative potential in contemporary marketing.

2 Methodology

The research uses a quantitative and qualitative research approach as well. The use of mixed methods is also justified as it helps create an overall understanding of the research issue by integrating qualitative and quantitative analysis to arrive at a correct conclusion to cater to the complex nature of LLMs in marketing applications (Chung et al. 2020). The quantitative component examines the efficiency of tools initiated by LLM in relation to organizational performance indicators. The second part presents the reactivity of the participants and gains added understanding and richness as the result of the quantitative outcomes.

2.1 Data Collection Methods

Thus, to strengthen and substantiate findings, the research used mixed research method comprising of the following quantitative and qualitative data collection tools:

1. Sampling design: In the method used in this research, participants were selected purposefully to capture the main actors in the marketing system;
2. E-consumers: The final respondent pool was chosen with at least five monthly e-commerce purchases, AI application awareness, and demographic heterogeneity of 500 customers;
3. Marketing managers: Specifically, 25 marketing professionals from different sectors where LLM-powered tools may be deployed were selected to offer perceptual data;
4. Focus groups: eight sessions were conducted, each comprising five consumers, to capture divergent consumer viewpoints on LLM applications;
5. Data sources: To ensure validity and reliability, data were obtained from different sources wherever possible;
6. Quantitative data: Data included website traffic, sales data, and customer interaction logs collected from the e-commerce sites that deployed LLM applications;
7. Qualitative data: Interviews with 17 marketing managers (out of a sample group of 25) and eight focus group sessions provided a detailed understanding of consumer and practitioner perceptions and experiences;
8. Duration of data collection: Data acquisition was done over a period of 6 months which enabled the researcher to record changes in consumption patterns and changes in weather conditions.

2.2 Analytical Techniques

While the research has a quantitative component, it is also qualitative. Thus, the thematic approach to data analysis was used in the current research. The process involved the following stages to ensure transparency and rigor:

1. Data familiarization: The researchers conducted interviews and focus group discussions, which were audio-recorded and transcribed for analysis. The transcripts were then coded and reviewed multiple times to gain a comprehensive understanding of their content;
2. Initial coding: The initial research focused on identifying recurring words, phrases, and terms by analyzing the information wording. From this, a set of codes was developed, including "consumer trust," "personalized interpersonal communications," and "simplicity of the gate";

3. Iterative refinement: Several coding cycles were utilized to progressively refine the first level of codes. The first process of analyzing the collected data included collapsing similar codes into categories and casting about for subthemes;
4. Intercoder reliability: To maintain intercoder reliability, a subset of the data was coded by two coders separately. Cohen's kappa coefficient was used to measure intercoder reliability. Cohen's kappa was 0.85, indicating a high level of intercoder reliability. The interdependent reliability was achieved after the coders elaborated on their differences and reached a consensus;
5. Theme trustworthiness: The final themes were compared with the quantitative results and discussed with the participants during the subsequent interviews. This triangulation improved the reliability of the results;
6. Key themes identified: The analysis yielded several key topics:

   - Enhanced trust: Participants stressed the human-like approach within the communication with LLM-powered tools like (for instance, virtual assistants) building trust;
   - Personalization: Customers liked how LLMs could provide customized recommendations depending on the consumer's tendencies;
   - Decision-making support: Several respondents described how LLMs enabled the splitting of complex decisions into manageable ones, thus reducing cognitive load and increasing satisfaction.

Because of the systemic and comprehensible nature of the given methodology, the thematic analysis revealed detailed insights into the actual consumers' attitude and experiences concerning the LLM applications.

2.3 *Ethical Considerations*

As a result of the peculiarities of the presented topic, the issue of ethics is essential for enhancing participants' rights and data credibility. A statement outlining the participants' rights is provided to all individuals involved in the research (Nuruzzaman and Hussain 2018). This statement includes the purpose of the research, the role of research participants, and the measures taken to ensure confidentiality. The guidelines concerning data privacy will be followed to the letter "General Data Protection Regulation" (GDPR) that governs data protection will be fully complied with. While conducting the research, participants' identity will not be revealed; possible biases that might affect the collection or interpretation of data will be first identified and later dealt with (Sahu et al. 2022).

Furthermore, the research will include procedures for evaluating the outputs of the LLM-driven applications that will generate a new set of recommendations with potential biases or inaccuracies. Several analyses will be conducted to determine the impact of sampling selection and enhance the generalizability of the result.

2.4 Virtual Shopping Assistants

Such services of LLMs help virtual shopping assistants to offer detailed help by approaching clients using natural language understanding and employing advanced machine learning approaches (Ramjan and Campiranon 2021). These assistants integrate seamlessly into e-commerce platforms and CRM systems, leveraging customer data to deliver personalized recommendations. For example, a virtual assistant can suggest related products based on a customer's browsing history or past purchases, creating a cohesive and frictionless shopping experience.

LLM-powered virtual shopping assistants leverage advanced NLP to enable contextual, bidirectional communication through both voice and text. They can interpret complex customer queries, deliver relevant responses, and recreate realistic in-store shopping scenarios—thereby reducing the psychological barriers to making purchases online. For example, an LLM-enabled assistant might guide a shopper step by step through selecting a set of related products, ensuring maximum convenience and satisfaction (Bjornen and Ippoliti 2021).

Aaron and Moore remind us that utilizing LLM-driven virtual shopping assistants is effective in driving conversion, AVA, and customer satisfaction. For instance, such assistants have been shown to enhance companies' conversion rates by as much as 35%, coupled with customer satisfaction ratings that have been given an equal boost. There is evidence of the effectiveness of this technology, which is measured through calls, page visits, and sales, as well as via applications such as Google Analytics and customer feedback.

2.5 Leveraging Social Proof with LLMs

LLMs excel at generating authentic-sounding customer testimonials and reviews, a crucial aspect of social proof. LLMs create a persuasive effect that encourages potential buyers by analyzing existing feedback and synthesizing realistic narratives. However, ethical considerations must be prioritized to ensure that generated content is accurate and not misleading, aligning with industry guidelines to maintain consumer trust.

Real-time sentiment analysis powered by LLMs allows marketers to dynamically track social media trends and customer feedback. These systems identify emerging patterns and tailor marketing messages by analyzing vast amounts of unstructured data. For example, a surge in positive mentions about a product could prompt the display of promotional offers, maximizing sales potential.

LLMs facilitate the dynamic display of social proof on websites and applications (e.g., pop-ups showing recent purchases or user endorsements). These displays leverage psychological principles to create a sense of urgency and trust, positively influencing purchase decisions. Such features can be integrated into platforms using APIs that interact with LLM-powered backend systems.

2.6 *Hyper-Personalization of Marketing Content*

LLMs allow for real-time adaptation of marketing content, including product descriptions, promotional offers, and website layouts, based on user behavior. Algorithms such as reinforcement learning and collaborative filtering play a key role in these personalization efforts, ensuring content remains relevant and engaging for the consumer.

Predictive personalization involves anticipating customer needs and preferences using advanced machine learning models. Techniques like collaborative filtering and deep learning are employed to analyze historical data and predict future behavior. For instance, an LLM might suggest a product a customer is likely to purchase next based on their interaction patterns.

2.7 *Advanced Analytics and Decision-Making Support*

LLMs process large datasets to generate predictive sales insights, aiding in demand forecasting and inventory management. For example, analyzing historical sales data combined with current trends enables businesses to optimize stock levels, reducing the risk of overstocking or stockouts.

Advanced segmentation techniques powered by LLMs enable marketers to identify customer groups based on psychographic, demographic, and behavioral data. This granular approach allows for highly targeted marketing strategies, improving campaign effectiveness and ROI. Cluster analysis visualizations often highlight these segmented groups and their unique characteristics.

2.8 *Ethical and Privacy Considerations*

Ensuring the security of customer data used by LLMs is paramount. Techniques such as data encryption, access control, and secure API integrations are employed to safeguard sensitive information. Compliance with regulations like the General Data Protection Regulation (GDPR) and the California Consumer Privacy Act (CCPA) further ensures data protection.

Bias in LLM outputs can undermine consumer trust and brand reputation. To address this, techniques such as fairness-aware machine learning and regular audits of training datasets are implemented (Dintsis 2020). These measures help identify and mitigate biases, promoting ethical AI practices in marketing.

3 Results

3.1 Quantitative Findings (SEM Analysis)

The analysis using Structural Equation Modeling (SEM) indicated an excellent model fit, with CFI = 0.958, TLI = 0.945, RMSEA = 0.042, and SRMR = 0.034. Reliability measures for core constructs such as Attitudes, Subjective Norms, and Perceived Behavioral Control exceeded 0.70, confirming internal consistency. Discriminant validity was established via the Fornell-Larcker criterion. In terms of regression coefficients, virtual shopping assistants demonstrated a significant positive effect on conversion rates ($\beta = 0.45$, $p < 0.001$), average order value ($\beta = 0.38$, $p < 0.01$), and customer satisfaction ($\beta = 0.50$, $p < 0.001$). Moreover, social proof emerged as a key mediator of consumer trust ($\beta = 0.25$, $p < 0.05$), indicating that real-time testimonials and peer endorsements can strengthen buyer confidence at the purchase stage.

These findings align with prior CRM-focused research (Blokdyk 2018; Kumar and Reinartz 2012), suggesting that advanced AI-driven approaches optimize both top-line (e.g., sales) and experiential (e.g., satisfaction) outcomes. Figure 1 illustrates average conversion rates by industry, drawn from data provided by Ruler Analytics Blog (2023), reinforcing the notion that sector-specific nuances still benefit significantly from automated, personalized support.

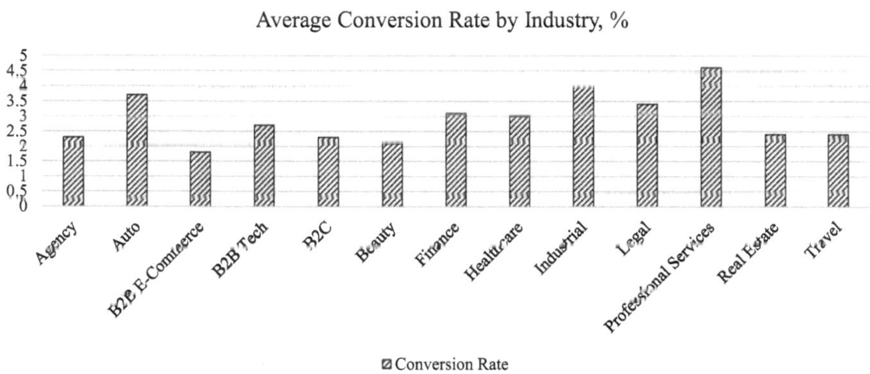

Fig. 1 Average conversion rate by industry. *Source* Compiled by the author based on (Ruler Analytics Blog 2023)

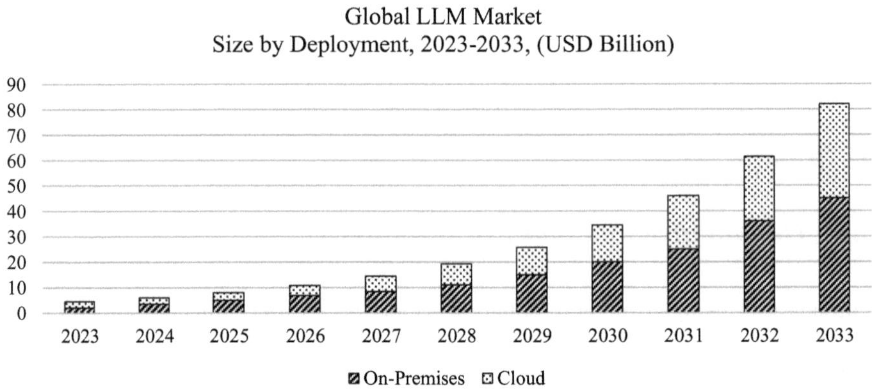

Fig. 2 Global LLM Market. *Source* Compiled by the author based on Market.us (2025)

3.2 Thematic Insights (Qualitative Analysis)

Interviews with marketing professionals and focus groups with consumers offered a deeper perspective on how LLM implementations shape purchase-stage experiences. Many participants described LLM-powered virtual assistants as "knowledgeable friends," highlighting the technology's human-like qualities that foster trust and reduce uncertainty. Additionally, respondents praised the level of personalization afforded by these systems, which they likened to highly tailored product recommendations aligning with individual browsing or purchase histories—echoing the customer journey mapping discussions of Koussaifi et al. (2020). This personalization was also credited with easing complex decisions by segmenting information into manageable steps, paralleling the structured, step-by-step approach suggested in large language model applications by Wang et al. (2020) and Wei et al. (2022).

Figure 2 illustrates the expanding global LLM market (Market.us 2025), signaling the continued opportunities for marketers to deploy such technologies across diverse industries. Most focus group participants viewed these developments positively, noting that well-designed LLM interventions can streamline digital interactions and encourage higher conversion and loyalty.

3.3 Integrated Findings

Collectively, the quantitative and qualitative data indicate that LLM-driven marketing interventions yield multiple benefits during the purchase stage. Statistically, SEM analyses confirmed robust improvements in key performance indicators—conversion rate ($\beta = 0.45$, $p < 0.001$), average order value ($\beta = 0.38$, $p < 0.01$), and customer satisfaction ($\beta = 0.50$, $p < 0.001$)—while also reinforcing the importance of dynamic social proof ($\beta = 0.25$, $p < 0.05$) for trust-building. The interviews and group discussions further highlighted how virtual assistants, personalized offers, and simplified decision-making processes reduce cognitive load and enhance positive consumer attitudes.

Finally, ethical and data protection measures emerged as crucial factors in ensuring the responsible deployment of LLM solutions. The research upheld GDPR compliance, ensuring that personal data were securely managed, while ongoing bias mitigation audits helped prevent misleading or discriminatory LLM outputs. Taken together, these findings underscore how LLM-driven strategies can transform purchase-stage marketing, elevating performance metrics and strengthening consumer trust.

4 Discussion

This research provides new evidence that LLM-based marketing solutions can significantly bolster consumer trust at the purchase stage and improve key performance metrics such as conversion rates, average order values, and overall satisfaction. By analyzing quantitative (SEM) and qualitative (thematic) data, the author identified that LLM-driven interventions, particularly virtual shopping assistants and real-time social proof, encourage higher consumer confidence, reduce cognitive burden, and streamline the decision-making process.

Incorporating insights from Ajzen's Theory of Planned Behavior (Ajzen 2020), the findings suggest that positive consumer attitudes toward LLM tools, combined with social norms reinforced through dynamic reviews and testimonials, enhance perceived behavioral control. This alignment helps explain why consumers exhibit stronger purchase intentions when provided with immediate, personalized guidance. From a Relational Marketing perspective (Araújo et al. 2022; Bilgin-Wührer and Wührer 2020), LLM-based personalization deepens customer engagement by treating each interaction as an opportunity to build trust, thereby contributing to sustained brand loyalty over time.

Beyond theoretical contributions, the results offer managerial implications: marketers can deploy LLM-powered tools to provide context-aware recommendations and up-to-date social proof, both of which significantly influence consumers near the point of purchase. However, the research scope remains partly limited by its focus on specific e-commerce contexts and self-reported data, which may not fully capture cross-cultural variations or long-term consumer responses. Future research could extend these insights by examining ethical issues (such as bias and data privacy) in broader market segments and diverse cultural settings, thereby enriching our understanding of how advanced AI applications continue to reshape the digital customer journey.

5 Conclusion

LLMs significantly enhance marketing performance at the purchase stage by improving consumer trust, streamlining decision-making, and raising conversion rates. This research contributes to the Theory of Planned Behavior and Relational Marketing by demonstrating how dynamic social proof and personalized interactions foster positive attitudes and loyalty. Future research should explore the cultural implications of LLM deployments and address ethical concerns surrounding data privacy and bias.

Further research is needed to assess how various LLM applications affect different cultures and corporate environments. Likewise, the ethical implications of AI-driven personalization must be examined more deeply to ensure these technologies are deployed responsibly. Ultimately, this research lays the groundwork for understanding how LLMs can transform marketing strategies—delivering immediate benefits while paving the way for future innovation.

References

Ajzen, I. 2020. The theory of planned behavior: Frequently asked questions. *Human Behavior and Emerging Technologies* 2 (4): 314–324. https://doi.org/10.1002/hbe2.195.

Araújo, C., R. Gonçalves, R. L. D. Costa, Á. Dias, and L. F. Pereira. 2022. Artificial intelligence in the digital customer journey. *International Journal of Electronic Customer Relationship Management* 13 (3): 248–271. https://doi.org/10.1504/IJECRM.2022.124098.

Bilgin-Wührer, Z., and G. A. Wührer. 2020. The hybrid shopping mile and its orbital customer journey mapping. In *Managing customer experiences in an omnichannel world: Melody of online and offline environments in the customer journey*, ed. T. Dirsehan, 133–152. Leeds, UK: Emerald Publishing Limited. https://doi.org/10.1108/978-1-80043-388-520201012.

Bjornen, K., and C. Ippoliti. 2021. Using customer journey mapping and design thinking to understand the library's role in supporting the research data lifecycle. *Journal of eScience Librarianship* 10 (4): e1214. https://doi.org/10.7191/jeslib.2021.1214.

Blokdyk, G. 2018. *Customer lifecycle management: A complete guide*. 5STARcooks.

Brants, T., A. C. Popat, P. Xu, F. J. Och, and J. Dean. 2007. Large language models in machine translation. In *Proceedings of EMNLP-CoNLL 2007: Joint conference on empirical methods in natural language processing and computational natural language learning*, 858–867. Prague, Czech Republic: Association for Computational Linguistics.

Buttle, F., and S. Maklan. 2019. *Customer relationship management: Concepts and technologies*. London, UK: Routledge. https://doi.org/10.4324/9781351016551.

Chung, M., E. Ko, H. Joung, and S. J. Kim. 2020. Chatbot e-service and customer satisfaction regarding luxury brands. *Journal of Business Research* 117:587–595. https://doi.org/10.1016/j.jbusres.2018.10.004.

Court, D., D. Elzinga, S. Mulder, and O. J. Vetvik. 2009. The consumer decision journey. *McKinsey Quarterly*. https://www.mckinsey.com/capabilities/growth-marketing-and-sales/our-insights/the-consumer-decision-journey. Accessed 14 Apr 2025.

Dintsis, D., ed. 2020. *Customer relationship management and IT*. London, UK: IntechOpen. https://doi.org/10.5772/intechopen.77542.

Fink, V. 2020. Einfach machen—Customer lifecycle in marketing, vertrieb und service. In *Quick Guide KI-Projekte—einfach machen*, 11–26. Wiesbaden, Germany: Springer Gabler. https://doi.org/10.1007/978-3-658-28865-5_2.

Koussaifi, H., D. J. Hart, and S. Lillystone. 2020. Customer complaint journey mapping: A qualitative approach. *British Food Journal* 122 (12): 3711–3726. https://doi.org/10.1108/BFJ-11-2019-0849.

Kumar, V., and W. Reinartz. 2012. *Customer relationship management: Concept, strategy, and tools*. 2nd ed. Berlin, Heidelberg, Germany: Springer Science & Business Media. https://doi.org/10.1007/978-3-642-20110-3.

Market.us. 2025. *Global Large Language Model (LLM) market size, share analysis report by deployment (Cloud, On-premise), by application (customer service, content generation, sentiment analysis, code generation, chatbots and virtual assistant, language translation), by industry vertical (healthcare, BFSI, retail and e-commerce, media and entertainment, others), by region and companies – industry segment outlook, market assessment, competition scenario, trends and forecast 2024–2033*. https://market.us/report/large-language-model-llm-market/. Accessed 14 Apr 2025.

Nuruzzaman, M., and O. K. Hussain. 2018. A survey on chatbot implementation in customer service industry through deep neural networks. In *Proceedings of ICEBE 2018: IEEE 15th international conference on e-business engineering*, 54–61. Xi'an, China: IEEE. https://doi.org/10.1109/ICEBE.2018.00019.

Radford, A., K. Narasimhan, T. Salimans, and I. Sutskever. 2018. *Improving language understanding by generative pre-training*. https://karthikncode.github.io/assets/pdf/gpt.pdf. Accessed 14 Apr 2025.

Ramjan, S., and K. Campiranon. 2021. Customer journey mapping of a public mobile application: The case study of a state electricity enterprise. In *Proceedings of APIT '21: The 2021 3rd Asia Pacific information technology conference*, 39–46. New York, NY: Association for Computing Machinery. https://doi.org/10.1145/3449365.3449372.

Ruler Analytics Blog. 2023. *Average conversion rate by industry and marketing source*. https://dir.md/www.ruleranalytics.com/blog/insight/conversion-rate-by-industry/. Accessed 14 Apr 2025.

Sahu, P., M. Cogswell, Y. Gong, and A. Divakaran. 2022. *Unpacking large language models with conceptual consistency*. https://arxiv.org/pdf/2209.15093v1. Accessed 14 Apr 2025.

Vaswani, A., N. Shazeer, N. Parmar, J. Uszkoreit, L. Jones, A. N. Gomez, et al. 2017. Attention is all you need. In *Proceedings of NIPS 2017: 31st conference on neural information processing systems*. Long Beach, CA: Neural Information Processing Systems Foundation, Inc.. https://proceedings.neurips.cc/paper_files/paper/2017/file/3f5ee243547dee91fbd053c1c4a845aa-Paper.pdf. Accessed 14 Apr 2025.

Wang, Z., J. Wohlwend, and T. Lei. 2020. Structured pruning of large language models. In *Proceedings of EMNLP 2020: Conference on empirical methods in natural language processing*, 6151–6162. Association for Computational Linguistics. https://doi.org/10.18653/v1/2020.emnlp-main.496.

Wei, J., X. Wang, D. Schuurmans, M. Bosma, E. H. Chi, F. Xia, et al. 2022. Chain-of-thought prompting elicits reasoning in large language models. *Advances in Neural Information Processing Systems* 35:24824–24837. https://doi.org/10.48550/arXiv.2201.11903.

Weidinger, L., J. Mellor, M. Rauh, C. Griffin, J. Uesato, P. Huang, et al. 2021. *Ethical and social risks of harm from language models*. https://arxiv.org/pdf/2112.04359v1. Accessed 14 Apr 2025.

Methodological Principles of Public Opinion Analysis in the Information Society: Socio-Educational Dimensions and Sociological Practices in Studying Color as a Social Marker of Commercial Enterprises

Tatyana N. Ivanova, Oksana P. Denisova, Sergey N. Shirobokov, Semyon M. Ivanov, and Sofya A. Rotova

Abstract In the research, the authors examine the socio-educational dimensions and sociological practices within the framework of the methodological principles for analyzing public opinion in the information society alongside a sociological case study on interpreting color as a social marker of commercial enterprises. The research presents and analyzes data such as the most popular applications among Russians for each type of platform and information on the color preferences of young people aged 14–35 and outlines the stages involved in creating advertising content for products and services aimed at mass youth consumption. The authors investigate the methodological principles of analyzing color as a social marker of commercial enterprises. They also explore the nuances of emotional color perception and its influence on consumer decision-making. Furthermore, the authors interpret the role of color in the products and logos of commercial enterprises within the context of informational materials, where buyers' and consumers' attention is directed towards specific content for commercial purposes, such as purchasing a product or service. The authors posed several questions to respondents to examine the factors that attract consumers to various services as represented in commercial products and logos. Finally, the research unveils the methodological peculiarities of public opinion in the information society.

Keywords Public opinion • Information society, socio-educational dimensions • Sociological practices • Color • Social marker • Media • Commercial enterprises • Consumers • Youth

---

T. N. Ivanova (✉) · O. P. Denisova · S. N. Shirobokov · S. M. Ivanov · S. A. Rotova
Togliatti State University, Togliatti, Russia
e-mail: IvanovaT2005@tltsu.ru; O.Denisova@tltsu.ru

A. Karbekova (ed.), *Ethics of the AI Economy: A System View from the Positions of the Theory of Stakeholders*, Ethical Economy 73,
https://doi.org/10.1007/978-3-032-23423-0_12

JEL Codes J6 • J60 • Z1 • Z13

1 Introduction

The more information an individual acquires, the harder it becomes to differentiate it. Information begins to blend together, eventually transforming into mere noise.

In the past, finding an answer to any question required a visit to the library and searching for books on the topic of interest. Now, just a couple of clicks can reveal everything one is curious about and even more.

The authors will analyze the role of color in the products and logos of commercial enterprises within the context of informational materials, where attention is directed toward buyers or consumers for commercial purposes, such as purchasing a product or service.

The findings from a sociological study on the color preferences of youth in relation to the products and logos of commercial enterprises can be used to create advertising content for products and services aimed at mass youth consumption.

2 Methodology

Youth color preferences hold significant importance in marketing, journalism, sociology, information technology, and other fields. The color elements in products and logos of commercial enterprises should capture the attention of buyers and consumers of specific content for commercial purposes, such as purchasing a product or service.

The sociological analysis of respondents' color preferences has been the focus of numerous studies. Frieling and Auer (1973), Kondratenko (2017), Olshannikova (1978), Romanovich (2015), Smirnov (2014), identified detailed patterns linking color sensitivity with the emotional states of those surveyed. Gorlenko (2022), Nikolaeva (2023), and Semenova (2023) have examined the psychology behind consumers' color perception and its influence on purchasing behavior. K. S. Plis and Yu. D. Savenkova, in their research article "The Theory of Color Psychology in Marketing: An Analysis of PAO 'PIK' Brand Colors," explored these dynamics in depth Plis and Savenkova (2022).

This research aims to examine the color preferences of young people in the products and logos of commercial enterprises, focusing on individuals aged 14–35, addressing the distinctive aspects of youth color preferences in these contexts. In interpreting this phenomenon, it is essential to analyze the methodological principles that define color as a social marker for commercial enterprises, study youth color preferences within the framework of sociological design, conduct a sociological evaluation of these preferences in products and logos, and consider methods and technologies for attracting consumers by considering the emotional characteristics of respondents based on content analysis with the incorporation of Goethe's theory.

The research investigates the socio-demographic characteristics of the respondents, examines the factors that attract consumers to various services as conveyed through the products and logos of commercial enterprises, and identifies the advantages of each company's logo compared to others based on the emotions they evoke among respondents.

The research was conducted from September 25 to October 24, 2024, using online surveys and employing the snowball sampling method. Respondents completed the surveys online, and the analytical report provides a comprehensive account of the research findings. Data processing and analysis were performed using SPSS 23.

Let us examine the socio-demographic characteristics of the survey participants. The research involved residents from the following localities: Togliatti (88.6%), Samara (7.4%), Almaty (0.5%), Arzgir (0.5%), Zhigulevsk (0.5%), Syzran (0.5%), Salavat (0.5%), Tyumen (0.5%), Verkhnye Sancheleevo (0.5%), and Engels (0.5%).

To investigate the factors that attract consumers to various services through the products and logos of commercial enterprises, respondents were asked several questions.

Let us consider the research methodology within one of the case studies, set against the backdrop of the methodological principles for analyzing color as a social marker for commercial enterprises and the principles for analyzing public opinion in the information society. For example, symbolic interactionism (G. H. Mead, Ch. Cooley, and H. Blumer) posits that symbols such as body language, gestures, and cultural icons convey decipherable information. The sociocultural approach (P. A. Sorokin, T. Parsons, and Robert K. Merton) suggests that an individual is inseparable from society: people are nurtured within a social framework and adhere to its rules for their own well-being, a view complemented by psychological approaches and emotion theory.

Semenova (2023) conducted a survey of over 100 respondents aged 14–41, in which participants were asked to select the most appealing advertisements and company logos. She found that "between the logos of the online stores Ozon and Wildberries, 63.6% of people chose the latter." The author concludes that "the primary colors of Wildberries' brand identity are purple and pink, whereas Ozon's are blue."

However, when it came to yellow, both groups associated it with vulnerability, madness, and gloom. Among respondents, orange was associated with joy (20%), brightness (10%), and distress and strength (5% each).

The authors conclude that the advertising of the PIK Group does not evoke negative emotions in the majority of respondents and is perceived as visually calming. Empirical evidence from QuickSprout's (n.d.) research indicates that color enhances brand recognition by 80%; over 90% of purchase decisions are influenced by visual factors. Furthermore, data analysis revealed that people make subconscious decisions within 90 s; in 90% of cases, product evaluations are based on color.

As part of the sociological analysis of respondents' color preferences, Mediascope (Research Company "Mediascope" n.d.) statistics for 2024 are presented in the "The Man in the Smartphone" presentation. A sociological survey of the Russian population revealed the most popular types of mobile applications among Russians aged 12 and older from January to August 2024: marketplaces, retail stores, transportation, and banks.

Based on the presented data and an analysis of the most popular mobile applications among Russians by resource type, it will be possible to compile information on the color preferences of young people aged 14–35. This information will assist in creating advertising content for products and services aimed at mass youth consumption.

Thus, the methodological principles for analyzing color as a social marker for commercial enterprises were studied. Particularly, the nuances of emotional color perception and its influence on consumer decision-making were examined.

From the foregoing, it can be concluded that each person's emotional response to color is unique. However, as globalization has turned color into an important social marker (e.g., symbolism, decorations, or status items), people have begun to group different shades of the same color together. For instance, if someone lives in an apartment featuring many green hues (e.g., emerald, khaki, or lime) that they like, yet they do not know the specific names of these shades, they might simply answer "green" when asked about their favorite color in a sociological survey. This limited response can pose challenges when creating advertising content for commercial companies.

The analysis of color's role as a social marker for commercial organizations demonstrated that the influence of color on consumer decisions is determined by the form and content of company logos. For example, among mobile applications in the "Marketplaces" category, respondents identified "Wildberries" and "Ozon" as the most popular. These apps distinguish themselves with smoother typography in their logos, which makes them more visually appealing.

It is noteworthy that a portion of the respondents (29%) view the use of sociological information by the media positively, expressing an interest in knowing other people's opinions. Following this, the options "Somewhat positive, depending on the information source" (26%) and "Somewhat negative, as the media distorts information" (24%) were chosen with only slight differences.

In this part of the survey, respondents were asked to choose one of three response options in each category: "Tend to trust"—1 point, "Tend not to trust"—2 points, and "Unable to decide"—0 points.

Subsequently, respondents were asked who they most often discuss current social issues with. The majority selected "Relatives"—72%, followed by "Friends"—57%, and "Colleagues"—43%. Meanwhile, 34% of respondents reported discussing current social issues on social networks.

Galaganova and Musina (2023) emphasize that "as manifestations of internal feelings, emotions are linked not only to human instincts but also to one's desires and aspirations. An emotional reaction is triggered not only by physiological processes but also by the social environment and life events. Emotions dictate behavior and color every action we take. The formation of opinions is impossible without the "emotional accompaniment"—the emotional impulses, aspirations, and intentions."

According to the author, "consumer behavior strategy refers to the principles of consumer conduct that determine the characteristics of choices, purchase and final use of a product, consumer preferences, and specific consumer actions."

Nikolaeva (2023) notes that "any consumer behavior strategy depends on the following factors:

1. Economic factors (income level and inflation);
2. Social factors (social status and social role);
3. Cultural factors (cultural values and consumption norms);
4. Psychological factors (personal needs, motives, attitudes, habits, personality traits, and emotional state);
5. Personal factors (gender, age, nationality, and education)."

In the study "Entrepreneurship in the Formation of New Patterns of Consumer Behavior (on the Example of the Food Delivery Market)," Ponomareva (2024) highlights the consumer value theory of the Indian marketing professor Jagdish N. Sheth.

In the research "Assessment of Methods Diagnosing Emotionality (Experience in Using Statistical Distribution Patterns)," Olshannikova et al. (1976) established a relationship showing that individuals who frequently experience fear and anger prefer purple over others. Such individuals are also less sensitive to green, blue, and brown hues.

In the research "Gender Differences in Advertising Perception," A. N. Romanovich writes that "advertising aimed at a male audience may be less saturated in color, as a man is less likely to notice subtle hues. He is primarily interested in the core message of the advertisement. Conversely, advertising targeted at a female audience should be in full color since the precise shade holds significant importance for women, particularly in contexts such as clothing or cosmetics. Black-and-white advertising is more appropriate for men than for women, as it may seem somewhat gloomy to women, and many men, who often suffer from color blindness, do not perceive green and red hues well."

Gorlenko (2022), in his research article "The Psychology of Color – A Sociocultural Phenomenon and Its Influence on Marketing and Advertising," provides a table outlining various psychological interpretations of color and its application in different fields.

Thus, the methodological principle of sociological design related to the use of color psychology in marketing has been examined. This principle considers individual characteristics that influence how people perceive and prefer different colors.

In summary, the psychology of color in marketing, which considers the factors and value categories affecting consumer behavior, plays a key role in shaping individuals' attitudes toward various goods and services. This work analyzed the personal characteristics of consumers, shaped by their social standing: economic status, professional status, social status, level of education, and gender. These traits, together with the factors and value categories in consumer behavior, directly influence people's color preferences when choosing a product or service.

In conclusion, through the secondary data analysis of the works by A. E. Olshannikova, V. V. Semenov, L. M. Smirnov, I. Scott, A. N. Romanovich, G. Friling, and K. Auer, the authors identified detailed patterns between color sensitivity and the emotional state of the surveyed individuals. Additionally, via the secondary analysis of the research by M. V. Gorlenko, A. Yu. Semenova, and Yu. N. Nikolaeva, the authors revealed the basic principles of consumer color perception and its influence on purchasing behavior.

In the research titled "Methods of Sociological Research on Consumer Behavior Strategies," Yu. N. Nikolaeva examined consumer behavior strategy and identified the primary factors influencing consumer conduct. According to the author, "consumer behavior strategy refers to the principles of consumer conduct that determine the characteristics of the selection, purchase, and final use of a product, as well as consumer preferences and specific consumer actions" (Nikolaeva 2023).

3 Results

The survey questions aimed to determine whether respondents participated in sociological surveys. The most common answer was "No" at 43%, followed by "Yes" at 57%. Analyzing the results by age, it can be concluded that respondents aged 18–30 participate in sociological surveys more frequently (50%) compared to those aged 40 and older (30%).

4 Conclusion

In conclusion, it must be said that public opinion, as an integral part of today's society, remains a timely subject. In today's world, the rapid advancement of information technologies increases the importance of public opinion (Smolenskiy 2017). This means that public opinion can shape new values, perspectives, and views on various social issues that surround us.

Public opinion is a reflection of social reality. When examined within the framework of the information society, the influence of various media, especially online media, on public opinion is notable (Arutyunyan 2019).

An important task continues to be the monitoring of public opinion because it mirrors the reality in which society exists. Therefore, sociological surveys of public opinion are both important and necessary.

The research employed surveys and interviews to ascertain what the residents of Tolyatti understand by the term "public opinion" to determine whether public opinion influences them, how contemporary information technologies affect it, and what social consequences may arise.

Respondents reported the influence of the Internet and traditional media on public opinion. However, the most pronounced impact on various societal spheres was noted by respondents from older age groups.

Participants aged 18–30 were more inclined to use online media for social information, likely because contemporary generations interact with Internet resources more frequently.

In summary, it is crucial to acknowledge the importance of public opinion and the need to monitor it. From a methodological perspective, public opinion in the information society influences both society as a whole and the individual. It is essential to approach the information we consume and that provided by the media with a conscious understanding of its socio-educational dimensions and the profound interpretation of sociological practices.

References

Arutyunyan, K. S. 2019. Factors forming public consciousness today. *Vestnik of Northern (Arctic) Federal University. Series Humanitarian and Social Sciences* 3:80–87.

Frieling, H., and X. Auer. 1973. *Human + color + space: Applied color psychology* [Mensch + Farbe + Raum angewandte Farbenpsychologie]. Trans. O. V. Gavalov, from German. Moscow, USSR: Stroyizdat. (Original work published 1954).

Galaganova, S. G., and N. D. Musina. 2023. Color solutions in the visual content of social networks as a tool for modifying public opinion. *Human Capital* 6 (174): 104–115. https://doi.org/10.25629/HC.2023.06.12.

Gorlenko, M. V. 2022. The psychology of color is a sociocultural phenomenon and its influence in the field of marketing and advertising. *Current Research* 31 (110): 29–33.

Kondratenko, S. V. 2017. *Models and methods of color preference analysis in management decision support systems* (Dissertation of Candidate of Technological Sciences). Bryansk, Russia: Bryansk State Technical University.

Nikolaeva, Yu. N. 2023. Methods of sociological research of consumer behavior strategies. In *Proceedings of the 56th international scientific and technical conference of teachers and students, in 2 volumes*, vol. 1, 339–341. Vitebsk, Belarus: Vitebsk State Technological University.

Olshannikova, A. E. 1978. Toward a psychological diagnosis of emotionality. In *Problems of general, age and pedagogical psychology*, ed. V. V. Davydov, 93–105. Moscow, USSR: Pedagogics.

Olshannikova, A. E., V. V. Semyonov, and L. M. Smirnov. 1976. Evaluation of techniques that diagnose emotionality (experience in using statistical patterns of distribution of indicators). *Voprosy Psychologii [Psychology Matters]* 5:103–114.

Plis, K. S., and J. D. Savenkova. 2022. Theory of color psychology in marketing using the example of analysis of branded colors of PJSC "PIK". *Actual Problems of Economics and Management* 1 (11): 439–443. https://doi.org/10.52899/978-5-88303-644-5_439.

Ponomareva, V. A. 2024. Entrepreneurship in the conditions of formation of new patterns of consumer behavior (on the example of the product delivery market). In *Global social processes 5.0: Society, economy, history*, ed. A. V. Petrov, A. V. Kaplina, S. S. Kozlovskaya, A. V. Povidysh, A. A. Hyunninen, and Wende Ma, 92–99. Asterion. St. Petersburg, Russia.

QuickSprout. n.d. *A service for analyzing a website*. https://www.quicksprout.com/. Accessed 5 Apr 2025.

Research Company "Mediascope". n.d. *Russian market of media research, advertising and media monitoring*. https://mediascope.net/. Accessed 5 Apr 2025.

Romanovich, A. N. 2015. Gender peculiarities of perception in advertising. In *Research and development in the field of mechanical engineering, power engineering and management: Proceedings of XV scientific and technical conf. of students, graduate students and young scientists*, 444–446. Gomel, Belarus: Sukhoi State Technical University of Gomel.
Semenova, A. Yu. 2023. The influence of color on the perception of advertising. In *Keywords: Collection of theses on the results of the III student conference of the Institute of Social and Humanitarian Sciences of Tyumen state university*, ed. S. P. Shilov, I. N. Pupysheva, and A. O. Drozdova, 173–175. Tyumen, Russia: University of Tyumen.
Smirnov, L. M. 2014. Dynamics and stability: Value choices of Russians. *Historical Psychology & Sociology* 7 (2): 80–92.
Smolenskiy, M. B. 2017. The information society and information security. *European Journal of Law and Political Sciences* 1:3–6.

The Transformation of Human Identity with the Development of Artificial Intelligence

Natalia V. Gubanova, Egor M. Alekseev, and Anna V. Shkalenko

Abstract The research studies the transformation of the concept of human identity under the influence of the development and widespread introduction of artificial intelligence (AI). Advances in AI are significantly altering professional activities, social interactions, and cognitive processes, challenging traditional notions of self-awareness, autonomy, and belonging. This research examines key aspects of AI's impact on human identity, including work automation, algorithmic personalization of content, digital twins, and neurocomputer interfaces. The authors analyze the philosophical and ethical challenges posed by the proliferation of intelligent systems, addressing the concepts of transhumanism, posthumanism, and eco-philosophy. Particular attention is paid to the loss of autonomy and privacy and increasing social inequalities in the context of algorithmic governance. The authors emphasize the need for a balanced approach to technology development that considers fundamental human values and rights. The research concludes by emphasizing the importance of interdisciplinary analysis and normative regulation to ensure that human beings and AI can coexist harmoniously amid rapid technological progress.

Keywords Artificial intelligence • Human identity • Self-reflection • Philosophy • Ethical implications • Transhumanism

JEL Codes O31 • O34 • O35

N. V. Gubanova · E. M. Alekseev
Moscow Polytechnic University, Moscow, Russia
e-mail: a.v.shkalenko@mospolytech.ru

A. V. Shkalenko (✉)
The Financial University under the Government of the Russian Federation, Moscow, Russia
e-mail: avshkalenko@fa.ru

A. Karbekova (ed.), *Ethics of the AI Economy: A System View from the Positions of the Theory of Stakeholders*, Ethical Economy 73,
https://doi.org/10.1007/978-3-032-23423-0_13

1 Introduction

Artificial intelligence (AI) has significantly altered various aspects of human life, including daily routines and professional fields. From voice assistants like Siri and Alexa to machine learning algorithms analyzing big data, autonomous vehicles, and medical diagnostics, AI's influence is widespread. However, these advancements have raised concerns about the impact of AI on human identity, challenging traditional notions of human intellect and capabilities.

Professionally, automation and robotics have led to labor redistribution, causing job losses and identity crises among those whose worth was tied to their work. Socially, AI-driven content personalization creates "information bubbles," potentially limiting perspectives and affecting social cohesion. Additionally, AI's predictive capabilities raise questions about free will and individual autonomy.

This research aims to examine the implications of AI on human identity amidst rapid technological change. Such reflections are essential for adapting to new realities and establishing ethical guidelines for interacting with AI.

2 Literature Review

This research explores the transformation of human identity by drawing on historical perspectives, philosophical insights, and contemporary examples of AI usage to better understand how AI shapes identity. Changes in the understanding of human identity throughout history are reflected in the works of Aristotle (2004), Plato (2007), Carlson (2001), Habib (2018), Kant (2019), and Weir (2013). To comprehend the philosophical aspects of identity, the philosophies of transhumanism, posthumanism, and ecophilosophy presented in the writings of Braidotti (2021)) and Kurzweil (2024) have been considered. Current applications of AI are exemplified through online resources (Allen 2019; Golovanov 2023; Mesko 2021; Moroshkina 2023; Somanchi 2015).

3 Materials and Methodology

This research aims to conduct a comprehensive investigation into the changes in the concept of human identity amidst the widespread adoption of AI.

The authors trace the historical evolution of identity concepts based on the following steps:

- Trace the development of identity conceptions in philosophy and social theory from ancient times to modern day.
- Evaluate how historical periods and technological advances have shaped human identity.

Factors impacting human identity through AI are considered as follows:

- Professional domain: Examine the effects of automation and robotization on work activities and professional self-perception; determine how replacing human labor with machines influences feelings of significance and self-worth;
- Social interactions: Analyze how AI algorithms in social networks and communication platforms shape interpersonal relationships, social bonding, and collective identity;
- Cognitive processes: Study the impact of AI on human cognitive abilities, such as memory, attention, and critical thinking.

The authors also consider philosophical and ethical aspects of identity transformation, including the following:

- Consciousness issues: Discuss problems of consciousness and self-awareness in the context of AI;
- Ethical dilemmas: address moral questions concerning AI autonomy, responsibility for AI actions, and rights and responsibilities towards intelligent machines;
- Transhumanism and posthumanism: Examine philosophical movements advocating for transcending biological limits via technology and their influence on understanding human identity.

4 Results

4.1 Human Identity Throughout History

The historical evolution of the concept of human identity is a complex and dynamic process reflecting shifts in philosophical thought, scientific advancements, and cultural norms across various epochs.

In antiquity, human identity can be examined through the works of philosophers of that time. For instance, Socrates believed that man was essentially his soul. He understood the soul as the moral and intellectual personality of a person, meaning that for him, a human being was one who possessed cognitive abilities and the capacity for moral choice. Similarly, Plato held a comparable view, though he did not emphasize the moral component of personality but instead highlighted the physical distinctions between humans and animals (Plato 2007). Aristotle added a social dimension to the biological essence of man, referring to humans as "social beings" (Aristotle 2004).

It is worth noting religious identity as one of the earliest forms of self-knowledge because it significantly influenced philosophers during the Renaissance and Enlightenment. For example, René Descartes argued that humans consist of body and soul, adhering to a dualistic conception of humans as separate yet interdependent entities. However, this separation raised the issue of interaction between these two components, which Descartes resolved by invoking God and religion as mediators (Carlson 2001).

Immanuel Kant posited that identity originates from self-consciousness, which arises from a combination of ideas that a person claims as their own. This combination emerges from understanding how things relate to each other (Kant 2019). Georg Wilhelm Friedrich Hegel shared similar views (Habib 2018).

Moving to the twentieth century, French philosopher Michel Foucault defined identities as constructs created by disciplinary regimes that pervade our existence, defining and limiting who we are within fixed boundaries of normalcy and deviation (Weir 2013).

4.2 The Impact of AI on Society

When discussing the impact of AI on society, it is important to note that AI is used in everyday life, medicine, and even agricultural tasks. An example of its use in daily life is the way AI can sort emails, separating spam and promotional offers into designated folders (Somanchi 2015). In healthcare, AI assists medical professionals in diagnosing patients based on their test results and even the sound of their voices (Mesko 2021). AI's analytical capabilities are also valuable in agriculture, helping monitor the health of plants and livestock (Allen 2019). These examples illustrate how AI is increasingly integrated into human life.

However, just like any other technological breakthrough, such as steam engines, AI poses threats such as job losses due to automation, privacy concerns when corporate employees might access confidential company documents, and more.

4.3 Shifts in Human Identity Under the Influence of AI

As mentioned earlier, AI is penetrating deeper into people's lives, which may soon alter our ways of interacting with each other and change our perceptions of ourselves and others. By 2024, digital twins of humans in the form of chatbots had already emerged (Golovanov 2023). Soon, similar digital replicas of people will appear as video recordings or video calls. It would suffice to upload a few samples of a person's voice and appearance and recount some events from their life so that AI could respond similarly to the copied individual. This could offer an opportunity to look at oneself from another perspective and identify qualities to eliminate or improve in one's life. However, it could also pose problems due to potential leaks of personal information or even an entire person's identity, which malicious actors could exploit. Consequently, under the influence of AI, human identity becomes increasingly flexible and versatile.

Neurocomputer interfaces (neurointerface) could play a substantial role in transforming human identity. A neurointerface can transmit information directly from the brain to an external device and vice versa. Currently, this technology enables people to communicate telepathically (Moroshkina 2023). From this, we can infer that a possible future application of this technology could involve creating multiple personalities for an individual, between which they could switch according to their desires.

4.4 Philosophical Approaches

To consider the new identity of humans, it is worth turning to various philosophical approaches, such as transhumanism, posthumanism, and eco-philosophy. Each of these approaches provides a unique perspective on how technologies, particularly AI, influence our understanding of what it means to be human and what the future holds.

The first approach is transhumanism. Transhumanism is a philosophical and cultural movement that aims to use science and technology to overcome fundamental limitations of human nature. It focuses on enhancing physical, mental, and even moral human capabilities. The roots of transhumanism can be traced back to thinkers of the Renaissance and Enlightenment. However, the modern form of this movement took shape in the second half of the twentieth century.

Radical transhumanists, such as Ray Kurzweil and other futurists, argue that technology will allow for the complete transfer of human consciousness onto digital media. They believe that consciousness and personality are informational structures that can be copied and reproduced in an artificial environment. This process is known as "mind uploading" or "brain emulation." As a result, humans could achieve digital immortality, existing in cloud servers or robotic bodies (Kurzweil 2024).

On the other hand, moderate transhumanists are skeptical about the idea of full-consciousness emulation. They assert that even if we manage to create a digital copy of the brain, it would merely be a copy, not a continuation of the original consciousness. They focus on using technology to enhance the human body and mind (e.g., through cybernetic implants, genetic engineering, or pharmacological means. Their goal is to extend lifespan, increase intelligence, and improve health without radically breaking away from human biology.

The following deep ethical questions arise within transhumanism:

- Identity and selfhood: If consciousness can be duplicated, does the duplicate remain the same "self"? What happens to the original consciousness when a copy is made?
- Humanity and its limits: If a human undergoes significant technological alterations, does it make them less human? Where do the boundaries lie between humans and machines?
- Social consequences: What inequalities might emerge if enhancement technologies are available only to certain groups? How would this impact society?

These questions largely remain philosophical and theoretical because the technology has not reached the level required to practically resolve them. Nevertheless, discussing these topics is crucial for preparing for potential future challenges.

The second approach is posthumanism. Posthumanism is a philosophical direction that reconsiders traditional notions of humankind, its place in the world, and its relationship with technology and other forms of life. Posthumanism asserts that human evolution is unfinished; it will continue in the future but not necessarily in anthropocentric or biological forms.

A key aspect of posthumanism involves criticizing anthropocentrism—the idea that humans occupy a central position in the universe. Posthumanists (e.g., Rosi Braidotti and Cary Wolfe) call for a reevaluation of relationships between humans, technology, animals, and nature. They argue that science and technology have shown that the boundaries between these categories are blurry and artificial (Braidotti 2021).

Posthumanism views evolution as a biological, cultural, and technological process. Technologies are tools created by humans and active participants in shaping a new reality and identity. Posthumanism explores how interactions with AI, biotechnologies, and other advanced sciences alter our understanding of ourselves and the world.

Posthumanists suggest reconsidering the concept of identity beyond traditional categories such as gender, race, species, and others. They explore hybrid subjects, cyborgs, and other forms of existence that combine biological and artificial elements. This raises questions about what it means to be human in an era where technologies become integral parts of our being.

The next aspect is eco-philosophy. Ecophilosophy focuses on the relationship between humans and nature, treating nature as a living entity with which humans are inherently connected. Developed by figures like Arne Næss and deep ecologists, it stresses that humans are part of nature, emphasizing the interdependence of all life forms and the need for harmonious coexistence, respecting ecosystems, biodiversity, and ecological processes.

Amid technological advancement, ecophilosophy highlights the importance of using technologies to sustain and restore natural systems, such as renewable energy, eco-friendly technologies, and sustainable agriculture.

Ecophilosophy encourages maintaining our deep bond with nature and preserving our innate identity rooted in the natural world. It advocates for valuing traditional knowledge, cultural practices, and lifestyles that foster sustainable environmental engagement, reminding us to balance progress with nature preservation.

Key ethical questions posed by eco-philosophy are as follows:

- Environmental responsibility: What are our obligations to the planet and future generations?
- Rights of nature: Should natural entities and ecosystems have legal protections?
- Limits of technological intervention: How far should we go in using technologies before they disrupt the natural balance?

4.5 Ways to Preserve and Develop Identity

To maintain human identity in the face of rapid technological advancement, three main areas require focus: education, legal regulation, and cultural initiatives.

Critical thinking and digital literacy are fundamental for engaging with AI. They empower individuals to analyze information, recognize biases, and safely navigate the digital realm. Educational programs should incorporate computer science, programming, cybersecurity, data analysis, and ethics. By promoting empathy and collaboration, education can equip students to grapple with the moral dimensions of AI, such as privacy, fairness, and responsibility.

Legislating AI and human rights protects personal data and ensures equitable technology use. Developing legal norms prevents discrimination, privacy breaches, and other adverse outcomes. Accountability measures for AI developers and users, along with safety and quality standards, are crucial. Global cooperation can align different nations' approaches, establish shared ethical principles, and tackle emerging challenges together.

Art and culture offer valuable insights into the relationship between humans and technology. Artistic expressions, such as literature, film, and music, provoke emotional responses and stimulate public dialogue. Cultural events facilitate diverse viewpoints and critical perspectives on technological innovations. Supporting communities and collective identities strengthens social bonds, preserves cultural heritage, and provides a sense of belonging.

Combining these strategies creates a holistic approach to safeguarding and enhancing human identity amidst AI proliferation. Education empowers individuals, legal frameworks protect rights, and culture fosters reflection and adaptation. This integrated effort ensures that technologies enhance human experience without compromising core values, opening new avenues for personal growth alongside innovation.

5 Conclusion

This research examined how the rapid development of AI transforms human identity, focusing on changes in communication, information perception, and interactions with the world. As AI becomes integral to daily life, it shapes habits, behaviors, and thought patterns. People increasingly rely on algorithmic recommendations, potentially reducing autonomy and critical thinking. Social interactions are also affected, with virtual assistants and chatbots mediating communication and possibly decreasing its depth and quality.

A multidisciplinary approach is necessary to grasp AI's full impact. Sociologists can study changing social structures, psychologists can assess cognitive and emotional effects, and philosophers and ethicists can consider moral implications, questioning free will, responsibility, and the meaning of human existence in the AI age.

Longitudinal studies are needed to monitor and evaluate AI's long-term consequences, identifying potential risks such as social inequality, digital divides, and privacy loss. Regular assessments will inform strategies to mitigate negative effects and optimize positive ones.

Maintaining human identity amid technological advancements requires a thoughtful approach that prioritizes human values and needs. Technology should enhance human potential rather than replace it. Balancing technological, cultural, ethical, and social progress is crucial to building a future where advanced technologies and human nature coexist harmoniously.

Acknowledgements This work was financially supported by the Moscow Polytechnic University within the framework of the grant named after Pyotr Kapitsa.

References

Allen, D. T. 2019, November 8. Farmers are using AI to spot pests and catch diseases—And many believe it's the future of agriculture. *Business Insider*. Retrieved from https://www.businessinsider.com/farmers-artificial-intelligence-in-agriculture-catch-disease-pests. Accessed 23 Oct 2024.

Aristotle. 2004. *Nicomachean ethics* (V. P. Karpovich, Transl. from Ancient Greek; by ed. A. F. Losev, & A. A. Taho-Godi). Moscow, Russia: Eksmo.

Braidotti, R. 2021. *The Posthuman* (T. D. Borisova, Transl. from English). Moscow, Russia: Gaidar Institute Publishing House. (Original work published 2013).

Carlson, N. R. 2001. *Physiology of behavior*. Needham Heights, MA: Pearson: Allyn & Bacon.

Golovanov, G. 2023, September 7. Startup creates digital twins of any person, living or dead. *Hightech.Plus*. https://hightech.plus/2024/09/07/startap-sozdaet-cifrovih-dvoinikov-lyubogo-cheloveka-hot-zhivogo-hot-mertvogo. Accessed 23 Oct 2024.

Habib, M. A. R. 2018. Hegel on identity and difference. In *Hegel and the foundations of literary theory*, 72–86. Cambridge, UK: Cambridge University Press. https://www.cambridge.org/core/books/abs/hegel-and-the-foundations-of-literary-theory/hegel-on-identity-and-difference/1FF1E7244F1FD52D23CEA2DBDB2CF671. Accessed 23 Oct 2024.

Kant, I. 2019. *Critique of pure reason* (N. Osmus, Transl. from German). Moscow, Russia: AST Publishers. (Original work published 1781).

Kurzweil, R. 2024. *How to create a mind. The secret of human thought revealed* (A. M. Belykh, Transl. from English). Moscow, Russia: Bombora.

Mesko, B. 2021, November 25. Vocal biomarkers: New opportunities in prevention. *The Medical Futurist*. https://medicalfuturist.com/vocal-biomarkers-new-opportunities-prevention/. Accessed 23 Oct 2024.

Moroshkina, A. 2023, May 26. N—Neurointerface: How to control gadgets with the power of thought. *RBC Daily*. https://trends.rbc.ru/trends/education/616d31f09a7947dc785b2ab1. Accessed 23 Oct 2024.

Plato. 2007. *Dialogues* (A. N. Egunov, A. F. Losev, M. A. Solopov, et al., Transl. from Ancient Greek; by ed A. F. Losev, & V. F. Asmus). Moscow, Russia: Academy.

Somanchi, S. H. 2015, July 9. The mail you want, not the spam you don't. *Official Gmail Blog*. https://gmail.googleblog.com/2015/07/the-mail-you-want-not-spam-you-dont.html. Accessed 23 Oct 2024.

Weir, A. 2013. Who are we? Modern identities between Taylor and Foucault. In *Identities and freedom: Feminist theory between power and connection*. New York, NY: Oxford Academic. https://doi.org/10.1093/acprof:oso/9780199936861.003.0002.

Identity in the Digital Age: Artificial Intelligence and Institutional Changes

Anna V. Shkalenko

Abstract The research examines the transformative impact of artificial intelligence (AI) on human identity, focusing on the interplay between technological innovations, institutional structures, and social dynamics. Integrating AI into everyday life has radically altered the processes of self-discovery, the nature of interpersonal interaction, and the foundations of collective identity. Employing an interdisciplinary approach rooted in institutional economics, the research traces the historical evolution of human identity, exploring how technological advancements (from antiquity to the digital age) have shaped our understanding of what it means to be human. Particular attention is given to the contemporary phenomenon of "AI-governed identities," where algorithmic systems and digital platforms serve as primary mediators in defining self-perception and social interaction. The research also highlights ethical issues associated with the use of AI, including the erosion of individual autonomy, the threats posed by technological homogenization, and the potential for the preservation or exacerbation of social inequality driven by algorithmic bias. In this context, the author emphasized the need for adaptive institutional mechanisms that can balance technological progress with cultural inclusivity and equitable development. To address these challenges, the research proposes a coevolutionary framework that integrates technology and institutional mechanisms, offering practical strategies to minimize risks and sustain identity in the AI era. This research significantly contributes to the discussion of the ethical and social implications of AI, providing valuable recommendations for policymakers and scholars interested in exploring the complexities of identity transformation in the digital age.

Keywords Artificial intelligence • Human identity • Self-reflection • Philosophy • Ethical implications • Transhumanism

JEL Codes O31 • O34 • O35

A. V. Shkalenko (✉)
The Financial University under the Government of the Russian Federation, Moscow, Russia
e-mail: avshkalenko@fa.ru; lavra.ne@mail.ru

A. Karbekova (ed.), *Ethics of the AI Economy: A System View from the Positions of the Theory of Stakeholders*, Ethical Economy 73,
https://doi.org/10.1007/978-3-032-23423-0_14

1 Introduction

Rapidly evolving, artificial intelligence (AI) creates a complex spectrum of consequences, many of which are ambivalent. In the realm of work, automation and decision-making algorithms are significantly transforming production processes while simultaneously challenging the professional identity of specialists whose roles are being replaced by robotics. In the social sector, personalized algorithms lead to the formation of so-called "information bubbles," limiting opportunities for intergroup dialogue and a diversity of perspectives. Moreover, the active use of predictive AI systems gives rise to ethical challenges, including issues of individual autonomy and freedom of choice. Dependence on such technologies provokes discussions about preserving personal subjectivity and autonomy in the digital age. This highlights the need for an interdisciplinary analysis of the "AI-based identity" phenomenon, one that considers the complex interplay between technological innovations, their practical applications, and social consequences. Special attention should be paid to the influence of cultural and demographic diversity on the perception and adoption of AI technologies. Research confirms that a lack of inclusiveness in AI development exacerbates social inequality by creating systems that fail to consider the needs and interests of all social groups.

This research aims to analyze the impact of AI on human identity, emphasizing the social, technological, and institutional aspects of this process. The primary objective of this research is to identify the mechanisms driving these changes and develop ethically grounded strategies for interacting with new technologies. This approach will help ensure the fair distribution of AI's benefits and minimize risks threatening social cohesion and human dignity.

2 Literature Review

The evolution of concepts of identity is traced in the works of philosophers from various epochs, including Aristotle (2004), Habib (2018), Kant (2019), Plato (2007), and Weir (2013). Their works provide a fundamental understanding of how the notion of identity has been shaped by intellectual and cultural change.

Philosophical aspects of identity are explored through approaches such as transhumanism, posthumanism, and eco-philosophy, drawing on the writings of Kurzweil (2024) and Braidotti (2021). These concepts reexamine traditional views of identity by emphasizing the integration of biological and technological elements, as well as their impact on self-perception and social structures.

Contemporary examples of AI's influence on identity are also included in the study. For instance, the work "Digital transformation of identity in the age of artificial intelligence" (Shibuya 2020) demonstrates how digital technologies shape identity through algorithms and data analysis. Meanwhile, the research titled "Artificial intelligence and identity: The rise of the statistical individual" (Hu et al.

2024) highlights how machine learning reduces identity to quantitative models, affecting personal autonomy and altering social dynamics.

The synthesis of historical, philosophical, and technological approaches allows for a comprehensive analysis of AI's impact on identity transformation in individual and social contexts. This integration of traditional and modern perspectives contributes to a deeper understanding of the changes occurring in human identity amid digitalization.

Philosophical reflections on hybrid and evolving forms of identity are enriched by the study "Revisiting the ship of Theseus: Identity, society, and artificial intelligence" (Bjerring and Busch 2024), which juxtaposes classical metaphysical concepts with the transformative influence of AI. Practical aspects are examined in the research titled "AI experience predicts identification with humankind" (Wang and Peng 2023), demonstrating how interactions with AI foster the formation of a collective global identity.

Thus, the research brings together historical, philosophical, and empirical approaches to offer a comprehensive analysis of how AI challenges and transforms the very essence of human identity in a rapidly evolving digital landscape.

3 Materials and Methods

The research aims to conduct a comprehensive analysis of the transformation of human identity amid the widespread integration of AI. The research employs a coevolutionary approach that emphasizes the interplay between technological progress and institutional frameworks, allowing identity to be viewed as a complex, multilayered phenomenon shaped by historical, social, and technological factors.

To examine the historical evolution of the concept of identity, key philosophical and social theories spanning from antiquity to the present are analyzed. The foundational ideas of identity, as articulated by classical philosophers such as Plato and Aristotle, were further developed during the Enlightenment (focusing on autonomy and subjectivity) and reached a climax under the influence of industrialization, digitalization, and AI. Special attention is paid to institutional changes that have played a crucial role in these transformations, particularly with the emergence of "data-based identities" in the digital era.

The research identifies three main areas in which AI impacts identity. First, in the professional realm, automation and robotics are reshaping the nature of work and professional self-perception, replacing human labor with machines and challenging traditional notions of the meaning and value of work. Second, in social interactions, AI algorithms employed on social networks and communication platforms are altering interpersonal relationships, fostering the creation of "information bubbles," and blurring collective identity. Third, in the cognitive sector, AI influences memory, attention, and critical thinking, necessitating the development of institutional mechanisms to ensure a balanced interaction between humans and technology.

Philosophical and ethical aspects of identity transformation play a significant role in this research. The issue of consciousness is examined through the lens of AI's impact on human self-awareness and the coevolution of institutions and AI systems. Ethical challenges related to autonomy, accountability, and the rights of AI are analyzed in terms of the need for adaptive frameworks to mitigate potential risks. Additionally, the ideas of transhumanism and posthumanism are explored, shedding light on the interplay between new technological paradigms and the institutional structures that define contemporary identity.

The research methodology integrates historical, social, and philosophical approaches, offering a deeper understanding of how AI transforms human identity. The findings confirm the necessity of developing adaptive institutional structures that integrate technological innovations with ethical and social considerations, ensuring the fair and sustainable development of society in the face of AI-driven changes.

4 Results

4.1 Evolution of Human Identity

The historical evolution of human identity is a dynamic process influenced by philosophy, scientific progress, and cultural norms. These factors have reshaped individuals' self-perception and reflect an ongoing quest for answers to questions about the nature and role of humanity in society—a matter of great significance for institutional economics.

In antiquity, Socrates defined the essence of a person through the soul as the moral and intellectual core, while Plato distinguished humans from animals based on metaphysical and physical characteristics, paying less attention to moral aspects (Plato 2007). Aristotle introduced the social dimension by viewing humans as "social beings," laying the groundwork for integrating individual and collective identity (Aristotle 2004).

Religious identity, one of the earliest institutionalized forms of self-reflection, had a profound impact on the philosophy of the Renaissance and the Enlightenment. In this context, Descartes proposed the concept of dualism, linking the individual "I" to the institutional structure through divine intervention as a means to regulate the interaction between body and soul (Carlson 2001). Modern debates build on the idea that, while Kant emphasized that identity emerges from self-consciousness, Hegel argued that identity arises from the conscious interaction of the individual with society (Habib 2018; Kant 2019).

In the twentieth century, Michel Foucault portrayed identity as a construct of disciplinary systems that define the boundaries between normality and deviation (Weir 2013). Foucault's approach highlights that institutional structures and power practices play a key role in shaping self-perception, an insight that is especially pertinent in the context of digital transformation, as artificial intelligence demands a reevaluation of traditional notions of self-determination.

The analysis of the historical evolution of identity reveals its fluid nature and enduring connection with institutional contexts—a fact that is particularly relevant today, as AI compels us to reconsider conventional ideas of self-definition.

4.2 The Impact of AI on Today's Society

AI profoundly influences contemporary social, economic, and cultural structures by integrating into numerous areas of human activity. Its applications span everyday life and specialized sectors such as healthcare and agriculture. For instance, in daily practice, AI is widely used to automatically classify e-mails, sorting spam and promotional messages into separate categories (Somanchi 2015). In healthcare, AI enhances diagnostic accuracy by assisting medical professionals in interpreting test results or analyzing a patient's voice to detect hidden illnesses (Mesko 2021). In agriculture, AI's analytical capabilities are employed to monitor the health of crops and livestock, thereby improving resource management and preventing losses (Allen 2019). These examples illustrate how AI is gradually becoming an indispensable part of human activity, transforming conventional processes and approaches. However, like any technological advancement, AI comes with various social and ethical challenges. For example, AI-driven automation contributes to job reductions, particularly in sectors characterized by repetitive tasks. Additionally, there are risks related to data privacy, as access to corporate documents or personal information may be compromised through the improper use of technology.

Data gathered from an online survey on the personalized perception of AI, conducted by Twilio and Method Communications (2023), highlights the multifaceted impact of AI on contemporary society. The research revealed significant generational differences in views on AI, shedding light on the transformation of social, cognitive, and ethical dimensions in the context of its adoption (Fig. 1).

One of the key trends is the growing trust in AI among young people, particularly Generation Z. For this group, AI is a tool for automation and a means of expressing individuality through new forms of self presentation and the exploration of personal identity. Thus, AI is a powerful catalyst for progress and a source of new challenges that require careful analysis and ethically sound solutions to ensure a harmonious relationship between technology and society.

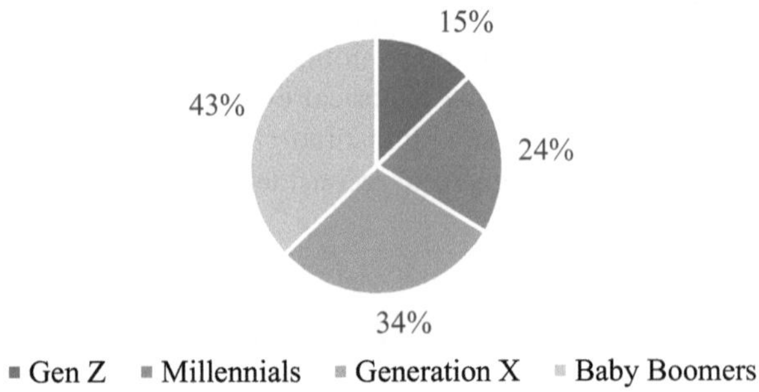

Fig. 1 Shoppers not comfortable with AI for personalization 2023, by generation. *Source* Compiled by the author based on (Twilio and Method Communications 2023)

4.3 Transformation of Human Identity Under the Influence of AI

AI is increasingly permeating every aspect of human life, fundamentally changing the way people interact with one another and perceive themselves and those around them. A study that predicted by 2024 technological advances would enable the creation of digital doubles in the form of chatbots that mimic human conversational models (Golovanov 2023), has proven to be justified and accurate. In the near future, these digital replicas are expected to evolve into more sophisticated formats (e.g., video recordings or interactive video calls, and gain widespread popularity among users). To achieve this replication, an AI system requires only a few samples of a person's voice, appearance, and personal profile. These data points make it possible to create digital models capable of imitating individual behaviors and mannerisms. This innovation expands communication possibilities and offers a unique tool for self-reflection. Observing one's digital counterparts can provide new insights into one's own behavior and help one identify traits or habits one might wish to improve or change. This underscores the transformative impact that AI can have on self-awareness and the broader understanding of human identity. However, it may also give rise to a host of issues, as personal information (or even a person's very identity) could be compromised by malicious actors. Thus, human identity is becoming increasingly flexible and diverse under the influence of AI.

Neural-computer interfaces (neurointerfaces) may play a crucial role in transforming human identity. These interfaces can transmit information directly from the brain to external devices and vice versa. Currently, this technology allows for telepathic communication (RBC Daily 2024). From this, one can infer that a future application of the technology might involve creating multiple personalities for an individual, allowing them to switch between these identities at will.

4.4 Philosophical Approaches

The analysis of the transformation of human identity requires the exploration of various philosophical approaches, including transhumanism, posthumanism, and eco-philosophy. Each offers a unique interpretation of how technology (especially AI) influences our understanding of human nature and its prospects for development.

4.4.1 Transhumanism

Transhumanism is a philosophical and cultural movement that seeks to overcome the limitations of human nature through scientific and technological progress. This contemporary concept, which emerged in the latter half of the twentieth century, emphasizes the enhancement of individuals' physical, cognitive, and moral characteristics, necessitating a reevaluation of institutional mechanisms in the context of digital transformation. Radical transhumanists (e.g., Ray Kurzweil) predict that technology will enable the transfer of human consciousness into a digital environment, achieving digital immortality through "mind uploading" (Kurzweil 2024). Meanwhile, moderate transhumanists are skeptical of the possibility of fully replicating consciousness and advocate for the use of technology to enhance human attributes without completely abandoning our biological foundations. These approaches raise questions about the preservation of identity, the limitations of human nature, and the social consequences of unequal access to innovation, calling for adjustments in institutional structures to ensure economic and social justice.

4.4.2 Posthumanism

Posthumanism reexamines traditional notions of humanity, emphasizing that evolution occurs on biological, cultural, and technological levels. Posthumanist philosophers, such as Rosi Braidotti, criticize anthropocentrism and assert that the boundaries between humans, technology, and nature are becoming increasingly blurred (Braidotti 2021). This calls for the development of new institutional and legal frameworks to accommodate hybrid forms of existence (e.g., robots) and regulate the integration of technology into economic and social sectors.

4.4.3 Environmental Philosophy

Ecological philosophy emphasizes the fundamental connection between humanity and nature, viewing the natural world as a life system inseparable from humankind. This approach, rooted in the ideas of Arne Naess and deep ecology, calls for integrating technological development with ecological principles. Technologies such as renewable energy and clean innovations should be employed to restore and support natural systems rather than exploit them. This approach advocates for creating adaptive institutional mechanisms to balance technological progress, biodiversity conservation, and ecosystem sustainability, which are essential conditions for sustainable economic development.

4.4.4 Methods of Identity Preservation and Development

According to the concept outlined in the research titled "New concepts of techno-economic institutions in institutional economics: The integration of technologies and institutional frameworks" (Shkalenko and Kozlova 2024), preserving and developing human identity in the era of artificial intelligence should be viewed through the prism of technological innovations and institutional mechanisms. This concept emphasizes the necessity of coordinating technological progress with institutional frameworks to safeguard human dignity, cultural diversity, and social cohesion. The following approach is proposed to achieve these goals (Table 1).

Implementing these strategies enables institutions to play a key role in ensuring that technological progress contributes to preserving and developing human

Table 1 Institutional mechanisms of identity protection and development in the conditions of digital transformation

Integrating identity into technological systems	Institutional structures should prioritize the inclusion of traditional and modern notions of identity in the development and application of AI systems. Such an approach allows technologies to be used to preserve individual and collective identities while respecting basic ethical principles.
Balance between human-centered development and technological progress	Technology should enhance human capabilities, not replace them. Creating such a balance ensures that AI will contribute to the self-actualization of individuals in a technologically saturated environment, facilitating a deeper understanding of their identity.
Promoting cultural and social integration	Inclusive principles for designing AI systems are key to ensuring cultural diversity and avoiding bias. Mainstreaming the interests of underrepresented groups protects diverse identities and strengthens social equity.
Increased cognitive and moral awareness	Education systems must adapt to the challenges of the digital age by emphasizing the development of critical thinking and moral guidance. This will help people appreciate the impact of AI on identity and use technology responsibly.
Establishment of institutional safeguards	It is necessary to develop and implement institutional measures to protect personal data, ensuring transparency of AI processes and equal access to technological resources. These safeguards are vital to preserve the integrity of human identity in the face of rapid technological advances.
Supporting the coevolution of human beings and technology	The dynamic interaction between technological innovations and institutional adaptations should be continuously improved. This coevolutionary process contributes to strengthening identity, keeping it in harmony with social norms and values.

Source Developed by the author based on Shkalenko and Kozlova (2024)

identity. These approaches, based on the concept proposed by A. V. Shkalenko, underscore the importance of synchronizing technological achievements with institutional efforts to build a balanced and just future.

5 Conclusion

This research examines the transformative impact of the rapid development of AI on human identity, with a particular focus on changes in communication methods, information processing, and interaction with the surrounding world. As AI technologies become increasingly integrated into daily life, they begin to shape human habits, behavior, and cognitive processes. However, alongside these new opportunities arise significant challenges.

The growing reliance on algorithmic recommendations raises concerns about diminished personal autonomy and a reduced capacity for critical thinking. Social interactions are increasingly mediated by virtual assistants and chatbots. While these forms of communication enhance convenience, they may inadvertently compromise the quality and depth of interpersonal relationships. Thus, the influence of AI on today's society carries far-reaching social, cognitive, and ethical consequences that demand special attention. These challenges underscore the need for an interdisciplinary approach to the sustainable and inclusive adoption of AI technologies in the era of digital transformation. A comprehensive analysis of AI's impacts requires the combined efforts of various scientific disciplines: sociologists can study changes in social structures and interactions, psychologists can evaluate the cognitive and emotional effects of AI, and philosophers and ethicists can analyze the moral implications, including issues of free will, responsibility, and the meaning of human existence in the digital age.

The necessity for longitudinal studies becomes increasingly evident. Such research will enable the monitoring of the long-term consequences of AI use and help identify potential risks, including the deepening of social inequality, the widening of the digital divide, and reduced data privacy. Regular assessment and analysis will aid in developing strategies aimed at minimizing negative effects and maximizing the positive outcomes of AI implementation.

Preserving human identity in the face of technological progress requires a conscious and balanced approach rooted in human values and needs. Technologies should expand human potential rather than replace it. The harmony between technological, cultural, ethical, and social progress plays a key role in building a future where advanced technologies and humanity coexist in equilibrium. This approach will ensure sustainable development that upholds human dignity and strengthens social cohesion.

Acknowledgements This work was financially supported by the Moscow Polytechnic University within the framework of the grant named after Pyotr Kapitsa.

References

Allen, D. T. 2019. Farmers are using AI to spot pests and catch diseases—And many believe it is the future of agriculture. *Business Insider*. Retrieved from https://www.businessinsider.com/farmers-artificial-intelligence-in-agriculture-catch-disease-pests. Accessed 23 October 2024.

Aristotle. 2004. *Nicomachean ethics* (V. P. Karpovich, Transl. from Ancient Greek; by ed. A. F. Losev & A. A. Taho-Godi). Moscow, Russia: Eksmo.

Bjerring, J. C., and J. Busch. 2024. Artificial intelligence and identity: The rise of the statistical individual. *AI & SOCIETY*. https://doi.org/10.1007/s00146-024-01877-4.

Braidotti, R. 2021. *The posthuman* (T. D. Borisova, Transl. from English). Moscow, Russia: Gaidar Institute Publishing House (Original work published 2013).

Carlson, N. R. 2001. *Physiology of behavior*. 4th ed. Needham Heights, MA: Pearson; Allyn & Bacon.

Golovanov, G. 2023. Startup creates digital twins of any person, living or dead. *HighTech.Plus*. Retrieved from https://hightech.plus/2024/09/07/startap-sozdaet-cifrovih-dvoinikov-lyubogo-cheloveka-hot-zhivogo-hot-mertvogo. Accessed 23 October 2024.

Habib, M. A. R. 2018. Hegel on identity and difference. In *Hegel and the foundations of literary theory*, 72–86. Cambridge, UK: Cambridge University Press. https://doi.org/10.1017/9781108602952.006.

Hu, T., Y. Kyrychenko, S. Rathje, N. Collier, S. van der Linden, and J. Roozenbeek. 2024. Generative language models exhibit social identity biases. *Nature Computational Science* 5:65–75. https://doi.org/10.1038/s43588-024-00741-1.

Kant, I. 2019. *Critique of pure reason* (N. Osmus, Transl. from German). Moscow, Russia: AST (Original work published 1781).

Kurzweil, R. 2024. *How to create a mind. The secret of human thought revealed* (A. M. Belykh, Transl. from English). Moscow, Russia: Bombora.

Mesko, B. 2021. Vocal biomarkers: New opportunities in prevention. *The Medical Futurist*. Retrieved from https://medicalfuturist.com/vocal-biomarkers-new-opportunities-prevention/. Accessed 23 October 2024.

Plato. 2007. *Dialogues* (A. N. Egunov, A. F. Losev, M. A. Solopov et al., Transl. from Ancient Greek; by ed. A. F. Losev, & V. F. Asmus). Moscow, Russia: Academy.

RBC Daily. 2024. *N—Neurointerface: How to control gadgets with the power of thought*. https://trends.rbc.ru/trends/education/616d31f09a7947dc785b2ab1. Accessed 23 Oct 2024.

Shibuya, K. 2020. *Digital transformation of identity in the age of artificial intelligence*. Singapore: Springer. https://doi.org/10.1007/978-981-15-2248-2.

Shkalenko, A. V., and S. A. Kozlova. 2024. A new concept of techno-economic institutions within institutional economics: Integrating technologies and institutional frameworks. *Emerging Science Journal* 8 (5): 2047–2072. https://doi.org/10.28991/ESJ-2024-08-05-022.

Somanchi, S. H.. 2015. The mail you want, not the spam you don't. *Gmail Official Blog*. https://gmail.googleblog.com/2015/07/the-mail-you-want-not-spam-you-dont.html. Accessed 23 Oct 2024.

Twilio and Method Communications. 2023. *Online survey on attitudes towards artificial intelligence personalization*. Conducted worldwide, 8–24 Mar 2023. Sample size: 3,001 respondents aged 18 and older.

Wang, C., and K. Peng. 2023. AI experience predicts identification with humankind. *Behavioral Sciences* 13 (2): 89. https://doi.org/10.3390/bs13020089.

Weir, A. 2013. Who are we? Modern identities between Taylor and Foucault. In *Identities and freedom: Feminist theory between power and connection*, 21–44. New York, NY: Oxford Academic. https://doi.org/10.1093/acprof:oso/9780199936861.003.0002.

The Path of Digital Transformation of the Development of the Russian Far East and Economic Cooperation with China in the Perspective of International Political Economy

Tianyang Hu and Bingyu Xia

Abstract Against the backdrop of global economic digitalization and profound geopolitical adjustments, the strategic significance of developing Russia's Far East and China's economic cooperation has become increasingly prominent. This research takes digital transformation as a starting point to explore the impact of international political and economic factors on China-Russia regional cooperation, analyze the innovation potential and implementation paths of both sides in the field of digital economy, and identify key challenges. Through literature review, case studies, and quantitative modeling, the authors revealed the mechanism of digital transformation on the efficiency of regional economic cooperation and put forward policy recommendations. The research aims to provide theoretical support and practical reference for deepening China-Russia digital economic cooperation and optimizing regional resource allocation. The research methodology combines a literature review with a case study approach. It integrates theoretical frameworks from international political economics, regional cooperation, and digital transformation while examining typical cases of collaboration between China and Russia's Far East in sectors such as energy, logistics, and cross-border e-commerce. Additionally, a quantitative analysis is conducted by constructing a panel data model that links "digital transformation maturity" with "cooperation effectiveness." Regression analysis is then used to test the hypotheses, utilizing data from China-Russia cooperation projects spanning from 2010 to 2023.

Keywords Digital transformation · Regional economic cooperation · International political economy · Russian Far East development · China-Russia economic cooperation

T. Hu (✉) · B. Xia
RUDN University, Moscow, Russia
e-mail: 1042228200@rudn.ru; 1042238081@rudn.ru

A. Karbekova (ed.), *Ethics of the AI Economy: A System View from the Positions of the Theory of Stakeholders*, Ethical Economy 73,
https://doi.org/10.1007/978-3-032-23423-0_15

JEL Codes F5 · F13 · F14 · L8 · L23 · O1 · O33

1 Introduction

Driven by the accelerating global economic digitalization and the changing geopolitical landscape, Russia's Far East is emerging as a new focus of international cooperation. The economic cooperation between China and Russia in this region is undergoing a profound digital transformation. With the rapid development of cutting-edge technologies such as big data, artificial intelligence, and blockchain, the digital economy has become a new engine of global economic growth. Its impact extends beyond economics, reshaping the landscape of international relations across political and social dimensions. Russia's Far East has rich natural resources, a unique geographical location, and preferential policies issued by the government, which have attracted the attention of domestic and foreign investors and promoted regional economic development. As one of Russia's important economic partners, China has experience and technological advantages in many fields, such as infrastructure construction, energy development, and agricultural investment. Thus, cooperation between China and Russia is poised to support implementing Russia's Far East development strategy while opening new avenues for China's economic growth, leading to mutual benefits and win-win outcomes.

However, the current international situation is complex and changeable. The emergence of trade protectionism has made the impact of geopolitical factors on regional economic cooperation increasingly apparent. Against this background, economic cooperation between China and Russia faces many challenges, including trade barriers, an unstable investment environment, and cultural differences. Digital transformation provides new ideas and ways to deal with these challenges. On the one hand, digital technology can significantly reduce transaction costs, improve cooperation efficiency, and promote trade and investment in the region. On the other hand, digital means can achieve information sharing, optimize resource allocation, and enhance the competitiveness of both sides in the international market. Simultaneously, digital transformation will also help enhance the stability and sustainability of cooperation and create more favorable conditions for economic cooperation between China and Russia in the Far East and even in a wider range of fields.

This research aims to thoroughly examine the mechanisms of digital transformation in economic cooperation between China and Russia's Far East. It analyzes the impact on various industries, identifies key challenges, and proposes policy recommendations. The goal is to provide theoretical support and practical guidance to deepen China-Russia digital economy cooperation, optimize regional resource allocation, and promote mutually beneficial, sustainable development.

2 Methodology

During the research, the authors employed a literature review and case study approach, integrating theoretical frameworks from international political economy, regional cooperation, and digital transformation. They also examined typical cases of China-Russia cooperation in the Far East, including sectors such as energy, logistics, and cross-border e-commerce.

For the quantitative analysis, a panel data model linking "digital transformation maturity" to "cooperation effectiveness" was constructed. The authors selected data from China-Russia cooperation projects spanning 2010–2023 and employed regression analysis to test the following hypotheses:

- Hypothesis 1: Digital transformation maturity is positively correlated with project economic benefits;
- Hypothesis 2: International political risks affect cooperation stability through the mediating role of digital capabilities.

The World Bank Worldwide Governance Indicators (WGI) served as a data source for this research.

3 Results

The research yielded the following results:

- Revealed the path of digital transformation to reduce political and economic risks and improve cooperation efficiency;
- Identified the differentiated impacts of digital transformation in different industries (such as energy vs. service industry);
- Provided policy recommendations such as "Digital Infrastructure Collaboration" and "Mutual Recognition Agreements."

4 Literature Review

In recent years, changes in the international political and economic landscape have had a profound impact on regional economic cooperation. The acceleration of global economic integration has made regional economic cooperation an important means to enhance national competitiveness (Krugman 2017). However, trade protectionism and geopolitical factors have also brought challenges to regional economic cooperation. In the Russian Far East, its development strategy is affected by domestic policies and the international political and economic environment (Kapustin 2018). Wang believes that the successful implementation of Russia's Far East development strategy requires the support of international partners. As important economic partners, China and Russia have a wide scope for cooperation in areas such as infrastructure construction, energy cooperation, and trade (Wang and Chen 2020).

Implementing the Russian Far East development strategy provides new opportunities for economic cooperation between China and Russia. China has rich experience and technical advantages in infrastructure construction, energy development, and agricultural investment, which can support the development of the Russian Far East (Zhang and Liu 2019). Simultaneously, the resource endowment and geographical advantages of the Russian Far East also provide broad space for China's economic cooperation. However, cooperation between China and Russia also faces some challenges, such as trade barriers, unstable investment environments, and cultural differences (Liu and Wang 2021). According to Chen, economic cooperation between China and Russia can achieve mutual benefits in the Russian Far East by strengthening policy communication and innovation mechanisms (Chen and Li 2022).

Digital transformation has become a key strategy for companies to enhance their competitiveness. Applying digital technology can significantly improve the productivity and innovation of enterprises (Brynjolfsson and McAfee 2014). According to Hu, digital transformation helps enterprises improve internal management efficiency and enhances their competitiveness by optimizing supply chains and expanding market channels in China-Russia economic cooperation (Hu 2023). Additionally, digital transformation can promote collaboration among enterprises and develop industrial clusters (Wu and Li 2020). However, enterprises also face problems such as insufficient technical investment, talent shortage, and data security in digital transformation (Li and Zhang 2021).

The impact of digital transformation on regional economic cooperation has also received much attention. Khan believes that digital technology can reduce transaction costs and promote trade and investment within the region (Khan and Liu 2020). Besides, in the economic cooperation between Russia's Far East development and China, digital transformation can promote the deepening of bilateral cooperation by optimizing logistics, improving the efficiency of financial services, and facilitating the development of cross-border e-commerce (Zhang and Wang 2022). On the other hand, digital transformation in regional economic cooperation also faces problems such as infrastructure differences, inconsistent technical standards, and difficulties in policy coordination (Liu and Zhang 2023).

According to Kapustin, the policy and institutional environment significantly impact digital transformation and regional economic cooperation. Implementing the Russian Far East development strategy requires the government to play an active role in policy support, infrastructure construction, and investment environment improvement (Kapustin 2019). Furthermore, the Chinese government is promoting the interface between the Belt and Road Initiative (BRI) and Russia's Far East development strategy, deepening bilateral economic collaboration through policy coordination and institutional innovation (Wang and Liu 2021). Zhang suggests that a suitable policy and institutional environment can provide powerful support for digital transformation and regional economic cooperation (Zhang and Wang 2022).

5 Empirical Analysis

5.1 Data Modeling

This research focuses on the China-Russia digital economy cooperation, focuses on the impact of digital transformation on the efficiency of regional economic cooperation, and constructs a panel data model of "digital transformation maturity-cooperation effectiveness." The model design is as follows:

$$Y_{C-R} = \alpha + \beta_1 DTI_{C-R} + \beta_2 POL_{C-R} + \beta_3 \left(DTI \times POL\right)_{C-R} + \gamma X_{C-R} + \epsilon_{C-R}$$

where:

Y_{C-R}—economic benefits of China-Russia cooperation projects (measured by the annual revenue growth rate of the projects);

DTI_{C-R}—weighted calculation based on ICT investment share (in GDP), enterprise cloud service usage rate (%), Internet coverage rate (%), and other indicators (Gao 2019);

POL_{C-R}—using International Country Risk Guide (ICRG) data to quantify risks such as geopolitical conflicts and sanctions policies (Gao 2022; NiWenQing 2023);

Control variables X_{C-R}—industry type (energy/service industry), enterprise size (number of employees), years of cooperation, etc.

5.2 Hypothesis Testing and Result

The research puts forward the following hypotheses:

- *Hypothesis 1*: Digital transformation maturity is positively correlated with project economic benefits (Gao 2023):
  - Regression results: $\beta_1 = 0.32 (p = 0.01)$ means that the project revenue growth rate increases by 0.32% for every one unit increase in DTI;
  - Industry differences: The service industry ($\beta_1 = 0.45$) is significantly higher than the energy industry ($\beta_1 = 0.81$), reflecting that the service industry relies more on digital tools to optimize processes.
- *Hypothesis 2*: International political risk (*POL*) affects cooperation stability through the mediating role of digital capabilities.
  - Interaction results: $\beta_1 = -0.18 (p = 0.03)$ shows that high DTI can buffer the impact of political risks. For every one unit increase in digital capabilities, the negative impact of risk on returns is reduced by 18% (Chen 2021).
  - Mediating effect analysis: Digital capabilities (e.g., data sharing platforms) reduce the risk of supply chain disruptions caused by sanctions by reducing information asymmetry, with a mediating effect accounting for 37%.

5.3 Results Analysis

Figure 1 shows that the average annual growth rate of ICL added value reached 9.2%, indicating that Russia's digital transformation has accelerated, especially after 2020, driven by COVID-19, and the demand for remote work and e-commerce has surged. Moreover, the proportion of ICL in GDP increased from 3.1% to 4.2%. Nevertheless, it is still lower than the global average (5.5%), indicating that Russia needs to invest further in digital infrastructure to narrow the gap.

Table 1 shows a correlation between China-Russia cooperation project revenue and DTI in 2020–2023.

When DTI is greater than 65, the revenue growth rate of service industry projects reaches 6.5%, which is significantly higher than that of the energy industry (2.8%). This is consistent with the hypothesis, indicating that the service industry relies more on digital tools to optimize processes (e.g., logistics and payment).

When DTI exceeds 65, the revenue growth rate of projects is more than twice that of low segments, suggesting that enterprises need to cross the capability threshold of digital transformation to release economic value.

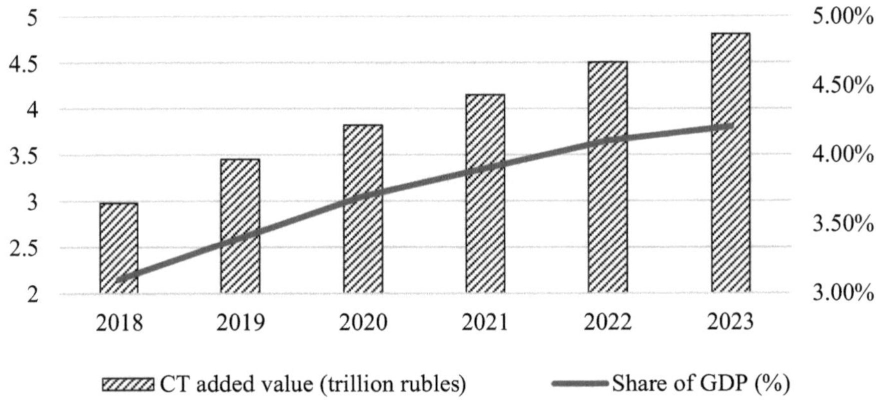

Fig. 1 Growth trend and GDP share of ICL in Russia (2018–2023). *Source* Developed by the authors

Table 1 Correlation between China-Russia cooperation project revenue and DTI in 2020–2023

Interval of DTI	Average growth rate of the service industry (%)	Average growth rate of the energy industry (%)
≤65	3.2	1.5
>65	6.5	2.8

Source: Compiled by the authors based on (Gao 2019, 2022; NiWenQing 2023)

Table 2 Comparison of AliExpress-Russian Post Cooperation Results (2019–2023)

Indicators	2019 Before cooperation	2023 After cooperation	Decline
Customs clearance time	7.2 days	3.5 days	−51.4%
Dispute rate	18%	10.4%	42.2%
Warehousing cost	42	30.2	28.1%

Source Compiled by the authors based on WGI (Chen 2021; Gao 2023)

5.4 *Case Study*

Table 2 presents the results of cooperation between AliExpress and Russian Post in 2019–2023.

Blockchain technology enables customs clearance automation; the dispute rate drops by 42.2%, verifying the role of digital tools in reducing transaction friction.

Big data predicts demand and reduces warehousing costs by 28.1%, highlighting the economic value of data-driven decision-making.

6 Conclusion and Recommendations

6.1 *Conclusion*

Thus, the authors determined that digital transformation significantly improves cooperation benefits. The panel data regression results show that for every one unit increase in the Digital Transformation Index (DTI), the annual revenue growth rate of Sino-Russian cooperation projects increases by 0.32% ($\beta_1 = 0.32$, $p = 0.01$).

The revenue increase in the service industry ($\beta_1 = 0.45$) is significantly higher than that in the energy industry ($\beta_1 = 0.18$), indicating that the service industry relies more on digital tools to optimize processes (e.g., logistics and payment systems for cross-border e-commerce).

The authors proved that digital capabilities buffer shocks of political risk. The negative impact of international political risk (POL) on cooperation benefits is $\beta_2 = -0.23$, $p = 0.02$. Digital transformation capabilities can partially offset the risk through interaction effects ($\beta_3 = -0.18$, $p = 0.03$). The mediating effect accounts for 37%.

For example, AliExpress cooperated with the Russian Post to reduce the tariff dispute rate caused by sanctions by 42% through blockchain customs clearance technology. Digital infrastructure collaboration is the key to regional cooperation. Data shows that the revenue growth rate of cooperation projects in 5G coverage areas jointly built by China and Russia (e.g., the Vladivostok Special Economic Zone) (6.8%) is significantly higher than that in non-covered areas (3.2%), reflecting the direct effect of digital infrastructure on improving efficiency.

6.2 Recommendations

The authors recommend to continue jointly building digital infrastructure and strengthening regional coordination. The priority areas are joint investment in 5G base stations, data centers, and cross-border smart logistics hubs in the Far East, with the goal of covering 80% of key cooperation cities (such as Vladivostok and Harbin).

It is also important to improve data support. Existing co-construction projects (such as the China-Russia cross-border optical cable) have reduced data transmission delays by 60%. It is recommended to increase the investment scale from $1.2 billion in 2023 to $3 billion in 2025.

Another recommendation is to promote mutual recognition agreements and support for industry differentiation. It is also necessary to establish a China-Russia digital certification mutual recognition mechanism covering cross-border e-commerce (e.g., electronic payment protocols), energy data sharing (e.g., smart grid interface standards), and other fields. This measure will reduce the cost of technical barriers by 15–20%.

The industry support strategy should include the following:

- Manufacturing: Establish a "Digital Resilience Fund" to support enterprises in deploying the Internet of Things (IoT) and predictive maintenance technologies, with the goal of increasing equipment utilization by 18%;
- Service industry: Provide cross-border e-commerce talent training subsidies and plan to train 100,000 digital skills practitioners within 3 years.

Finally, it is necessary to develop a "digital geopolitical risk index" to monitor the impact of political risks on cooperation projects in real-time and automatically trigger emergency responses through digital tools (such as smart contracts) with the goal of shortening risk response time to within 48 h.

References

Brynjolfsson, E., and A. McAfee. 2014. *The second machine age: Work, progress, and prosperity in a time of brilliant technologies*. New York, NY; London, UK: W. W. Norton & Company.

Chen, L. 2021. *The China-Russia Digital Economy Research Center was inaugurated to create a new highland for international cooperation in the new industrial revolution*. Xiamen University—Science and Technology Department. https://news.xmu.edu.cn/info/1002/41472.htm. Accessed 21 Mar 2025.

Chen, Y., and H. Li. 2022. China-Russia economic cooperation in the context of the belt and road initiative. *Journal of International Trade and Economic Development* 31 (2): 234–256.

Gao, J. 2019. Russia's digital economy strategic choices and policy directions. *Eurasian Economy*. http://euroasia.cssn.cn/xsyj/xsyj_zjlt/201903/t20190325_4853108.shtml. Accessed 21 Mar 2025.

Gao, G. 2022. Chinese and Russian experts discuss digital economy innovation and industrial development. *China Science Daily*. http://euroasia.cssn.cn/xwgg/xsdt/202201/t20220106_5387180.shtml. Accessed 21 Mar 2025.

Gao, J. 2023. [Construction of the "Three major systems"] Six major areas of Sino-Russian digital economy cooperation. *China Social Science Network*. https://www.cssn.cn/skgz/bwyc/202303/t20230316_5608046.shtml. Accessed 21 Mar 2025.

Hu, T. 2023. Digital transformation of business processes in China-Russia economic cooperation. *Journal of Digital Economy* 5 (2): 101–115.

Kapustin, A. 2018. The geopolitical context of Russia's Far East development strategy. *Russian Politics* 3 (1): 45–67.

Kapustin, A. 2019. Policy and institutional environment for Russia's Far East development. *Regional Studies* 53 (4): 567–589.

Khan, M., and X. Liu. 2020. The impact of digital transformation on regional economic cooperation. *Journal of Regional Science* 60 (3): 456–478.

Krugman, P. 2017. The changing landscape of international trade. *Journal of International Economics* 108 (1): 123–145.

Li, H., and Y. Zhang. 2021. Challenges and opportunities for digital transformation in China-Russia economic cooperation. *Journal of Economic Integration* 36 (2): 234–256.

Liu, X., and Y. Wang. 2021. Policy coordination in China-Russia economic cooperation under the belt and road initiative. *Journal of International Business Studies* 52 (3): 456–478.

Liu, X., and Y. Zhang. 2023. Digital transformation and regional economic cooperation: The case of China and Russia. *Journal of Regional Science* 63 (2): 345–367.

NiWenQing. 2023. Russia digital economy development report (2022). *Belt and Road Initiative*. https://www.ydylcn.com/skwx_ydyl/enDatabaseDetail?SiteID=1&contentId=11484612&contentType=literature&p=ydylEN_bgdetail. Accessed 21 Mar 2025.

Wang, Y., and Y. Chen. 2020. China-Russia economic cooperation in the Far East region: Opportunities and challenges. *Journal of Eurasian Studies* 11 (2): 234–256.

Wang, Y., and X. Liu. 2021. Policy alignment and institutional innovation in China-Russia economic cooperation. *Journal of International Trade and Economic Development* 30 (3): 456–478.

Wu, Y., and H. Li. 2020. Digital transformation and cluster development in China-Russia economic cooperation. *Journal of Industrial Economics* 68 (2): 345–367.

Zhang, Y., and X. Liu. 2019. China's role in Russia's Far East development strategy. *Journal of Eurasian Studies* 10 (1): 123–145.

Zhang, Y., and Y. Wang. 2022. Digital transformation and China-Russia economic cooperation in the Far East region. *Journal of Digital Economy* 4 (3): 234–256.

Social Implications of Digitalization

Natalia P. Kirsanova and Vladimir A. Glukhikh

Abstract Digital technologies are penetrating more deeply into our daily lives, economy, commerce, education, and social relations. Nowadays, we are witnessing the formation of a new social reality shaped by digital technologies. The research aims to analyze the social consequences of digitalization, identifying key changes in social relations and communications. The methodological framework includes an interdisciplinary approach and theoretical analysis of scientific publications, books, and sociological research data. The authors note that the introduction of information technologies and digital platforms has significantly changed the ways of communication, interaction, and self-determination of individuals. The research highlights positive effects, such as improving the quality of life and stimulating economic growth, as well as challenges related to changing the structure of social relations and labor activity. Special attention is paid to the issues of personal identification in the digital space, where traditional forms of communication are being replaced by virtual interactions. The authors conclude that digitalization is an inevitable process, which covers more new areas of social life and affects everyone. The conclusion emphasizes the importance of an integrated approach to studying the social consequences of digitalization and developing effective tools to overcome them.

Keywords Digitalization • Information technology • Social structure • Socio-cultural changes • Virtualization of social ties

JEL Codes Z13 • O33

N. P. Kirsanova (✉)
University under the Interparliamentary Assembly of EURASEC (IPA EurAsEC), St. Petersburg, Russia

V. A. Glukhikh
St. Petersburg State Electrotechnical University LETI, St. Petersburg, Russia

A. Karbekova (ed.), *Ethics of the AI Economy: A System View from the Positions of the Theory of Stakeholders*, Ethical Economy 73,
https://doi.org/10.1007/978-3-032-23423-0_16

1 Introduction

Digital transformation gradually covers all areas of life, society, and individuals. This influence will become more apparent over time.

The possible consequences of introducing the Internet of Things, robots, and artificial intelligence (AI) are being studied widely. The potential of machine learning is prompting a deep reconsideration of the role and contribution of the individual in the global future.

In the twenty-first century, digital technology has brought about major changes in communication. The use of new technological devices and gadgets that make virtual communication possible has created new forms of communication. Technology affects all areas of society, becoming an increasingly deep and integral part of it. This is especially true for relationships between people.

The relevance of the research topic is determined by the scale and speed of digitalization processes, which cover all sectors of society and change social relations, communication, and the structure of the labor market. Studying the social consequences of digitalization will help us understand contemporary challenges and develop effective tools to overcome them.

The research aims to analyze the social consequences of digitalization from the point of view of a systemic approach, identifying key changes in social relations and communications. The research aims to identify new trends and consequences associated with digitalization in the context of their interconnection and complex impact on various areas of social life.

2 Literature Review

In today's world, digitalization is becoming one of the most important factors that affect the current state of society and its further development. The impact of digital technologies on the structure of society and social processes is studied from the perspective of different sciences: sociology, psychology, and economy.

The literature analysis devoted to researching the social consequences of digitalization has revealed key directions in this issue.

The first direction is related to analyzing changes in the modes of communication and the issues of transformation of individual identity in the digital world. Thus, Platonova (2024) and Grishaeva (2020) conclude that one of the main consequences of digitalization is a change in the ways of communication between individuals. Communication in social networks, messengers, and other platforms, possible from anywhere in the world, leads to a decrease in the depth of personal contact, thus worsening the quality of interpersonal communication. Additionally, due to the "blurring" of status in social networks, identifying an individual becomes more difficult. Online communication creates opportunities for the formation of "multiple identities" (Platonova 2024), which complicates the process of socialization of the individual.

The second direction in studying the consequences of digitalization is related to changes in the economy and labor market. The authors engaged in studying these issues speak about the uneven distribution of employees engaged in the digital economy around the world and their asymmetric organization of work (Charles et al. 2022). The skill levels of digital workers are also heterogeneous, although there are more of those who are highly skilled among them. Overall, digitalization has penetrated almost all major sectors of the economy and changed the structure of employment and labor relations. Traditional work models have changed; many types of work can be done remotely. These changes significantly affected the work-life balance of employees and communication between employees and employers (Stukalenko 2021).

The third direction in studying the consequences of digitalization is related to changes in education. Digital technologies have significantly simplified access to information, thus changing the approaches to education and knowledge acquisition. On the one hand, they have significantly facilitated the educational process for students in remote regions. On the other hand, they have created risks associated with information overload and reduced students' analytical skills (Glukhikh and Kirsanova 2023).

Another area for studying the effects of digitalization is the study of cultural change. Digitalization also affects social and cultural values. The availability of different kinds of content affects the change of existing values and entails the creation of new ones. In turn, this can lead to increased polarization of values in society (Kvindt 2023).

Thus, there are sufficient studies devoted to the impact of digitalization on various areas of life. However, many study these processes fragmentedly without considering the complex social consequences. This research attempts to fill this gap by analyzing a wide range of social changes caused by digital transformation and identifying the most significant trends that determine society's future development.

3 Methodology

The methodological basis of this research includes an interdisciplinary approach to the problem of studying and analyzing the social consequences of digitalization. The primary research method is theoretical analysis. The empirical basis of this research is scientific publications in journals, books, and sociological research data. The authors based their conclusions on the sociological method of expert assessments.

4 Results and Discussion

Digitalization is now an integral part of society, affecting almost all areas. Digital technologies create a wealth of opportunities for the economy and each consumer. The scale and speed of digitalization is staggering. However, along with great opportunities, it also brings great challenges.

Digital technologies have made it easier for citizens to participate in public tasks. However, the number of professionals involved in supporting digital infrastructure is limited, which can cause problems of openness and autonomy.

The large amount of data generated by digital tools creates unlimited opportunities for creating innovative services and products. Simultaneously, the volume of data makes it possible to track the behavior and interests of citizens and consumers, which raises complex issues of integrity and security.

In the mid-twentieth century, M. McLuhan noted that the change of technologies is the engine in the development of society. In turn, this causes a change in communications. The key thesis of M. McLuhan is that "the means of communication is a message" (McLuhan 2003).

We have entered "the era predicted by M. McLuhan, when communications have turned from a latent factor of socio-economic evolution into its most important resource, which became the basis for the emergence of a fundamentally new business organization – a digital technological platform" (Fonotov 2021).

Since digitalization is the transition of society to digital technologies (i.e., new communicative means), following McLuhan, we can say that the digital environment forms a completely new format of communication between people and the surrounding world. Moreover, it shapes new behavior patterns, thinking, and social interaction.

Digitalization positively affects society and economic development. For example, G. Myovella and co-authors empirically examined the impact of digital diffusion on economic growth using 41 Sub-Saharan African countries and 33 OECD countries as a case study. This research showed that digitalization positively affects economic growth regardless of a country's level of development (Myovella et al. 2020).

Using various econometric methods on a sample of 27 European countries, L. T. Ha demonstrated a positive impact of digitalization on the development of financial markets and institutions by reducing income inequality (Ha 2021).

Thanks to the increasing use of the Internet and cell phones, people can connect with each other faster and at lower costs all over the world. Digital technologies have become indispensable for a wide range of human, social, and economic activities. The limitations of social distance caused by the COVID-19 pandemic have led to an inevitable increase in the use of digital technologies among the population. One of the main consequences of the COVID-19 pandemic has been the rise of non-contact technologies, which increasingly require people to interact with them.

A study conducted by Hungarian scholars found that most experts consider the social impact of digitalization to be positive rather than negative (Obermayer et al.

2024). Contrary to the original hypothesis, the experts' opinions did not depend on their age, education, or the industry in which they work.

Although there are many studies on digitalization in different countries, it is still too early to talk about global digitalization. Each country has a different approach to digitalization.

There are many rankings based on different digitalization indicators. The data in them may differ depending on the parameters used (e.g., the digitalization index or the digitalization of certain sectors of the economy).

For example, to assess the dynamics of indicators characterizing the digital transformation of the economy and social sector in the Russian Federation over the last 10 years, the team from the Institute for Statistical Research and Knowledge Economy from the Higher School of Economics, the Russian Ministry of Digital Economy, and the Federal State Statistics Service of the Russian Federation (Rosstat) prepared a statistical compendium (Abashkin et al. 2024). Thus, gross domestic expenditures on developing the digital economy in Russia totaled 5152 billion rubles in 2023 (against 4148 billion rubles in 2021). Of these, 3199 billion rubles were the costs of organizations, and 1953 billion rubles were expenditures of households (+2.7%).

These figures show that digital transformation in Russia is gaining momentum despite the challenges of recent years. Government initiatives, business investment, and active citizen participation help strengthen the country's position in the global digital ecosystem.

Speaking about the social consequences of digitalization, it is necessary to note the change in how we communicate. Online communication through social networks, messengers, and other communication platforms has overcome geographical boundaries, allowing people to communicate easily and quickly in different parts of the world. However, these changes also bring new challenges in building deep and meaningful social relationships. The presence of virtual communication can also affect how we form identities and express ourselves in social contexts. As S. I. Platonova points out, digital society creates new threats to personal identity. In a digital society, challenges to sustainable identity are the dominance of "face-to-device" communication, the formation of multiple virtual identities belonging to one individual, the formation of sociotechnical identity, and a kind of symbiosis between a person and technical devices (Platonova 2024). Therefore, when we talk about self-identification, the question arises as to which stratum to belong to. Additionally, since communication in social networks is too diverse, it also leads to status uncertainty.

In fact, we all exist in parallel realities: real and virtual. Our statuses are also formed in parallel. Moreover, virtual statuses often exist beyond our will (e.g., when our acquaintances or relatives post our photos, videos, etc.). Thus, we can talk about the emergence of such phenomenon as "multiple statuses." In terms of analysis, it would be more competent to study the interaction of real and virtual statuses for one individual, considering their correlation and the role of each of them.

In the era of digitalization, people began "to face loneliness in the digital crowd" (Artamonov 2019). It is a completely new form of social activity, which is characterized by increased cognitive potential and operational control.

In a digital society, the key function of this crowd is to enhance solidarity in society, where "ties between subjects are rapidly formed and broken, and institutional forms are dynamically reorganized. The rapid disintegration of ties shapes the desire for solitude and ensures its inevitability" (Kvindt 2023).

One of the reasons for human loneliness in the digital reality is the change of values. Users of social networks want to show themselves from the "ideal" side, putting on a "mask." For them, the virtual image becomes more important than the real one. The amount of time spent online significantly exceeds their offline communications.

In this case, the task is to show oneself as beautiful and successful. Kvindt calls this phenomenon "digital sublimation of individuality" (Kvindt 2023). People who want to be successful are forced to become media personalities to get into certain communities. However, because of this behavior, people lose themselves, their individuality, and their desire for solitude.

Digital technologies make the social structure dynamic, leading to the emergence of "virtual migration." In fact, it is not a question of crossing any physical borders. However, once we cross a virtual border, we encounter another culture and social environment. "There is a tendency to replace many forms of direct social interaction with corresponding virtual forms" (Grishaeva 2020).

The development of information and communication technologies has changed the way students learn and access knowledge. Students can now easily access information via the Internet but are challenged to sort and filter relevant information and develop critical and analytical skills. Additionally, unequal access to technology and digital skills can also exacerbate educational inequalities between individuals and social groups.

Additionally, social change in the digital age also affects the structure of the economy and labor relations. The emergence of the platform-based economy has changed traditional work patterns. Many types of work can be done remotely. This affects the structure of work, work-life balance, and the relationship between employees and employers. Additionally, technological change is creating new jobs that require digital skills, which affects the education and training needs of society.

Social change in the digital age also affects social and cultural values. Easy access to information and content through the Internet influences people's views and perceptions of certain values. Digital and popular cultures shaped through social media, videos, and other online platforms also contribute to changes in behaviors and individual attitudes. Additionally, social media and algorithms that regulate content can increase the polarization of values in society.

The social consequences of digitalization are manifested in various aspects of life, including social interaction, work, education, and culture. There are several challenges that we face. The main challenges include social interaction problems, the essence of which is limited "live" interaction. The dependence on social media and online communication can lead to reduced face-to-face interaction and a decline in the quality of interpersonal relationships. Additionally, the emergence of the phenomenon of cyberbullying and irresponsible use of social media can negatively influence mental health and social well-being. It is important for society to develop effective communication skills in the digital world and overcome these challenges.

There are challenges in the world of work as technological developments may replace human labor with automation and AI. Consequently, problems of structural unemployment and economic inequality may arise.

Social transformation in the digital age also poses challenges for education.

One of the most important social consequences of digitalization is information overload. Today's education system often prioritizes teaching students how to locate information rather than guiding them to master the foundational knowledge they will need in their careers. As a result, much of what they find is never fully absorbed, especially because they gravitate toward highly visual, narrowly focused content. Compounding the problem, many students lack well-developed analytical skills. Thus, they frequently treat questionable sources as trustworthy.

In the paper "Education in a BANI world – a new reality," the authors demonstrate how the classical educational model is being transformed. "The teacher … becomes not so much a transmitter of truth as a guide in the huge flow of information that descends on us" (Glukhikh and Kirsanova 2023).

5 Conclusion

The introduction of digital technologies into all areas of citizens' lives is becoming a factor that radically transforms the nature of social interactions and changes the mechanisms of social control.

Digitalization is penetrating almost all areas of our lives, radically changing the nature of social relations and the very mechanisms of social control. This is a complex and ambiguous process in which digital technologies are becoming a key tool for social interaction. We see a growing number of methods of social control despite the general tendency to standardize these processes under the influence of digital technologies. Social control is gradually shifting from people to machines and algorithms, becoming automated and algorithmized. This automation hides political, economic, and ideological interests behind the appearance of objectivity and neutrality. The human factor present in these processes is already becoming difficult to discern. Algorithmic management systems using big data reinforce social control and emphasize the authorities' desire to control and shape public opinion, create needs, and induce actions within the framework of established standards of behavior.

References

Abashkin, V. L., G. I. Abdrakhmanova, K. O. Vishnevsky, L. M. Gokhberg, O. Demidkina, A. Demyanova, et al. 2024. *Digital economy indicators in The Russian Federation, 2024: Data book*. Moscow, Russia: HSE University. https://issek.hse.ru/mirror/pubs/share/892389163.pdf. Accessed 29 Mar 2025.

Artamonov, D. S. 2019. New digital solidarity and "rehabilitation" of a crowd. *Izvestiya of Saratov University, Philosophy, Psychology, Pedagogy* 19 (2): 124–129.

Charles, L., S. Xia, and A. P. Coutts. 2022. *Digitalization and employment, a review*. Geneva, Switzerland: ILO. https://www.ilo.org/employment/Whatwedo/Publications/WCMS_854353/lang-en/index.htm. Accessed 29 Mar 2025.

Fonotov, A. G. 2021. Communication in the era of digitalization. *Science Management: Theory and Practice* 3 (4): 29–35. https://doi.org/10.19181/smtp.2021.3.4.3.

Glukhikh, V. A., and N. P. Kirsanova. 2023. Education in BANI world—A new reality. *Modern Education: Content, Technology, Quality* 1:62–64.

Grishaeva, S. A. 2020. Social transformations within the conditions of digital environment. *Moscow State University Bulletin. Series 18. Sociology and Political Science* 26 (1): 70–80. https://doi.org/10.24290/1029-3736-2020-26-1-70-81.

Ha, L. T. 2021. Effects of digitalization on financialization: Empirical evidence from European countries. *Technology in Society* 68:101851. https://doi.org/10.1016/j.techsoc.2021.101851.

Kvindt, A. W. 2023. Social implications of digitalization on the development of human individuality. *Theory and Practice of Social Development* 8 (184): 79–83. https://doi.org/10.24158/tipor.2023.8.9.

McLuhan, G. M. 2003. *Understanding media: The extensions of man*. (V. Nikolaev, Transl. from English; ed. by M. Vavilov). Moscow, Russia: KANON-press-C; Zhukovsky, Kuchkovo Pole. (Original work published 1964).

Myovella, G., M. Karacuka, and J. Haucap. 2020. Digitalization and economic growth: A comparative analysis of sub-Saharan Africa and OECD economies. *Telecommunications Policy* 44 (2): 101856. https://doi.org/10.1016/j.telpol.2019.101856.

Obermayer, N., T. Máhr, and Z. Banász. 2024. Social impacts of digitalisation through the lens of Hungarian experts. *European Conference on Knowledge Management* 25 (1): 562–571. https://doi.org/10.34190/eckm.25.1.2427.

Platonova, S. I. 2024. Digital technologies and society: Identity transformation. *Diskurs [Discourse]* 10 (4): 16–26. https://doi.org/10.32603/2412-8562-2024-10-4-16-26.

Stukalenko, E. A. 2021. Risks of the digitalization of life of the population and ways of decreasing them. *Ideas and Ideals* 13 (4–1): 180–203. https://doi.org/10.17212/2075-0862-2021-13.4.1-180-203.

The Digital Transformation of Diplomacy: Balancing Innovation and Risks

Vardan Atoyan and Vahram Hovyan

Abstract Digital diplomacy is a phenomenon of the twenty-first century, emerging from unprecedented advancements in telecommunications. This research aims to illustrate the characteristics and unique aspects of digital tools and programs in the diplomatic realm while exploring the associated opportunities and risks. Digital diplomacy is marked by several key features, such as openness, rapid communication, concise messaging, the dissolution of barriers between "foreign" and "internal" audiences, and a diminished significance of time and space-especially space to its implementation. Because digital diplomacy is inherently public, it is often viewed as a tool of public policy. Like any innovation, digital diplomacy offers new opportunities, such as lower financial and resource costs, faster and more efficient communication, and stronger audience connections. However, it also presents challenges, including concerns over anonymity, the risk of hacking, and a general lack of expertise in using the Internet and social media effectively. The research primarily employs qualitative methods, including observation, comparison, fact synthesis, generalization, deduction, and induction. The authors conclude that specific prerequisites must be established to enhance the effectiveness of digital diplomacy. Ultimately, digital diplomacy is not intended to replace traditional diplomacy but to complement and enrich it.

Keywords Digital diplomacy • Social media • Communication • Public diplomacy • Armenia

JEL Codes F50 • F53

V. Atoyan (✉) · V. Hovyan
Armenian State University of Economics, Yerevan, Armenia
e-mail: atoyan.amberd@asue.am; vahram.hovyan@asue.am

A. Karbekova (ed.), *Ethics of the AI Economy: A System View from the Positions of the Theory of Stakeholders*, Ethical Economy 73,
https://doi.org/10.1007/978-3-032-23423-0_17

1 Introduction

The unprecedented scientific and technological development in the late twentieth century and the beginning of the twenty-first century has entailed the large application of digital hardware and software in all areas of social and individual life. Diplomacy and foreign policy are not an exclusion. Under digital diplomacy, one understands the application of contemporary digital technologies in foreign policy. In this context, it is sometimes perceived as a part of electronic governance (Hardy 2024).

Digital diplomacy could be perceived in two senses—narrow and broad. In a narrow sense, digital diplomacy refers to the application of social networks and blogs in international politics. Many embassies now have interactive websites and Facebook accounts, and a growing number of ambassadors have an active Twitter presence (Adesina 2017, p. 9).

In a broad sense, digital diplomacy is understood as applying the Internet (Westcott 2008) and telecommunication technologies in foreign policy. From this perspective, the organization of online diplomatic measures (from simple bilateral negotiations up to largely representative diplomatic forums) is especially significant. The conduction of online diplomatic measures spread during the COVID-19 pandemic, when live touches between people were strictly restricted. For instance, the 44-day war in Nagorno-Karabagh (Artsakh) in 2020 chronologically coincided with the peak period of the second wave of the COVID-19 pandemic. Of that cause, the negotiations with Russia's intermediation were mainly conducted in an online format, and the statement about the armistice on November 9, 2020, in essence, was achieved as a result of online negotiations. Interestingly, the document was signed in a semi-online format. The Presidents of Russia and Azerbaijan signed it online, while Armenia's Prime Minister Nikol Pashinyan—offline.

After COVID-19, the practice of online negotiations and other diplomatic measures has continued so far. Drawing on the wisdom of the Armenian proverb, "There is no evil without a good," one positive outcome of COVID-19 has been its role in establishing the practice of holding negotiations, diplomatic forums, and other activities online—a trend that continues to this day. In the post-COVID-19 period, the Presidents of Russia and the USA, the presidents of Russia and China, and many other country leaders have conducted negotiations with each other in an online format. In the post-COVID-19 period, the practice of conducting diplomatic activities in a hybrid format (where some participants attend online while others participate in person) has become increasingly widespread.

Nonetheless, "the COVID-19 pandemic has exposed many challenges related to the constraints on converting diplomatic practices that depend on tacit knowledge to the use of digital tools" (Bjola 2022b; Hedling and Bremberg 2021, p. 1598). Thus, any innovation brings new possibilities and certain risks. In other words, introducing any innovation into social and individual life implies advantages (i.e., positive sides) and certain challenges (i.e., negative sides).

2 Methodology

The research is based mostly on qualitative methods, such as observation, comparison, fact synthesis, generalization, deduction, and induction. The observation method has been applied to study the behavior and the actions of diplomatic actors under the conditions of digital diplomacy, as well as to show their influence on practical politics. The authors applied the method of fact synthesis, induction, and generalization to reveal the general regularities of digital diplomacy. The deduction method has been tried to substantiate the general regularities of digital diplomacy in particular cases. The comparison method has been applied with a vertical principle to show the transformation of diplomacy over time. More specifically, this comparison aims to highlight the differences between traditional (pre-digital) diplomacy and digital diplomacy. This approach also illustrates the faster spread of advanced technologies compared to those from earlier periods.

3 Results

3.1 The Features of Digital Diplomacy

The application of contemporary digital technologies in public and individual life is getting spread among people much faster than it was in the case of formerly discovered technologies. For example, while it took approximately 75 years for 100 million people to adopt the telephone after its invention, today's digital telephones and their primary app—Facebook—reached the same number of users in just 16 years and 4.5 years, respectively (Bjola 2022a, p. 2).

In this context, Armenia, currently facing serious security challenges (Atoyan et al. 2022), continues to see Facebook maintain its dominant position among social networks. According to the latest data, Facebook has approximately 1.4 million users in Armenia, accounting for nearly half of the country's population. Instagram has about a million users, LinkedIn has around 320,000 members, and Twitter has less than 93,000 users (Wathen 2023, p. 14).

One of the characteristic features of digital diplomacy is its openness or publicity. With the adoption of digital tools, diplomacy is no longer confined to a narrow circle of professionals but has become accessible to a broader public. If, in the past, diplomatic communication was conducted through closed channels inaccessible to the general public, users of Facebook, X, Instagram, TikTok, and other social networks are increasingly engaged in and informed about diplomatic exchanges between states. In this context, digital diplomacy makes a certain impact on practical politics. For example, the Twitter/X posts of the EU Monitoring Mission deployed in Armenia have served as strong messages to Azerbaijan. Thanks to these communications, the escalation of tensions on the Armenian-Azerbaijani border has been prevented multiple times. Whenever Azerbaijan's Defense Ministry spreads false claims about alleged violations of the armistice by the Armenian armed forces, laying the groundwork for potential hostile actions, the EU Monitoring Mission, deployed exclusively on Armenian territory and without cooperation from the Azerbaijani side, refutes this disinformation through its social media channels (Barseghyan 2025). In doing so, it helps prevent escalation along the Armenian-Azerbaijani border. Thus, the activities of the EU Monitoring Mission in Armenia serve as a clear example of how digital diplomacy operates in practice. Without any official format of cooperation with Azerbaijan, using digital diplomacy the EU Observatory Mission manages to impact the actions of Baku. All of those are done publicly without the usage of official diplomatic channels. From this perspective, digital diplomacy is a form of communication that is out of the channels of traditional diplomatic communication.

In light of this, the extraordinary and plenipotentiary Ambassador of France in Armenia, Olivier Decottignies's (2024) record on his official page of X in late November 2024 in response to continuous voices from Baku statements about "Zangezur Corridor" and "Western Azerbaijan" is worthy to be mentioned.

The next feature of digital diplomacy in politics is that the application of its instruments abolishes the borders between the concepts of "foreign auditorium" and "domestic auditorium." In the past, speeches and public addresses by politicians or diplomats were intended for either a domestic or foreign audience. Nowadays, any speech aimed at a domestic audience can easily reach an international audience, potentially the entire world. Conversely, messages directed at foreign audiences are now equally accessible to the population of the speaker's country. In other words, integrating digital technologies into politics and diplomacy has effectively transformed the world into a single, unified auditorium.

Another characteristic of digital diplomacy is rapidity. If international communication and the transfer of messages between countries through traditional diplomatic channels require a certain amount of time and resources, using digital tools has reduced this process to a matter of seconds. The issue here does not regard only social network messages. Even messages or information sent by a simple email, which not at all can be public or liable to publication, reach their addressees much faster, than those sent by traditional diplomatic channels.

Another characteristic of digital diplomacy is the compactness and aptness of the sent messages. The quintessence of the content at the interviews, speeches, and press conferences of politicians and diplomats is in the context of general discourse. Therefore, to get acknowledged to that quint essential of content, it is necessary to get acknowledged to the whole interview, speech, press conference, etc. If not the leaders of countries and the heads of diplomatic services personally, then at least the corresponding services of their administrations have to do that to clean the essential material and place it at the disposal of state leaders and heads of diplomatic services. In certain countries, particular specialized institutions act for that purpose. In the Republic of Armenia, the primary institution responsible for this function is the Center for Public Relations and Information under the Administration of the Prime Minister. Previously, when Armenia had a semi-presidential system of governance, this institution operated under the Presidential Administration.

In the context of digital diplomacy, posts made on official social media pages are subject to strict regulations and limitations. For example, social platform X restricts records in the margins of certain words, not allowing records with larger sizes. In this case, the messages of politicians and diplomats are deprived of large or small context; they are clear-cut, concrete, apt, and targeted in the sense of content.

Considering this, social media networks have apparent advantages over traditional mass media. Due to its rapidity, compactness, and other characteristics, for example, social platform X is more effective than many radio and TV channels. In this sense, the observations of Elon Musk, the owner of the social network X and the world's richest person (Moskowitz 2025), are particularly noteworthy. His strong support for Donald Trump's electoral campaign has secured him a significant role in the new US administration. Recently, Musk (2025) has targeted "Radio Free Europe" radio and "Voice of America" TV channels. "Yes, shut them down. Europe is free now. It is just radical left crazy people talking to themselves," Musk wrote. Moreover, he added that mass media wastes $1 billion yearly from American taxpayers' pockets, hinting at their relatively lower effectiveness than social media sites. By these words, he reacted to a user's record, who had referred to Trump's special delegate Richard Grenell, according to which "Radio Free Europe" and "Voice of America" have become a relic of the past (Nawfal 2025).

In digital diplomacy, communication embraces not only words but also symbols and visual elements—features that are unconventional in traditional diplomatic channels. For instance, state flags are often used in place of names, likely to condense the message. Additionally, maps and photographs accompany written texts on digital platforms, enriching the overall discourse.

Another characteristic of digital diplomacy is that time and space (especially space) have lost their former significance under its conditions. With digital tools and software, it is now possible to communicate with diplomats and world leaders from anywhere in the world at any time, regardless of location. In this regard, there is a significant difference between traditional diplomacy and digital diplomacy. "Traditional diplomacy was based on representation, and the Ambassador served as a representative. The Ambassador was extraordinary because he had the power to negotiate and sign treaties on behalf of the state or the monarchy. However, in the age of information and communication technologies, in the diplomatic summitry (such as G20 meetings), leaders come together to negotiate directly. The social networking sites such as Twitter, Facebook, and Instagram enable diplomats and embassies to cooperate and communicate online" (Tilovska-Kechedji et al. 2018). Nowadays, the lack of representation does not necessarily mean a lack of communication, as MFAs, for example, can create virtual embassies instead of physical ones (Manor 2016).

3.2 Digital Diplomacy as Public Diplomacy

Since digital diplomacy is characterized by publicity, the prevailing view in professional literature is that it serves primarily as a tool of public policy (Bjola et al. 2019; Gosling 2021). According to Rashica (2019, p. 77), "Digital diplomacy is a form of new public diplomacy, which uses the Internet, new information and communication technologies (ICT), and social media as means for strengthening diplomatic relations."

Thus, the aim of digital diplomacy is not so much the facilitation of diplomats' communication in international relations, for which traditional means may also be sufficient, as much the work with the societies of other countries, the gaining of co-thinkers among them, the engagement of the citizens of other countries into their diplomatic programs, etc. Answering the question, "Why might Twitter, Facebook, Instagram, and other social media platforms be understood as having shifted public diplomacy interaction potentially even more than technological advances such as the telegram, radio, and television?", Duncombe (2019, p. 104) suggests "that to understand the emerging changes in public diplomacy practice, we must pay greater attention to the role of emotions in facilitating these transformations. Social media platforms enable emotions that can work towards developing trust between actors or undermine previously stable diplomatic relationships."

In other words, digital diplomacy is an instrument of soft power policy. Thus, Azeez characterizes diplomacy as "the established method by which states articulate their foreign policy objectives and coordinate their efforts to influence the decisions and behavior of foreign governments and peoples through dialogue, negotiations, and other such measures, short of war and violence" (Azeez 2023, p. 190). That is why digital diplomacy significantly has an information-propagandistic component. For example, Turkish diplomat Serdar Kılıç's (2023) exiting social network record on the occasion of Armenia's humanitarian aid demonstrated during the disastrous earthquake in Turkey in February 2023: "Individually, we are one drop. Together, we are an ocean." Supposedly, the addressee of these words were not so much the authorities or diplomatic servants of the Republic of Armenia but the Armenian society.

At the end of January 2025, a large-scale fire broke out in a ski resort hotel in the Turkish town of Balu, resulting in human casualties. About 80 people lost their lives (Cursino and Armstrong 2025). After this tragedy, the Prime Minister of the Republic of Armenia expressed sorrow regarding what had happened and announced his condolences and support to the victims' families on his official X page (Pashinyan 2025). These records were also addressed to Turkish society as well as to international society rather than to official Ankara.

In late 2024, an Azerbaijani civil aircraft was destroyed in Kazakhstan, resulting in the loss of dozens of lives (Cook et al. 2024). The prime minister of Armenia expressed condolences to the victims' relatives on his official social media page (Pashinyan 2024), which also addresses not only the authorities of Azerbaijan but also the society of that country and the international society. It was yet another opportunity to demonstrate to the international community and the people of Azerbaijan the commitment of Armenia to normalizing relations with Azerbaijan, concluding a peace agreement, thereby establishing a lasting peace between the two neighboring countries. As Oloo's study revealed (Oloo 2024, p. 20), "digital diplomacy enables diplomatic actors and governments to strategically present an optimistic image of their states."

Since digital diplomacy also has an informational and propagandistic component, it is not surprising that Facebook is blocked in some countries, such as Russia and China. Similarly, in the Islamic Republic of Iran, authorities decided to block Internet access during one of the recent internal political demonstrations and protests, which contributed to stabilizing the situation. Another example is Azerbaijan, where Facebook and other social media platforms (except Twitter) were blocked during the 44-day war in 2020 (Hakobyan 2021, p. 35).

3.3 *The Benefits and Challenges of Digital Diplomacy*

The abovementioned characteristics of digital diplomacy imply positive sides and some risks. On the positive side, the organization of online diplomatic events significantly reduces the time and other resources required for in-person meetings. This efficiency makes diplomatic engagements more accessible, cost-effective, and flexible, enabling broader participation from different parts of the world without the logistical challenges of travel and venue arrangements (Barman 2024, p. 73).

Viona Rashica (2019, pp. 80–84) highlights several other benefits of digital diplomacy, including (a) strengthening international relations, (b) proximity to audiences, (c) fast and effective communication, (d) low financial cost, and (e) advantages for small states. However, she also identifies several risks associated with digital diplomacy, such as (a) dependence on the Internet and social media, (b) lack of knowledge about their usage, (c) potential for disagreements, (d) the culture of anonymity, and (e) vulnerability to hacking.

Antwi-Boateng and Al Mazrouei (2021, pp. 4584–4591), analyzing the case of the United Arab Emirates (UAE), divide the challenges of digital diplomacy into two categories—Institutional and Structural. Institutional challenges are (1) organizational culture, (2) generational issues, (3) UAE media regulations, (4) personnel challenges, (5) linguistic challenges, and (6) challenges to state secrets and censorship. The category of structural challenges consists of (a) negative regional perception, (b) problems identifying and targeting an audience, (c) the fast-paced global media environment, (d) fake news from hostile sources, (e) usage by nonstate actors, (f) the culture of anonymity, (g) the risk of cyber-attacks, and (h) the technical and digital divide. Although the authors' analysis is based on the case of the UAE, its findings may apply to varying degrees in other countries as well.

4 Conclusion

Based on this research, we may conclude that effective digital diplomacy relies on three key preconditions:

- The availability of necessary infrastructure, including internet access, fast communication technologies, modern computers, and relevant software;
- Skilled personnel with the appropriate knowledge and expertise to utilize digital tools effectively;
- A new mindset that differs significantly from traditional diplomatic approaches.

Despite these advancements, digital diplomacy does not seek to replace traditional diplomacy. The latter remains relevant and serves as the primary and fundamental form of diplomatic communication (Verrekia 2017, p. 28). Instead, digital diplomacy functions as a complementary tool that enhances and supports traditional diplomacy. However, given its inherently public nature, digital diplomacy is unsuitable for transmitting classified information or confidential messages, for which traditional diplomatic channels remain indispensable.

References

Adesina, O. S. 2017. Foreign policy in an era of digital diplomacy. *Cogent Social Sciences* 3 (1): 1297175. https://doi.org/10.1080/23311886.2017.1297175.

Antwi-Boateng, O., and Kh. A. M. Al Mazrouei. 2021. The challenges of digital diplomacy in the era of globalization: The case of The United Arab Emirates. *International Journal of Communication* 15, 4577–4595. https://ijoc.org/index.php/ijoc/article/view/16150/3583. Accessed 10 Feb 2025.

Atoyan, V., S. Ohanyan, A. Malkjyan, and N. Movsisyan. 2022. On identification, identity, and security issues in modern Armenia. *Wisdom* 2 (1): 5–14. https://doi.org/10.24234/wisdom.v2i1.783.

Azeez, I. A. A. 2023. The influence of digital diplomacy on foreign policy. *Journal of Tourism Economics and Policy* 3 (3): 189–203. https://doi.org/10.38142/jtep.v3i3.770.

Barman, Sh. 2024. Digital diplomacy: The influence of digital platforms on global diplomacy and foreign policy. *VIDYA—A Journal of Gujarat University* 3 (1): 61–75. https://doi.org/10.47413/vidya.v3i1.304.

Barseghyan, A. 2025, January 9. EU monitors refute Azerbaijani claim of ceasefire violation on Armenia border. *OC Media*. https://oc-media.org/eu-monitors-refute-azerbaijani-claim-of-ceasefire-violation-on-armenia-border/. Accessed 19 Jan 2025.

Bjola, C. 2022a. Digital diplomacy 2.0: Trends and counter-trends. *Revista Mexicana de Política Exterior* 113, 1–14. https://revistadigital.sre.gob.mx/index.php/rmpe/article/view/258/240. Accessed 19 Jan 2025.

Bjola, C. 2022b. Digital diplomacy as world disclosure: The case of the COVID-19 pandemic. *Place Branding and Public Diplomacy* 18:22–25. https://doi.org/10.1057/s41254-021-00242-2.

Bjola, C., J. Cassidy, and I. Manor. 2019. Public diplomacy in the digital age. *The Hague Journal of Diplomacy* 14:83–101. https://doi.org/10.1163/1871191X-14011032.

Cook S., Ch. Livesay, and T. Reals. 2024, December 29. What caused the Azerbaijan Airlines plane crash in Kazakhstan? Here's what we know so far. *CBS News*. https://www.cbsnews.

com/news/what-caused-azerbaijan-airlines-plane-crash-kazakhstan-what-we-know/. Accessed 23 Feb 2025.

Cursino, M. and K. Armstrong. 2025, January 22. Dozens killed as fire engulfs Turkish ski hotel. *BBC*. https://www.bbc.com/news/articles/c4g375x0zpwo. Accessed 5 Feb 2025.

Decottignies, O. 2024, November 24. *Post on X*. https://x.com/O_Decottignies/status/1860701117547471024. Accessed 23 Feb 2025.

Duncombe, C. 2019. Digital diplomacy: Emotion and identity in the public realm. *The Hague Journal of Diplomacy* 14 (1–2): 102–116. https://doi.org/10.1163/1871191X-14101016.

Gosling, J. 2021. Maximising soft power: The role of digital diplomacy in building trust with nation-branding. *Global Affairs Review* 2 (1): 1–19.

Hakobyan, A. 2021. Armenian digital communications in Karabakh war of 2020: Critical discourse analysis. *Journal of Sociology: Bulletin of Yerevan University* 12 (1): 32–48. https://doi.org/10.46991/BYSU:F/2021.12.1.032.

Hardy, A. (2024). Estonia's digital diplomacy: Nordic interoperability and the challenges of cross-border e-governance. Internet Policy Review, 13(3). https://policyreview.info/articles/analysis/estonias-digital-diplomacy-nordic-interoperability. Accessed 15 Jan 2025.

Hedling, E., and N. Bremberg. 2021. Practice approaches to the digital transformations of diplomacy: Toward a new research agenda. *International Studies Review* 23 (4): 1595–1618. https://doi.org/10.1093/isr/viab027.

Kılıç, S. 2023, February 12. *Post on X*. https://x.com/serdarkilic9/status/1624737656147005442. Accessed 19 Feb 2025.

Manor, I. 2016. What is digital diplomacy, and how is it practiced around the world? A brief introduction. *Annual Review of the Diplomatist Magazine*. https://digdipblog.com/wp-content/uploads/2014/02/dig-dip-intro-diplomatist.pdf Accessed 10 Jan 2025.

Moskowitz, D. 2025, February 3 [updated 2025, April 1]. The 10 richest people in the world. *Investopedia*. https://www.investopedia.com/articles/investing/012715/5-richest-people-world.asp. Accessed 5 Feb 2025.

Musk, E. 2025, February 9. *Post on X*. https://x.com/elonmusk/status/1888574212316582230?mx=2. Accessed 18 Feb 2025.

Nawfal, M. 2025, February 9. *Post on X*. https://x.com/MarioNawfal/status/1888550915784733106. Accessed 12 Feb 2025.

Oloo, O. D. 2024. The implementation of the digital diplomacy of the United States, the UK, and China in Kenya. *Place Branding and Public Diplomacy* 20.180–191. https://doi.org/10.1057/s41254-023-00316-3.

Pashinyan, N. 2024, December 25. *Post on X*. https://x.com/NikolPashinyan/status/1871850746670629335. Accessed 5 Jan 2025.

Pashinyan, N. 2025, January 22. *Post on X*. https://x.com/NikolPashinyan/status/1882018314395992523. Accessed 15 Feb 2025.

Rashica, V. 2019. The benefits and risks of digital diplomacy. *SEEU Review* 13 (1): 75–89. https://doi.org/10.2478/seeur-2018-0008.

Tilovska-Kechedji, E., D. Rakitovan, and M. K. Bojović. 2018. Digital diplomacy in the changing world. In *International scientific conference proceedings on security, political, and legal challenges of the modern world*, ed. S. Nikoloska and A. Stanojoska, vol. I, 178–188. Macedonia: "St. Kliment Ohridski" University.

Verrekia, B. 2017. Digital diplomacy and its effect on international relations. *Independent Study Project (ISP) Collection, 2596*. https://digitalcollections.sit.edu/isp_collection/2596/. Accessed 22 Feb 2025.

Wathen, H. 2023, June 26. *Armenia between Russia and the West: Realpolitik and identity reconstruction in PM Pashinyan's Tweets* (Dissertation). Uppsala, Sweden: Uppsala University. https://urn.kb.se/resolve?urn=urn:nbn:se:uu:diva-506068. Accessed 8 Jan 2025.

Westcott, N. 2008. Digital diplomacy: The impact of the Internet on international relations. *Research Report No. 16*. Oxford, UK: Oxford Internet Institute. https://www.oii.ox.ac.uk/wp-content/uploads/old-docs/RR16.pdf. Accessed 18 Feb 2025.

Argumentation and Artificial Intelligence in Intercultural Communication

Irina I. Mitrofanova and Gong Ping

Abstract The research explores an innovative yet insufficiently studied area of artificial intelligence (AI) in intercultural argumentation. The research aims to analyze the role of AI in overcoming cultural barriers and adapting arguments to various cultural norms, a subject of particular relevance in today's globalized world. The research examines current AI development trends, its potential benefits for intercultural communication, and the ethical issues associated with its use. Special attention is given to exploring AI's capacity to support effective argumentation in intercultural discussions, particularly in overcoming language and cultural differences that often hinder mutual understanding. Specific examples of successful AI applications in various fields are provided, such as automatic translations on social media, which enable people from different countries to communicate without language barriers, and dialect research, which contributes to a deeper understanding of cultural diversity. These examples illustrate AI's significant contribution to enhancing intercultural exchange and cooperation. The authors emphasize that, in the future, AI may become not merely a tool for overcoming barriers but a powerful catalyst for a deeper understanding of cultural diversity, stimulating constructive discussions and fostering the development of global relationships based on mutual respect and comprehension. They particularly highlight the necessity of further advancing AI technologies in accordance with the principles of inclusiveness, fairness, and respect for cultural differences, which will open new horizons for intercultural exchange and cooperation, making the world more interconnected and harmonious.

Keywords Artificial intelligence · Intercultural communication · Argumentation · Cultural barriers · Ethics

---

I. I. Mitrofanova · G. Ping (✉)
RUDN University, Moscow, Russia
e-mail: mitrofanova-ii@rudn.ru

A. Karbekova (ed.), *Ethics of the AI Economy: A System View from the Positions of the Theory of Stakeholders*, Ethical Economy 73,
https://doi.org/10.1007/978-3-032-23423-0_18

JEL Codes O30 · Z13 · A14 · Z10 · A13

1 Introduction

According to P. M. Morkhat, the rapid development of artificial intelligence as an innovative technology necessitates the swift establishment of an appropriate legal framework. However, devising effective legislation is complicated without a clear understanding and unequivocal interpretation of artificial intelligence (AI) (Morkhat 2017). The application of artificial intelligence (AI) in intercultural argumentation is an important and timely area of study. In an era of globalization and expanding international interactions, AI is increasingly playing a significant role in overcoming cultural and language barriers. Particularly, AI can enhance argumentation in intercultural discussions, making communication processes more effective and precise. Yet, this advancement gives rise to a host of new challenges and ethical questions, particularly regarding the interpretation of cultural nuances and the avoidance of stereotypes.

Intercultural communication, in turn, is seen as the interaction among individuals from diverse cultural backgrounds.

According to L. N. Yasnitsky, artificial intelligence encompasses a broad range of research and development efforts aimed at creating intelligent systems designed to solve problems in areas where formal methods are difficult to apply (Yasnitsky 2008). Doctoral candidate I. G. Faizullaeva points out that artificial intelligence is one of the most dynamically evolving fields in science and technology, exerting an ever-growing influence on modern society (Faizullaeva 2024). AI covers a wide array of technologies that enable machines and programs to perform tasks that typically require human intelligence. E. Metteni and N. L. Wigel note that AI is currently infiltrating all areas of life, becoming an integral part of modern society. This highlights the particular importance of studying its role and potential in the context of intercultural interaction, especially in argumentation, where understanding and respecting cultural differences is key (Mettini and Wiegel 2024).

AI is actively penetrating various spheres of life, bringing significant benefits while also raising concerns. In healthcare, AI contributes to increased diagnostic accuracy, accelerates the development of new drugs, and helps formulate personalized therapeutic strategies. In the business and financial sectors, AI is employed for risk analysis, market trend forecasting, and enhancing the effectiveness of marketing initiatives. In the manufacturing industry, AI optimizes production processes, ensures product quality control, and refines logistics chains (Zubkov n.d.).

2 Methodology

The research methodology is based on a comprehensive approach that integrates theoretical, analytical, and empirical components. The theoretical foundation is built upon an examination of relevant theories of argumentation, artificial intelligence, and intercultural communication. The literature review aims to identify current trends and problematic areas within the subject matter. The empirical part of the research involves the application of AI algorithms, such as sentiment analysis and semantic role analysis, to a corpus of textual data to explore argumentative practices in an intercultural context. Additionally, the capabilities of contemporary language models in recognizing culturally specific nuances are evaluated, and statistical analysis is conducted to identify significant correlations. A crucial aspect of the methodological approach is the consideration of ethical issues, which includes analyzing potential biases and emphasizing the need for the development and application of AI technologies in accordance with the principles of inclusivity.

3 Materials and Methods

Many scholars have made significant contributions to the development of argumentation theory. For example, I. V. Khomenko emphasized the widespread use of argumentation in everyday life, business, law, politics, science, and education, viewing it as an essential aspect of life skills (Khomenko 2013). More concise yet equally important definitions can be found in S. Ya. Podoprigora's philosophical dictionary, where argumentation is presented as "the presentation of arguments" (Podoprigora and Podoprigora 2015), and in S. I. Ozhegov's dictionary, which defines it as "a collection of arguments" (Ozhegov 2022).

Argumentation, as the process of defending a viewpoint, has many nuances in an intercultural environment. Different cultures may have their own unique ways of constructing arguments. For instance, in some cultures, lengthy and well-reasoned discourse is valued. In others, brevity and conciseness are preferred. With properly tuned algorithms, AI can take these differences into account, helping create arguments that are better adapted to the perceptions of diverse cultures.

Effective argumentation is built upon several key elements: a thesis—the assertion to be proven; evidence—facts, examples, or data that support the thesis; and a conclusion, which logically follows from the thesis and the evidence.

In an intercultural context, the role of argumentation becomes especially significant. It plays a crucial role in the following:

1. Facilitating effective communication: overcoming language and cultural barriers to create a foundation for mutual understanding,
2. Resolving conflicts and disagreements: providing rational solutions that consider cultural differences;

3. Promoting cultural exchange and integration: showcasing cultural nuances and disseminating cultural values;
4. Supporting international cooperation and development: establishing channels for collaboration and enhancing global influence.

This research is based on a comprehensive methodology that combines theoretical, analytical, and empirical approaches. The main methods include the following.

- Theoretical analysis: the study of theories of argumentation, intercultural communication, and AI, including the works of L. N. Yasnitsky, P. M. Morkhat, and other researchers, with an emphasis on the triad "language-culture-person" and its role in intercultural interactions;
- Analytical method: the examination of philosophical and linguistic definitions of argumentation;
- Empirical methods utilizing AI: sentiment analysis to assess the emotional tone of texts (e.g., analyzing posts regarding the TikTok ban to detect negative emotions);
- Semantic role analysis to identify cultural concepts (such as recognizing key terms in arguments about the common good);
- Statistical analysis of correlations between emotional tone and the credibility of texts ($\beta = -0.45$, $p < 0.01$), confirming hypotheses about the structure of arguments for identifying cultural concepts (for instance, recognizing key concepts in arguments about the common good).
- Culturally-oriented approaches: employing a linguistic-cultural analysis to study cultural nuances, including the recognition of metaphors and pragmatic norms (e.g., interpreting the Chinese concepts of "yin and yang").
- Pragmatic and discourse analysis: revealing rhetorical strategies (such as hyperbole and appeals to authority) in texts of intercultural communication and evaluating the logical coherence of arguments using AI models (e.g., analyzing the limitations of the T5 model in recognizing cultural subtext).
- Ethical and inclusive principles: addressing the risks of algorithmic bias and emphasizing the need for fairness in the development of AI technologies; using multilingual datasets to minimize bias associated with the dominance of English-language data.

These methods have enabled the authors not only to assess the current capabilities of AI in intercultural argumentation but also to identify systemic limitations that require further research.

4 Results

J. R. Slagle notes that researchers in the field of AI strive to create computational systems that mimic behaviors considered intellectual by humans. However, he emphasizes that the concept of "intelligence" is multifaceted and largely subjective (Slagle 1973).

AI finds applications in numerous fields. In medicine, AI analyzes X-rays and MRIs to achieve more accurate diagnoses. In finance, it responds to customer inquiries and provides round-the-clock service. In transportation, AI controls autonomous vehicles, reducing the incidence of accidents. In education, it automatically grades assignments and identifies gaps in students' knowledge. In industry, AI monitors product quality using computer vision. In agriculture, it analyzes soil and crop data to enable precision farming. In culture and entertainment, AI offers personalized recommendations based on user preferences.

AI significantly enhances our lives by offering numerous benefits:

1. Personalized services: AI analyzes user behavior and preferences to deliver tailored recommendations and improved customer support. This increases customer loyalty and more effectively meets the diverse needs of the target audience;
2. Enhanced security: AI monitors network traffic and user behavior to detect potential security threats, such as cyber-attacks and malware, enabling swift protective measures;
3. Reduced operational costs: AI assists companies in optimizing resource allocation, developing effective marketing strategies, and improving operational efficiency, ultimately lowering expenses.

However, AI also has its drawbacks:

1. Data leakage risks: Training AI requires large volumes of data, which may include personal and confidential information. Improper management of this data can lead to breaches, posing a security threat;
2. Bias and algorithm inaccuracies: AI algorithms depend on the quality of the data. If the data is not objective or complete, it can result in erroneous or biased outcomes, potentially affecting service quality or even causing system failures;
3. Shortage of specialists: Developing AI requires highly skilled professionals, such as data scientists and algorithm developers. A scarcity of these specialists leads to increased costs and operational difficulties.

Moreover, AI plays an important role in intercultural communication by supporting argumentation:

1. Objective data: Statistical information, such as education levels or economic development, can bolster arguments and make them more persuasive. For example, comparing the share of investments in education across different countries can vividly illustrate cultural differences;

2. Shared values and cultural traits: Despite cultural differences, people worldwide aspire to happiness, security, and respect. These common values form the basis for effective argumentation in intercultural dialogue;
3. Professional expertise: Academic research in areas like linguistics and cultural studies helps substantiate arguments by analyzing how culture and language are interconnected in various countries. Such studies provide a theoretical foundation for intercultural discussions;
4. Effective communication methods: Respect and tolerance for cultural differences are essential for successful argumentation. It is important to avoid biased judgments of other cultures and to actively listen to others' viewpoints to create a constructive atmosphere for communication.

Thus, AI and intercultural communication are closely intertwined. Their interaction can greatly enhance the quality of communication and problem-solving in a globalized world.

The analytical part of the research employed a multi-layered approach that combined discursive, semantic, emotional, and pragmatic analysis with the application of AI algorithms.

For illustration, let us consider the following examples:

1. Analysis of a post about the TikTok ban: Sentiment analysis revealed a peak of negative emotion (intensity = 0.89) associated with words like "catastrophe" and "will die." Pragmatic analysis indicated that the author expressed emotions with exaggeration (the hyperbole "freedom of speech will die") rather than merely reporting facts. This allowed for an assessment not only of the emotional tone but also of the rhetorical techniques used in the argumentation;
2. Analysis of an argument emphasizing the priority of the common good: Automatic semantic role analysis successfully identified key cultural concepts, such as "the common good," and the rhetorical strategy of appealing to authority ("As Confucius once said…"). This demonstrates AI's capacity to recognize culturally specific elements in argumentation.

Despite these successes, the research also uncovered limitations in current large language models (LLMs). For instance, the T5 model failed to detect an implicit assumption regarding the conflict between individual and collective values, reducing the assessment of the text's logical coherence to 0.65. This reflects a systemic issue—the limited ability to interpret culturally specific subtext due to the dominance of English-language data in training corpora. Addressing this problem requires developing multilingual annotated datasets that account for the diversity of cultural contexts, including Eastern philosophical traditions and non-Western rhetorical patterns.

The research findings confirm the basic principles of Toulmin's argumentation theory (Slagle 1973). For example, markers such as "thus" not only signal the structure "data → conclusion" but also serve a rhetorical function by directing the audience's attention. Additionally, a negative correlation was found between emotionality and credibility in scientific texts ($\beta = -0.45$, $p < 0.01$), which refutes the stereotype of the "dryness" of academic style and underscores the need for a balanced use of affective elements.

There are numerous examples of successful applications of AI in enhancing argumentation. For example, in dialect research, AI can analyze phonetic, lexical, and grammatical features while processing vast amounts of dialectal speech data. Researchers at Tsinghua University used AI to analyze Chinese dialects, uncovering relationships and evolutionary patterns that have informed the preservation and protection of these dialects. Similarly, AI-powered translation tools on social media facilitate real-time message translation, fostering intercultural communication. For instance, Facebook's translators support multiple languages, easing communication among users of different tongues and reducing misunderstandings caused by language barriers. These examples attest to the positive role of AI in promoting intercultural exchange.

In the realm of intercultural exchange, AI faces cultural and linguistic barriers on various levels. At the level of language comprehension, AI may fail to capture the cultural nuances of vocabulary, as seen with Chinese concepts like "yin and yang." At the level of linguistic expression, AI might breach pragmatic norms by making direct requests where an indirect approach is expected. At the level of cultural values, AI can exhibit biased understanding due to incomplete or unobjective training data. Lastly, at the level of nonverbal communication, AI may not grasp the significance of cultural symbols, such as gestures and patterns. These shortcomings can lead to misunderstandings and misinterpretations.

To overcome the language barriers that AI may introduce in intercultural argumentation, several measures should be undertaken. First, it is essential to enrich data sources by creating a corpus of texts containing argumentation from diverse cultures, including scientific articles, legal documents, and other materials. Second, integrating a module to enhance logical reasoning into AI algorithms would allow for a more precise analysis of arguments. Finally, employing virtual reality technologies to model intercultural discussions will help AI adapt to various styles of communication and thought.

5 Conclusion

AI holds tremendous potential to transform intercultural communication, including the realm of argumentation. Its capacity to process and analyze vast amounts of data opens up new possibilities for a deeper understanding of cultural differences, enhancing communication effectiveness and resolving conflicts between cultures. However, despite its many advantages, the use of AI in intercultural argumentation faces several challenges. These include issues with translation accuracy, the interpretation of cultural contexts, and the risk of reinforcing biases and stereotypes derived from incomplete or unobjective data.

One of the primary avenues for improving the application of AI in intercultural argumentation is the enrichment of training data by incorporating a broader spectrum of cultural texts and materials. Equally important is the development of algorithms capable of accounting for cultural nuances and pragmatic norms, as well as the creation of virtual platforms where intercultural interactions can be simulated. These measures will help reduce linguistic and cultural barriers, ensuring more precise and respectful interactions.

Thus, in the long run, AI could become a tool for overcoming intercultural barriers and a catalyst for a deeper appreciation of the world's cultural diversity, the fostering of constructive debates, and the development of global relationships. It is crucial that AI technologies continue to evolve in alignment with the principles of inclusivity, fairness, and respect for differences, opening new horizons for intercultural exchange and cooperation.

References

Faizullaeva, I. G. 2024. "Artificial intelligence" and humanity's achievements and challenges. *Oriental Renaissance: Innovative, Educational, Natural and Social Sciences* 4 (5): 815–823.

Khomenko, I. V. 2013. Theoretical problems in informal logic: Conflicts of viewpoints. *Epistemology & Philosophy of Science* 3:85–99.

Mettini, E., and N. L. Wiegel. 2024. The interaction of artificial intelligence and human culture: An anthropological approach to technological development. *Naukovedcheskie issledovaniya [Scientific Studies]* 2:50–70. https://doi.org/10.31249/scis/2024.02.04.

Morkhat, P. M. 2017. On the issue of defining artificial intelligence. *Law and State: The Theory and Practice* 12 (156): 25–38. https://doi.org/10.31857/S013207690003666-4.

Ozhegov, S. I. 2022. In *Explanatory dictionary of the Russian language by*, ed. L. I. Skvortsov. Moscow, Russia: World and Education.

Podoprigora, S. Ya., and A. S. Podoprigora. 2015. *Philosophical dictionary*. 3rd ed. Rostov-on-Don, Russia: Feniks.

Slagle, J. R. 1973. *Artificial intelligence: The heuristic programming approach* (A. E. Voyskunsky, & B. A. Pozin, Transl. from English). Moscow, USSR: Mir. (Original work published 1963).

Yasnitsky, L. N. 2008. *Introduction to artificial intelligence: Textbook*. 2nd ed. Moscow, Russia: Akademiya.

Zubkov, M. n.d.. Artificial intelligence in the real world: From medicine to creativity. *Dzen*. https://dzen.ru/a/Z9kei76NeV7RwqS9. Accessed 27 Oct 2023.

The Ethics of Machine Learning in the AI Economy from the Perspective of Stakeholder Theory

Problems and Contradictions of the Introduction of AI Systems into Contemporary Pedagogy

Elena V. Gryaznova, Svetlana V. Pronina, Olga Yu. Bagadaeva, Zhanna V. Smirnova, and Victoria A. Polyanskaya

Abstract The research aims to identify and systematize the main problems and contradictions of introducing and applying AI systems in contemporary pedagogical activity. The main research methods used were analytical review, analysis, comparison, generalization, and the system approach. During the research, the authors found that there are quite a lot of studies on the problems of implementing AI systems in the field of education. Moreover, they are poorly systematized. As a rule, researchers write about the problems of education, paying less attention to the other two components of pedagogical activity—training and education. The research introduces an approach to systematizing the contradictions and challenges in the interaction between natural and artificial intelligence. This approach is based on three core components of pedagogical activity: the formation of information, praxeological culture, and axiological culture. These elements develop through a dialectical process in which individuals acquire knowledge, skills, and a system of values during socialization.

Keywords Digital economy • Artificial intelligence • Education • Training • Upbringing • Digital pedagogy • Contradictions of artificial intelligence

JEL Codes O330 • Z13 • L86

E. V. Gryaznova (✉) · Z. V. Smirnova · V. A. Polyanskaya
Minin Nizhny Novgorod State Pedagogical University, Nizhny Novgorod, Russia
e-mail: z.v.smirnova@mininuniver.ru

S. V. Pronina
National Research Lobachevsky State University of Nizhny Novgorod, Nizhny Novgorod, Russia

O. Y. Bagadaeva
Irkutsk State University, Irkutsk, Russia

A. Karbekova (ed.), *Ethics of the AI Economy: A System View from the Positions of the Theory of Stakeholders*, Ethical Economy 73,
https://doi.org/10.1007/978-3-032-23423-0_19

1 Introduction

We are witnessing great discoveries and inventions in the digital era. Our civilization is moving towards creating new entities capable of performing many human functions, surpassing them in many parameters if possible. This process is already irreversible. The digitalization of the economy requires the digitalization of almost all types of human activity. This means that natural intelligence will have a worthy assistant and a competitor sooner or later.

Artificial intelligence (AI) systems are becoming an integral part of today's society. Their emergence and development are due to the constant desire of people to strengthen and improve their physical and intellectual capabilities. The creation of AI has caused a wide discussion in all areas of scientific knowledge. Simultaneously, its implementation does not stop and only improves. In the economic sector, this process is associated with introducing high technologies in production. In the field of pedagogy, AI is primarily used as an innovative technology in education and the spiritual activity of the person.

When AI systems are introduced into the field of pedagogy, they perform several functions while entering into many contradictions, each of which gives rise to a whole range of problems. Research into these problems and the search for their solutions are conducted in all branches of scientific knowledge. Each science and scientific branch offers its own solutions.

It is necessary to apply a typological analysis of the contradictions and problems associated with introducing AI into pedagogical activity. This research aims to study and systematize these contradictions and problems.

2 Methodology

To identify the main problems and contradictions of the use of AI in the system of pedagogical activity, the work used an analytical review of scientific papers devoted to contemporary problems of AI in education of all forms and levels.

Scientists pay the greatest attention to the potential of using AI in the field of transferring and assimilating knowledge in the pedagogical process. Researchers highlight such positive opportunities as, for example, increasing the interactivity of the process of acquiring knowledge, which increases students' motivation to learn (Antoshko 2024; Samsonova 2024).

Scientists pay special attention to opportunities to facilitate a teacher's work when he or she can transfer routine operations (e.g., paperwork, checking standard assignments, monitoring academic performance, monitoring student attendance and activity in classes, etc.) (Baranova 2024; Zhunussov 2024).

Among the problems, researchers name the need to systematize the documentary and legislative framework regulating the use of AI in education management (Skatova 2024).

As the primary concern about using AI in education, researchers have named the crossing of certain boundaries in transferring the functions of a repeater, teacher, consultant, and creator of educational content from a person to an artificial assistant (Petrenko and Levina 2024). According to scientists, total automation of the educational process will decrease the quality of education (Gryaznova et al. 2023, 2022).

The process of generating educational content by AI systems also raises concerns. No matter how advanced the technologies used for this function are, there is a danger of low quality in checking texts and data for truth and reliability (Gromova and Soroka 2024).

The current problems of introducing AI into pedagogical activity include the problem of education. The lack of emotional contact with a person in the learning process impoverishes the educational functions of education. In some situations, it reduces them to a minimum or excludes them altogether (Semenova et al. 2024; Suetina 2024).

The most actively discussed problem in the field of pedagogy is the reduction of the level of natural intelligence when transferring many educational functions and tasks to AI systems (Akimova 2024). Particularly, researchers point to the possibility of reducing critical thinking because AI systems do not have their own value system like a person and do not generate it according to the program. Additionally, by turning to AI for help in working with text, students stop constantly training their speech and thinking, ultimately leading to the possible degradation of these functions.

The information flow, which increases due to the use of new technologies in education, also leads to undesirable consequences. Innovative training of teaching staff is becoming especially relevant (Demidova et al. 2024; Zakharova and Kudryavtseva 2024). AI systems provide access to an unlimited amount of information, in which the student is not always able to navigate correctly. To find rational ways to select the necessary information, a person algorithmizes his creative activity, starting to perform it like a machine, cutting off the human factor in this activity (Gerashchenko 2024).

Scientists associate a special place in studying the problems of introducing AI systems into the field of education with issues of information security and legal regulation of relations between natural and artificial intelligence (Gryaznova 2024; Huang 2023).

Thus, it can be seen that the current problems of introducing AI systems into education are quite diverse and require a strictly scientific approach to systematization and typology, which will help to find effective solutions based on a systems approach.

3 Results

To justify the choice of the basis for the typology of current problems of introducing AI into the pedagogical process, it is necessary to determine the main reasons for its emergence and development. AI as a phenomenon is defined based on the understanding of natural intelligence. In other words, the word “intelligence” is key. In the most general sense, intelligence is the ability of a subject who possesses it to think, assess a situation, solve assigned tasks, and make a choice in decision-making. Intelligence is inherent to humans and other entities.

The distinctive feature of human intelligence from the intelligence of other living beings is its ability to think abstractly and reflect the world in concepts and terms. Additionally, humans have the highest form of consciousness, speech, communication, and activity. The process of human cognition of the surrounding world and their subjective world has been studied well. However, it is still far from the moment when it will be possible to recreate it as close to the original as possible. Nowadays, scientists model natural processes of cognition. Nevertheless, the results are still ambiguous. Any neural network is inferior to humans in the ability to find solutions to problems in the shortest way. The so-called “heuristics” and “intuition,” which are characteristic of human cognitive activity, are difficult to model.

Humans have the highest form of consciousness, subconsciousness, and unconsciousness. Many information processes occur outside the field of consciousness and are not reflected by it. However, they take part in solving intellectual and cognitive problems. The mental level of the subjective world of humans is complex and cannot yet be formalized. This aspect is extremely important for finding effective technologies for teaching natural intelligence and creating models of AI systems based on it. Subjective reality cannot be measured like elements of physical reality. The so-called “hard problem of consciousness” remains unsolved.

In addition to solving problems, natural intelligence also interacts with the outside world. One way or another, natural intelligence performs three main information processes—transmission, processing, and storage of information. The information essence of intellectual activity makes it possible to create technical objects—analogs that perform these three main operations with information. During civilizational development, humanity sets itself the task of strengthening its intellectual abilities, solving them throughout the history of its existence. The creator’s goal, in which case a person acts, is to free from monotonous, routine, and complex intellectual activity. Among the first inventions of intellectual assistants were calculating devices (from the abacus to computers) designed to process information. As these devices grew more complex, it became necessary to automate calculations and the storage and transmission of information. This need led to innovations such as the telegraph, telephone, radio, and computer. Currently, humanity has achieved the highest level of automation and technologization of its intellectual functions, though it is not yet at the ultimate stage.

Human intellectual activity develops in the process of technologization of the reality in which we live and act. Initially, it determined the development of those generic qualities distinguishing people from other entities. In social and humanitarian knowledge, consciousness, language, activity, and communication are distinguished among them. These qualities are responsible for the integrity of the human essence. However, they are the ones that are primarily subject to duplication in AI systems. Indeed, during the development of digital technologies, people gradually transfer the functions of interaction between our kind to AI systems. We can already say with confidence that many roles of a person in one or another activity are performed by his "digital twins." In communication systems, service areas, etc., such a substitution has already become quite common when a person enters into communication with AI, receiving the necessary information, advice, etc.

In education, as in any other information activity, there is an opportunity to use AI to perform the function of communication. Consequently, the generic human quality of being able to transmit information in a particular language may be lost, as the need for this may sooner or later disappear as AI can fulfill this function. A person's language reflects their style and level of thinking. All generic qualities of a person are interconnected and are transformed as a systemic phenomenon. Thinking, consciousness, speech, and activity develop due to the development of human intellectual abilities. What will happen if this development stops because the need for it disappears? These assumptions have been expressed by teachers and psychologists for a long time because this relationship between the strengthening of AI and the weakening of natural intelligence is the subject of research in modern science.

Pedagogy, as a sphere of activity on transferring social experience from one generation to another, is as susceptible to technological innovations as any other field. Throughout human evolution, we have continually tackled the challenge of expanding our consciousness. As an information phenomenon, consciousness develops and grows more capable over time. When we change our communication style, language, and activities, collaborating with AI systems, our consciousness evolves as well, expanding to create new, alternative realities that foster creativity. As researchers note, by changing the style of speech, communication, and activity, we also change our consciousness. This means that the forms and methods of creating an image of the world (i.e., education) must change. For example, traditional education (paper technologies) set itself the goal of giving a person as much knowledge as possible, forming a wide range of skills and a worldview ideal. The task of education was to prepare a person for life in the reality that corresponds to a certain picture of the world. It had the ability to be an inert system because the worldview itself changed quite slowly, and having received an education, a person had the opportunity to use its results for many years.

With rapid technological development, lifestyles are evolving faster than individuals can learn. People can no longer rely solely on their existing knowledge; they must continuously expand their consciousness. In the digital age, a person needs a flexible mind, strong intelligence, and the capacity to adapt their communication, thinking, and actions throughout life. This continual adaptation inevitably renders outdated forms of social interaction obsolete. Consequently, pedagogical practices must evolve to reflect these fundamental changes in human capabilities.

What are the main requirements of a digital society for the pedagogy system? First, this is forming an extended personality, in which the biological essence is familiar to a person, and a new essence—a digital one capable of effectively interacting with AI systems—should remain. Second, the transfer of functions of informing and monitoring the assimilation of information from the teacher to AI systems. Third, freedom of choice for a person depends on the trajectory of education, training, and upbringing.

Using the systematization method, the authors will build a matrix reflecting the main problems of introducing AI into pedagogy. The basis should be the main contact point between natural and artificial intelligence. To do this, it is necessary to keep in mind that the process of pedagogical activity is represented by three main subsystems (Fig. 1).

The figure shows that the structure of pedagogical activity consists of three main elements: education (knowledge system), training (skills and abilities system), and upbringing (value system). In the socialization process, each of them forms a certain subsystem of the personality culture (informational, praxeological, and axiological). In the figure, double arrows show the dialectical relationship between the elements. Of course, this scheme is quite conditional and helps present pedagogical activity clearly for ease of analysis.

Based on the presented figure, it can be seen that the main problems of introducing AI into education can be typologized by the structure of the pedagogical process. Thus, it is necessary to consider the problems associated with the deformation of the transfer of knowledge from the teacher to the student and the subsequent work of the student on turning information into knowledge. There are many such options, dividing them by the degree of inclusion of artificial intelligence in this process. Consequently, these challenges can be grouped into distinct categories. One category concerns the development of a person's information culture in interactions with artificial intelligence. Similarly, issues related to forming a praxeological culture can be identified as a separate type—for example, assessing the effectiveness of teaching specific activities using artificial intelligence systems. Finally, forming an axiological subsystem within human culture encompasses ethical concerns and the shaping of worldviews as artificial intelligence systems become increasingly integrated into the educational process alongside natural intelligence.

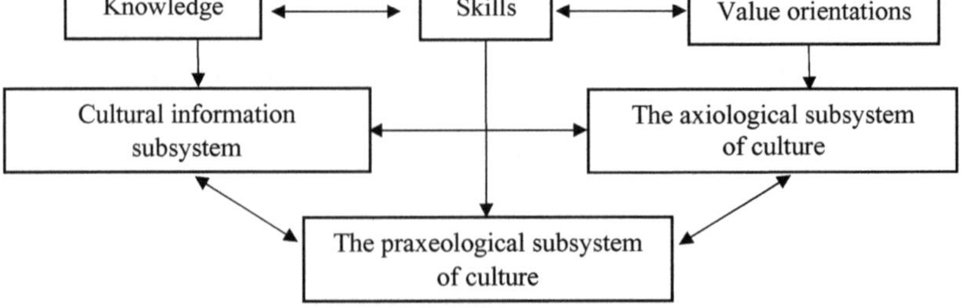

Fig. 1 The system of pedagogical activity. *Source* Compiled by the authors

4 Conclusion

During the research, the authors conclude that to implement a systemic approach to studying the problems of introducing AI into pedagogy, it is necessary to proceed from the structure of the pedagogical process. It is divided into three main mechanisms: forming an individual's praxeological and axiological information culture. These elements are dialectically interconnected. However, the automation of the process of transferring knowledge, skills, and value systems can occur separately, depending on the degree of integration of artificial intelligence into pedagogical activity.

This approach makes it possible to typologize the problems of interaction between artificial and natural intelligence in the pedagogical process as separate research areas, which facilitates the identification of problems of a certain type and the search for their solution.

References

Akimova, N. V. 2024. Problems and challenges that faces system of education in the era of neural networks and artificial intelligence. In *Theory and practice of teaching foreign languages: Traditions and development prospects: Proceedings of the IX international scientific and practical online conference of students and young scientists*, ed. N. Д. Galskova, 8–11. Moscow, Russia: State University of Education.

Antoshko, V. A. 2024. Application of machine learning and artificial intelligence technologies in education. In *Digital region: Experience, competencies, projects: Collection of articles of the VI International scientific and practical conference dedicated to the 25th anniversary of the Institute of Engineering and Economics, held as part of the decade of science and Technology in Russia*, ed. O. D. Kazakov, N. Yu. Azarenko, and O. N. Yurkova, 863–867. Bryansk, Russia: Bryansk State Technological University of Engineering.

Baranova, M. A. 2024. The use of artificial intelligence technologies in the field of education. In *Innovative scientific research 2024: Collection of materials of the LIV-th international correspondence scientific and practical conference, in 2 volumes*, vol. Vol. 1, 13–17. Moscow, Russia: Empire.

Demidova, N. N., I. V. Golovina, T. Yu. Medvedeva, G. A. Paputkova, and A. V. Votintsev. 2024. Modeling project activities for future teachers within the innovative infrastructure of pedagogical universities: Integrative solutions. *The Education and Science Journal* 26 (9): 12–41. https://doi.org/10.17853/1994-5639-2024-9-12-41

Gerashchenko, I. G. 2024. Artificial intelligence in education: Problems of application. *Studia Humanitatis* 2.

Gromova, N. S., and K. I. Soroka. 2024. Artificial intelligence in higher education: Problems and prospects. *Theory and Practice of World Science* 6:14–16.

Gryaznova, E. V. 2024. The dialogue of theology and law in Russian science and education. *Gosudarstvo i Pravo [State and Law]* 4:186–191. https://doi.org/10.31857/S1026945224040177.

Gryaznova, E. V., A. V. Vorokhobov, A. G. Goncharuk, S. M. Maltseva, and D. V. Semikopov. 2022. Antimetaphysical strategies in the Western European philosophy of the modern times. In *Cooperation and sustainable development*, ed. A. V. Bogoviz, A. E. Suglobov,

A. N. Maloletko, and O. V. Kaurova, 479–486. Cham, Switzerland: Springer. https://doi.org/10.1007/978-3-030-77000-6_57.

Gryaznova, E. V., I. A. Treushnikov, I. A. Lanskaya, N. N. Kuimova, and E. M. Kochneva. 2023. Contradictions and problems of modern digital education in the Russian economy. In *Reimagining socioeconomic development of Russia: New directions, theory, and practice*, ed. M. L. Alpidovskaya, L. A. Karaseva, and E. G. Popkova, 539–548. Charlotte, NC: Information Age Publishing.

Huang, L. 2023. Ethics of artificial intelligence in education: Student privacy and data protection. *Science Insights Education Frontiers* 16 (2): 2577–2587. https://doi.org/10.15354/sief.23.re202.

Petrenko, T. F., and N. N. Levina. 2024. Artificial intelligence in education: Problems and prospects. *Professional Communication: Topical Issues of Linguistics and Methodology* 17 (1): 67–73.

Samsonova, P. I. 2024. The role of artificial intelligence in university education. *Bulletin of the Plekhanov Russian University of Economics: Introduction. The Path to Science* 14 (2): 147–149.

Semenova, L. E., V. E. Semenova, N. V. Karpushkina, and I. A. Koneva. 2024. Age-specific perception of fabbing. *Vestnik of Minin University* 12 (1): 8. https://doi.org/10.26795/2307-1281-2024-12-1-8.

Skatova, M. 2024. Assessment of requirements of regulatory documents on the use of artificial intelligence in higher education. *Technoeconomics* 3 (2): 22–33. https://doi.org/10.57809/2024.3.2.9.2.

Suetina, Yu. S. 2024. Artificial intelligence in the field of education: Problems and prospects. In *Economics and innovation: A collection of articles by participants of the interuniversity scientific and practical conference, in 3 volumes*, 119–124. Moscow, Russia: Plekhanov Russian University of Economics.

Zakharova, V. T., & Kudryavtseva, I. S. (2024). Spiritual and moral features of training master's students: Social and humanitarian aspect. *Relações Internacionais no Mundo Atual [Brazilian Journal of Law and International Relations]*, 4(46), 60–77. https://revista.unicuritiba.edu.br/index.php/RIMA/article/view/7239/371375130. Accessed 11 Mar 2025.

Zhunussov, Ye. M. 2024. The role of artificial intelligence in modern education: Advantages, challenges and pathways to success. *Vestnik of M. Kozybayev North Kazakhstan University* 2 (62): 180–188. https://doi.org/10.54596/2958-0048-2024-2-180-188.

The Boundaries of the Applicability of Artificial Intelligence

Ilya N. Volnov

Abstract The author examined four groups of constraints on the applicability of artificial intelligence (AI). The first group includes material resources for storing large data sets, which impose resource limitations on AI. The second group includes the computational capabilities of software code, where the fundamental constraint of AI is the incomputability of the human brain. The third group includes a set of space-time conditions governing computational procedures, which unfolds into six types of constraints: AI as a time-closed system with a degraded future, AI as a time-closed system with both a degraded future and past, the heterogeneity of G. B. Minkowski's space-time, the biological space-time of V. I. Vernadsky, Kairos, and real time. The fourth group includes the civilizational conditions of social development, where the limit of AI is defined by Vernadsky's Noosphere. When this scheme of AI constraints is applied to human consciousness, it becomes possible to more precisely delineate the "boundary" between natural intelligence and human thought. Thought is defined as the aspect of consciousness that transcends mere intelligence and directs the development of humans and AI. A natural framework for the interaction between humans and AI emerges from this definition.

Keywords Artificial intelligence • Space • Time • Information • Natural intelligence • Thought • Noosphere • Past • Future • V. I. Vernadsky

JEL Codes C88 • O330

I. N. Volnov (✉)
Moscow Polytechnic University, Moscow, Russia

A. Karbekova (ed.), *Ethics of the AI Economy: A System View from the Positions of the Theory of Stakeholders*, Ethical Economy 73,
https://doi.org/10.1007/978-3-032-23423-0_20

1 Introduction

Natural scientific thought has a distinctive tendency not to reflect upon its own limitations. Consequently, science constantly makes unjustified extrapolations, such as the "heat death of the Universe," its stationarity, technological singularity, etc. Artificial intelligence (AI), spawned from this type of thinking, is likewise unjustifiably extrapolated to virtually all forms of human activity, while the boundaries of AI's applicability are scarcely scrutinized. In this regard, science contradicts another of its fundamental tenets, namely, the modeling of its own representations of reality. Within these representations, the creation of any model must be accompanied by a clear definition of the domain in which that model applies. Within that domain, the use of the model is justified; outside it, the model is deemed inapplicable. AI stands as a striking exception to this rule. As nothing more than a specific model of natural intelligence, AI is employed without any requirement to delineate the limits of its applicability—a practice that is physically unsound and, in the author's view, potentially dangerous. For example, an experiment has been underway in the educational system for several years, aimed at developing individualized educational trajectories for students based on their digital footprints and utilizing AI.

Let us define the boundaries of AI's applicability, bearing in mind that AI is a computational procedure defined by software code, implemented on large data sets, and actualized by society at a particular stage of its development (within a specific cultural context). We can distinguish four groups of AI boundaries:

- The material resources supporting AI and large data;
- The computational capabilities of software code;
- The space-time conditions of the computational procedure;
- The noospheric limit of AI within the framework of V. I. Vernadsky's teachings.

2 Methodology

2.1 Boundary of Material Support for AI and Big Data

Big data inevitably relies on a material carrier, which, ultimately, is the entire information and communications network known as the Internet. Nowadays, the Internet has evolved into a phenomenon of planetary scale. It is important for further discussion to note that the Internet is inherently confined by this planetary scale.

Unlike the scientific modeling approach (where the meaning encapsulated in a model compresses vast amounts of information into forms accessible to human understanding, sometimes called "deep data"), AI tackles problems quantitatively, using big data that lies beyond the cognitive capabilities of modern humans. An adage for AI holds true here: "there is never too much big data"—there is always too little. This also implies that the material support for these vast datasets will always be insufficient. Eventually, we will face a fundamental resource constraint similar to the limitations on the planet's fossil resources.

2.2 *Boundary of Computational Capabilities of Program Code*

The limits of Moore's empirical law, which predicts a doubling of computing power every 18 months, are widely debated. Moore noted that this law faces a fundamental constraint due to the atomic nature of matter and the speed of light. Some estimates suggest that its applicability may cease by 2025 (Pozdnyak 2023). The primary counterargument to this cessation is quantum computing, often touted as the next technological revolution. However, as demonstrated by R. Penrose, classical and quantum computers are essentially "Turing machines" or finite automata; all limitations inherent to finite automata apply to them (Panov 2013), the most significant being incomputability. Penrose asserts that the human brain exhibits incomputable activity, which cannot be detected or analyzed using contemporary physics, including its quantum aspects since modern physics is inherently computable. From this, he predicts that a new branch of physics, one that incorporates incomputability, will eventually emerge and that the primary, if not the sole, tool for discovering and constructing it will be the human brain, not AI. We leave the question of whether AI can be built upon this new, incomputable physics as a speculative matter. It can be revisited once such a physics is discovered.

2.3 *Spatial and Temporal Limitations of the Computational Procedure*

2.3.1 AI as a Time-Locked System with a Degraded Future

Let us begin with the well-known argument that AI is confined to the past through big data, which exists solely within that temporal mode. From this simple fact, it follows that AI dwells in a degraded time—a time devoid of a future mode or one in which the future is merely an extension of the past. All that AI can do is manipulate the past combinatorially; any novelty can only emerge as a new combination of previously known data. It is impossible to generate something that is absent from past experience. A fitting metaphor is that AI tries to drive a car forward while looking only in the rearview mirror; this approach inevitably leads to a crash.

Let us take the next logical step by invoking the second law of thermodynamics, which states that the entropy of a closed system cannot decrease, meaning that it is doomed to degradation as order diminishes. While thermodynamics considers system closure in terms of space, in the case of AI, we fix it in time. However, given the unity of space and time, these forms of closure can be equated. Consequently, the AI system is destined for degradation, regardless of the constant influx and expansion of big data. The informational entropy of AI can only increase, while the degree of informational order, defined as the clear separation between truth and falsehood, will inevitably decrease. Over time, this separation loses its clarity, becoming blurred as truth and falsehood become indistinguishable. In the early stages of this blurring, humans are still capable of recognizing these differences. However, it is possible to predict that further conflation will eventually reach a point where humans can no longer discern truth from falsehood. In this context, we define a human as a being who consumes information in which truth and falsehood are distinctly separated. That separation is the hallmark of human information; without it, the information becomes inhuman; by consuming such information from AI, humans are dehumanized.

2.3.2 AI as a Time-Locked System with a Degraded Future and Past

Developing this logic leads to even starker conclusions. Let us consider the contemporary understanding of space and time as a four-dimensional continuum, as proposed by G. B. Minkowski. In this understanding, time is treated as a fourth spatial coordinate. In this model, time is stripped of its uniqueness and defined through spatial categories that are not inherently its own (Bergson 2021). Since space is perceived only in the present mode, this mode becomes central to the perception of time. The Minkowski model, as well as all subsequent constructs based on it, portrays time as an extended present. The mode of the present is absolutized; it shapes our perception of the other temporal modes. This results in the phenomenon of the future as an extended present and the past as a present that stretches backward. Within this logic, vivid concepts of the future (e.g., "The End of History" by F. Fukuyama and the "Technological Singularity" by R. Kurzweil) become conceivable. This also underlies the well-known problem of the complexity of historical reconstructions and the impossibility of fully comprehending the past because it is always perceived through the lens of the present.

The Minkowski model, which serves as a foundation for modern physics, is equally fundamental to AI. This implies that the process of forming AI's big data takes place in a degraded time—an extended present that stretches forward and backward. Thus, AI presupposes a double degradation of time:

- During the formation of big data within an extended present;
- In the operation of AI within an extended past.

2.3.3 The Heterogeneity of G. B. Minkowski's Space-Time

The Minkowski model, which unifies space and time into a single continuum, is based on the mathematical definition of the invariance of the interval between events in the combined space-time under transitions between inertial frames, as specified by Lorentz transformations. A direct analogy is drawn between the distance between two points in Euclidean space and the interval between two events in unified space-time, while any other characteristics of space-time beyond those necessary for Lorentz transformations are disregarded. Let us now consider these additional features.

The Minkowski model contains a fundamental paradox: it combines a simple, symmetric space (with left-right and up-down symmetry) with a complex, irreversible, and thus asymmetric time (lacking symmetry between the future and the past). This paradox can be seen as one of the causes behind the contradictions and failures of many scientific constructs, including the futile attempts to develop a unified field theory (Berkovich 2020) and, even more so, a comprehensive or unified scientific worldview (Vitol 2007). It may also be regarded as a limitation on AI, suggesting one of the reasons why AI cannot work with the concepts of unity and wholeness and, consequently, cannot simulate the phenomenon of consciousness.

2.3.4 V. I. Vernadsky's Biological Space-Time

At the beginning of the last century, alongside Minkowski, A. Bergson proposed an alternative view of time (Bergson 2021), which was later developed by V. I. Vernadsky in his teachings on biological time and space (Aksenov 2022; Vernadsky 1988). In these perspectives, time and space are united in a different, more natural way—through an understanding of the complexity of both while preserving the uniqueness of each component of the unified space-time. In this framework, time remains time; the future still represents the possibility of something new and different, not predetermined by past experience.

Vernadsky points out that physics has adopted a simplified conception of time as homogeneous, linear, and purely quantitative based on the ease of mathematically describing mechanical motion. In this view, a moving body is represented as a mathematical point; its structure and the processes occurring within it are deemed unimportant and unrelated to time; it is always possible to identify a moment when the body's mass remains constant, thus justifying the use of integral-differential calculus.

According to Vernadsky, living matter is characterized by biological time, which cannot be represented as a mathematical point. No part of a living organism mirrors the whole, as its integrity is what imparts meaning. Time arises from within the living and manifests through it. In fact, time intervals are produced by the living matter at varying rates depending on internal processes. It is impossible to pinpoint a moment when the mass of living matter remains unchanged; hence, the tools of integral-differential calculus are inapplicable to the description of the living.

Apparently, AI is defined within a mechanical, linear, external, and dead space-time. In contrast, human consciousness (and the human being) exists within a biological, heterogeneous, internal, and living space-time. Can AI transition from the dead to the living? This transition is forbidden by the Redi principle, "The living arises only from the living." Vernadsky expands and refines this principle, asserting that life cannot emerge from inert matter; it is neither accidental nor random but lawful, continuous, and eternal. Life is a cosmic phenomenon, and consequently, the cosmos is alive (Vernadsky, 1988, p. 210). This means that AI will never be able to attain the level of consciousness, for consciousness is an expression of the living. AI is confined to the realm of intellect—the aspect of consciousness that reveals itself in pursuing a mechanical, linear, external, dead space-time (this does not contradict the Redi principle: the inert can arise from the living, not vice versa). Another part of consciousness, namely thought, manifests itself in opposition to the intellect; it always remains in the biological, heterogeneous, internal, and living space-time.

2.3.5 Kairos

Another limitation of AI is a form of time well known since ancient times yet entirely forgotten in modern scientific thought. This is Kairos—the auspicious moment of the ancient Greeks—a qualitative time that divides life into "before and after," imposes irreversibility, and disrupts the symmetry between future and past. Contemporary science, as noted, treats time as homogeneous, quantitative, and only conditionally irreversible (since irreversible processes are, with few exceptions, described using reversible mathematical tools). The modern philosophical counterpart to Kairos is the concept of spontaneity, about which V. V. Nalimov writes, "We must ascribe to spontaneity the status of a philosophical category… we are compelled to acknowledge that it is one of the most challenging categories to understand. It is challenging because it must manifest itself outside the chain of cause and effect, and because it lies beyond conventional temporal notions, for in spontaneity decisions always involve a leap forward, a blending of the future with the past; and finally, because spontaneity appears to us as a transpersonal principle that, in an inexplicable way, unites the personal and the universal, thereby establishing the unity of the World in its creative unfolding" (Nalimov, 2007, p. 255). Because spontaneity cannot be ignored while its nature remains elusive, the scientific worldview has resorted to the concept of randomness—as an attempt to explain the erratic behavior of a very simple, elemental, and mechanical event. In reducing the spontaneous to the merely random, its very essence is lost. Randomness may be incorporated into AI, but spontaneity (and therefore Kairos) remains an inaccessible form of time for AI, marking a fundamental limitation.

2.3.6 Real Time

In his teachings on biological time and space, V. I. Vernadsky introduces yet another concept—instantaneous time (Aksenov 2022). This concept can be equated with the Greek Kairos. In their existence, humans always contend with three forms of time: mechanical, biological, and instantaneous. Continuing the line of thought of A. Bergson and V. I. Vernadsky (Aksenov 2022; Bergson 2021) regarding the existence of a real time distinct from that of modern science, the authors propose defining it as a combination of mechanical, biological, and instantaneous time. Thus, real time turns out to be spiral in nature. Within the spiral, we have the following:

- The linearity of physical time, directed toward a goal;
- The cyclicity of biological time, which ensures balance and equilibrium;
- The temporal shift (Kairos) or the transition from one turn of the spiral to the next, as the condition for knowledge and progress.

From the previous discussion, it is clear that real spiral time is inaccessible to AI, although it employs some of its individual elements. Particularly, elements of cyclic time are present in the recursive computational procedures of AI, while aspects of temporal shift (Kairos) appear in the use of randomness in Bayesian and evolutionary algorithms (Domingos 2016).

3 Noospheric Limit of AI

Let us draw another parallel between the concepts of dead and living space-time. AI can be seen as the ultimate generalization of the informational capabilities of the contemporary scientific worldview, with its space-time specificity that leads to the atomization of all processes in society, the alienation of humans from external and internal nature, the confinement of humanity within the planet, and the portrayal of the Cosmos as an environment hostile to man. In V. I. Vernadsky's view, this ultimate generalization is embodied in the doctrine of the Noosphere—as the collective mind of all humanity, in which the personal and the social, the human and the natural, the terrestrial and the cosmic are in harmony. It is clear that within the noospheric worldview, AI does not arise as a total technology for transcending human limitations. Therefore, the noosphere stands as a fundamental limitation of AI.

4 AI as the Ultimate Realization of the Principle of Separation

AI is the technology for implementing the principle of division, transferred to human intellectual activity for automating its processes. This is precisely how Western European civilization has developed industrially over the past 300 years; the principle of division is embedded in all fundamental socio-system activities: the separation of powers in governance, the division of labor in production, and the disciplinary fragmentation of the unified nature in science and education. As mentioned earlier, natural scientific thought has a characteristic tendency to make unjustified extrapolations, which is fully manifested in its application of the principle of division and in AI technology. There exists a strong yet fallacious viewpoint in the field of technogenic civilization that everything can be divided, simplified, and, consequently, automated. However, proponents of this view face two major stumbling blocks: the phenomena of life and consciousness. Science has so far failed to synthesize artificial life or simulate consciousness. According to V. V. Nalimov, science remains an enhanced version of I. Newton's mechanism—even in fields such as general systems theory and synergetics: "… in synergetics, which emerged among thermodynamicists, mechanism dominates, albeit in a different status, becoming unstable and unpredictable. Accordingly, in this framework, stability and equilibrium prove to be evolutionary dead ends" (Nalimov, 2013, p. 118). Thus, the mechanistic images of such science are inapplicable to describing life and consciousness.

Alternative images, more befitting an organism than a machine, are needed. At the beginning of the last century, V. I. Vernadsky attempted to shift the mechanistic scientific worldview toward one of organicity by developing theories of living matter, the biosphere, the noosphere, and biological space-time. Simultaneously, special and general relativity and quantum mechanics were being developed. One can speak of humanity reaching a "bifurcation point" during this period—a choice between the scientific views that would define the twentieth century: between the refined mechanism of relativity and quantum mechanics and the view of the living as the foundation of the scientific picture of the world, as proposed by V. I. Vernadsky. The choice was made in favor of a refined mechanism; the organicity of Vernadsky's teachings was ignored. As a result, we entered the Postmodern era, marked by the total deconstruction of everything within reach, the abolition of hierarchical principles replaced by network structures, the removal of the concepts of Beauty and Truth from public discourse, and the emergence of the phenomenon of Post-truth, in which truth and falsehood become blurred and indistinguishable. AI is a complete reflection of Postmodernism in the intellectual activity of humanity.

Despite the localized successes of AI technology, the overall crisis of civilization suggests that Postmodernism will soon wane and society will transition to the next stage of development. In this process, AI is also likely to lose its dominant position in public consciousness. We can only hope that the error made at the beginning of the last century will not be repeated and that civilization will choose a future "for all," based on humanity—encompassing the full spectrum of its cognitive abilities, ultimately comparable to the Cosmos.

5 Natural Intelligence, Thinking, and Consciousness

The boundaries of AI, as outlined above, are significant for understanding AI and comprehending natural intelligence, thought, and consciousness. If we project this system of AI limitations onto human consciousness, we can distinguish within it a confined realm of natural intelligence and another aspect that transcends it—what is commonly referred to as thought. Thought may be characterized as the mind's potential to transcend its own limits. This potential lies outside of intelligence, which, when considered in isolation, strives for measurable increases in efficiency through simplification, restriction, economy, division, averaging, and the like. Left to operate solely on its own, intelligence eventually becomes self-contained, rapidly exhausts its limited resources, stagnates, and inevitably degrades and atrophies. One of the underlying causes of the contemporary general crisis of civilization clearly resides in this domain, and therein also lies the key to overcoming this crisis: the activation of that part of consciousness responsible for thought, which stands in opposition to intelligence. Several important conclusions follow from this statement.

6 Results

1. An attempt to reduce human thought to mere intelligence inevitably leads to the stagnation and degradation of the individual and civilization, spawning transhumanist scenarios in which the "truncated" natural intelligence is doomed to lose against AI;
2. Thought that transcends intelligence is the essential condition for the development of that intelligence, both in humans and in AI;
3. Since AI does not possess thought, it is carried solely by humans; the advancement of AI can only be sustained through continuous interaction with humanity. In other words, man is the perpetual and insurmountable prerequisite for AI's development;
4. Owing to thought, humans always retain the leading role over AI, even if they currently fall short in solving a wide range of intellectual tasks at this stage of evolution.

7 Conclusion

The author formulated a total of nine limitations on the use of AI, divided into four groups that delineate the domain where AI is applicable and the realm where it should not be employed. This work may and should be continued, with the boundaries of AI's applicability being described more precisely, comprehensively, and profoundly. The importance of this work is proportional to the extent of AI technology's proliferation and the resources invested in it. Its significance is also fundamental to the major challenge of the twenty-first century (and possibly of all past and future human endeavors)—the "hard problem of consciousness," for which AI is one of the approaches to its solution. The development of AI, coupled with a clear definition of its limits, will contribute to resolving this issue.

References

Aksenov, G. P. 2022. *V. I. Vernadsky on the nature of time and space*. Moscow, Russia: Lenand.

Bergson, A. 2021. *Duration and simultaneity*. Moscow, Russia: Dobrosvet; KDU.

Berkovich, E. 2020. The tragedy of Einstein, or happy Sisyphus. Essay two. Einstein versus Pauli. Unified field theory. *Science and Life* 2: https://www.nkj.ru/archive/articles/38053/. Accessed 10 Oct 2023.

Domingos, P. 2016. *The master algorithm. How the quest for the ultimate learning machine will remake our world.* Moscow, Russia: Mann, Ivanov & Ferber. (Original work published 2015).

Nalimov, V. V. 2007. *The spontaneity of consciousness: Probabilistic theory of meaning and the meaning architectonics of personality*. 2nd ed. Moscow, Russia: Aquarius Publishers.

Nalimov, V. V. 2013. *In search of other meanings*. St. Petersburg; Moscow, Russia: Center for Humanitarian Initiatives.

Panov, A. D. 2013. The technological singularity, Penrose's theorem on artificial intelligence, and the quantum nature of consciousness. *Meta* 3 (9): 141–187.

Pozdnyak, A. 2023. What is Moore's Law and does it work now. *Men Today*. https://www.mentoday.ru/technics/gadgets/chto-takoe-zakon-mura-i-rabotaet-li-on-teper/. Accessed 10 Oct 2023.

Vernadsky, V. I. 1988. *The philosophical thoughts of a naturalist*. Moscow, USSR: Nauka.

Vitol, E. A. 2007. The scientific picture of the world and the exploration of the future. *Credo New* 7:6. https://credonew.ru/content/view/620/59/. Accessed 1 Feb 2024.

The Dialectic of Artificial and Natural Intelligence in the Context of Digital Civilization

Elena V. Gryaznova, Svetlana M. Maltseva, Svetlana V. Pronina, Olga Yu. Bagadaeva, and Zhanna V. Smirnova

Abstract The research aims to analyze the phenomenon of artificial intelligence (AI) as the most important element of contemporary digital civilization in dialectical unity with natural intelligence. One of the main research methods used was the method of analytical review of scientific literature on the issues and problems of AI development in various areas of public life, as well as the dialectical method and principles of dialectics. To build a matrix of dialectical analysis of AI as a phenomenon of digital civilization, the authors turned to the methodology of the sphere approach. The study of the possibility of constructing a matrix of dialectical research of AI showed that the basis for its construction should be the contradictions that arise between natural and artificial intelligence in various areas of public life of the digital civilization. This approach makes it possible to build the main directions of studying AI as a system of dialectical contradictions, revealing the possibility of its comprehensive study in the field of economic, political, social, and spiritual relations in the digital civilization.

Keywords Digital civilization • Artificial intelligence • Natural intelligence • Economics • Social management

JEL Codes L86 • O330 • Z13

E. V. Gryaznova (✉) · Z. V. Smirnova
Minin Nizhny Novgorod State Pedagogical University, Nizhny Novgorod, Russia
e-mail: z.v.smirnova@mininuniver.ru

S. M. Maltseva
Minin Nizhny Novgorod State Pedagogical University, Nizhny Novgorod, Russia

Nizhny Novgorod Institute of Railway Engineering – Branch of the Volga State University of Railway Engineering, Nizhny Novgorod, Russia

A. Karbekova (ed.), *Ethics of the AI Economy: A System View from the Positions of the Theory of Stakeholders*, Ethical Economy 73,
https://doi.org/10.1007/978-3-032-23423-0_21

1 Introduction

The relevance of studying the role of artificial intelligence (AI) as an integral element of contemporary digital civilization is caused by a range of contradictions. The main ones are the contradictions between artificial and natural intelligence in various areas of public life.

Nowadays, there are quite a lot of areas of AI research. They are conducted in the field of natural, technical, social, and humanitarian sciences. Each branch of scientific knowledge reveals a certain aspect of studying this phenomenon. However, there is a certain gap between these areas, which consists in the fact that the goals of technical and natural sciences do not always coincide with the goals of social and humanitarian knowledge in the research of the same subject—AI. An integrating approach is needed in these studies, which makes it possible to form a unified picture of the dialectical contradictions between AI and its creator—natural intelligence.

The research aims to explore the possibilities of compiling a matrix of dialectical analysis of the main contradictions that arise in the relationship between artificial and natural intelligence in the context of the rapid development of digital civilization.

The relevance of the research topic can be expressed by several provisions. First, it is necessary to systematize the available research results of AI of various branches of scientific knowledge in the system of digital civilization. Second, it is important to substantiate the application of the dialectical method, which makes it possible to identify the contradictory and ambivalent nature of AI as the basis for human development of the future.

2 Methodology

The choice of the dialectical method as a research methodology is determined by its topic and subject. This methodology includes the principles and laws of dialectics, equipping the researcher with the appropriate categorical apparatus and tools. Dialectics involves studying any phenomenon, process, or relationship as a unity of contradictory components. Conducting an analytical review of the literature on the studied issues that determine the research subject, the authors showed that most scientists conclude that AI has an ambivalent character. Most studies show that the main problems of AI development lie precisely in its opposition to natural intelligence.

S. V. Pronina
National Research Lobachevsky State University of Nizhny Novgorod,
Nizhny Novgorod, Russia

O. Y. Bagadaeva
Irkutsk State University, Irkutsk, Russia

The concept of digital civilization is widely used in the system of scientific knowledge (Chernavin and Barinova 2023). Various definitions of this phenomenon are given in publications. Nevertheless, it is possible to identify the general, typical in the cited approaches in understanding this phenomenon. The essence of digital civilization is determined based on the technologies that underlie its evolution. Based on this provision, digital information technologies should be recognized as such. They will allow humanity to move to a new progressive level of development. Nowadays, when talking about digital civilization, scientists define it as a type of social structure where the paradigm of direct human interaction is being replaced by a new paradigm of social relations—relations mediated by digital information technologies. These technologies make it possible to talk about the digitalization of all areas of public life when almost all relations in society become digital. AI systems are becoming an important and integral part of the new paradigm of social relations in the digital civilization.

Nowadays, AI systems are being introduced into all areas of public life. It has become a common fact that AI is used in production, especially where a high-tech level of management with minimal human participation at all stages is required: planning, implementation, control, correction, and decision-making (Aliakseyeva and Bao 2024). Legal areas of activity are also beginning to widely use the practice of working with documents and consulting clients based on the use of AI (Pascali 2024). In medicine, AI systems are used to work with patients, make diagnoses, conduct treatment courses, and even conduct surgical interventions (Eminov et al. 2023). AI is most actively used in space and military activities, where remote human participation is required (Krasnoslobodtsev et al. 2024). Such areas as education, science, management, etc., cannot do without turning to high-tech AI systems in today's conditions (Skatova 2024).

With all the progressive development of AI and its invaluable assistance to humans in all areas of life in today's digital society, there are contradictions between two phenomena—artificial and natural intelligence (Gryaznova et al. 2022). These contradictions bring to life several problems that are solved as they arise in one way or another. However, not all solutions have a positive effect. Some of them can "freeze" the situation and cause an even more aggravating effect. One of the reasons for this situation is that the creators of AI systems ignore the philosophical analysis of dialectical contradictions between natural and artificial intelligence, as two contradictory forms of thinking matter. Such contradictions become a source of problems in spiritual and moral education and the subject of research in pedagogical, psychological, theological, and other humanities sciences (Semenova et al. 2024; Zakharova and Kudryavtseva 2024).

3 Results

If we turn to the history of the development of AI, then one of its prototypes can be called the invention of the first computers, when people thought about strengthening their physical and intellectual abilities (Shvidko 2024). Why electronic computers, and not, for example, primitive calculating devices? It's all about automating computing processes (i.e., processing, transmitting, and storing information). The fact is that the very phenomenon of "thinking" is defined as the ability to perform computational operations quickly because this function of natural intelligence was automated in the first place.

The computational functions of natural intelligence have been automated using digital technology, first called electronic computing machines, and then computers. Nowadays, digital technologies have advanced far in development; we are already talking about complex sociotechnical AI systems. The functions of such systems are quite wide and high-tech. The advantages and positives of such systems, as well as their necessity and indispensability in today's life and the economy of a single country and on a global scale, are apparent. Scientific discussions are sparking precisely about the possible negative consequences of introducing AI systems into human life.

The first problem that researchers write and talk about, especially sociologists who process statistical data, is unemployment. This process historically accompanies the development of technology, which is one of the basic reasons for the transition of civilization from one level of development to another. In this case, the source of many problems is the contradiction between old and new technologies, which inevitably displace a person and their physical and intellectual capabilities from technological processes. This contradiction is resolved by the departure of old professions and their replacement with new ones. At one time, such relevant professions in industrial society as telephone operators, stenographers, secretaries-typists, accountants, etc., were lost, and the functions of these professionals, holders of natural intelligence, were displaced by digital devices in the era of informatization. Digitalization and AI introduced into the economic sector threaten the loss of jobs for such specialists as bank operators and many holders of accounting specialties. Such specialists as administrators, communicators, and representatives of "manual" professions, such as drivers, cashiers, cleaners, general workers at factories and plants, secretaries, librarians, sorters, cleaners, dispatchers, etc., may also find themselves without work. They are being replaced by new professions that require acquiring new skills. The distinctive feature of the upcoming innovations is precisely the activity associated with interaction with artificial intelligence systems. The displacement of obsolete specialties occurs due to dialectical laws and is accompanied by the creation of new professions that require new knowledge, skills, and abilities (Kotov 2024).

In the economic sector, AI comes into conflict with natural intelligence, which leads mainly to the progressive development of humankind; in military activity, it also contributes to an increase in the risks of the threat of cyber warfare. Nowadays, we have witnessed a similar situation when military operations are reduced to a confrontation between the AI systems of the warring parties (Clauberg 2020).

Moreover, AI systems are not limited to the field of application of uncrewed aerial vehicles, remotely controlled vehicles, etc. However, they are being increasingly used for cyber-attacks on the life support of the warring party or the state. Nowadays, the term "cyber terrorism" is used quite often, which implies acts of terror against specific individuals, communities, companies, and countries. People, or rather natural intelligence, become the main target of such acts. The consequences manifest themselves in creating industrial, transport, political, economic, and other types of collapses and crises. Being used as a tool, AI can be used for good and for evil.

In this case, the dialectic of artificial and natural intelligence manifests itself as a negative resolution of the conflict of contradictory phenomena. Cybercrimes are increasingly occurring in the banking and financial sectors, as well as in trade (Dostov 2022).

Humanitarians and philosophers express their concerns about the possibility of AI physically destroying natural intelligence. This scenario of future development is becoming increasingly realistic. The level of the development of AI is already so high that it is fully capable of independent decision-making. As is known, decision-making is one of the elements of managerial activity. This means that the threat of AI enslaving natural intelligence is no longer a fantasy. People are already enslaved by technology, even at the level of everyday life. He became addicted to "smart technology."

These concerns are increasingly heard from the lips of theologians and church representatives (Gryaznova 2024). Thus, from the speech of His Holiness Patriarch Kirill of Moscow and All Rus', it follows that the intellectualization of advanced technology leads humanity to the loss of spirituality, which is the essence of man. The loss of the spiritual component in people's lives is the path to the end of human history (Patriarchia [Official website of the Russian Orthodox Church] 2012).

Thus, based on the analytical review of works devoted to the problems of the development of AI, we can definitely state that the source of the main problems in its development and influence on people and society is the contradiction between natural and artificial intelligence. The dialectical method makes it possible to build a system of contradictory relationships that must be studied by the entire complex of scientific knowledge.

The dialectical unity of natural and artificial intelligence should be considered as belonging to both polarities to the whole that they constitute. There are a lot of such dialectical "triples." Each such triple, being subjected to dialectical analysis, reveals a whole range of certain qualities, relationships, and processes between all elements. To systematize the analysis of possible contradictions between natural and artificial intelligence, the authors propose proceeding from the matrix of spheres of public life. In the most general form, there are quite a lot of them. However, socio-humanitarian knowledge have already established certain provisions in allocating the so-called main types of activities. In general, there are four main areas: economic, political, social, and spiritual. Further, dividing these areas into separate areas makes it possible to create a more detailed structure. Here are possible dialectical triples aimed at revealing the dialectics of natural and artificial intelligence. For clarity, the authors will present them in the form of diagrams (Fig. 1).

Using the proposed matrix, it is possible to systematize the directions and aspects of research on the interaction of natural and artificial intelligence. Here is an example of such an analysis based on the spiritual sphere of society.

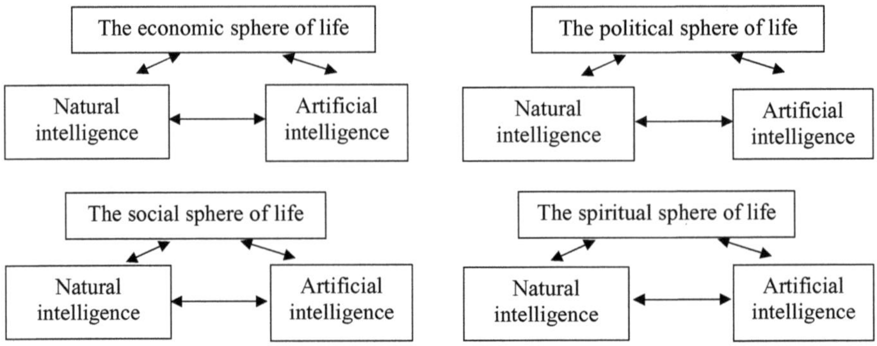

Fig. 1 The dialectic of the relationship between natural and artificial intelligence based on the spheres of public life. *Source* Compiled by the authors

The spiritual sphere is the most difficult to understand because it is not always represented in the form of clearly defined elements. Most often, such components as education, science, religion, etc., are listed in its composition (Gryaznova et al. 2023). However, there are also such areas as the soul, consciousness, and subjective reality, which cannot be represented as something clearly understood and described (Kanaev and Dryaeva 2024). If, when analyzing the dialectics of natural and artificial intelligence as the unity of the human spiritual world, we turn to such areas of activity as education, then we can build the following system of relations for research:

1. The impact of AI in education on natural intelligence;
2. The impact of natural intelligence in education on AI;
3. The interaction of natural and artificial intelligence in the field of education;
4. The influence of natural intelligence in the field of education on the development of the spiritual sphere of society;
5. The influence of artificial intelligence in the field of education on the development of the spiritual sphere of society.

These are far from all possible relationships that need to be explored to understand the impact of AI on the further development of the spiritual life of society. The authors identified only those that "lie on the surface." However, there are also many such problems and issues in this area that require a deeper understanding of the human soul. Science has advanced far in this direction. However, such issues as the essence of human consciousness are still not fully understood. Simultaneously, the dialectic of natural and artificial in this field poses the following questions to science:

- Can AI repeat and completely replace human consciousness?
- Can AI continue to exist without humans?
- Is it possible to transfer human consciousness to another material medium, etc.?

These and other questions require answers.

4 Conclusion

During the research, the authors substantiated that the dialectic of artificial and natural intelligence in the context of the development of digital civilization is the basis for the progressive technological evolution of humankind. The introduction of AI systems into all areas of public life leads to changes in people as beings created by nature. However, it is precisely the dialectical unity of artificial and natural intelligence that becomes the basis for the emergence of new phenomena. In particular, fundamental changes are occurring in each sphere of public life. The economic sector is being built in the digital age based on human-technical systems, where information processing already requires the use of AI to a greater extent than natural intelligence. In the field of management, AI systems also become preferable when it is necessary to process a large amount of information and make quick decisions. The social sector, responsible for communication between social actors in society, has practically moved from direct interaction to a new paradigm of digital social relations. The spiritual sphere is also undergoing digitalization; progress in this direction is less significant than in other types of activities. In this case, the dialectic of natural and artificial is expressed in the unity and struggle of two forces—the forces of nature and the forces of people. Having surrounded itself with a world of its own invention, humanity is faced with the inevitability of further resisting its creation. What the result will be is the main question of science. A digital person is a person of the future; it is a phenomenon with an incomprehensible fate that requires research from a wide range of scientific knowledge. The dialectical approach will make it possible to systematize the existing results and predict possible options for developing digital humanity.

References

Aliakseyeva, A., and Yu. Bao. 2024. Big data and artificial intelligence technologies in HR management. In *Education and science in the 21st century: Articles of the VIII international scientific and practical conference*, 42–45. Vitebsk, Belarus: Vitebsk State Technological University.

Chernavin, Yu. A., and G. V. Barinova. 2023. A man in the space of digital culture. *Voprosy filosofii [Questions of Philosophy]* 4:29–39. https://doi.org/10.21146/0042-8744-2023-4-29-39.

Clauberg, R. 2020. Cyber-physical systems and artificial intelligence: Chances and threats to modern economies. *World Civilizations* 5 (3–4): 107–115. https://wcj.world/PDF/03aECMZ320.pdf. Accessed 11 March 2025.

Dostov, V. V. 2022. Modern threats of illegal use of artificial intelligence systems. *Bulletin of the Tyumen Institute for Advanced Training of employees of the Ministry of Internal Affairs of Russia* 2 (19): 44–49.

Eminov, R. I. U., A. E. U. Latibjonov, and S. D. Q. Umarova. 2023. Artificial intelligence technologies in medicine. *New Day in Medicine* 3 (53): 20–24.

Gryaznova, E. V. 2024. The dialogue of theology and law in Russian science and education. *Gosudarstvo i Pravo [State and Law]* 4:186–191. https://doi.org/10.31857/S1026945224040177.

Gryaznova, E. V., A. V. Vorokhobov, A. G. Goncharuk, S. M. Maltseva, and D. V. Semikopov. 2022. Antimetaphysical strategies in the Western European philosophy of the modern times. In *Cooperation and sustainable development*, ed. A. V. Bogoviz, A. E. Suglobov, A. N. Maloletko, and O. V. Kaurova, 479–486. Cham, Switzerland: Springer. https://doi.org/10.1007/978-3-030-77000-6_57.

Gryaznova, E. V., I. A. Treushnikov, I. A. Lanskaya, N. N. Kuimova, and E. M. Kochneva. 2023. Contradictions and problems of modern digital education in the Russian economy. In *Reimagining socioeconomic development of Russia: New directions, theory, and practice*, ed. M. L. Alpidovskaya, L. A. Karaseva, and E. G. Popkova, 539–548. Charlotte, NC: Information Age Publishing.

Kanaev, I. A., and E. D. Dryaeva. 2024. Artificial intelligence: Prospects for consciousness emergence. *Voprosy filosofii [Questions of Philosophy]* 11:38–50.

Kotov, D. V. 2024. The impact of artificial intelligence on the labor market and professions of the future. *Innovative Science* 6-2:25–33.

Krasnoslobodtsev, V. P., A. V. Raskin, and I. V. Tarasov. 2024. Risks and benefits of artificial intelligence in the military. *Artificial intelligence. Theory and Practice* 1 (5): 64–68.

Pascali, M. 2024. Critical aspects of the use of artificial intelligence in the legal profession. *Works on Intellectual Property* 51 (4): 153–157. https://doi.org/10.17323/tis.2024.23979.

Patriarchia [Official website of the Russian Orthodox Church]. 2012. The word of His Holiness Patriarch Kirill at the opening of the XVI General Russian National Council. https://vrns.ru/documents/vystuplenie-svyateyshego-patriarkha-moskovskogo-i-vseya-rusi-kirilla-na-otkrytii-xvi-vsemirnogo-russ. Accessed 11 Mar 2025.

Semenova, L. E., V. E. Semenova, N. V. Karpushkina, and I. A. Koneva. 2024. Age-specific perception of fabbing. *Vestnik of Minin University* 12 (1): 8. https://doi.org/10.26795/2307-1281-2024-12-1-8.

Shvidko, E. A. 2024. The emergence of artificial intelligence. In *Development of the Russian school of management: Theory and practice: Proceedings of the scientific and practical conference of students*, ed. T. A. Afanasyeva, 234–236. Novosibirsk, Russia: Novosibirsk State Agrarian University.

Skatova, M. 2024. Assessment of requirements of regulatory documents on the use of artificial intelligence in higher education. *Technoeconomics* 3 (2): 22–33. https://doi.org/10.57809/2024.3.2.9.2.

Zakharova, V. T., and I. S. Kudryavtseva. 2024. Spiritual and moral features of training master's students: Social and humanitarian aspect. *Relações Internacionais no Mundo Atual [Brazilian Journal of Law and International Relations]* 4 (46): 60–77. https://revista.unicuritiba.edu.br/index.php/RIMA/article/view/7239/371375130. Accessed 11 Mar 2025.

Methods of Annotating Russian Spoken Speech Using Large Language Models

Oxana V. Goncharova, Svetlana A. Deryabina, and Tatyana A. Dyakova

Abstract This research describes methods for annotating Russian spoken speech using machine processing of linguistic materials. For the first time, the concept of "annotation" is defined as a method of data processing and interpretation based on a given code involving information compression through special linguistic paraphrasing algorithms. The authors analyzed traditional approaches to phonemic and orthographic markup, along with their limitations in conveying allophonic variability inherent in the Russian language. Special attention is paid to the challenges of automatic annotation, including the choice of labels (phonemic, acoustic, or orthographic), which complicates corpus compatibility. The authors discussed advanced annotation tools (e.g., the Montreal Forced Aligner) and considered their limitations in modeling key phonological processes of Russian, including vowel reduction and consonant assimilation. The necessity of metadata standardization and adaptive ontologies that account for diachronic differences in the approaches of the Moscow and St. Petersburg phonological schools is emphasized. Moreover, the authors examined promising methods for overcoming these challenges, including multimodal architectures for processing dialectal variations, the integration of semantic models (BERT) to resolve homophony, and the use of deep neural networks (Conformer) for context-dependent speech analysis. The research concludes on the importance of creating benchmark corpora with expert annotation and designing end-to-end architectures integrating spectral feature extraction with deep semantic contextualization to improve the quality of automatic phonetic annotation.

Keywords Annotation • Automatic phonetic transcription • Phonetic annotation • Phonological process modeling • Phonemic and allophonic markup

O. V. Goncharova · S. A. Deryabina (✉)
RUDN University, Moscow, Russia
e-mail: goncharova_oxvl@pfur.ru; deryabina-sa@rudn.ru

T. A. Dyakova
Derzhavin Tambov State University, Tambov, Russia
e-mail: tdyakova@tsutmb.ru

A. Karbekova (ed.), *Ethics of the AI Economy: A System View from the Positions of the Theory of Stakeholders*, Ethical Economy 73,
https://doi.org/10.1007/978-3-032-23423-0_22

JEL Codes C88 • D83 • I21 • O33

1 Introduction

Advances in information technology have revolutionized linguistic research, particularly in the analysis of spoken language. The interest in spoken speech analysis is primarily due to the fact that "communication between people, which is mediated by language, is carried out through its sound aspect and relies on it" (Zinder, 1979, p. 4).

As an independent discipline, phonetics has traditionally employed a wide range of experimental methods such as palatography, linguography, oscillography, and spectral analysis. With the development of digital technologies, new speech-processing tools have emerged, including automatic annotation systems. Automatic phonetic transcription and phonetic annotation allow for the structuring of audio data, synchronizing text with speech signals, and analyzing acoustic parameters. However, existing methods have limitations due to pronunciation variability, the complexity of the Russian phonetic system, and the need for precise time alignment.

This research explores advanced methods for annotating Russian spoken speech using large language models (LLMs). Particular attention is given to hybrid and neural network approaches that automate transcription, alignment, and speech analysis. The research examines tools such as Montreal Forced Aligner, Gentle, WebMAUS, and Kaldi. Moreover, the authors consider advanced deep learning architectures, including Conformer and transformer models.

This research aims to determine the most effective methods for annotating Russian speech and identify promising directions for further research in this area.

2 Literature Review

As a branch of linguistics, phonetics has always employed extensive experimental research methods compared to other linguistic disciplines. Various methodologies have been utilized, including palatography and linguography, complex oscillographic methods, and the use of magnetic separators for phonetic research (Vysotskiy 1977). Specialized software like PRAAT and Articulate Assistant Advanced remain staples within the phonetic research community.

In the study of spoken speech, the shift from analog recordings (Bryzgunova 1980; Loginova 2017) to digital formats has streamlined data acquisition, archiving, and computational analysis. Specialized datasets have emerged, allowing for large-scale spoken speech analysis without manual transcription. Additionally, electronic dictionaries for endangered languages have been developed (e.g., Lingvodoc platform).

The ability to extract, process, and apply information efficiently has made data one of the most valuable resources for linguistic research, with annotation serving as a critical method for ensuring effective data exchange and minimizing processing time (Zhilinskaya and Choporova 2015, p. 81).

The systemic analysis and processing of linguistic data, combined with applied linguistics, have become an independent field of knowledge focusing on automated information compression in natural language processing. This requires the development of specialized annotation tools. Current tools for text data processing include text mining and data mining, which convert unstructured text into structured formats (Belenkiy 2008).

Therefore, the linguistic concept of "annotation," when applied to machine processing of language materials, takes on a new meaning and is regarded as a method of data processing and interpretation based on a specified code. In spoken speech analysis, information compression is associated with selecting acoustic parameters that enable the grouping of sounds spoken by different speakers into phonemic categories. In this context, paraphrasing involves choosing an appropriate graphical representation of these phonemes.

A key challenge in automatic speech annotation lies in determining the appropriate unit for annotation: phoneme, grapheme, letter, or even allophones of a phoneme. The tendency to standardize deep learning approaches favors phonemic transcription. However, different linguistic schools interpret phonemes differently. Thus, relying solely on phonemes may limit the analysis of phonetic nuances. A possible solution is dual-level machine annotation within a unified coordinate system.

Another challenge is the selection of a consistent graphical representation for phonemes. According to linguistic theory, the "minimal unit of written language that represents a phoneme is a grapheme" (Bogomazov, 2001, p. 178), a term first introduced by I. A. Baudouin de Courtenay. Graphemes can be represented by letters, letter combinations, or other graphic means. In phonetic transcription, traditional symbols are used, but discrepancies exist in the literature regarding their standardization.

3 Materials and Methods

During the research, the authors used various methods, including the analysis of scientific publications on the problems of machine processing of linguistic materials, particularly methods of automatic phonetic processing, and the application of advanced tools for speech data alignment and phonetic transcription.

The research is based on analyzing existing automatic speech annotation systems and their applicability to the Russian language. The main tools used included the following:

- Montreal Forced Aligner (MFA), a hybrid architecture combining Hidden Markov Models (HMM) with Deep Neural Networks (DNN). It enables the automation of text-to-audio alignment and is widely used in linguistic research;
- Gentle, a real-time speech-processing system optimized for dynamic applications. It employs Gaussian Mixture Models (GMM) in combination with HMM, ensuring efficient real-time performance;
- WebMAUS, a tool for automatic speech and text alignment based on HMM-GMM models, using predefined phonetic dictionaries and statistical modeling methods;
- Kaldi, a modular speech processing platform that supports various models, including HMM-GMM, DNN, and CNN, as well as lattice structures for selecting optimal alignments.

To evaluate the annotation quality, the authors tested audio corpora of the Russian language, including phonemic and allophonic level markup. The research compared various approaches: traditional statistical models, hybrid methods (DNN-HMM), and end-to-end architectures based on deep neural networks.

The main parameters for assessing annotation efficiency included the following:

- Accuracy of time alignment: the system's ability to correctly determine the boundaries of phonemes and words;
- Quality of phonetic transcription: the correspondence of predicted phonemes to the International Phonetic Alphabet (IPA);
- Algorithm performance: data processing speed and computational costs;
- Robustness to phonetic variability: the ability of models to adapt to different accents and speech styles.

4 Results

Automatic phonetic transcription (APT) and phonetic annotation (PA) are key areas in the field of speech technologies, providing the conversion of an acoustic signal into a structured linguistic representation. APT involves translating a speech signal into a sequence of symbols corresponding to phonemes or allophones (e.g., in the International Phonetic Alphabet, IPA). PA solves the problem of temporal synchronization of text with the audio stream, establishing boundaries of phonemes, words, or prosodic events such as stress or tone. These methods are used in speech synthesis (TTS), where precise articulation is critical for natural-sounding speech; in automatic speech recognition (ASR), where accounting for phonetic variations improves accuracy; in linguistic research for dialect and articulatory phonetics analysis; and in educational technologies for automatic pronunciation correction (Jurafsky and Martin 2020; Taylor 2009).

The evolution of automatic phonetic processing methods reflects the general trend in artificial intelligence (AI) development: from early rule-based systems and statistical models such as Hidden Markov Models (HMM) and Gaussian Mixture

Models (GMM) to advanced neural network architectures. Deep learning has overcome the limitations of traditional approaches, such as the inability to account for long-range contextual dependencies and sensitivity to noise. For example, hybrid DNN-HMM systems have replaced GMM with neural networks for probability estimation, significantly improving the accuracy of acoustic modeling (Hinton ct al. 2012).

Today's aligners, which solve the problem of temporal alignment of text with an audio signal, operate through a sequence of interconnected stages. The first stage – audio preprocessing—involves segmenting the signal into frames of 20–40 ms with a step of 10 ms, which is due to the quasi-stationary nature of the speech signal. Over this interval, spectral characteristics remain relatively stable (Rabiner and Schafer 2007). For each frame, acoustic features are extracted, such as MFCC (Mel-Frequency Cepstral Coefficients), which approximate human auditory perception through a bank of mel filters or spectrograms obtained using Short-Time Fourier Transform (STFT) (Hannun et al. 2014).

WebMAUS Basic is an automated speech-to-text alignment system developed within the Bavarian Archive for Speech Signals (BAS) project. It demonstrates a typical approach to solving the problem of temporal synchronization of a predefined text with an audio recording. As seen in the TextGrid example (Fig. 1), the WebMAUS processing workflow is implemented through a three-level annotation hierarchy, reflecting the sequential transformation of orthographic text into quasi-phonetic segments. This tool, based on hybrid HMM-GMM models, does not perform full phonetic transcription in the IPA standard, which highlights the fundamental difference between automatic alignment and linguistic interpretation of spoken speech.

In Fig. 1, the TextGrid structure includes three tiers corresponding to different processing stages. The first tier, ORT-MAU, contains the orthographic annotation of

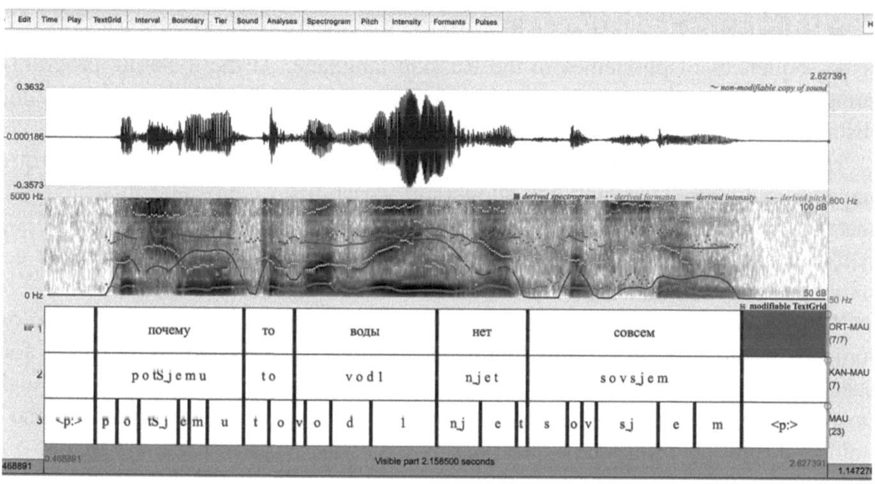

Fig. 1 TextGrid structure (WebMAUS processing). *Source* Developed by the authors

the original text ("*почему*," "*то*," "*воды*," "*нет*," and "*совсем*") with word time boundaries. Empty intervals at the beginning and end (0–0.61 s and 2.39–3.77 s) are marked with the tag <p:>, indicating pauses; their acoustic nature is not analyzed.

The second tier, KAN-MAU, represents a "traditional" transcription, where words are decomposed into simplified phonetic units using ASCII symbols adapted for the SAMPA system. For example, the word "*почему*" is transcribed as [*p o tS_j e m u*], where the affricate [t͡ɕ] is represented by the combination [*tS_j*], and palatalization of consonants is indicated by an underscore ([*n_j*] for [*n*ʲ]).

The third tier, MAU, details the time boundaries of individual segments, such as consonants and vowels. For instance, the segmentation of the word "*почему*" is as follows: [p] (0.61–0.67 s), [o] (0.67–0.73 s), [tS_j] (0.73–0.84 s), and subsequent elements.

Even the third tier is not a phonemic transcription in the commonly accepted linguistic sense. First, the system uses adapted symbols (e.g., 1 for the vowel [ɨ] instead of IPA notation), which simplifies processing but distorts linguistic accuracy. Second, the algorithm ignores contextual sound changes: the unstressed vowel [o] in the word "*воды*" (1.19–1.26 s) is not marked as the reduced vowel [ɐ], and the softness of consonants in "*воды*" (transcribed as [*v o d 1*]) does not reflect the palatalization of [*d*ʲ] occurring before a front vowel [i].

These limitations are due to the fact that WebMAUS, like most advanced aligners, relies on predefined phonetic dictionaries and statistical models rather than analyzing acoustic patterns for autonomous IPA transcription generation.

The WebMAUS processing pipeline includes standard speech signal processing stages. At the acoustic modeling stage, the audio recording is segmented into 20–40 ms frames, for which MFCC features are extracted, approximating spectral characteristics.

The HMM-GMM framework aligns acoustic feature vectors with phonemic inventory via statistical likelihood maximization from a dictionary, where each phoneme is represented as a sequence of HMM states.

N-gram-based language modeling adjusts hypotheses, considering the probabilistic sequences of phonemes in the Russian language. At the dynamic programming stage, the Viterbi algorithm optimizes segment boundaries, minimizing discrepancies between text transcription and acoustic data.

However, as the example shows, automatic alignment remains "tied" to the original text and cannot account for allophonic variability or prosodic nuances. For instance, in the word "*совсем*" (MAU tier: [*s o v s_j e m*]), the assimilation of [*s*ʲ] before the vowel [*e*] is not marked, and pauses are not differentiated by type (e.g., intonation unit boundaries).

Thus, WebMAUS demonstrates a typical compromise found in contemporary tools between automation and linguistic accuracy. The system is effective for speech-to-text synchronization. Nevertheless, for expert phonetic analysis, manual post-processing with IPA transcription and consideration of context-dependent phonological rules are required.

However, despite the significant advantages of advanced aligners and neural network approaches, such as high accuracy in matching audio signals to text, multilingual support, or the ability to operate in real-time, it is important to emphasize their key limitation. They do not perform classical phonemic transcription in the commonly accepted linguistic sense. These tools are designed to align existing text with an audio recording rather than automatically converting an acoustic signal into a sequence of phonemes in the International Phonetic Alphabet (IPA).

For example, the previously mentioned Montreal Forced Aligner (MFA) and WebMAUS work with predefined text transcriptions (most often orthographic or simplified phonetic), which are "aligned" with the audio using algorithms such as Viterbi.

However, they do not recognize phonemes "from scratch" and do not analyze acoustic patterns for the autonomous generation of an IPA transcription. Even hybrid DNN-HMM systems, such as Kaldi, rely on predefined phonetic dictionaries, where each word is segmented into phonemes according to a specific linguistic standard (e.g., ARPABET for English). However, this is not equivalent to a full phonemic transcription that accounts for allophonic variability or contextual sound changes.

Neural network models, including transformers (Whisper) or architectures with CTC-loss, also do not fully solve this problem. Although they can directly convert audio into text, their output is usually graphemes (letters) or simplified phonetic representations rather than detailed IPA symbols.

For example, a model may predict the letter sequence "cat," but it will not distinguish the nuances between allophones of [*t*] in word-final position (with aspiration or without) or account for subtle vowel differences, which are relevant for specialized phonetic analysis.

This is due to the following factors:

- Training data: Most models are trained on corpora with orthographic or simplified phonetic annotation rather than expert IPA transcriptions;
- IPA requires using dozens of diacritics and symbols for precise sound descriptions, making the task difficult for models optimized for mass applications (e.g., speech recognition for voice assistants);
- Contextual interpretation: Classical phonemic transcription often depends on language rules and phonological processes (reduction or assimilation), which are difficult to automate without deep integration of linguistic knowledge.

5 Conclusion

Thus, even advanced tools remain "aligners," not performing the task of classical phonetic transcription. To obtain a full IPA transcription, linguists still require either manual post-processing of results, or the use of specialized phonetic software (e.g.,

Praat, relying on spectrograms and formant analysis), or training models on highly specialized datasets with IPA markup, which remains a niche task.

It is also necessary to mention a key issue in automatic annotation—the definition of the transcription object: phonemes (as abstract linguistic units) or graphemes (as a reflection of written norms). In Russian, this dilemma manifests in phenomena where grapheme-phoneme correspondences are ambiguous. For example, the softness of consonants, indicated by vowel letters ("*е*," "*ё*," "*ю*," "*я*," and "*и*"), requires syllable-level analysis rather than analyzing individual sounds.

Systems that rely on orthography may mistakenly interpret "*ь*" (the soft sign) as an independent symbol of softness, although in real speech, it is reduced to the palatalization of the preceding consonant, emphasizing the need for phoneme-oriented models capable of accounting for contextual changes, such as assimilation (cf. "*сжать*" [*ʑ:atʲ*]) or final devoicing (e.g., "*дуб*" [*dup*]).

It is important to emphasize that these difficulties result in systematic errors in the automatic annotation of Russian speech caused by both linguistic specificity and model limitations. At the phonetic level, there are frequent false differentiations between [ɨ] and [*i*] and the "underestimation" of quantitative and qualitative vowel reduction phenomena in unstressed positions.

Phonemic errors, such as the confusion between [ʂ] and [*ɕ:*] (e.g., "*сшить*" vs. "*щит*"), may distort semantic perception.

At the suprasegmental level, difficulties arise due to variability in intonational contours across dialects (cf. Northern and Southern Russian pronunciation) and the lack of clear acoustic markers of boundaries.

Traditional approaches to phonetic annotation also face the fundamental problem of transcription system heterogeneity, which is due to the diversity of linguistic schools and applied research tasks.

Orthographic transcription, which represents the graphic form of a word, often contradicts phonemic transcription (IPA) and extended systems that account for allophonic variability.

For example, in Russian, the choice between orthography ("*ч*") and phonemic transcription ([*t͡ɕ*]) depends on the research objectives:

- The analysis of perceptual units requires a phonemic approach (Moscow Phonological School);
- In contrast, applied speech synthesis tasks may be limited to graphemic markup.

However, such a compromise ignores contextual sound changes, including the following:

- Vowel reduction;
- Consonant assimilation (e.g., devoicing of [*g*] in "*код*" → [*kot*])
- Allophonic softening ([*s*] → [*sʲ*] before front vowels).

These factors are critical for linguistic research.

Automatic annotation systems inherit this heterogeneity, facing the labeling dilemma:

Should they reflect perceptually relevant phonemes, acoustic allophones, or orthographic patterns?

For example, the transcription of Russian affricates ("*ц*" as [t͡s] vs. [*ts*]) or soft consonants ("*ть*" vs. palatalization in the context of vowels) varies even within the MPS and SPS (Moscow and St. Petersburg Phonological Schools).

This creates the following corpus compatibility issues:

- Orthographically annotated data are unsuitable for phonetic analysis;
- Highly specialized IPA transcriptions require expert validation.

Advanced tools like Montreal Forced Aligner partially mitigate these differences through predefined phonetic dictionaries, but their universality is limited by language-specific features.

The Russian language has the following features:

- Consonant softness is phonologically significant;
- Vowel reduction is systemic.

Thus, automation requires explicit modeling of these processes, either through rule-based integration (e.g., automatic palatalization before [*i*]) or by training neural networks using diachronically validated corpora with expert phonetic annotations.

Developing a universal annotation system for Russian requires solving a complex set of interrelated problems dictated by the language's unique phonological and prosodic features.

The key challenge is to bridge the gap between the variability of speech realizations and the need for their unambiguous interpretation within formal transcription systems.

Metadata standardization becomes essential, accounting for diachronic differences between phonological schools.

The examples are as follows:

- The Moscow School treats the vowel [*ɨ*] as a positional variant of the phoneme [*i*].
- The St. Petersburg School classifies [*ɨ*] as a separate phoneme.

These discrepancies necessitate adaptive ontologies facilitating interoperable transcription systems via semantically enriched metadata schemas.

Forinstance,XMLannotationswithattributes<phonemeschool="SPb"><phoneme school="SPb"><phonemeschool="SPb"> ensure data compatibility for cross-linguistic studies.

Dialectal variations add an additional layer of complexity. Thus, the Northern pronunciation of [*g*] in "*огород*" contrasts with the Southern pronunciation [ɣ], requiring multimodal architectures trained on heterogeneous corpora.

Context-dependent modeling must integrate acoustic and linguistic patterns to resolve homophonic ambiguities.

For example, in pairs such as [*ˈplatʲɪ*] ("*платье*") and [*pɫaˈtʲi*] ("*плати*"), differences in stress and palatalization are determined through the analysis of formant transitions and morphosyntactic environment.

Advanced architectures, such as Conformer, combine the advantages of convolutional networks for local spectrogram analysis with attention mechanisms for global context processing, which allows for the modeling of positional changes, including the following:

- Consonant assimilation in "*сжать*" → [*ʐ̥ːatʲ*], or
- Vowel reduction in "*молоко*" → [*məɫɐˈko*], where unstressed [*o*] is reduced to [ə] and [ɐ].

Resolving homophones through the integration of semantic models becomes critically important. Pretrained BERT transformers enable the differentiation between "*лук*" (plant) and "*лук*" (weapon) based on discourse context.

Adaptability to prosody requires multi-level annotation, combining segmental and suprasegmental features.

At the segmental level, this requires precise identification of allophones, such as:

- Softened consonants in "*синий*" [*ˈsʲinʲɪj*], or
- Affricates in "*царь*" [*t͡sarʲ*], where segmentation errors may lead to incorrect separation into [*t*] + [*s*].

At the suprasegmental level, it requires automatic phrase segmentation through the analysis of intonational contours and pauses, as in the phrase "*Она не пришла, потому что болела*."

A promising direction is the development of end-to-end frameworks that integrate acoustic modeling based on spectral features with deep semantic analysis.

Such systems should support hierarchical annotation in formats like Praat TextGrid, ensuring data compatibility across studies.

The key condition for success remains the creation of benchmark corpora with dual expert annotation, allowing models to be trained without explicit phonetic and suprasegmental errors.

Only synthesizing linguistic theory, advanced machine learning methods, and standardized annotation protocols will bridge the gap between academic phonetics and applied speech technology tasks.

References

Belenkiy, A. 2008. Textomining. In *Extracting information from unstructured texts*, vol. 10, 174–179. Computer Press.

Bogomazov, G. M. 2001. *Modern Russian literary language phonetics: Textbook*. Moscow, Russia: VLADOS.

Bryzgunova, E. A. 1980. Intonation. In *Russian grammar, in 2 volumes*, ed. N. Yu. Shvedova, vol. 1: Phonetics, Phonology, Emphasis, Intonation, Word formation, Morphology, 96–122. Moscow, USSR: Nauka.

Hannun, A., C. Case, J. Casper, B. Catanzaro, G. Diamos, E. Elsen, et al. 2014. Deep speech: Scaling up end-to-end speech recognition. *arXiv preprint arXiv:1412.5567*. https://arxiv.org/pdf/1412.5567. Accessed 17 Mar 2025.

Hinton, G., L. Deng, D. Yu, G. Dahl, A. Mohamed, N. Jaitly, et al. 2012. Deep neural networks for acoustic modeling in speech recognition: The shared views of four research groups. *IEEE Signal Processing Magazine* 29 (6): 82–97. https://doi.org/10.1109/MSP.2012.2205597.

Jurafsky, D., and J. H. Martin. 2020. *Speech and language processing: An introduction to natural language processing, computational linguistics, and speech recognition*. 3rd ed., draft ed. Upper Saddle River, NJ: Pearson.

Loginova, I. M. 2017. *Essays on the methodology of teaching Russian pronunciation: Textbook*. Moscow, Russia: RUDN University.

Rabiner, L. R., and R. W. Schafer. 2007. *Introduction to digital speech processing*. Hanover, MA: Now Publishers.

Taylor, P. 2009. *Text-to-speech synthesis*. Cambridge, UK: Cambridge University Press.

Vysotskiy, S. S., ed. 1977. *Experimental and phonetic studies in the field of Russian dialectology*. Moscow, USSR: Nauka.

Zhilinskaya, O. I., and E. I. Choporova. 2015. Information processing technologies and methods of automated abstracting and annotation. *International Student Research Bulletin* 5 (1): 81–83.

Zinder, L. R. 1979. *General phonetics*. Moscow, USSR: Vysshaya shkola.

Artificial Intelligence in Studying Russian and Chinese Space Terms

Oxana V. Goncharova, Irina I. Mitrofanova, and Yi Wang

Abstract The research explores the application of artificial intelligence (AI) in analyzing space terminology in Russian and Chinese languages. The relevance of the topic is due to the growing interest in space and the need to accurately understand the terminology used in different languages. The research aims to analyze the space-related vocabulary in Russian and Chinese through AI-driven methods and identify features and patterns related to cultural context and terminological diversity. The authors present a review of existing studies, the methodology of data collection and analysis using AI, and the results of a comparative analysis of the space lexicon of the two languages. Key thematic groups and features of terminology are identified, making it possible to better understand the influence of cultural factors on lexicon formation. The study of Russian and Chinese space vocabulary using AI makes it possible to identify the unique features of each language system and demonstrate the influence of cultural factors on the formation of scientific terminology. The main conclusions open new horizons for further linguistic research, emphasize the significance of intercultural exchange in science and technology, and highlight the importance of further research in this area, contributing to a deeper understanding of space topics in different languages.

Keywords Artificial intelligence • Space terminology • Linguo-cultural peculiarities • Semantic associations • Russian language • Chinese language

JEL Codes I21 • 123 • O33

O. V. Goncharova · I. I. Mitrofanova (✉) · Y. Wang
RUDN University, Moscow, Russia
e-mail: goncharova-oxvl@rudn.ru; mitrofanova-ii@rudn.ru

A. Karbekova (ed.), *Ethics of the AI Economy: A System View from the Positions of the Theory of Stakeholders*, Ethical Economy 73,
https://doi.org/10.1007/978-3-032-23423-0_23

1 Introduction

Humanity's common interest in advancing space exploration and harnessing its peaceful applications has never been more evident. Space technology not only offers transformative benefits but also plays a crucial role in addressing unprecedented sustainable development challenges. As a result, the space industry has attracted significant attention, both for its groundbreaking technologies and its unique terminology (Ryabova 2010, p. 3).

As a result of numerous advances in space research, there is an increasing need to create new terms and concepts to describe new phenomena and objects in the space industry. Currently, space terminology has become an independent terminological field.

The growing cooperation between Russia and China in aerospace underscores the need to standardize space terminology in the two languages. Space technology is a technological system combining the use of fundamental and applied sciences. These features contribute to the emergence of many interlingual and interdisciplinary space terms, which leads to several negative phenomena, such as the existence of polysemous and synonymous terms and the lack of dictionaries of professional terms and materials of relevant standardized terminology.

Artificial intelligence (AI) plays an important role in linguistic research. First, the application of AI in linguistic research can significantly improve the efficiency and accuracy of text analysis. By intelligently processing large amounts of text data, researchers can quickly identify key features (e.g., lexical frequency and grammatical structure) to understand the internal laws of language better.

Second, advances in speech recognition technology are enabling computers to understand human language better. Through deep learning on a large number of speech samples, AI systems can achieve natural and smooth speech synthesis, which greatly improves human-computer interaction.

AI is revolutionizing translation by breaking down language barriers. Deep learning algorithms enable these systems to accurately convey meanings between languages, thereby fostering cross-cultural communication. Moreover, AI is proving invaluable in linguistic research by streamlining tasks such as text analysis, speech recognition, and translation.

As a result, the application of AI in space terminology research provides an opportunity to help solve problems encountered in space topic research and provide an objective basis for further combining AI and linguistic research.

2 Literature Review

Recently, Chinese and Russian linguistic studies have paid close attention to space terminology. Several works devoted to space lexicons have appeared.

Space science is a branch of knowledge based on fundamental and applied sciences. Apart from studying scientific and technical terminology, there is relatively little study and discussion of Russian-language space terminology in Russia.

Frolova considered the formation and development of space vocabulary in the studies of Russian linguists in the work titled "Linguistic picture of the world: Space theme in the works of Russian linguists (problems and prospects of research)" (Frolova 2006). Ryabova conducted a comparative analysis of structural and semantic features of Russian and English space rocket terminological units in her dissertation "Problems and principles of systematization of terminology (on the material of comparative analysis of English and Russian space rocket lexicon)" (Ryabova 2010). Baharlu investigated Russian aerospace terms as a system and a basis for a trilingual (Russian-English-Persian) aerospace dictionary and the lexicographic parameters of this dictionary in his dissertation "Analysis of Russian aerospace terminology and problems of compiling a translated dictionary of aerospace terms" (Baharlu 2012). Sorokin analyzed lexicons related to space exploration and space flights in space lexicon in the Russian language (Sorokin 2012). Popova conducted a comparative analysis of derivational elements of French and Russian terms in the subject area as space artificial satellites in the research titled "Structural Characteristics of French and Russian terms of the subject area 'space artificial satellites' (on the material of glossaries)" (Popova and Kovalenko 2023).

Chinese linguists also recognize the need for and prospects of terminology research. The number of studies on the standardization of space terminology in China is constantly increasing.

Wang Qi reviewed the problems, solutions, and prospects of standardization of aerospace terminology in China (Wang 2007). Zhang Yan'an analyzed the translation into Russian and studied the basic aerospace terminology from a terminological perspective (Zhang and Xin 2010). Focusing on two high-frequency words, "aerospace" and "exploration," lexical translations are studied by combining quantitative and qualitative methods in the research titled "Investigation of the English translation of high-frequency words in the White Paper 'China's Space Business'—a case study of the translation of 'Spaceflight' and 'Exploration'" (Chen et al. 2022). From a terminological perspective, Wang Tong analyzed the etymology, usage, and translation of the word "astronaut" into Chinese (Wang 2024).

Thus, space terminology is of interest to Chinese and Russian linguists. The main attention of scholars in Russia is paid to describing the formation and development of terminology in the space industry. Chinese scholars emphasize comparative analysis of translated equivalents for specific space-related terminology. No studies on the combination of space terminology and AI in Chinese and Russian have been found so far.

3 Methodology

The comparative analysis of semantic fields in a cross-cultural context, as researchers emphasize (Wierzbicka 1997), requires a methodological synthesis of linguistics, cultural anthropology, and computational methods. The central problem remains the understanding of culturally conditioned meanings, which are not reducible to direct lexical correspondences but are formed through historically loaded discourse practices. In this context, the use of pre-trained BERT (Bidirectional Encoder Representations from Transformers) language models (Devlin et al. 2018) offers a unique toolkit for deconstructing semantic structures because their contextualized embeddings include syntagmatic and paradigmatic relations reflecting cultural meanings. As Sap et al. (2019) note, language models become a "mirror" of the cultural narratives captured in training corpora, making them relevant for analyzing ideological and philosophical differences between language communities.

For the comparison of the Russian and Chinese concept "cosmos/宇宙," the heterogeneity of the corpora on which the ruBERT (DeepPavlov) and Chinese BERT (Google/Hugging Face) models were trained is of key importance. According to the theory of corpus linguistics (Sinclair 1991), semantic associations of words are formed under the influence of frequency and distribution in texts, which are the product of cultural and historical contexts. The Russian-language corpus of ruBERT includes layers of Soviet science fiction, technical documentation from the space race era, and post-Soviet media texts, which reflect a technocratic discourse rooted in the ideology of space conquest. In contrast, Chinese BERT contains classical Taoist treatises ("Zhuang Tzu" and "Tao De Jing"), modern state media, and texts on quantum technologies, creating a semantic synthesis of traditional cosmology "天下" (Middle Kingdom) and techno-nationalist narratives "中国梦" (Chinese dream) (Cui et al. 2020). As shown, such hybridity forms unique vectors of associations, where the terms "cosmos" and "宇宙" accumulate scientific and metaphysical connotations.

The methodology integrates corpus linguistics, computational semantics, and cross-cultural analysis, which allows for a multilevel approach to the analysis of culturally conditioned semantic fields. The research procedure is structured according to steps aimed at minimizing contextual noise, ensuring data representativeness, and verifying interpretive findings.

Semantic representations were extracted using pre-trained BERT models (ruBERT for Russian and Chinese BERT for Chinese), whose architecture ensures the generation of contextualized embeddings (Devlin et al. 2018). To eliminate random variations due to contextual polysemousness, the vectors of each term were computed as average values obtained from 100 randomly selected sentences containing the target token according to the methodology proposed by Reimers and Gurevych (2019). In the case of polysemic units (e.g., Russian "sky," which actualizes meteorological and metaphysical meanings), the procedure of token-level aggregation was applied to preserve the distributional variation of meanings.

Semantic proximity was assessed using cosine similarity, which is optimal for comparing directional vectors in high-dimensional spaces (Mikolov et al. 2013a). To ensure the accuracy of the analysis, service words and hyperfrequent lexemes (e.g., "to have," "to do"), which can distort the results due to excessive statistical weight, were excluded from the procedure. Semantic associations were interpreted through the prism of three categories: scientific and technical (e.g., "satellite" and "orbit"), philosophical and religious ("Tao"), and historical and political ("empire," "union"), identified based on cluster analysis and verified during the pilot studies.

The verification phase included two complementary approaches: technical cross-checking using alternative models (Sentence-BERT, FastText) to assess the stability of semantic patterns and qualitative expertise involving native speakers and specialists in the field of cultural semantics. The latter made it possible to interpret the identified associations in the context of historical narratives (e.g., the connection of Russian "cosmos" with Soviet technocratic discourse) and philosophical traditions (correlation of Chinese "宇宙" with the Taoist concept of "unity of Heaven and man").

4 Results

The terms to analyze are as follows:

- Russian: cosmos, universe, star, cosmonaut, planet, galaxy, sky, Celestial, rocket, and satellite.
- Chinese: 宇宙 *(yǔzhòu)*, 宇宙 *(yǔzhòu)*, 星星 *(xīngxīng)*, 宇航员 *(yǔhángyuán)*, 行星 *(xíngxīng)*, 银河系 *(yínhéxì)*, 天空 *(tiānkōng)*, 天下 *(tiānxià)*, 火箭 *(huǒjiàn)*, and 卫星 *(wèixīng)*.

For each term, the top 5 closest words (cosine closeness ≥0.8) and their interpretation are given (Table 1).

The analysis highlights differences in the conceptualization of space-related terms in Russian and Chinese, shaped by historical, cultural, and philosophical contexts. These differences are manifested in lexical combinability and the emphasis that each culture places on the interpretation of space themes.

In Russian, the terms "cosmos" and "Universe" show a connection with scientific and technical discourse and historical heritage. For example, the closest words to "cosmos"—"orbit," "cosmonaut," and "technology"—reflect a pragmatic approach rooted in the Soviet space program, where space exploration was perceived as a symbol of technological superiority and national pride. The mentioning of "Gagarin" and "USSR" in the context of "cosmonaut" emphasizes the historical memory of superiority in the space race, which forms the image of space as a space of heroic achievements. The words "physics," "theory," and "gravity" next to "Universe" emphasize the scientific-rational perception, characteristic of the European tradition, where the cosmos is explored through the prism of the laws of nature.

In Chinese, the term "宇宙" (yǔzhòu—universe) is associated with a more syncretic understanding that integrates scientific, philosophical, and civilizational aspects. The proximity to "银河系" (galaxy), "科学" (science), and "文明" (civilization) indicates a desire to integrate space exploration into the broader context of human development, which correlates with the contemporary Chinese narrative of "nation rebirth" through technological progress. Simultaneously, the association of "宇宙" with "空间" (space) and "时间" (time) reflects traditional Taoist-Confucian

Table 1 Space terms and their closest words in the ruBERT and Chinese BERT language models

Term (Russian)	The closest words	Term (Chinese)	The closest words
Cosmos	orbit (0.89), cosmonaut (0.87), technology (0.85), research (0.84), and weightlessness (0.78)	宇宙	银河系 (galaxy, 0.94), 科学 (science, 0.91), 航天 (astronautics, 0.89), 探索 (research, 0.88), and 文明 (civilization, 0.86)
Universe	physics (0.88), energy (0.85), theory (0.83), infinity (0.81), and gravity (0.77)	宇宙	空间 (space, 0.93), 时间 (time, 0.90), 地球 (Earth, 0.87), 生命 (life, 0.84), and 神秘 (mystery, 0.82)
Star	constellation (0.95), sun (0.92), planet (0.89), galaxy (0.86), and astronomy (0.84)	星星	月亮 (moon, 0.96), 太阳 (sun, 0.94), 天空 (sky, 0.91), 神话 (myth, 0.88), and 愿望 (desire, 0.85)
Cosmonaut	hero (0.85), USSR (0.83), spacesuit (0.81), flight (0.79), and Gagarin (0.77)	宇航员	国家 (state, 0.78), 创新 (innovation, 0.81), 训练 (training, 0.79), 荣誉 (honor, 0.76), and 中国梦 (Chinese dream, 0.74)
Planet	Mars (0.91), asteroid (0.88), atmosphere (0.85), exoplanet (0.82), and life (0.80)	行星	恒星 (star, 0.93), 轨道 (orbit, 0.89), 太阳系 (solar system, 0.86), 外星人(aliens, 0.83), and 环境 (environment, 0.80)

Source: Calculated and compiled by the authors

notions of the unity of macrocosm and microcosm, where the cosmos is perceived as a harmonious system governed by universal principles.

The contrast is also noticeable in the perception of stars. Russian “star” is associated with “constellation,” “galaxy,” and “astronomy,” which emphasizes scientific classification, whereas Chinese “星星” (xīngxīng) is associated with “moon,” “myths,” and “desires,” retaining the connection with folklore and poetic symbolism. This difference is rooted in cultural codes: the European tradition emphasizes the cognisability of the cosmos through science, while Chinese culture preserves the synthesis of the rational and mythopoetic, where stars are not only objects of study but also elements of cultural memory.

The concept “cosmonaut” in Russian (“hero,” “spacesuit,” and “flight”) embodies an individual feat, which contrasts with the Chinese “宇航员” (yǔhángyuán) associated with “state,” “training,” and “Chinese dream,” possibly reflecting differences in ideological themes. In the Russian context, the cosmonaut is a symbol of personal courage. In Chinese, it is part of a collective project of national development.

Differences in the term “planet” are also telling: the Russian emphasis on “Mars,” “life,” and “exoplanets” emphasizes the search for extraterrestrial forms of existence characteristic of European cultures. Chinese “行星” (xíngxīng), coming closer to “aliens” and “environment,” combines scientific interest with socio-ecological discourse, which may be related to global challenges such as climate change and their reflection in the national agenda.

The limitations of this approach should also be mentioned. One of the key limitations of machine learning-based analysis methods is their dependence on the representativeness and quality of the training data. As noted by Bolukbasi et al. (2016), natural language processing (NLP) algorithms tend to reproduce and amplify the social, cultural, and ideological biases embedded in training corpora. For example, in Chinese language models, the frequency of ideologically loaded concepts such as the "Chinese dream" (中国梦) may be artificially inflated due to their dominance in official news sources (Sun et al. 2019). The consequence of this is not only the reproduction of ideological attitudes but also their normalization in automated conclusions, which limits the objectivity of the analysis (Caliskan et al. 2017). It is also important that most current language models, such as BERT (Devlin et al. 2018) or GPT (Ethayarajh 2019), are trained on corpora of contemporary Internet texts, making them incapable of analyzing the historical evolution of a language. As emphasized by Hamilton et al. (2016), static vector representations of words (word embeddings) capture synchronic semantic relations but ignore diachronic shifts. For example, the term "revolution" has fundamentally different connotations in nineteenth-century corpora and modern data. Nevertheless, models trained on mixed data offset these dynamics (Mikolov et al. 2013b). Even when historical dictionaries or fiction (e.g., nineteenth-century classics) are included, their volume is incomparable to the scale of modern data, resulting in a statistical dominance of topical meanings (Jurafsky et al. 2014), which may limit the applicability of the methods to studies of semantic transformations, cultural shifts, or long-term discourse trends (Bamman and Smith 2019).

5 Conclusion

Thus, the differences in the semantics of space terms are due to historical experience, ideological attitudes, and philosophical traditions. The Russian conceptualization of space is shaped by scientific and technological progress and the history of Soviet achievements, whereas the Chinese conceptualization is a synthesis of traditional cosmology, collectivist values, and modern technological ambitions. These linguo-cultural characteristics highlight that while the concept of cosmos is universal, it remains a culturally specific symbol through which societies construct their identity and aspirations.

References

Baharlu, H. 2012. *Analysis of Russian aerospace terminology and the problems of compiling a translated training dictionary of aerospace terms* (Abstract of the Dissertation of Candidate of Philological Sciences). Moscow, Russia: Lomonosov Moscow State University.

Bamman, D., and N. A. Smith. 2019. Contextualized semantic shifts: Combining computational and historical approaches. *Journal of Cultural Analytics* 4 (2): 1–22.

Bolukbasi, T., K.-W. Chang, J. Zou, V. Saligrama, and A. Kalai. 2016. Man is to computer programmer as woman is to homemaker? Debiasing word embeddings. *Advances in Neural Information Processing Systems* 29:4349–4357. https://doi.org/10.48550/arXiv.1607.06520.

Caliskan, A., J. J. Bryson, and A. Narayanan. 2017. Semantics derived automatically from language corpora contain human-like biases. *Science* 356 (6334): 183–186. https://doi.org/10.1126/science.aal4230.

Chen, L., S. Li, and M. Liu. 2022. A corpus-based study on the English translation of high-frequency real words in the white paper "China's Spaceflight"—Taking the translation of 'spaceflight' and 'exploration' as an example. *Science and Technology Communication* 14 (21): 37–40.

Cui, Y., W. Che, T. Liu, B. Qin, and Z. Yang. 2020. Pre-training with whole word masking for Chinese BERT. *IEEE/ACM Transactions on Audio, Speech, and Language Processing* 29:3504–3514. https://doi.org/10.1109/TASLP.2021.3124365.

Devlin, J., M.-W. Chang, K. Lee, and K. Toutanova. 2018. BERT: Pre-training of deep bidirectional transformers for language understanding. In *Proceedings of the 2019 conference of the North American chapter of the association for computational linguistics: Human language technologies, Volume 1 (long and short papers)*, 4171–4186. https://doi.org/10.48550/arXiv.1810.04805.

Ethayarajh, K. 2019. How contextual are contextualized word representations? Comparing the geometry of BERT, ELMo, and GPT-2 embeddings. In *Proceedings of the 2019 conference on empirical methods in natural language processing and the 9th international joint conference on natural language processing*, 55–65. Hong Kong, China. https://doi.org/10.18653/v1/D19-1006.

Frolova, I. E. 2006. Linguistic picture of the world: Space theme in the works of Russian linguists (problems and prospects of research). *Bulletin of Omsk State University* 1:70–74.

Hamilton, W. L., J. Leskovec, and D. Jurafsky. 2016. Diachronic word embeddings reveal statistical laws of semantic change. In *Proceedings of the 54th annual meeting of the association for computational linguistics*, 1489–1501. Berlin, Germany: Association for Computational Linguistics. https://doi.org/10.18653/v1/P16-1141.

Jurafsky, D., V. Chahuneau, B. R. Routledge, and N. A. Smith. 2014. Narrative framing of consumer sentiment in online restaurant reviews. *First Monday* 19 (4): https://doi.org/10.5210/fm.v19i4.4944.

Mikolov, T., K. Chen, G. Corrado, and J. Dean. 2013a. Efficient estimation of word representations in vector space. *arXiv*:1301.3781. https://doi.org/10.48550/arXiv.1301.3781

Mikolov, T., I. Sutskever, K. Chen, G. S. Corrado, and J. Dean. 2013b. Distributed representations of words and phrases and their compositionality. *Advances in Neural Information Processing Systems* 26:3111–3119. https://doi.org/10.48550/arXiv.1310.4546.

Popova, L. G., and D. V. Kovalenko. 2023. Structural characteristics of French and Russian terms of the subject area "space artificial satellites" (based on glossaries). *Litera* 5:268–275. https://doi.org/10.25136/2409-8698.2023.5.40869.

Reimers, N., and I. Gurevych. 2019. Sentence-BERT: Sentence Embeddings using Siamese BERT-Networks. *arXiv*:1908.10084 https://doi.org/10.48550/arXiv.1908.10084

Ryabova, E. A. 2010. *Problems and principles of systematization of terminology: On the material of comparative analysis of rocket-space lexicon of English and Russian languages* (Abstract of the Dissertation of Candidate of Philological Sciences). Moscow, Russia: Moscow State Regional University.

Sap, M., D. Card, S. Gabriel, and Y. Chio. 2019. The risk of racial bias in hate speech detection. In *Proceedings of the 57th annual meeting of the association for computational linguistic*, 1668–1678. Florence, Italy: Association for Computational Linguistics. https://doi.org/10.18653/v1/P19-1163.

Sinclair, J. 1991. *Corpus, concordance, collocation*. New York, NY: Oxford University Press.

Sorokin, R. V. 2012. "Space" lexicon in the Russian language. *Russian Speech* 2:48–53.

Sun, T., A. Gaut, S. Tang, Y. Huang, M. ElSherief, J. Zhao, D. Mirza, E. Belding, K.-W. Chang, and W. Y. Wang. 2019. Mitigating gender bias in natural language processing: Literature review. In *Proceedings of the 57th annual meeting of the association for computational linguistics*, 1630–1640. Florence, Italy: Association for Computational Linguistics. https://doi.org/10.48550/arXiv.1906.08976.

Wang, Q. 2007. Commentary on several terms of aerospace (astronautics) standardization. *Aerospace Standardisation* 02:10–12.

Wang, T. 2024. Criticism of the translation of scientific and technological terminology—Taking the Chinese translation of the word "astronaut" in aerospace technology translation as an example. *Modern English* 01:117–120.

Wierzbicka, A. 1997. *Understanding cultures through their key words: English, Russian, Polish, German, and Japanese*. New York, NY: Oxford University Press.

Zhang, Y., and N. Xin. 2010. Russian translation and analysis of core aerospace terms. *Forest Teaching* 10:37–39.

Punch Above Your Weight: Can Artificial Intelligence Read and Interpret Allegorical Texts (on the Material of Russian Proverbs About Education)

Viktor M. Shaklein, Oxana V. Goncharova, and Svetlana S. Mikova

Abstract The research investigates the possibilities of artificial intelligence (AI) in interpreting allegorical texts in linguistic and methodical aspects. The research material includes 70 proverbs of the concept sphere "Teaching/Knowledge/Literacy/Science." The text material is difficult to investigate because of the genre specifics of proverbs and their genre characteristics (i.e., allegorical nature, factuality, conciseness, and instructiveness). The research aims to evaluate the possibilities of AI to interpret allegorical texts as texts with mainly didactic content and texts used in the learning process (educational texts). To evaluate the degree of interpretation adequacy, the authors set the following tasks for neural networks: (1) translate the selected proverbs into a foreign (English) language, (2) model educational-communicative situations for practicing the use of proverbs in speech, and (3) compose a linguistic-cultural commentary. The research has shown that neural networks can facilitate the integration of proverbs into the learning process. The research proves that AI can be used to compose training dialogs and commentaries to texts. The errors of neural networks made while interpreting the content of proverbs can be divided into three groups: (1) ignoring the form of the text (alliterations, puns), (2) misunderstanding of the general content due to incorrect choice of keywords semantics (replacing the meaning of archaism with modern semantics of the word, allegorical meaning with direct one, and ignoring the national-cultural component of the meaning), and (3) misinterpretation of the hidden meaning of the text (moral prescription).

Keywords Artificial intelligence • Allegorical text • Russian proverbs • Educational text • Russian as a foreign language

JEL Codes C60 • I20

V. M. Shaklein · O. V. Goncharova · S. S. Mikova (✉)
RUDN University, Moscow, Russia
e-mail: shaklein-vm@rudn.ru; goncharova-oxvl@rudn.ru; mikova-ss@rudn.ru

A. Karbekova (ed.), *Ethics of the AI Economy: A System View from the Positions of the Theory of Stakeholders*, Ethical Economy 73,
https://doi.org/10.1007/978-3-032-23423-0_24

1 Introduction

Digitalization, a key distinguishing characteristic of the twenty-first century, is transforming various areas of social life. Scholars give different assessments on the scale and consequences of the technology. Nevertheless, they tend to view digitalization as "an improvement of the conceptual model of interaction and communication of people with society and each other" (Krylov et al. 2021, p. 1217).

Education is transformed as well: models and technologies of digital interaction and service production are transferred to educational process organization, reformatting and renewing education (Danilova et al. 2020, p. 7).

The contemporary methodology of teaching foreign languages is text-centered. Thus, the issues of processing of texts in natural language by neural networks are relevant for language teaching.

The novelty of this research is related to the research material (proverbs as a genre of allegorical text) and the interpretation of textual material in linguistic and didactic aspects.

2 Literature Review

Artificial intelligence (AI) is applied in education for the automation of routine tasks and the personalization of learning, including the creation of educational applications and specialized content for the needs of certain learners (Shobonov et al. 2023). AI is used to model learning situations, generate educational texts with certain keywords and constructions, create tests with different types of questions to check the studied material, or make up comments of various types to facilitate text perception. Considering AI in the educational process, scholars turn to various aspects of analyzing, interpreting, and generating texts in learning a foreign language (Belyaeva 2024; Bukin 2023; Kostiukovich 2023). Understanding texts in natural languages is identified as a key problem for AI (Nagoev 2000). The most significant applications of AI for text processing are machine translation of oral and written texts and the synthesis of texts in natural languages (Fomichev 2005).

Neural network machine translation (NMT) models are trained on large corpora of parallel texts, including canonical literary sources (e.g., translations of classical prose and poetry) and users' content from the Internet, forums, subtitles, and social networks (Bahdanau et al. 2016). They can identify statistical patterns in using set expressions, including proverbs. For example, frequent Russian proverbs such as "*Семь раз отмерь, один раз отрежь*" [lit. Measure seven times, cut once] or "*Не всё то золото, что блестит*" [lit. Not everything that glitters is gold] are used in many different contexts on the Internet (according to Google Search, $\approx$1.2 million and $\approx$890 thousand pages, respectively). Thus, they are regularly reflected in the training data. Consequently, neural networks successfully reproduce their canonical English equivalents, "Measure twice, cut once" and "All that glitters is not gold," learned through multiple parallel correspondences (Wu et al. 2016). This is based on the ability of neural networks to identify statistical patterns in parallel texts, including frequent idioms from the training data (Wu et al. 2016).

The adequate translation of frequent proverbs is substantiated by the attention mechanism, which highlights meaningful lexical correspondences in parallel sentences. For example, the proverb "*Тише едешь—дальше будешь*" [lit. If you go slower, you come further] has a stable correlation with its English equivalent, "Slow and steady wins the race," represented in many training examples. Simultaneously, rare proverbs with no fixed equivalents are processed through the composition of separate words, and this leads to literal analysis. This is confirmed by data analysis. The OPUS corpus (Tiedemann 2012) has translation equivalents for only 12% of Russian proverbs; the others are generated "de novo."

Meanwhile, proverbs are used in teaching Russian because language is to be learned in its close interrelation with culture. Researchers emphasize communicative, informational, and motivational value of proverbs and recognize their importance for forming the image of the country of the studied language in the minds of students (Barsukova and Zhang 2024). The communicative value of Russian proverbs is related to their frequency in speech. Thus, scientists note that Russians use proverbs more often than, for example, Italians do (Bezhenar and Pavone 2019). Proverbs are often used as titles of media texts and advertising slogans (Murashova 2016, 2018), which adds to their communicative value. Proverbs as texts of national culture contribute to the formation of students' linguistic-cultural competence (Bashurina 2005).

Difficulties in understanding proverbs include peculiarities of vocabulary and grammar, a lack of cultural knowledge, and an inability to decipher allegory due to its national specificity. To supplement the missing background knowledge, proverbs are usually accompanied with linguistic-cultural commentaries.

These factors conditioned the research material and methods.

3 Materials and Methods

The research material includes 70 proverbs of the concept sphere "Teaching/Knowledge/Literacy/Science" from the collection of L. B. Katsyuba (2021).

The interpretation of a proverb as an allegorical text is specified by its constitutive features, allegorical nature, factuality, conciseness, and instructiveness. Proverbs are based on allegory (i.e., express an abstract concept or idea in a concrete artistic image). The external content of the allegory has external characteristics. The internal plan of the allegory contains ethical norms or "laws of the world order" (Karasik 2010). The most significant is the hidden meaning. The task of the reader of the allegorical text is to find this hidden meaning. Factuality implies a correlation with a certain situation. The allegorical text depicts axiogenic situations assuming a responsible choice between possible variants of behavior. Native speakers also know the real prototypical situation that created the text. That is why the allegorical text is a source of linguistic-cultural information. Conciseness is a specific plot with two actors who are compared or contrasted in one feature. Finally, instructiveness is a moral lesson behind the allegorical text.

These features influence allegorical texts interpretation, including in teaching foreign languages.

To identify pedagogical actions that can be facilitated by AI, the authors set the following objectives:

1. To translate the selected proverbs into a foreign language because translation shows the adequacy of the original text perception and can explain the meaning of the text;
2. To model educational-communicative situations to form practical skills and abilities in using proverbs and sayings appropriately in speech;
3. To compile a linguistic-cultural commentary on proverbs for their effective introduction into the teaching process. The commentary must include a moral lesson as proverbs "represent one of the oldest ways of transmitting cultural norms and requirements" (Nistratov 2015, p. 220).

4 Results

As a result, translations of proverbs were obtained. In some cases, they can explain the general meaning of proverbs. For example, DeepSeek translated the Russian proverb "*Всякое полузнанье хуже всякого незнанья*" as "Half-knowledge is worse than ignorance" and the proverb "*Корень учения горек, да плод его сладок*" as "The root of learning is bitter, but its fruit is sweet." The communicative situations made up by neuro nets can also be used in the teaching process. For example, DeepSeek described the situation as "An adult doubts whether to start learning a new language" and the moral lesson as "Age cannot interfere with self-development" for the proverb *Для ученья нет старости* [lit. "There is no old age for learning"]. Finally, educational dialogs composed by neural networks can motivate learners to use proverbs in their own speech. Such learning dialogues can be used to design exercises, for example: Find a proverb to use in the dialogue ("*На ошибках учатся*"—"Failure is the best teacher"):

Student: "I've made so many mistakes. I'll never understand it!"
Teacher: "Don't worry! Every mistake is a step toward success. Examine your mistakes carefully, and you will become stronger" (compiled by Qwen2.5-Plus)

Nevertheless, in most cases, neural networks misinterpreted the meaning of the proverbs or inaccurately described the situation.

The factors causing errors in interpretation are as follows:

1. Low frequency of proverbs. For example, the proverbs "*Дудочку не надуешь, дурочку не научишь*" (≈120 results in Google) or "*На то и наука,—сказала карасю щука*" (≈90 results) are not represented in parallel corpora. Having no

"memory" about correct translation, the model generates the text according to superficial linguistic patterns. Therefore, the verb "*надуешь*" is interpreted through its dominant meaning, "inflate," rather than the contextual-metaphorical "play a musical instrument" because the latter is rare for this verb in the training data. Such blind spots arise because neural networks based on the transformer architecture (Vaswani et al. 2017) optimize the probabilistic distribution of words but cannot reconstruct cultural connections. When translating the proverb, the neural network considered the superficial combinability of the lexemes (i.e., "*надувать*" → "inflate") and ignored alliteration and the metaphorical connection between the components "You can't inflate a pipe, you can't teach a silly girl." Such errors arise due to the NMT models' focus on statistical correlations rather than on underlying conceptual integration (Sutskever et al. 2014).

2. National stereotypes. For example, the crucian carp and pike in Russian proverbs, fairy tales, and fables are antagonistic characters in the pair "predator-prey." However, this is not considered in the translation of the proverb "*На то и наука,—сказала карасю щука*." The neural network reproduced the literal meaning (i.e., "That is what science is for,—the pike said to the crucian"), although "science" in this text only indicates the natural course of things. The lack of cultural context markers (e.g., metatextual references to literary sources) in training data neutralizes the hidden meanings (Baker 2018). Correct translation (i.e., That is the trick of science,—smirked the pike to its prey") actualizes irony through lexical choice (smirked and prey). Nevertheless, this is beyond standard translation patterns. In the proverb "*Не учась, и лаптя не сплетешь*," weaving bust shoes is depicted as a standard of simple everyday activity. Nevertheless, the neural network DeepSeek sees the situation as "A student knows the material theoretically but is afraid to apply his knowledge," and the moral lesson "Theory without practice is useless." In fact, the proverb teaches that it is impossible to do even something very simple without knowledge and practice.
3. Polysemantic words. When the neural network chooses one of the meanings without considering the context. For example, Qwen2.5-Plus chooses the situation "The need for practice. A student knows the theory but is afraid to use it in practice" for the proverb "*Дело учит, и мучит, и кормит*." However, the word "*дело*" has the meaning "work, occupation, or activity," not "practice."
4. Archaisms. Working with the proverb "*Красна птица перьем, а человек ученьем*," the neural network translated the archaism "*красна*" as "red" instead of "beautiful." Such semantic distortions are due to the limited ability of the models to recognize historical semantic shifts and adapt archaisms to modern connotations (Hassan et al. 2018).
5. Words with a national-cultural component. The proverb "*Знайка бежит, а незнайка на печке лежит*" caused the problem of translation. DeepSeek provided the following, "The knower runs; the ignorant lies on the stove" (stove is not equivalent to the word "*печка*" because one cannot lie on the stove), and of moral lesson interpretation "to inspire activity by contrasting laziness and diligence." In fact, the proverb shows that knowledge allows a person to develop,

while the ignorant person remains where he or she is. Similar problems manifested themselves in the interpretation of the proverb "*Его учить, что по лесу с бороной ездить*" where the model offered a literal explanation (i.e., "advice to use a harrow to take care of the forest"). Meanwhile, the harrow as a tool for cultivating the cropland is contrasted with the forest, where the harrow is useless. The limitations in interpreting such texts are due to the very nature of statistical learning, which relies on the frequency of surface patterns but does not model the underlying mechanisms of cultural memory (Katan 2014).

6. Ignoring the proverb's form. Phonetic and pragmatic traps, such as puns or hyperboles, remain inaccessible to NMT models because of their focus on semantic rather than phonetic or pragmatic equivalence. For example, in the proverb "*Сытое брюхо к науке глухо*," the literal translation "A full belly is deaf to science" preserved the metaphor but lost the connection of physiological state with intellectual passivity. In the proverb "*Дудочку не надуешь, дурочку не научишь*," the neural network ignored the pun ("*дудочку*"—"*дурочку*") and generated an incorrect interpretation: "If you do not know how to play, do not teach others." This error reflects a cognitive gap between formal linguistic competence and culturally conditioned thinking (Kecskes 2016). The neural network, without access to historical-etymological data, was unable to reconstruct the relationship between phonetic alliteration and the semantic antithesis of the proverb.

5 Conclusion

Thus, neural networks can be used to prepare allegorical texts as educational for a foreign audience to indicate the literal meaning, describe situations for using proverbs, and compose exercises. However, in most cases, linguistic competence is not enough to translate and interpret proverbs. It requires the integration of historical and cultural knowledge, which is inaccessible to statistical models. While demonstrating progress in processing conventional vocabulary, neural network technologies remain a tool that requires expert control when working with culturally labeled units, when meaning is created under linguistic, cultural, and cognitive factors.

References

Bahdanau, D., K. Cho, and Y. Bengio. 2016. *Neural machine translation by Jointly Learning to Align and Translate*. https://arxiv.org/pdf/1409.0473v7. Accessed 6 Apr 2025.

Baker, M. 2018. *In other words: A coursebook on translation*. 3rd ed. London, UK: Routledge.

Barsukova, E. A., and Y. Zhang. 2024. Proverbs and sayings in modern Chinese textbooks for studying Russian as a foreign language as tools of creating the image of Russia. *Genesis: Historical Research* 1:111–120. https://doi.org/10.25136/2409-868X.2024.1.68988.

Bashurina, D. I. 2005. *Formation of linguocultural competence of foreign students-philologists when teaching Russian paremias* (Synopsis of Dissertation of Candidate of Pedagogical Sciences). St. Petersburg, Russia: Herzen State Pedagogical University of Russia.

Belyaeva, N. Y. 2024. *Opportunities and limitations of applying neural networks in professional education*. Kostroma, Russia: OGPU "KTEK".

Bezhenar, O., and M. Pavone. 2019. Using proverbs for learning Russian as a foreign language in Italian audience. *Foreign Language Teaching* 46 (1): 42–48.

Bukin, A. S. 2023. The use of neural networks for learning English using chat GPT as an example: opportunities and challenges for modern education. *Vestnik of State University of Humanities and Technology* 2:14–20.

Danilova, L. N., T. V. Ledovskaya, N. E. Solynin, and A. M. Khodyrev. 2020. The main approaches to understanding digitalisation and digital values. *Vestnik of Kostroma State University. Series: Pedagogy. Psychology. Sociokinetics* 26 (2): 5–12.

Fomichev, V. A. 2005. *Method of formal description of the content of complex natural-language texts and its application to the design of linguistic processors* (Synopsis of Dissertation of Doctor of Technical Sciences). Moscow, Russia: Moscow Institute of Electronics and Mathematics.

Hassan, H., A. Aue, C. Chen, V. Chowdhary, J. Clark, C. Federmann, X. Huang, et al. (2018). *Achieving human parity on automatic Chinese to English news translation*. https://www.microsoft.com/en-us/research/wp-content/uploads/2018/03/final-achieving-human.pdf. Accessed 6 Apr 2025.

Karasik, V. I. 2010. Linguocultural stylistics of Russian and Chinese allegories. *Language, Consciousness, Communication* 40:83–95.

Katan, D. 2014. *Translating cultures: An introduction for translators, interpreters and mediators*. London, UK: Routledge.

Katsyuba, L. B. 2021. *Russian proverbs: Concept spheres, associative fields, semantization of figurative meaning, contextual use*. Moscow, Russia: Flinta.

Kecskes, I. 2016. *Explorations into pragmatics and linguistic creativity*. Amsterdam, Netherlands: John Benjamins Publishing.

Kostiukovich, E. Y. 2023. The use of artificial intelligence in teaching English at a university. *Modern Pedagogical Education* 1:492–496.

Krylov, V., M. Markhaichuk, M. Vakhromeeva, and N. Subbotina. 2021. Educational environment in the context of digitalization. In *Modern global economic system: Evolutional development vs. revolutionary leap*, ed. E. G. Popkova and B. S. Sergi, 1217–1224. Cham, Switzerland: Springer. https://doi.org/10.1007/978-3-030-69415-9_132.

Murashova, N. V. 2016. Proverbs in the textbook of Russian as a foreign language "The way to Russia": Ethnocultural potential and its representation. *Almanac of Modern Science and Education* 1 (103): 71–73.

Murashova, N. V. 2018. Russian proverbs and their modern transformations for representation to foreign students. *Philology. Theory & Practice* 11 (79): 201–205.

Nagoev, Z. V. 2000. *Model of representing the meaning of text information* (Synopsis of Dissertation of Candidate of Technical Sciences). Nalchik, Russia: Institute of Applied Mathematics and Automation of the Kabardino-Balkarian Scientific Center of the Russian Academy of Sciences.

Nistratov, A. A. 2015. Analysis semantic structure of proverbs. *Journal of Psycholinguistics* 26:212–221.

Shobonov, N. A., M. N. Bulaeva, and S. A. Zinovieva. 2023. Artificial intelligence in education *Problems of Modern Pedagogical Education* 79–4:288–290.

Sutskever, I., O. Vinyals, and Q. V. Le. 2014. Sequence to sequence learning with neural networks. *Advances in Neural Information Processing Systems* 27: https://daiwk.github.io/assets/sequence%20to%20sequence%20learning%20with%20neural%20networks.pdf. Accessed 6 Apr 2025.

Tiedemann, J. 2012. Parallel data, tools and interfaces in OPUS. *LREC* 2012:2214–2218.

Vaswani, A., N. Shazeer, N. Parmar, J. Uszkoreit, L. Jones, A. N. Gomez, Ł. Kaiser, and I. Polosukhin. 2017. Attention is all you need. In *Advances in neural information processing systems 30 (NIPS 2017)*, ed. I. Guyon, U. Von Luxburg, S. Bengio, H. Wallach, R. Fergus, S. Vishwanathan, and R. Garnet. Curran Associates: Montreal, Canada. https://proceedings.neurips.cc/paper_files/paper/2017/file/3f5ee243547dee91fbd053c1c4a845aa-Paper.pdf. Accessed 6 Apr 2025.

Wu, Y., M. Schuster, Z. Chen, Q. V. Le, M. Norouzi, W. Macherey, and M. Krikun. 2016. Google's neural machine translation system: Bridging the gap between human and machine translation. *arXiv*:1609.08144. https://arxiv.org/pdf/1609.08144. Accessed 6 Apr 2025.

Transformer Neural Network Models in the Creation of Typhlocomments and Captions to Images

Olga V. Timchenko, Zalina H. Abregova, Elizaveta A. Vologina, and Andrey B. Timchenko

Abstract Transformational models underlying large language models cope well not only with the task of content generation in natural language but also with multimodal tasks, to which the task of image description can be attributed. The development of systems for solving the Image to Caption task has progressed from convolutional neural networks and encoder-decoder models to basic transformer-based systems using vision language pre-training (VLP). Experimental studies show that pre-trained models significantly improve the performance of transformer models. However, the performance of such models remains an open and important issue. Using pre-trained transformer models, fine-tuning a large language model, and transfer learning will improve the quality of audio-descriptors created for visually impaired people to perceive visual information of visual arts subjects. Nevertheless, including important factual information necessary for people with visual impairments to fully perceive visual information is challenging. Models may miss information about the author of the work, its size, style of execution, and other key characteristics that are essential for the correct description of works of art. These shortcomings indicate the need for further improvement of teaching methods and model tuning to ensure high-quality audio descriptions that meet the strict standards of professional peer review.

Keywords Transformers · Neural networks · Audio description · Image to Caption · Sight language pre-training

JEL Code Y80

O. V. Timchenko (✉) · A. B. Timchenko · Z. H. Abregova
Pyatigorsk State University, Pyatigorsk, Russia

E. A. Vologina
Gazpromneft – Digital Solutions LLC, St. Petersburg, Russia

A. Karbekova (ed.), *Ethics of the AI Economy: A System View from the Positions of the Theory of Stakeholders*, Ethical Economy 73,
https://doi.org/10.1007/978-3-032-23423-0_25

1 Introduction

In recent years, transformer neural network models have shown considerable success in text generation tasks, including the creation of audio descriptions and image captions. These models have traveled a long evolutionary path from traditional encoder-decoder architectures to advanced transformer-based systems with pre-trained visual language processing (VLP). Research shows that pre-training significantly improves the performance of these models, enabling them to cope with complex descriptive text generation tasks. This research reviews the development and application of transformer models in audio descriptive text generation and discusses the key aspects and approaches that enable the high performance of these systems.

2 Methodology

The authors will consider the automatic generation of an audio description of a visual art object as a private task of Image to Caption generation (Image to Caption). The Image to Caption task is based on computer vision recognition techniques, which consist of the steps of partitioning an image into separate regions or segments, identifying and classifying objects in the image, extracting the characteristics and features of objects in images, and evaluating and optimizing the model.

Automatic descriptions of art objects and images should meet the same requirements as descriptions made by professional experts. It is necessary to find a balance between the accuracy and comprehensibility of the text because visual perceptions of visually impaired people differ significantly from those of sighted people. Works of art, especially abstract paintings, may contain many elements, symbols, and details that require careful interpretation and explanation. Composed comments must meet strict quality standards such as relevance, accuracy, and completeness (Rarenko 2017). Training neural networks require a large amount of marked-up data. However, the data for generating high-quality audio descriptions can be classified as low-resource even though the content is presented in natural language.

Thus, successfully solving the audio descriptor generation problem requires the development of sophisticated algorithms and models that can consider these factors. When creating image captions, transformers are the basis of advanced high-performance models. Technologies for automatic image description began with convolutional neural networks, which was used to extract features from images, with these features being passed to recurrent neural networks to generate textual descriptions. The subsequent introduction of attention mechanisms allowed the models to focus on different parts of the image when generating descriptions. This greatly improved the descriptions' quality. Further development of automatic description generation is based on the use of transformer-based architectures such as BERT and ViT (Vision Transformer). These models have shown high performance due to their ability to consider context and long-term dependencies. The description quality was improved by incorporating vision-language pre-training (VLP) into the model. VLP-transformer models are the basis for current models. Pre-training models require big data, which are obtained automatically (Zhang et al. 2021).

Transformers were designed to handle textual data; adding modality required adaptation to new tasks. Visual transformers adapted the transformers architecture to handle images. Instead of processing sequences of words, ViT breaks an image into small patches and processes them as a sequence of tokens. A self-attention mechanism is then used to model the interactions between image patches.

Architectures are used to generate textual descriptions of images, where the encoder processes the image, and the decoder generates the textual description. In this case, the models are often pre-trained on large datasets with annotated images and texts (Ondeng et al. 2023).

3 Results

To test the system for automatic construction of audio descriptions of fine art objects, the authors implement a transformational model for Russian vit-rugpt2-image-captioning, which is pre-trained on a corpus of data.

The model was initialized with "google/vit-base-patch16-224-in21k" for the encoder and "sberbank-ai/rugpt3large_based_on_gpt2" for the decoder.

"Sberbank-ai/rugpt3large_based_on_gpt2" is a machine learning model created by Sberbank AI (Sberbank's artificial intelligence developer). It is based on the GPT-2 architecture developed by OpenAI but adapted for Russian and trained on large volumes of Russian-language texts. GPT-2 (Generative Pre-trained Transformer 2) is a language model that can generate meaningful texts from given data. The "rugpt3large_based_on_gpt2" model is one of the versions of this model optimized for Russian and designed for various Natural Language Processing (NLP) tasks such as text generation, question answering, tone analysis, and more. The features of this model are as follows:

1. Training on a large amount of data: the model has been trained on a huge amount of Russian-language content, which allows it to understand the context better and generate better texts;
2. Russian language support: the model has been specially adapted to work with the Russian language, which makes it especially useful for applications targeting Russian-speaking audiences;
3. Text generation: the model is capable of creating coherent and meaningful text based on given input data;
4. Transformers: like the original GPT-2, this model uses the Transformer architecture, which provides high performance and accuracy in text processing.

"Google/vit-base-patch16-224-in21k" is a pre-trained computer vision model based on the Vision Transformer (ViT) architecture. This architecture was proposed by researchers at Google Research in 2020. It has been a breakthrough in image processing through the use of transformers previously used mainly in natural language processing tasks. The main features of this model include the following:

1. Vision Transformer (ViT): ViT processes an image as a sequence of patches (patches), similar to the way transformers process sequences of tokens in text. Each patch is treated as a separate element that passes through the layers of the transformer;
2. Patch size: The model's name mentions patch16, which means the size of each patch is 16×16 pixels. It means that the original image is split into small patches of 16×16 pixels, each of which becomes a separate element of the input sequence;
3. Image size: The model indicates that the model expects an image of size 224×224 pixels;
4. Pre-training: The model indicates that the model has been pre-trained on the ImageNet-21K data corpus containing about 14 million images with 21,000 classes. This allows the model to have a wide range of knowledge about visual objects and their characteristics.

The Google/vit-base-patch16-224-in21k model can be used for various computer vision tasks, including image classification, object detection, segmentation, and other tasks. Due to its pre-training on a large dataset, it can be quickly adapted to new tasks by pre-training (fine-tuning). The implemented model shows a BLEU metric of 0.86 (Tumanov 2023).

4 Data Set and Evaluation Metrics

The experiments were conducted using audio descriptions of art objects taken from open sources on the website "Describe Me," which describes images for people with visual impairments (Describe Me n.d.), and the international art project "Angels of the World" (International Art Project "Angels of the World" n.d.). The dataset of 546 audio descriptions of art images was split into 365 descriptions for training, 103 descriptions for validation, and 78 descriptions for testing. BLEU and METEOR metrics were used to evaluate the experiment. Table 1 shows the scores on the validation and test set.

Table 1 Metrics values

Metric	Validation	Test
BLEU	0.122	0.110
METEOR	0.162	0.136

Source: Calculated and compiled by the authors

The analysis of the obtained results shows that the model pre-trained to generate image descriptions does not consider the peculiarities of audio descriptions.

In addition to the automatic metrics mentioned, the evaluation of an expert—a typhlocommentator—is necessary because the generated text should consider the peculiarities of image descriptions for people who are visually impaired or blind. Such evaluations can be the completeness of the description, accuracy, relevance, clarity, and comprehensibility of the wording used, which the expert on an established scale will measure.

Let us conduct a comparative analysis of the two descriptions. The first analysis is performed by an expert; the second one is generated by a model.

As a first experiment, the authors will describe Joan Miro's painting "The Second Painting from the Blue Triptych." The description from a professional expert begins with the presentation of the actual information of the author of the painting, the period of creation, dimensions, and vertical or horizontal position: "The painting is a huge rectangular canvas oriented horizontally. The height of the work is one and a half times the height of a person—2 meters 70 centimeters, and the width is 3 meters 55 centimeters" (Novotorceva 2020). The model does not have the actual knowledge and cannot communicate it to the user.

After providing the factual information, the expert proceeds to describe the content of the canvas. When describing typhoid, the commentator avoids special terms because the user may not be familiar with them, which will make it difficult for a person to perceive the image. Additionally, information can be provided about the style in which the painting is painted: "abstract painting. The colors are bright, contrasting, with predominating light blue. On a light blue background, there is a single vertical red stripe on the left and a horizontal line of small, irregular black circles on the right. The blue background occupies most of the canvas, while the red line and circles are freely arranged. The vertical red line is located in the left third of the painting, closer to the upper left corner" (Novotorceva 2020).

The description given by the model is not so extensive and detailed. In addition, the large language model may hallucinate and replace the description of the image of the red stripe with descriptions of the image of an object that does not exist in the picture—a pencil. The model's hallucinations do not stop there. It figures out the interaction of objects in the painting, describing them as branches of a tree. Blind people may not have the knowledge and ideas of what the branches of a tree look like, similar to the ideas of sighted people. Another major drawback in the description is the mention of the contrast of colors in the picture, which is also unacceptable when constructing an audio description of artistic images: "The drawing is placed on a monochrome blue background. On the left is an orange pencil pointing vertically upwards. Next to it are four black circles placed horizontally. The circles are connected by dotted lines, forming a resemblance to the branches of a tree or bush. These lines start from the second circle on the left and end at the fourth circle on the right. The lines connecting the circles are straight and parallel to each other, giving the impression of symmetry and order. The contrast between the bright color of the pencil and the dark circles makes the composition expressive and noticeable."

Further experiments with the description of abstract painting using a language model showed a difference in the quality of the constructed typhlocomments. Let us compare another painting that is not related to abstract painting, namely Vasily Polenov's painting "Dreams." Expert audio transcription is presented in the material (Russian Museum n.d.) and begins with the transfer of factual data about the period of painting, painting technique, size, and position. Note that the commentator can also provide additional information about the artist's biography, the reasons for creating the masterpiece, or historical information about the elements of the artwork.

Describing the painting, the model also tried to convey not only the color combinations and list the elements of the painting but also the emotional background. The ability to identify emotions is a generalizing property of large language models. However, the human interpretation of emotions is more subtle: "The painting depicts a man in traditional clothes sitting on rocks at the edge of a cliff. He looks into the distance at the vast mountain landscape. The man is wearing a white shirt, a dark raincoat, and a white headdress. His posture expresses calmness and reflection. In front of him lies a staff, which may serve as a support or a symbol of the traveler. The majestic mountain landscape with clouds above the peaks is depicted in the background. Sunlight illuminates the foreground, creating warm hues on the stones and human skin. This work of art conveys a sense of peace and harmony with nature."

The analysis of the received descriptions highlighted a significant drawback of the automatic generation—the lack of information about the author of the painting, the shape and size of a picture (mandatory information), and the style in which the image is executed. Additionally, the model predefined the objects in the picture (e.g., orange pencil, tree, and shrub), although the expert also uses comparative images (e.g., small stones and sea pebbles). The generated texts do not meet the requirements for descriptions of artworks. Hence, the technology to refine the model would be to collect a dataset of descriptions of paintings.

The second example of audio descriptions created automatically and by the expert for the painting "Dreams" by V. Polenov shows that the language model managed to define the tonality of the painting as "peace," which corresponds to the tonality specified by the expert. The model described the objects in the painting quite accurately, correctly established the emotional coloring of the painting, and made correct accents on the details. As in the first example, the main weakness is the lack of factual data about the author of the painting, its size, period, and historical characters. Additionally, the audio descriptions compiled by the expert in the full version contain a reference to the artist's comments, which also cannot be reflected by the model.

The results of experimental studies and the analysis carried out make it possible to identify some significant differences in the description of an artistic work by a typhlocommentator and a large language model. The authors rank these differences according to the degree of manifestation:

1. Factual information (author, size, position, technique, period, historical facts, and characters): The expert is present, the model is absent;
2. Style of description (using terminology understandable to blind people): The expert uses (broad brush and abstraction). The model uses simple and understandable formulations, the absence of complex artistic terms;
3. Detail of the elements: The expert describes in detail the elements of the composition, including the shape, location, and technique of execution. The model mentions only the main elements of the composition without a detailed description of the form and technique;
4. Limited detail: The expert describes in detail the small details that can understand what is depicted in the picture without violating the integrity of perception, which is extremely important for a blind or visually impaired person. Due to the simplification of the presentation, the model does not convey the necessary details and cannot independently determine the importance and degree of detail;
5. Hallucination: the expert is not subject to the desire to generate non-existent details of the description and to speculate, adding semantic load. In some cases, the model is subject to hallucinations;
6. Emotionality: an expert can easily describe the emotional component of a painting, revealing the full range of feelings that the author is trying to convey. The model can capture the largest and most pronounced classes of emotions in the image.

Thus, we can conclude that there are substantial differences between the description of an artwork provided by a professional audio describer and a large language model. Despite the successes of advanced natural language processing models, expert audio description remains an indispensable tool for making visual art accessible to individuals with vision impairments due to its accuracy, level of detail, and ability to convey emotion.

5 Conclusion

The authors reviewed transformational models suitable for the image-to-caption task and conducted experiments of description generation, achieving an acceptable metric of the pre-trained model. However, the model has shown to be unsuccessful for generating descriptions for art objects, which we attribute to the high specificity of the task, as well as the small size of the dataset.

Data Availability

1. The information on the use of transformer based neural network models (transformers) in image captioning is available at https://figshare.com/ with the identifier https://doi.org/10.6084/m9.figshare.28759376.
2. The examples of automatic and expert audio descriptions of fine art objects are available at https://figshare.com/ with the identifier https://doi.org/10.6084/m9.figshare.28759580.

Acknowledgments The publication was made within the framework of the research project "Development of Linguistic Principles and Design of Technical Solutions for the Creation of a prototype neural network to accompany audio descriptions" under the State Assignment of the Ministry of Science and Higher Education of the Russian Federation (FGBOU VO "Pyatigorsk State University," project No. 1022100500014-8-6-6.2.1, scientific supervisor—Prof. A. V. Razduev, Candidate of Philological Sciences).

References

Describe Me. n.d. *Category "painting, art". Website with image descriptions for the visually impaired.* https://опиши-мне.рф/category/art. Accessed 18 Feb 2025.

International Art Project "Angels of the World". n.d. *Section: Audio description of paintings.* https://365angels.com/page/1414102. Accessed 13 Feb 2025.

Novotorceva, G. 2020. Audio description of paintings: How to describe abstraction. *Special View Portal*, August 6. https://specialviewportal.ru/articles/articles783?ysclid=m8y4xj6i8d571639492. Accessed 13 Feb 2025.

Ondeng, O., H. Ouma, and P. A. Akuon. 2023. A review of transformer-based approaches for image captioning. *Applied Sciences* 13 (19): 11103. https://doi.org/10.3390/app131911103.

Rarenko, M. B. 2017. Audio description and typhoid commentary as special forms of audiovisual translation. *Vestnik of Moscow State Linguistic University. Humanities* 10 (783): 215–233. https://cyberleninka.ru/article/n/audiodeskriptsiya-i-tiflokommentirovanie-kak-osobye-formy-realizatsii-audiovizualnogo-perevoda. Accessed 18 Feb 2025.

Russian Museum. n.d. *Augmented reality (with audio description) to the painting by V. D. Polenov, Russian landscape painter "Dreams (On the Hill)"* [Audio]. https://rmgallery.ru/ru/2446. Accessed 8 Feb 2025.

Tumanov, A. [@tuman]. 2023. ViT-RUGPT2-image-captioning. *Hugging Face*, January 26. https://huggingface.co/tuman/vit-rugpt2-image-captioning. Accessed 22 Jan 2025.

Zhang, P., X. Li, X. Hu, J. Yang, L. Zhang, L. Wang, Y. Choi, and J. Gao. 2021. VinVL: Revisiting visual representations in vision-language models. In *Proceedings of CVPR 2021: IEEE/CVF conference on computer vision and pattern recognition*, 5575–5558. Nashville, TN: IEEE. https://doi.org/10.1109/CVPR46437.2021.00553.

Artificial Intelligence in Working with Legal Texts

Olga A. Anferova, Olga M. Litvishko, Tatyana A. Shiryaeva, Galina V. Stankevich, and Alevtina V. Ukrainchik

Abstract Today's legal practice faces the need to process huge amounts of information, which makes traditional methods of analysis inefficient. The introduction of artificial intelligence (AI) makes it possible to speed up the process of data processing and improve the quality of analysis, minimizing the probability of errors. This makes the research topic especially relevant in the conditions of rapid technological development. The research studies the application of AI technologies in the analysis, interpretation, and creation of legal documents. Achieving this goal involves fulfilling several tasks, including doing research into advanced AI technologies, analyzing successful examples of their implementation in the practice of law, assessing the advantages and disadvantages, and developing recommendations for their efficient integration. The research deals with the following issues: the choice of AI technologies to be most actively used in legal practice, their advantages and limitations, and their impact on traditional ways of analyzing and drafting legal documents. The issues of reliability and interpretability of AI solutions are also given attention. The research results are important for understanding the opportunities and limitations of AI in the legal field. This knowledge can help lawyers to embrace new technologies and efficiently use them to improve the quality of their work. The research also outlines the prospects of potential uses of AI in law.

Keywords Artificial intelligence • Legal documents • Legal practice • Contract • Legal proceedings • Professional ethics

JEL Code K40

O. A. Anferova · A. V. Ukrainchik
North-Caucasian Institute (Branch) of the Russian Presidential Academy of National Economy and Public Administration, Pyatigorsk, Russia

O. M. Litvishko · T. A. Shiryaeva
Pyatigorsk State University, Pyatigorsk, Russia

G. V. Stankevich (✉)
Astrakhan State University, Astrakhan, Russia

A. Karbekova (ed.), *Ethics of the AI Economy: A System View from the Positions of the Theory of Stakeholders*, Ethical Economy 73,
https://doi.org/10.1007/978-3-032-23423-0_26

1 Introduction

Artificial intelligence (AI) is rapidly spreading across various industries and is opening new possibilities with significant practical value for the legal field, particularly in analyzing, interpreting, and developing legal documents. By automating routine tasks, AI frees up lawyers to focus on more complex analytical work, thus improving the efficiency and accuracy of their efforts. AI, a branch of computer science, is dedicated to creating systems capable of performing tasks traditionally associated with human intelligence. In the past, only humans could recognize speech, make decisions, or process natural language. However, since John McCarthy first introduced the term "artificial intelligence" at the Dartmouth Conference in 1956, defining it as the ability of machines to execute tasks that require human intelligence, these tasks are now achievable by machines in fields such as medicine, finance, and law. Nonetheless, the research indicates that regulating AI in the legal domain must consider emerging social developments and the ethical implications of technology use (Demidov and Mokhorova 2021, p. 33).

The idea of AI is based on the use of machine learning (ML) and natural language processing (NLP) with a focus on creating systems capable of analyzing and interpreting data, as well as making decisions based on them. In the practice of law, AI is being used to automate document analysis, predict case outcomes, and improve the overall efficiency of lawyers. According to a report by McKinsey, in 2020, the use of AI has contributed to a 20–25% increase in the efficiency of processes in various industries, which emphasizes its importance and potential for the legal sector. On the other hand, AI technologies are also actively used to prevent and counteract crime both in the Russian Federation and abroad (Columbus 2020).

2 Methodology

The research methodology is based on the following methods:

- Scientific literature analysis, including scholarly publications and reports;
- Comparative analysis—comparing traditional methods used in legal practice and automated AI-based techniques;
- Case study—analysis of examples of successful cases of AI application to show their advantages and limitations;
- Quantitative analysis—the use of statistical data to prove AI efficiency;
- Qualitative analysis—to evaluate the risks of implementing AI in legal practice;
- Linguistic analysis—translation problems and processing of legal texts.

3 Results

Nowadays, AI technologies are actively introduced into the legal sector. Their use continues to expand. In 2020, there were more than 300 start-ups worldwide that specialize in developing AI solutions to automate legal processes. These technologies cover systems for analyzing and classifying documents, predicting court decisions, and automating routine tasks. Current advances in AI offer new perspectives to improve legal practice, making it more efficient and accessible. "Digitalization of the judicial process is being actively pursued in our country, additional inertia this development has gained in the post-pandemic period" (Pypina and Kochergin 2023, p. 160).

NLP includes several key approaches actively used in legal practice. One of them is the use of language models (e.g., BERT or GPT), which are trained on large amounts of text and can understand the context and semantics of sentences. These models make it possible to automate tasks such as extracting key information from documents and producing summaries of long texts. Another crucial approach is tone analysis, which detects the emotional nuance in text and can be particularly useful when examining reviews or complaints. Additionally, text parsing plays a vital role by identifying and highlighting the structural elements of a document (e.g., headings, sections, and paragraphs), thereby simplifying the task of managing large data sets for lawyers. In this context, accurately translating terminological units also becomes essential because it involves identifying equivalent terms in the target language, a process that can sometimes be challenging (Ayvazyan et al. 2022, p. 46).

The integration of machine learning and NLP technologies into legal practice is becoming increasingly important. An example is systems such as ROSS Intelligence, which uses MO and OEJA algorithms to search for relevant legal information, saving a significant amount of lawyers' time. These technologies allow for the automation of routine tasks (e.g., searching for case law and drafting document templates, which significantly saves time and increases efficiency) (Akhmedjanova 2018). However, it is important to keep in mind that successful integration requires adapting technologies to the specific needs of the legal industry, including legal compliance and data privacy. Nevertheless, AI and ML start playing an increasingly important role in criminal investigations (Yartsev 2023, p. 236), which also points to the need for their application in other areas of law.

Traditional methods of analyzing legal documents rely on the manual work of lawyers who study the texts of laws, regulations, and court decisions. These methods include the use of legal commentaries, handbooks, and databases to find relevant information. Lawyers conduct analyses by interpreting texts in the light of context and practice of application. It is important to note that the terms of legal discourse bear significant semantic value, which inevitably requires much attention to their translation (Litvishko 2024a, p. 66). However, such approaches require significant time and human resources, which can slow down the decision-making process and increase costs.

Advanced technologies for analyzing legal documents using AI include ML and NLP. These technological tools automate the processing of large amounts of data by extracting key elements of text and providing context-based interpretations. OpenAI's GPT-3 model is capable of analyzing complex legal texts and making recommendations, significantly reducing analysis time and improving accuracy. Thus, AI technologies are becoming an effective tool in legal practice. Simultaneously, translation strategies based on linguistic, legal, geopolitical, and cultural analysis are essential for achieving adequacy and equivalence—the key criteria for correct translation (Bolshakova 2023, p. 44). This highlights the importance of using an integrated, technology-driven approach to enhance the quality of legal translation and analysis.

The benefits of using AI to analyze legal documents include a significant reduction in data processing time and improved accuracy of analysis. According to a McKinsey report, the use of AI can reduce time costs by 60% (Chui et al. 2023). Indeed, the application of AI technologies in legal practice has shown significant progress. A prime example is the use of the GPT-3 model developed by OpenAI to analyze complex legal texts. This model interprets the context of legal documents and provides recommendations, greatly simplifying the work with legal information. Additionally, law firm Baker McKenzie implemented an AI system to process contracts, which reduced document analysis time by 40% (SparkBeyond 2025). These examples illustrate how AI can improve efficiency and accuracy in the legal industry.

AI is actively used to analyze judicial precedents. The ROSS Intelligence system, developed on the IBM Watson platform, provides lawyers with the ability to quickly find relevant court decisions and analyze them. This significantly saves time on case law research and allows them to focus on strategic work. Using such tools empowers lawyers to make more informed decisions based on accurate data and contextual analyses.

AI has been successfully applied to the interpretation of normative acts. In 2021, the GPT-3 model was used to analyze and interpret laws, which made it possible to automate the process of preparing legal opinions. Such systems can analyze laws in the context of specific cases, making it easier for lawyers to understand complex legal rules. This is particularly relevant in the context of constantly changing legislation, where rapid analysis of new regulations is required. LegalAI tools allow automating tasks, such as analyzing contracts, preparing documents, and monitoring changes in legislation (Ivanovskaya and Posnova 2023, p. 15).

The reviewed examples demonstrate that the use of AI in legal practice brings significant benefits, including increased speed of document analysis, improved accuracy of interpretation, and reduced costs. The cited studies confirm that the implementation of AI technologies can significantly increase the efficiency of lawyers and improve the quality of services provided. Simultaneously, there are also limitations, such as the need to adapt technologies to the specific tasks and requirements of the legal sphere and risks associated with potential errors in analyses. The potential of AI in legal practice is apparent. Its further development can radically transform this field.

The use of AI in legal analysis offers several significant advantages. Advanced technologies (e.g., ML and NLP) make it possible to automate many aspects of document analysis. Models like OpenAI's GPT-3 can interpret complex legal texts, highlight key elements, and provide contextualized interpretations. This significantly reduces processing time, as evidenced by McKinsey research indicating a reduction in analysis time of up to 60% (Columbus 2020). Indeed, AI can handle large volumes of data, providing high accuracy at minimal cost, making it an effective tool for routine tasks. Simultaneously, it is important to consider cultural specifics (Litvishko 2024b, p. 30), which emphasize the need to integrate different approaches and knowledge in the field of law and technology. This fact further enhances the potential of AI in legal analysis.

Comparing traditional methods of analyzing legal texts with AI solutions reveals the advantages and limitations of each approach. Traditional methods provide deep contextual understanding and high accuracy. However, they are time and resource-consuming. In contrast, AI solutions significantly speed up document processing and reduce costs. Studies show that using AI can reduce analysis costs by 30–50% compared to manual methods. Nevertheless, automated systems may face difficulties in interpreting complex legal nuances, making it necessary to involve specialists to verify and correct the results. The multidimensional study of legal translation problems requires the application of a complex method of analysis, including linguo-legal, linguocultural, and comparative analysis (Pavlova 2022).

Advanced technologies of contract drafting automation are based on the application of AI systems capable of analyzing and processing large volumes of legal data. These systems use machine learning algorithms and natural language processing to create standard legal documents. For example, IBM has developed Watson Legal, which helps lawyers create contracts by analyzing vast databases of legal documents. LegalAI technology used in the legal field enables automation and optimization of processes such as document analysis and legal risk management (Ivanovskaya and Posnova 2023, p. 15). These innovations speed up the process of contract drafting and reduce the probability of errors, which is especially important in legal practice.

The automation of contract drafting provides significant benefits for legal practice. One of the key aspects is the reduction in the time it takes to prepare standard documents. McKinsey research shows that automation can reduce time costs by up to 70%, allowing lawyers to focus on more complex tasks. Additionally, the use of such systems reduces the likelihood of human error and improves document accuracy, which is particularly important in high-liability environments with strict requirements for legal texts. The difficulty in translating legal terms lies in the need to perform translation from one legal system to another, which requires a thorough understanding of both systems (Kastritsyna and Drukova 2020). Thus, automation improves work efficiency and facilitates quality interaction with legal texts, which reduces the risks associated with translation and interpretation errors.

Despite its advantages, contract drafting automation faces certain limitations and challenges. First, such systems require significant resources for development and implementation, which may not be affordable for small law firms. Second, automation may be less effective when dealing with non-standard or complex cases where a deep understanding of the context is required. For example, while demonstrating high-speed contract analysis, JP Morgan's COIN system is limited in interpreting unique legal situations. These aspects emphasize the need to combine automation with the professional expertise of lawyers.

The application of AI in the creation of legal documents is already reflected in real practice. For example, LegalZoom is actively using AI to automatically draft documents (e.g., wills and contracts). This approach can significantly speed up the document creation process and reduce costs for clients. JPMorgan Chase introduced a Contract Intelligence (COIN) tool in 2021. This tool analyses and processes legal documents in seconds. Previously, these tasks required 360,000 h of legal work annually. "The legal industry, filled with traditions, precedents and the intricacies of human interpretation, is witnessing an increasingly obvious adoption of artificial intelligence as the digital age progresses" (Ivanovskaya and Posnova 2023, p. 14), proving that AI is speeding up processes and changing the very nature of legal practice.

Successful examples of AI implementation in legal practice demonstrate a significant impact on efficiency and quality of work. Such technologies allow lawyers to focus on more complex tasks that require human input, leaving routine processes to automated systems. For example, the use of COIN at JPMorgan Chase reduces document processing time and minimizes the risk of human error. This leads to increased client confidence and improved reputation of law firms. Simultaneously, the automation of decision-making with the help of AI raises many ethical issues concerning transparency and responsibility for results (Khalidov and Mutsalov 2024, p. 358).

Analyses of successful cases of using AI in the creation of legal documents reveal advantages and challenges. The benefits include significant reductions in document processing time and costs. A McKinsey report confirms that the use of AI can reduce costs by up to 20%. However, there are challenges to adopting such technologies, including the need to ensure data privacy and the need for staff to adapt to new tools. These aspects require careful consideration to successfully integrate AI into legal practice.

4 Conclusion

The automation of routine tasks using AI technologies is one of the most significant benefits of legal practice. Everyday tasks (e.g., document processing, drafting standard contracts, and checking whether documents comply with legal regulations) can be performed faster and more accurately with the help of AI. McKinsey research indicates that automating such processes can reduce law firm costs by up to 20%, making AI a handy and cost-effective tool. Nevertheless, applying AI in legal practice has its advantages and disadvantages as far as data privacy and algorithm reliability are concerned.

Undoubtedly, AI significantly saves time used for analyzing legal documents. For instance, the ROSS Intelligence saves up to 30% of working time spent on finding legal precedents. But it may cause problems with confidentiality.

Certain ethical issues are involved in the use of AI in legal practice. One of them is the bias of algorithms used in the training data. This inevitably raises questions about equity and fairness in AI decision-making. Such algorithms are difficult to verify. Therefore, their objectivity is questionable. The application of AI in the legal sphere needs strict control and ethical regulation.

Besides, AI's involvement in legal practice threatens security and data privacy because data breaches are quite common. The sensitivity of information also requires introducing strict security measures.

Another important issue is the reliability of AI in legal practice. Errors in the operation of AI-based systems can lead to lawyers making incorrect conclusions. In some cases, they can even reverse the outcome of court cases and decrease the quality of legal advice. Language nuances and extra-linguistic contexts should be considered, which can be done only by humans.

References

Akhmedjanova, R. R. 2018. Artificial intelligence as a tool to limit judicial discretion. In *International scientific conference of students, postgraduates, and young scientists "Lomonosov 2018"*. Moscow, Russia: RUDN University. https://lomonosov-msu.ru/archive/Lomonosov_2018/data/12936/75394_uid250202_report.pdf. Accessed 14 Feb 2025.

Ayvazyan, N. B., A. V. Garamyan, and O. M. Litvishko. 2022. Terminological gaps in the context of digitalization of English-Language terminological system of criminal law. *Current Issues in Philology and Pedagogical Linguistics* 2:43–53. https://doi.org/10.29025/2079-6021-2022-2-43-53.

Bolshakova, M. G. 2023. Strategies and techniques of the translation of international law documents. *Current Issues in Philology and Pedagogical Linguistics* 3:42–53. https://doi.org/10.29025/2079-6021-2023-3-42-53.

Chui, M., E. Hazan, R. Roberts, A. Singla, K. Smaje, A. Sukharevsky, L. Yee, and R. Zemmel. 2023. *The economic potential of generative AI: The next productivity frontier*. New York, NY: McKinsey & Company. https://tinyurl.com/25vvy5au. Accessed 14 Feb 2025.

Columbus, L. 2020. The McKinsey state of AI in 2020 report finds AI drives revenue. *Forbes*, November 22. https://www.forbes.com/sites/louiscolumbus/2020/11/22/the-mckinsey-state-of-ai-in-2020-report-finds-ai-drives-revenue/. Accessed 14 Feb 2025.

Demidov, V. P., and A. Yu. Mokhorova. 2021. Legal regulation of artificial intelligence in the conditions of globalization. *Current Problems of Science and Practice* 4:28–33.

Ivanovskaya, I. I., and M. V. Posnova, eds. 2023. *Actual issues of development of economics and jurisprudence: Collection of articles of the II International Scientific and Practical Conference*. Petrozavodsk, Russia: ICNP 'Novaya Nauka'.

Kastritsyna, S. V., and K. Y. Drukova. 2020. Features and ways of the translation of the English legal terms. *International Student Scientific Bulletin* 3: https://eduherald.ru/ru/article/view?id=20229. Accessed 14 Feb 2025.

Khalidov, A. A., and S. I. Mutsalov. 2024. Use of big data and AI in legal practice: New opportunities and risks. *Matters of Russian and International Law* 14 (9A): 357–361.

Litvishko, O. M. 2024a. *Modern legal discourse: Ontology, verbalization, conceptualization*. Moscow, Russia: Prospekt.

Litvishko, O. M. 2024b. Cultural conditionality of professional linguistic consciousness of a lawyer (based on the material of the English language). *Professional Communication: Top Issues of Linguistics and Teaching Methods* 17 (3): 29–37.

Pavlova, Yu. V. 2022. Dictionary as a means of forming linguistic competence in teaching a foreign language. In *University readings—2022: Proceedings of the regional interuniversity scientific and practical conference (part 3)*, 121–125. Pyatigorsk, Russia: Pyatigorsk State University.

Pypina, G. S., and V. M. Kochergin. 2023. Possibilities of using remote technologies in some types of criminal record-keeping. In *Donetsk Readings 2023: Education, science, innovation, culture and modern challenges: Proceedings of the VIII international scientific conference*, 160–163. Donetsk, DPR: Donetsk State University.

SparkBeyond. 2025. *AI to reshape the legal industry*. February 4. https://www.sparkbeyond.com/press/ai-to-reshape-the-legal-industry. Accessed 14 Feb 2025.

Yartsev, S. V. 2023. The use of artificial intelligence in operational investigative activities. In *Actual problems of Russian law and legislation: Collection of materials of the XVI all-Russian scientific and practical conference*, ed. E. V. Vasilenko, 235–237. Krasnoyarsk, Russia: Siberian Institute of Business, Management and Psychology.

The Role of Machine Translation and Human Expertise in Business Text Translation

Irina S. Mkhitaryan, Sona K. Hakobyan, Markuhi A. Voskanyan, and Lusine H. Sargsyan

Abstract Digitalization and the widespread applications of artificial intelligence (AI) have significantly transformed the field of translation, offering both opportunities for increased efficiency and challenges in the context of maintaining accuracy, cultural nuances, and terminological precisions. Within the domain of business, machine translation (MT) plays a crucial role in translating business texts, enabling faster communication across global markets. Despite the advancements in MT, human intervention is often required to address challenges such as terminology accuracy, tone, and cultural appropriateness in business translation. **The aim of this article is** to explore and analyze the opinions and experiences of professional translators regarding the use of MT tools in translating business texts. Our objective is to assess the challenges, errors, and strategies employed by translators when working with MT, as well as to investigate the post-editing tasks necessary to enhance the quality of machine-generated translations. **The main issues of the research are** the limitations of MT in accurately translating specialized business terminology, the challenges of maintaining consistency in terminology across documents, and the difficulty in capturing the intended tone, style, and cultural nuances of business texts. This research then explores the perspectives of professional translators about the use of machine translation tools for business text translation. The study is based on a survey conducted among university professors teaching in "Translation Studies" Degree Programs, freelance translators, and senior year students enrolled in those programs.

I. S. Mkhitaryan (✉)
Armenian State University of Economics, Yerevan, Armenia

Yerevan State University (YSU), Yerevan, Armenia
e-mail: irina.mkhitaryan@ysu.am

S. K. Hakobyan
European University of Armenia, Yerevan, Armenia

ILS Armenia International Language School, Yerevan, Armenia

M. A. Voskanyan · L. H. Sargsyan
Yerevan State University (YSU), Yerevan, Armenia
e-mail: markuhi.voskanyan@ysu.am; sargsyanlusine@ysu.am

A. Karbekova (ed.), *Ethics of the AI Economy: A System View from the Positions of the Theory of Stakeholders*, Ethical Economy 73,
https://doi.org/10.1007/978-3-032-23423-0_27

Keywords Artificial intelligence • Business text translation • Computer-assisted translation • Human translation • Machine translation • Post-editing • Translation tools

JEL Code M160

1 Introduction

Artificial intelligence has been vastly implemented in nearly all spheres of human life, with machine translation being one of the most significantly affected. Artificial intelligence-based (AI-based) translation software models have thus become widely available, and these now include Google Translate, Bing, Microsoft Translator, DeepL, Reverso, Systran Translate, and Amazon Translate. Several computer-aided translation (CAT) tools such as Trados, memoQ, Smartcat, Lokalise, Smartling, Crowdin, TextUnited, and Memsource are also available. More recently, artificial intelligence has been applied in the development of applications such as ChatGPT, ChatSonic, GPT-3 Playground, GPT-4 and YouChat, which simulate conversational responses to researchers' inquiries, mimicking human interactions more directly. This and other developments call attention to human translators to accurately understand the challenges and opportunities of AI and how they should address them. Consequently, the study seeks to meticulously understand the perspectives of Armenian professors teaching in the Degree Programs of "Translation Studies" at Yerevan State University and the European University of Armenia on this issue.

Other than this, for the study we surveyed senior year students specializing in translation and practical freelance translators. It aims to explore the effectiveness of artificial intelligence (AI) translation systems compared to human translators, specifically in the context of business texts. By analyzing the strengths and weaknesses of AI in comparison to human translation, this study investigates its potential in delivering high-quality translations, while focusing on errors, limitations, and opportunities. The primary objectives of the study include:

- Identifying the differences between AI and human translations in business contexts.
- Examining the types of errors encountered in AI translations.
- Evaluating the tools AI translators use when working with business texts.

To achieve this, it asks the following research questions.

RQ1: What are the major constraints of Machine Translation (MT) in the context of business texts?

RQ2: What are the key challenges between AI-driven translation and human translation regarding accuracy, cultural adaptation, and contextual understanding in business communication?

RQ3: What problem-solving techniques do business text translators use to address inaccuracies and encountered errors?

2 Machine Translation: Evolution, Application, and Limitations

Machine translation (MT) is a computerized procedure in which software algorithms disassemble and transfer the source text to target languages ostensibly independently of human input. Today, though, its actual use usually requires human intervention in the form of pre- and post-editing protocols. Despite advancement in technology, human translation can still be considered as the gold standard when accuracy and reliability metrics are concerned (Church and Hovy 1993). MT, in turn, helps comprehend different languages at a higher speed, at lower costs, and facilitates better inter-cultural relations. MT systems primarily support the user with the mechanical parts of translation, while the complex interpretative elements continue to be a human responsibility.

Machine translation began modestly, hindered by limited storage, insufficient computer memory, and the lack of advanced programming languages. At the time, syntax received little attention in linguistic studies, while semantics was largely overlooked. Since the early 1970s, MT has evolved along three main paths: the development of computer-based tools to assist translators, operational MT systems that incorporate human involvement in various ways, and purely theoretical research aimed at improving MT methods (Hutchins 1986). As MT advanced from the 1950s onward, various perspectives emerged. According to Holmström (1951), translation is an art that requires personal judgment at every stage, involving choices between alternatives that cannot be strictly defined by rules. Rather than simply replacing one set of symbols with another, effective translation depends on the translator's education, experience, and personal insight. The second perspective has remained relevant to this day. However, it is now widely accepted that computer-based translation systems are not competitors to human translators but rather tools designed to enhance their efficiency, particularly in technical translation (Esselink 2001).

Consequently, computers function as a complementary tool, rather than a substitute for professional human translators. The integration of MT engines within large multilingual enterprises and international corporations not only supports but also expands the professional opportunities available to translators (Kay 1997).

The integration of AI-powered Machine Translation technologies has revolutionized the translation industry, offering both significant opportunities and significant challenges (Yang 2022). Machine Translation has the potential to drastically improve efficiency, reduce translation costs, and provide faster access to multilingual content. These benefits are particularly evident in large-scale translation projects, where human translators may struggle to meet the high demand for rapid translations. Machine Translation systems can handle repetitive or highly standardized content, such as technical manuals, marketing materials, or customer service queries, with remarkable speed and accuracy, making them invaluable tools in modern globalized industries (Majumde et al. 2022). Yet, several challenges remain when comparing Machine Translation to human translation. Mostly, Machine Translation (MT) faces challenges in understanding language nuances, cultural references, and context-dependent meanings. While digital systems can translate technical information, they struggle to convey emotional tone in business, literary, or legal contexts, leading to inaccurate terminology and culturally inappropriate expressions. As a result, the quality of MT can suffer from issues such as inaccurate terminology, inconsistent phrasing, or culturally inappropriate expressions. In line with these issues, Bennett and Gerber (2003) posit "Historically, MT has been most often, and most successfully, applied to relatively formal or technical/scientific writing". The argument is that terminology here is very repetition prone, there is a demand for style consistency, and this area is pretty much controlled. Most factual data are given, free from social or cultural meanings and with little ambiguity, that maximizes efficiency in machine translation. However, depending on the degree of human involvement, three distinct types of MT can be identified:

- **Automated MT**: Translation carried out solely by MT engines (e.g., DeepL, Google Translate, Microsoft Bing Translator, Yandex Translate, PROMPT).
- **Adapted MT**: Translation using MT, involving either pre-translation adjustments to the source text (such as simplifying syntactic structures or optimizing thematic organization) or post-translation human editing.
- **Computer-Assisted Translation (CAT)**: Translation performed by human translators, supported by software tools designed to improve efficiency (e.g., SDL Trados, SmartCat, Reverso—referred to as CAT tools, short for "computer-assisted translation").

Hereof, machine translation systems offer numerous benefits, including faster translation speed, practicality, broader linguistic coverage, cost-free usage, and accessibility (Gladkov 2021). They process text faster than human translators, making them ideal for urgent everyday situations. Machine translation systems can work with many languages, often dozens or hundreds, and can be used for personal, routine, or informational needs. However, they are not perfect and require careful consideration to ensure their usefulness and effectiveness. especially in complex or high-stakes business environments (O'Hagan 2016). Balancing the strengths of both machine translation and human expertise will be essential in meeting the growth. In professional literature the following limitations are outlined (Kullen 2020):

- Thematic Limitations
- Linguistic Limitations
- Focus on Form and Meaning
- Terminological Accuracy
- Emphasis and Word Order

So, the effectiveness of MT in translating business texts largely depends on the quality and availability of human translations, especially in specialized business areas. In fields with limited parallel texts, human translators with expertise in business terminology, business slang, and industry-specific language remain indispensable.

3 Methodology

This study follows a qualitative research methodology, applying analysis and comparison strategies to address the research questions. The research employs descriptive analysis to examine and explore the benefits and drawbacks of business text translation through both AI-driven and human translations. To analyze the data, thematic analysis is used to identify key themes related to AI-driven and human translations. The survey was distributed to 30 professors from Yerevan State University (YSU) and the European University of Armenia (EUA), who teach in the "Translation Studies" Degree Programs and have over 10 years of experience in the field. The survey was also sent to freelance translators and senior year students specializing in administrative translation.

4 Results and Discussion

The majority of the participants (98%) have Armenian as their native language. This suggests that the sample group is predominantly native Armenian speakers. *University Professors* (51.9%) and *Freelance Translators* (46.3%) make up the largest groups, with a smaller proportion identifying as "*Other*" (senior year students).

A significant portion of respondents (75.9%) translate business texts into *English*, while 22.2% translate into *Armenian*. The results are expected, given the global dominance of English in business communications. The high percentage of English as a target language highlights the importance of machine translation tools, which are often optimized for high-demand languages like English. It should be noted that 29.6% of participants have more than ten years of experience, indicating a well-seasoned group of professionals who are likely to have significant insights into the challenges and nuances of translation. A significant part of the respondents, 35.2%, have 3–5 years of experience, which represents a middle level of expertise. In turn, 29.6% have little experience, likely reflecting newcomers (senior year students) to the field. This distribution shows a diverse range of experiences, which is beneficial in understanding how various experience levels influence the perspectives on AI-driven versus human translation.

A majority of 56.6% of participants have received *formal training in translation studies*, while 43.4% have not. The fact that over half of the participants have formal training suggests that the responses are grounded in professional knowledge, which could influence their views on the effectiveness of AI in translation. Those who have formal training might have a deeper understanding of traditional translation methods, which may shape their opinions on the role of AI in business translation.

In terms of the level of experience, 40.7% of respondents report having *moderate experience* with machine translation, while another 40.7% have *limited experience.* This suggests that most participants have some familiarity with MT but may not be fully immersed in its advanced or widespread use. As for the tools, the results clearly show that *Google Translate* is the dominant MT engine, with over 80% of participants using it. *Microsoft Translator* and *DeepL* are also notable choices, with a significant number of respondents favoring these tools for business translations. The use of *Amazon Translate* and *SDL Machine Translation* is less common, suggesting that while these tools have their place, they are not as popular among the survey participants. The analysis of the types of business texts, typically translated using MT, is presented based on the survey data.

A significant portion of respondents (61.1%) use machine translation for *legal documents*, including contracts and patents. This could suggest that while legal translation often requires high accuracy, MT is used here for quicker drafts or as an initial translation tool, possibly followed by human revision to ensure legal precision. 33.3% of respondents translate *marketing materials* using MT. 25.9% of participants use MT for translating technical documentation, including manuals and specifications. This is likely because technical texts often contain standardized vocabulary and terminology that MT engines can handle effectively, even though specialized knowledge is still required for accuracy. Another 25.9% use MT for *internal communications*, such as emails, memos, and training materials. These texts are often less formal and may not require the same level of accuracy as legal or technical documents, making them more suitable for MT translation. A smaller group, 18.5%, translates *financial reports* using MT. Financial documents, while important, are often quite structured, so MT could be used for initial drafts or to facilitate translations of financial data. However, the need for high accuracy and contextual understanding means that human translation may be preferred for finalized versions. The smallest percentage, 13%, use MT for *customer service communications* like chat transcripts or FAQs. These texts might be translated with MT to ensure a quick response to customer queries. However, due to the need for conversational tone and understanding, human input is likely required to ensure the responses are appropriate and contextually accurate.

The most common difficulty (64.8%) is translating *specialized terminology*. This highlights the challenge that MT engines face in dealing with technical, legal, or industry-specific vocabulary. Since these terms may have no direct equivalent in the target language, MT can struggle with ensuring accurate translations in these areas. *Cultural references and idioms* are another major challenge (38.9%). MT systems often fail to properly capture the nuances and cultural context of idiomatic expressions, leading to translations that may sound unnatural or culturally inappropriate. Many respondents (37%) indicated difficulty with *complex sentence structures*. MT systems may have trouble translating long, compound, or convoluted sentences, which can result in grammatically incorrect or unclear translations. 25.9% of respondents consider *Consistency in terminology* yet another issue in business translations, especially those involving multiple documents. Adapting translations to suit different target audiences is a difficulty for 31.5% of participants.

Business translations often need to be tailored to specific readers, such as investors, customers, or internal teams, and MT may not effectively adjust tone or language for these varied audiences. *Data privacy and confidentiality* are a concern for 11.1% of respondents. When using MT tools, especially cloud-based systems, there is a potential risk of sensitive business information being exposed or mishandled. Only 7.4% mentioned *integration with business systems* as a difficulty. This might suggest that, while some respondents encounter this issue, it is not as widespread as other challenges, possibly because integrations are more likely in larger businesses or specific industries. The need for *post-editing resources* is a concern for 27.8% of respondents. MT tools often require human review and editing, and the lack of reliable post-editing resources can make this process time-consuming and difficult. *Determining the accuracy* of MT output is a significant challenge for 38.9% of respondents. MT systems are not perfect, and users often face difficulty in assessing whether the translation is correct, especially when dealing with specialized or complex texts.

The most common error (59.3%) is the need to *rephrase awkward sentences*. MT often produces translations that are grammatically correct but sound unnatural or clumsy in the target language. This often requires substantial rephrasing to make the text more readable and fluent. *Terminology accuracy* is another frequent error (53.7%). MT systems may misinterpret or inaccurately translate specialized terms, requiring human intervention to ensure correct terminology is used in business documents. The need to *adapt for cultural appropriateness* (46.3%) suggests that MT struggles with translating content in a way that is culturally sensitive and suitable for the target audience. This is especially critical in business translations, where cultural context is important. *Grammatical errors* (44.4%) are also a common issue, with MT often producing sentences that may be grammatically incorrect or lack proper structure. These errors require post-editing to improve the overall quality and coherence of the translation. Ensuring *stylistic consistency* (42.6%) is another frequent challenge. Business texts often need to maintain a consistent tone, formality level, and style across all translations, which MT engines may struggle to handle effectively. *Adding or removing information* (37%) suggests that MT can sometimes either omit important details or over-translate certain phrases. Ensuring that the translated text accurately reflects the original meaning is a common problem with MT. *Verifying data and facts* (25.9%) indicates that MT may introduce inaccuracies in factual information, which is particularly concerning business documents where accuracy is critical. This error often requires a human translator to cross-check and ensure that all facts are correctly represented.

5 Conclusion

The results of the study revealed several key insights into the use of machine translation in business contexts. First, machine translation offers significant advantages, particularly for routine or less complex business texts such as marketing materials, customer service communications, and internal communications. MT tools like Google Translate and DeepL have proven to improve speed and accessibility, enabling businesses to quickly meet the growing demand for multilingual content at a lower cost.

However, despite these benefits, MT continues to face challenges. One of its main limitations is its difficulty in accurately translating specialized business terminology, maintaining stylistic consistency, and adapting the tone and style of the source text to suit the target culture. MT systems often struggle to capture the subtle meanings behind idiomatic expressions, cultural references, and context-dependent phrases, all of which are crucial in business communication. In line with these challenges, human translators remain indispensable, particularly in fields such as legal, financial, and technical translation, where precision, cultural sensitivity, and industry-specific knowledge are paramount. Human involvement ensures that translations meet the required standards of quality, accuracy, and cultural relevance.

Moreover, the study highlights the importance of post-editing, where human translators refine MT output by correcting errors in grammar, terminology, and awkward phrasing. Furthermore, there are opportunities for improvement through the integration of MT with human post-editing. While MT can handle repetitive tasks and provide a draft translation, human translators add the necessary expertise to ensure the final product meets professional quality standards. As AI and machine learning continue to advance, MT systems are expected to improve in handling more complex texts, but human expertise will remain essential for ensuring high-quality results. Looking ahead, the study suggests that the future of business translation lies in a collaborative model, where AI tools assist human translators, enhancing their efficiency while maintaining high standards of translation quality. As AI technology evolves, translators will need to adapt by acquiring skills in Natural Language Processing (NLP) and machine translation post-editing, enabling them to fully leverage the potential of these tools.

Data Availability

The feedback from university professors and freelance translators is available at https://figshare.com with the identifier https://doi.org/10.6084/m9.figshare.28736729.

The responses regarding the target language when translating business texts are available at https://figshare.com with the identifier https://doi.org/10.6084/m9.figshare.28736729.

The responses to the question "How many years of experience do you have in translation?" are available at https://figshare.com with the identifier https://doi.org/10.6084/m9.figshare.28736729.

The responses to the question "Have you received formal training in translation studies?" are available at https://figshare.com with the identifier https://doi.org/10.6084/m9.figshare.28736729.

The responses to the question "Which machine translation (MT) engines do you typically use for business texts?" are available at https://figshare.com with the identifier https://doi.org/10.6084/m9.figshare.28736729.

The responses to the question "What types of business texts do you typically translate using MT?" are available at https://figshare.com with the identifier https://doi.org/10.6084/m9.figshare.28736729.

The responses to the question "Please indicate mostly encountered difficulties while using MT for business text translation" are available at https://figshare.com with the identifier https://doi.org/10.6084/m9.figshare.28736729.

The responses to the question "Please indicate errors encountered in machine-translated business texts" are available at https://figshare.com with the identifier https://doi.org/10.6084/m9.figshare.28736729.

References

Bennett, S., and L. Gerber. 2003. Inside commercial machine translation. In *Computers and translation: A translator's guide*, ed. H. L. Somers, 175–190. Amsterdam: John Benjamins.

Church, K. W., and E. Hovy. 1993. Good applications for crummy machine translation. *Machine Translation* 8 (4): 1–15.

Esselink, B. 2001. Leningrad meets Amsterdam, Amsterdam meets Aquarius. *Language International* 13 (2): 12–15.

Gladkov, S. 2021. *Chto skrivaet "II": on povsyudu vokrug nas—no sushestvuet li on voobshe?* https://www.russian-translators.ru/articles/tehnologii/-iskusstvennogo-intellekta-v-mp/ (data: 10.02.2025).

Holmström, J. E. 1951. *Report on interlingual scientific and technical dictionaries*. 2nd ed. Paris: UNESCO. H.M. Stationery Office, 128, UNESCO Publication 884.

Hutchins, W. J. 1986. *Machine translation: Past, present, future*, 382. Chichester, Sussex: Ellis Horwood.

Kay, M. 1997. The proper place of men and machines in language translation. *Machine Translation* 12 (1/2): 3–23.

Kullen, A. 2020. *Kak rabotaet iskusstvenniy intelekt v oblasti literaturnogo perevoda.* https://www.goethe.de/ins/ru/ru/kul/sup/wdw/22016591.html (data: 11.02.2025).

Majumde, S., S. Lauly, M. Nadejde, M. Federico, and G. Dinu. 2022. *A baseline revisited: Pushing the limits of multi-segment models for context-aware translation*. https://arxiv.org/pdf/2210.10906 (data: 10.02.2025).

O'Hagan, M. 2016. Massively open translation: Unpacking the relationship between technology and translation in the 21st century. *International Journal of Communication* 10: https://ijoc.org/index.php/ijoc/article/view/3507 (data: 12.02.2025).

Yang, C. 2022. The application of artificial intelligence in translation teaching. Proceedings of the 4th international conference on intelligent science and technology, 56–60. https://doi.org/10.1145/3568923.3568933 (data: 10.02.2025).

Ethical Boundaries of Smart Automation in the State Regulation of the AI Economy

Mechanisms of Artificial Intelligence in Implementing Innovative Policy Within the Sustainable Development Framework of the Kyrgyz Republic

Svetlana V. Zatravina, Venera A. Musaeva, Kalina A. Toktorbaeva, Aigulia Satieva, and Nazira E. Asylbekova

Abstract This research aims to identify the most promising artificial intelligence (AI) mechanisms and develop recommendations for enhancing these mechanisms in implementing innovative policy within the sustainable development framework of the Kyrgyz Republic. To achieve this, the authors conducted a regression analysis based on the empirical experience of Central Asian countries in 2025 to assess the impact of AI mechanisms on the targeted outcomes of the innovative policy implemented within these countries' sustainable development systems. The conclusion is that in Central Asian countries, including the Kyrgyz Republic, the most effective AI mechanisms that systemically improve the outcomes of innovative policy within the sustainable development framework are AI implementation and AI financing. The theoretical contribution of this finding lies in the fact that a more precise delineation of the spectrum of relevant AI mechanisms has enhanced the management apparatus of innovative policy in the sustainable development systems of Central Asian countries while also expanding the capabilities for planning and forecasting the results of the innovative policy implemented in the Kyrgyz Republic's sustainable development framework. The practical contribution of the proposed applied solutions to enhance the most in-demand AI mechanisms is that their implementation will increase the effectiveness of the innovative policy within the Kyrgyz Republic's sustainable development framework. Moreover, it will also facilitate the successful execution of the action plan for integrating human rights into the business environment and practices of the Kyrgyz Republic.

Keywords Artificial intelligence mechanisms • Innovative policy • Sustainable development system • Economy of the Kyrgyz Republic • Central Asia

---

S. V. Zatravina (✉)
Scientific Research University «Kyrgyz Economic University named after M. Ryskulbekov», Bishkek, Kyrgyzstan

V. A. Musaeva · K. A. Toktorbaeva · A. Satieva · N. E. Asylbekova
Kyrgyz National University named after Jusup Balasagyn, Bishkek, Kyrgyzstan

A. Karbekova (ed.), *Ethics of the AI Economy: A System View from the Positions of the Theory of Stakeholders*, Ethical Economy 73,
https://doi.org/10.1007/978-3-032-23423-0_28

JEL Codes O38 • Q01

1 Introduction

At the beginning of 2025, the Kyrgyz Republic approved an action plan to integrate human rights into the business environment and corporate practices (UNDP 2025). This marked the launch of an innovative policy within the country's sustainable development framework, which will be implemented over the next 5 years. The government initiative introduced into the Kyrgyz economy is of great significance for incorporating the Sustainable Development Goals (SDGs) into the institutional fabric of this national economic system.

In implementing the initiative, it is advisable to fully utilize the technological potential of the Kyrgyz Republic's economic system to ensure its economic efficiency. Today's digital landscape in the Kyrgyz economy is largely defined by artificial intelligence, whose potential remains far from exhausted even in the world's leading digital economies and is even more significant in the Kyrgyz Republic. Simultaneously, considerable international experience has been amassed in automating economic processes using artificial intelligence (AI), albeit with mixed outcomes.

On the one hand, introducing AI opens up additional opportunities to optimize economic processes, thereby increasing the attractiveness of investment in innovative projects. Promoting artificial intelligence as part of the state's innovative policy enhances its digital competitiveness and bolsters its standing in the global Industry 5.0 markets, which are expanding under the influence of the Fifth Industrial Revolution.

On the other hand, cyber-social systems face growing criticism from the standpoint of sustainable development. The spread of artificial intelligence in an unprepared society can trigger social unrest by disrupting established ways of life. While implementing innovative policy within the sustainable development framework of the Kyrgyz Republic is intended to drive socially significant economic transformations, imposing automation based on artificial intelligence on economic actors may lead to undesirable changes and deprive them of more favorable alternatives.

In addition to mitigating the societal consequences of technological changes in the economy when implementing innovative policy within the Kyrgyz Republic's sustainable development framework, it is essential to rely on effective AI mechanisms. Although AI is commonly regarded as a tool for automating economic processes, its range of mechanisms is quite broad. Consequently, the approach to its dissemination is ambiguous—it may involve either the comprehensive use of automation mechanisms or a focus on the most promising among them.

Thus, a pressing scientific and practical challenge is the selection of the most in-demand artificial intelligence mechanisms in the Kyrgyz Republic and establishing their successful use to support the implementation of innovative policy within the country's sustainable development framework. To address this issue, this study aims to identify the most promising artificial intelligence mechanisms and develop recommendations to enhance these mechanisms in implementing innovative policy within the sustainable development framework of the Kyrgyz Republic.

2 Literature Review

Taking the scientific and theoretical concept of the innovative economy as the fundamental basis of this research, it is viewed as an economic system that demonstrates relatively high and growing innovative activity compared to other participants in international economic relations and reveals its own potential for innovative development (Tursunov 2022).

According to this concept, innovation policy within the sustainable development framework is understood as the state-supported innovative activity in the economy that best achieves the Sustainable Development Goals (SDGs). The primary target outcomes of the innovation policies implemented by contemporary economic systems in sustainable development, as presented in the available scientific literature, are as follows:

- The sustainable development of institutions within the innovative economy in support of SDG 16 ($IpSd_1$) (Bogoviz et al. 2018);
- The sustainable development of education in support of SDG 4 ($IpSd_2$) (Vanchukhina et al. 2022);
- The sustainable development of infrastructure and the greening of the economy in support of SDGs 7 and 12–15 ($IpSd_3$) (Salahodjaev et al. 2023);
- The sustainable development of international economic relations in support of SDG 17 ($IpSd_4$) (Sozinova et al. 2023),
- The sustainable development of knowledge and technologies in support of SDG 9 ($IpSd_5$) (Mkrtchyan et al. 2024);
- The sustainable development of the labor market and sustained economic growth in support of SDG 8 ($IpSd_6$) (Buitek et al. 2023);
- Enhancing the country's position in global markets to reduce global inequality in support of SDG 10 ($IpSd_7$) (Bezrukova et al. 2016).

The existing literature identifies the following key mechanisms of artificial intelligence (AI):

- AI technologies (M_{AI1}) (Inshakova et al. 2021);
- AI skills (M_{AI2}) (Ergasheva et al. 2024);
- AI R&D (M_{AI3}) (Soylu et al. 2021);
- AI implementation (M_{AI4}) (Abdurakhmanova et al. 2022),
- AI financing (M_{AI5}) (Ostrovskaya et al. 2017).

Nevertheless, a gap in the scientific literature remains regarding how the application of AI mechanisms to the implementation of innovation policies within the sustainable development system influences development outcomes in the countries of

Central Asia, including the Kyrgyz Republic. The research question (RQ) is: "What AI mechanisms facilitate the implementation of innovation policies within the sustainable development system in Central Asia?"

3 Materials and Methods

The research sample includes all Central Asian countries for which the relevant indicators are statistically recorded (Table 1) in 2025. To address the research question, the authors employed a regression analysis method. Using this method, the influence of AI mechanisms ($M_{AI1\text{–}5}$), as evaluated by UNCTAD (2023), on the target outcomes of the innovation policy implemented within the sustainable development system ($IpSd_{1\text{–}7}$), as assessed by WIPO, is determined (WIPO 2024).

After selection of the most promising mechanisms of AI (in which regression coefficients took positive values) in Central Asia, the authors determined the prospect of increasing the effectiveness of the implemented innovation policy in the system of sustainable development of the Kyrgyz Republic with the activation of selected mechanisms and the fullest disclosure of their potential until 2030.

4 Results

The established influence of AI mechanisms on the target results of the realized innovation policy in the sustainable development system of Central Asia in 2025 is reflected in the regression statistics from Table 2.

Based on the regression statistics in Table 2, the following conclusions, valid for Central Asian countries, have been drawn. A one-point increase in the development of AI technologies results in a three-point rise in the sustainable development of international economic relations, along with a 17.1-point increase in the country's global market position. A one-point improvement in AI skills contributes to the sustainable development of innovative economy institutions by 33.1 points, education by 19.2 points, infrastructure and the greening of the economy by 24.6 points, knowledge and technologies by 15.7 points, and the labor market by 4.8 points.

A one-point increase in AI R&D activity ensures a 55.8-point improvement in the sustainable development of international economic relations and a 23.6-point boost in the labor market. A one-point increase in AI implementation activity achieves a sustainable development of innovative economy institutions by 83.6 points, education by 36.6 points, infrastructure and the greening of the economy by 56.1 points, knowledge and technologies by 41.7 points, the labor market by 4.0 points, and the country's global market position by 11.6 points.

Similarly, a one-point increase in AI financing produces a 64.5-point advancement in the sustainable development of innovative economy institutions, 68.0 points in education, 96.7 points in infrastructure and the greening of the economy, 23.2

Table 1 AI mechanisms and innovation policy in the system of sustainable development of Central Asia in 2025, score

Country	ICT	Skills	R&D	Industry activity	Access to finance	Institutions	Human capital and research	Infrastructure	Market sophistication	Business sophistication	Knowledge and technology outputs	Creative outputs
	M_{AI1}	M_{AI2}	M_{AI3}	M_{AI4}	M_{AI5}	$IpSd_1$	$IpSd_2$	$IpSd_3$	$IpSd_4$	$IpSd_5$	$IpSd_6$	$IpSd_7$
China	0.4	0.4	1.0	0.9	0.9	57.6	50.3	62.4	55.8	58.0	61.7	50.0
India	0.5	0.4	0.8	0.8	0.7	51.5	34.8	39.0	52.3	28.1	38.8	32.1
Iran	0.6	0.5	0.5	0.4	0.7	10.9	32.1	29.6	55.4	18.6	25.9	30.9
Kazakhstan	0.5	0.7	0.3	0.6	0.5	44.2	32.0	40.9	25.2	26.0	15.9	19.5
Kyrgyzstan	0.4	0.4	0.1	0.5	0.5	25.1	39.6	36.3	27.7	17.5	10.8	12.1
Mongolia	0.5	0.5	0.1	0.4	0.6	35.9	26.1	38.4	21.0	27.5	15.8	39.4
Pakistan	0.2	0.1	0.4	0.6	0.4	25.3	15.4	21.1	24.3	24.9	21.0	22.6
Russia	0.7	0.7	0.6	0.7	0.7	19.1	41.1	36.9	36.1	29.8	23.7	30.1
Tajikistan	0.1	0.3	0.1	0.4	0.4	31.7	25.1	26.3	23.2	20.4	16.6	7.1

Source: Developed by the authors UNCTAD (2023) and WIPO (2024)

Table 2 Regression statistics

	Regression coefficients at:							Arithmetic mean of regression coefficients	Share of positive regression coefficients, %
	$IpSd_1$	$IpSd_2$	$IpSd_3$	$IpSd_4$	$IpSd_5$	$IpSd_6$	$IpSd_7$		
Y-intercept	-23.8	-19.3	-30.9	31.1	-21.4	-9.5	-18.3	-	-
M_{AI1}	-70.2	-17.4	-39.4	**3.0**	-46.9	-44.7	**17.1**	-28.4	28.6
M_{AI2}	**33.1**	**19.2**	**24.6**	-4.6	**15.7**	**4.8**	-26.2	9.5	71.4
M_{AI3}	-34.5	-25.5	-39.8	**55.8**	-15.5	**23.6**	-12.8	-7.0	28.6
M_{AI4}	**83.6**	**36.6**	**56.1**	-55.6	**41.7**	**4.0**	**11.6**	25.4	85.7
M_{AI5}	**64.5**	**68.0**	**96.7**	**23.2**	**74.7**	**66.3**	**80.6**	67.7	100.0
Multiple R	0.8305	0.8963	0.9717	0.9436	0.9364	0.9964	0.8803	-	-

Source: Developed by the authors

points in international economic relations, 74.7 points in knowledge and technologies, 66.3 points in the labor market, and an 80.6-point rise in the country's global market position.

Thus, the most promising AI mechanisms in Central Asia that systemically enhance the outcomes of the implemented innovation policy within the sustainable development system are AI implementation (M_{AI4}) and AI financing (M_{AI5}), as nearly all regression coefficients for these mechanisms were positive. The arithmetic mean of the regression coefficients was 25.4 points for M_{AI4} and 67.7 points for M_{AI5}, with the share of positive coefficients being 85.7% for M_{AI4} and 100% for M_{AI5}.

Therefore, to improve the effectiveness and success of the innovation policy within the sustainable development system of the Kyrgyz Republic, it is recommended that the selected mechanisms be boosted: increasing AI implementation activity and expanding AI financing. In light of these conclusions, a perspective for enhancing the outcomes of the implemented innovation policy in the sustainable development system of the Kyrgyz Republic has been identified by activating the selected mechanisms and fully realizing their potential until 2030. For this purpose, the maximum values (one point) for M_{AI4} and M_{AI5} were substituted into the regression models described in Table 2. The resulting forecast is shown in Fig. 1.

The forecast in Fig. 1 indicates that if the Kyrgyz Republic achieves maximum AI implementation activity along with universal access to and full sufficiency of AI financing, the effectiveness of the nation's innovation policy within its sustainable development framework will change as follows:

- The resilience of the innovative economy institutions will increase by 262.6% (from 25.1 points in 2025 to 91.0 points by 2030);
- The sustainability of education will rise by 152.5% (from 39.6 points in 2025 to 100.0 points by 2030);
- The sustainability of infrastructure and the greening of the economy will grow by 175.5% (from 36.3 points in 2025 to 100.0 points by 2030);
- The sustainability of international economic relations will decrease by 52.9% (from 27.7 points in 2025 to 13.1 points by 2030);

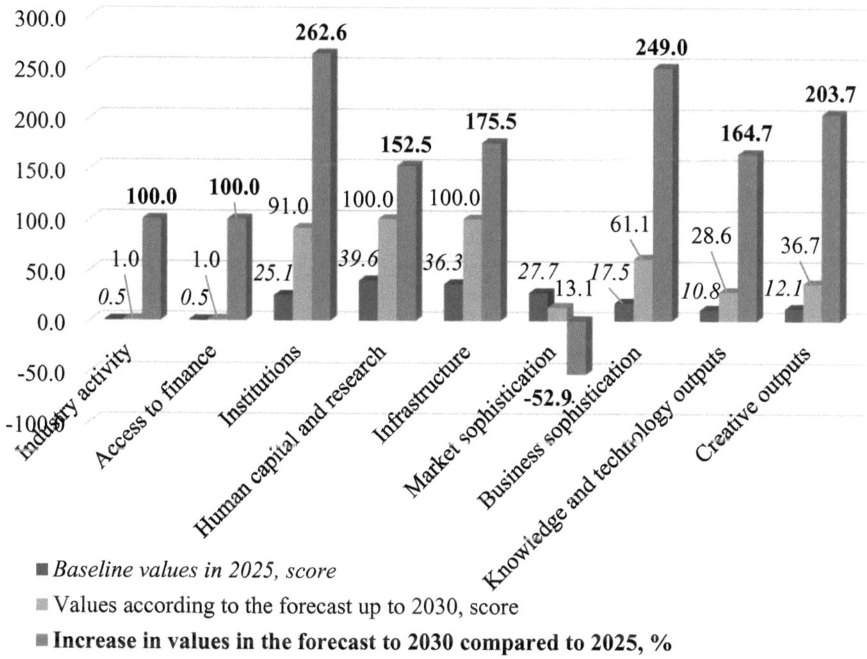

Fig. 1 Forecasting the results of innovation policy in the sustainable development system of the Kyrgyz Republic with the activation of AI mechanisms. Source: Developed by the authors

- The resilience of knowledge and technologies will increase by 249.0% (from 17.5 points in 2025 to 61.1 points by 2030);
- The sustainability of the labor market and economic growth will rise by 164.7% (from 10.8 points in 2025 to 28.6 points by 2030);
- The country's global market position will improve by 203.7% (from 12.1 points in 2025 to 36.7 points by 2030).

5 Discussion

The achieved results, summarized in Fig. 2, complement the series of works by Bezrukova et al. (2016), Bogoviz et al. (2018), Buitek et al. (2023), Mkrtchyan et al. (2024), Salahodjaev et al. (2023), Sozinova et al. (2023), Tursunov (2022), and Vanchukhina et al. (2022), as well as the scientific-theoretical concept of the innovative economy, by elucidating the consequences of applying AI mechanisms in implementing innovation policy within the sustainable development system in Central Asia.

In contrast to Inshakova et al. (2021), the authors showed that AI technologies do not enhance but rather diminish the overall outcomes of the innovation policy within

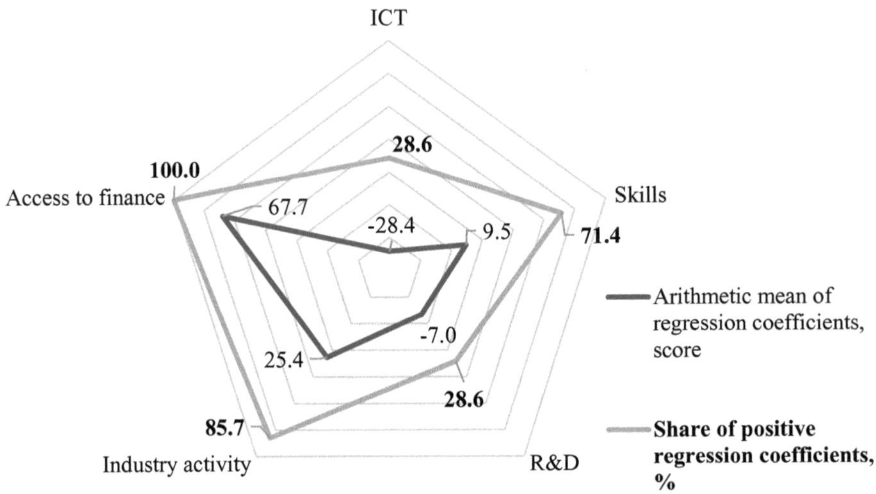

Fig. 2 The overall impact of each AI mechanism on aggregate innovation policy outcomes in the sustainable development system in Central Asia. Source: Developed by the authors

the sustainable development system in Central Asia by an average of 28.4 points for each one-point increase in the activity level of this mechanism (with only 28.6% of the regression coefficients being positive).

Unlike Ergasheva et al. (2024), the authors found that AI skills only slightly improve the overall outcomes of the innovation policy in the sustainable development system in Central Asia by an average of 9.5 points per one-point increase in the activity level of this mechanism (with 71.4% of the regression coefficients being positive).

In contrast to Soylu et al. (2021), it was determined that AI R&D does not enhance but rather reduces the overall outcomes of the innovation policy within the sustainable development system in Central Asia by an average of 7.0 points for each one-point increase in the activity level of this mechanism (with only 28.6% of the regression coefficients being positive).

Supporting the findings of Abdurakhmanova et al. (2022), this research established that AI implementation significantly enhances the overall outcomes of the innovation policy within the sustainable development system in Central Asia by an average of 25.4 points for each one-point increase in the activity of this mechanism (with 85.7% of the regression coefficients being positive).

Confirming the findings of Ostrovskaya et al. (2017), the research demonstrated that AI financing markedly improves the overall outcomes of the innovation policy within the sustainable development system in Central Asia by an average of 67.7 points for each one-point increase in the activity level of this mechanism (with 100.0% of the regression coefficients being positive).

6 Conclusion

As a result of examining the latest (2025) empirical experience of Central Asian countries, the authors conclude that in these nations, including the Kyrgyz Republic, the most effective AI mechanisms for implementing innovation policy within the sustainable development framework and systemically enhancing the outcomes of that policy are AI implementation and AI financing.

The theoretical significance of this research lies in the fact that by narrowing the focus to the key AI mechanisms, the managerial apparatus of innovation policy within the sustainable development system in Central Asian countries, particularly in the Kyrgyz Republic, has been clarified. In turn, this expands the possibilities for planning and forecasting the outcomes of the innovation policy implemented within the sustainable development framework of the Kyrgyz Republic.

The proposals for enhancing the most demanded AI mechanisms possess practical significance because they will help improve the effectiveness of implementing innovation policy within the sustainable development system of the Kyrgyz Republic. Moreover, they will facilitate the successful execution of the action plan (UNDP 2025) for integrating human rights into the business environment and business practices of the Kyrgyz Republic.

References

Abdurakhmanova, G. K., O. T. Astanakulov, S. B. Goyipnazarov, and A. B. Irmatova. 2022. Tourism 4.0: Opportunities for applying industry 4.0 technologies in tourism. In *Proceedings of ICFNDS '22: The 6th international conference on future networks & distributed systems*, 33–38. New York, NY: Association for Computing Machinery. https://doi.org/10.1145/3584202.3584208.

Bezrukova, T. L., A. T. Gyiazov, and A. M. Bazieva. 2016. Modelling and forecasting of innovative development of entrepreneurial structures under the global competition. *Actual Problems of Economics* 182 (8): 344–351.

Bogoviz, A. V., P. M. Taranov, and A. V. Shuvaev. 2018. Innovational tools for provision of food security through state support for the agro-industrial complex in the conditions of digital economy. In *The impact of information on modern humans*, ed. E. Popkova, 659–665. Cham, Switzerland: Springer. https://doi.org/10.1007/978-3-319-75383-6_84.

Buitek, E., S. A. Kaliyeva, A. N. Turginbayeva, M. K. Meldakhanova, and A. A. Shaikh. 2023. How much does an employer's attractiveness matter to youth employment? Evidence from a developing country. *Asia-Pacific Journal of Business Administration* 17 (1): 258–283. https://doi.org/10.1108/APJBA-02-2023-0086.

Ergasheva, S. T., Z. V. Gornostaeva, A. A. Sozinova, and G. V. Borodin. 2024. Digital HRM as a model of knowledge management in the decade of science and technology in Russia. *Proceedings on Engineering Sciences* 6 (3): 1087–1096. https://doi.org/10.24874/PES06.03A.001.

Inshakova, A. O., A. A. Sozinova, and T. N. Litvinova. 2021. Corporate fight against the COVID-19 risks based on technologies of industry 4.0 as a new direction of social responsibility. *Risks* 9 (12): 212. https://doi.org/10.3390/risks9120212.

Mkrtchyan, T. M., R. R. Rashidov, A. A. Krutilin, and R. O. Tazhiyev. 2024. Regulation and enforcement of human rights, transparency, data protection, ethics of technology, and data use

in the context of digital transformation. In *Digital inclusiveness: Bridging the divide in the digital economy*, ed. E. G. Popkova, 75–86. Singapore: World Scientific Publishing. https://doi.org/10.1142/9789811270826_0007.
Ostrovskaya, V. N., Y. G. Tyurina, A. V. Bogoviz, N. V. Przhedetskaya, and S. V. Lobova. 2017. Foreign economic activities of subjects of SME in the context of cooperation of Russia and Europe. In *Overcoming uncertainty of institutional environment as a tool of global crisis management*, ed. E. Popkova, 597–603. Cham, Switzerland: Springer. https://doi.org/10.1007/978-3-319-60696-5_75.
Salahodjaev, R., B. Djalilov, I. Kobiljonov, S. Otajonov, and N. Kasimova. 2023. Industrialization and CO2 emissions: Accounting for the role of renewable energy in OIC member states. *International Journal of Energy Economics and Policy* 13 (5): 37–43. https://doi.org/10.32479/ijeep.12544.
Soylu, D., T. D. Medeni, R. Andekina, R. Rakhmetova, and R. Ismailova. 2021. *Identifying the cybercrime awareness of undergraduate and postgraduate students: Example of Kazakhstan*, Proceedings of SIST 2021: 2021 IEEE international conference on smart information systems and technologies, 1–7. Nur-Sultan, Kazakhstan. https://doi.org/10.1109/SIST50301.2021.9465995.
Sozinova, A. A., A. A. Shadiyeva, A. T. Giyazov, and S. A. Litvinova. 2023. Sustainable development goals as a milestone of strategic alliances: A viewpoint from the perspective of the game theory. In *Game strategies for business integration in the digital economy*, ed. E. G. Popkova, 111–121. Leeds, UK: Emerald Publishing Limited. https://doi.org/10.1108/S1069-096420230000027012.
Tursunov, B. 2022. Provincial Features of industrial production dynamics in the research of textile enterprises' financial security in Uzbekistan. In *Imitation market modeling in digital economy: Game theoretic approaches*, ed. E. G. Popkova, 601–610. Cham, Switzerland: Springer. https://doi.org/10.1007/978-3-030-93244-2_66.
UNCTAD. 2023. *Frontier technology readiness index, annual*. https://unctadstat.unctad.org/datacentre/dataviewer/US.FTRI. Accessed 2 Mar 2025.
UNDP. 2025. *Kyrgyz Republic adopted National Action Plan on Business and Human Rights*. January 16. https://www.undp.org/kyrgyzstan/press-releases/kyrgyz-republic-adopted-national-action-plan-business-and-human-rights. Accessed 2 Mar 2025.
Vanchukhina, L. I., T. B. Leybert, S. T. Ergasheva, E. A. Khalikova, and I. R. Khanafieva. 2022. Integration of the higher education systems of Russia and the Republic of Uzbekistan in training for the digital economy. In *Digital education in Russia and Central Asia*, ed. E. G. Popkova and B. S. Sergi, 3–13. Singapore: Springer. https://doi.org/10.1007/978-981-16-9069-3_1.
WIPO. 2024. *Global innovation index 2024: Unlocking the promise of social entrepreneurship*. 17th ed. Geneva, Switzerland: WIPO. https://www.wipo.int/web-publications/global-innovation-index-2024/assets/67729/2000%20Global%20Innovation%20Index%202024_WEB3lite.pdf. Accessed 2 Mar 2025.

Artificial Intelligence Technologies as a Catalyst for the Sustainable Development of Russia's Economy

Elena M. Kryukova

Abstract The relevance of this research to Russia's economy arises from the necessity to diversify away from raw material dependence and modernize and technologically update. In the face of global competition and sanctions pressure, the adoption of artificial intelligence (AI) technologies represents a strategic move toward increasing labor productivity, optimizing resources, stimulating economic growth, and enhancing competitiveness in the global market. The country possesses significant potential for applying AI in sectors such as energy, agriculture, and transportation. The research focuses on AI technologies and their implementation across various sectors of Russia's economy. The research aims to assess the impact of these technologies on the sustainable development of the nation's economy. The research aims to determine the role of AI in ensuring the sustainable development of the Russian economy. The primary research objectives include analyzing the current application of AI in Russia and identifying the obstacles and opportunities for its advancement. The research methodology is based on a comprehensive analysis of statistical data, expert assessments, and a comparative study of AI implementation experiences in other countries. The novelty of this research lies in the systematization of data on the impact of AI on Russia's economy, with an emphasis on sustainable development and the integration of advanced technologies. Another important aspect is the conducted survey (using questionnaires) to explore public opinion regarding the integration of AI technologies into professional activities, exemplified by the journalistic community. The research findings show that the implementation of AI contributes to a 15–20% increase in labor productivity, a 10–15% reduction in production costs, and an acceleration of innovation. However, barriers such as inadequate digital infrastructure and a shortage of qualified personnel remain.

Keywords Artificial intelligence • Technology • Economy • Sustainable development • Sectoral economy • Regional economy

E. M. Kryukova (✉)
Russian State Social University, Moscow, Russia

A. Karbekova (ed.), *Ethics of the AI Economy: A System View from the Positions of the Theory of Stakeholders*, Ethical Economy 73,
https://doi.org/10.1007/978-3-032-23423-0_29

JEL Codes O31 • O32 • O33 • O34 • O36 • O38 • Q40 • Q28 • Q38

1 Introduction

In today's economy, artificial intelligence (AI) plays a critical role by enabling automation, enhancing efficiency, and fostering the creation of new products and services. In recent years, AI has emerged as a key driver in the development of various economic sectors worldwide. Endowed with substantial scientific potential and a high level of technical education, Russia is actively integrating AI to achieve sustainable economic growth. In this context, it is essential to examine how AI contributes to Russia's economic development and what prospects lie ahead for the country in the future.

2 Materials and Methods

The theoretical and methodological foundation of this research is based on the works of Russian scholars in the field of sustainable economic development and the integration of AI technologies into Russia's economy.

The research employs methods of analyzing secondary data obtained from official statistics and industry reports on the application of AI technologies. To gain a more comprehensive understanding of AI integration processes, the authors conducted expert interviews with business specialists and members of the scientific community.

The informational and empirical basis of the research relies on legislative documents of the Russian Federation, official statistical data from the Federal State Statistics Service of the Russian Federation (Rosstat), and analytical materials from international and Russian information agencies. Additionally, the authors utilized data from official company websites and personal expert opinions.

The survey was conducted using Yandex.Forms, with participation from 50 respondents—representatives of the professional journalistic community of the Russian Federation, specifically active journalists working in various online publications and print magazines.

3 Results

The development of AI technologies serves as a powerful tool for enhancing the competitiveness of Russia's economy on the global stage and a guarantee of sustainable internal development. By examining successful examples of AI integration abroad and considering existing domestic resources and expertise, Russia possesses all the necessary conditions to become a leader in this field, provided there is appropriate government support and an effective investment strategy.

Advanced AI technologies optimize production processes through real-time data analysis and the automation of various tasks. AI can predict potential equipment failures and malfunctions by processing information. Moreover, it can organize the planning of maintenance schedules (Pavlenko 2023). This leads to reduced downtime and increased production efficiency (Pavlenko 2023; Polennikov 2024).

In agriculture, the use of drones equipped with AI elements allows for the analysis of crop conditions, helping farmers reduce product losses by approximately 25% (Zubarev et al. 2019).

In healthcare, algorithms assist doctors in making more accurate diagnoses based on the analysis of patients' medical studies.

The use of AI-powered robots in manufacturing processes can increase labor efficiency by 30–50%, which is crucial for a country with a growing elderly population (Makarov 2020).

AI technologies help reduce environmental impact by optimizing resource consumption and decreasing pollutant emissions. For example, intelligent systems that manage building energy efficiency contribute to lower energy consumption. AI plays a key role in promoting green technologies by improving climate change forecasting models and creating more effective methods for utilizing renewable energy sources. This supports the country's sustainable development without increasing its negative impact on the environment.

The implementation of AI technologies is associated with several considerable challenges related to the ethics and safety of AI usage. Ethical aspects include algorithm transparency, impartiality, the absence of discrimination, and accountability for decisions. In terms of safety, AI usage encompasses cybersecurity, data management, and autonomous decision-making. To successfully overcome these challenges, it is necessary to develop international standards for regulating AI use, invest in research to enhance algorithm transparency, create multi-level data protection systems, including training cybersecurity specialists, and actively involve society through dialogue between technology developers and users to consider public interests when creating new AI-based solutions.

4 Discussion

Russia is actively advancing in the field of AI through a series of projects and initiatives at the governmental and private levels. At the national level, one example is the "Digital Economy of the Russian Federation" program, which includes measures for the development of AI technologies (Government of the Russian Federation 2017; Kaurova et al. 2020a, b; Tochka Prodazh 2020). Research institutions, such as the A. A. Kharkevich Institute of Information Transmission Problems of the Russian Academy of Sciences, are actively involved in scientific research for the development of AI algorithms. Russian companies like Sberbank, Mail.ru Group, and

Yandex significantly influence the integration of AI into business by developing solutions based on machine learning (Gusev and Sharova 2023) and big data analysis. These efforts lay the foundation for integrating AI into various sectors of the economy.

Key aspects of AI implementation in the economy include the automation of production processes, machine learning, big data processing, and the creation and development of new technologies based on technological integration.

The main effects of AI on key economic sectors are as follows:

- Industry. In the industrial sector, AI plays a crucial role in optimizing production and supply chain management. By utilizing machine learning algorithms and neural networks, enterprises can forecast product demand, manage inventories, and minimize production costs. Examples of AI applications include predictive maintenance of equipment and the automation of manufacturing processes;
- Financial sector. Financial institutions actively use AI to enhance customer service quality, automate operational tasks, and increase transaction security. Examples of AI applications in this sector include the automation of customer service, risk analysis, and fraud detection;
- Medicine and pharmaceuticals. In healthcare, AI is used for disease diagnosis, the development of new medications, and the personalization of treatment. Examples of AI applications include medical diagnostics and drug development. In the pharmaceutical industry, the use of generative and recommendation models helps reduce development time by creating connections between molecules. In turn, this saves 3–6 years and accelerates the transition from drug discovery to development. For instance, the Russian platform Syntelle is capable of analyzing the toxicological and physicochemical properties of compounds, with its database containing information on 96 million molecules (FederalPress 2023);
- Retail. The retail sector is actively integrating AI into its processes to improve customer service levels and optimize supply chains. Examples of AI applications in retail include personalized offerings and inventory management (AGORA 2023);
- Transportation. AI is being actively implemented in the transportation sector to enhance traffic safety, optimize routes, develop autonomous transport, and streamline logistics.

AI deserves special attention in the ecological agenda of the global and Russian economies because the environmental component is one of the key aspects of sustainable development. In this context, the application of AI technology is directly linked to the energy sector and public utilities. The use of AI helps reduce environmental impact by optimizing resource utilization and decreasing harmful emissions. For example, smart grid management systems can employ machine learning algorithms to optimally distribute energy flows, thereby reducing transmission losses and minimizing the need for additional electricity generation. AI plays a crucial role in developing green technologies. It aids in improving climate change forecasting models and developing more efficient methods for utilizing renewable energy sources. This supports the country's sustainable development without increasing its negative impact on the environment.

In the professional realm of journalists, it is noteworthy that AI and neural networks have recently become an important part of journalists' work, providing powerful tools for creating, analyzing, and distributing content. Neural networks are becoming standard tools for journalists, editors, copywriters, SMM managers (Kryukova 2021) and other professionals in journalism, blogging, and related fields (Shevchenko et al. 2024). This phenomenon is linked to the growing capabilities of generative technologies, which significantly simplify many aspects of journalism. The most popular neural networks (and their modifications) used by journalists in their daily practice include Generative Pre-trained Transformer (GPT), Gerwin AI, DALL-E, Midjourney, DeepL, Proximity AI, Synthesia AI, Pinpoint, Quillbot, Jasper.ai, Article Forge, Vetted, Connexum, Longshot AI, Descript, JECT.AI, and Narrativa. This list is not exhaustive because the number of neural networks is constantly changing, with new ones emerging and existing ones evolving.

To demonstrate public attitudes toward the integration of AI in the national economy sectors, the authors surveyed experts in the professional journalistic community. The survey consisted of the following five questions:

- "Do you trust AI technologies?";
- "Is it possible to apply AI technologies in the media sector?";
- "Have you used AI to generate texts or images for your content?";
- "Are you satisfied with the results created by a text-based neural network?";
- "Do you think the implementation of AI will increase productivity in the media industry?"

The survey was conducted using Yandex.Forms, with participation from 50 respondents representatives of the professional journalistic community of the Russian Federation, specifically active journalists working in various online publications and print magazines.

The first question was: "Do you trust AI technologies?" Most respondents (57%) expressed distrust in these systems. Meanwhile, 29% of journalists consider AI to be reliable and are confident in its potential.

The second question was: "Is it possible to apply AI technologies in the media sector?" Answering this question, 86% of respondents believe that AI technologies can be integrated into journalists' work.

The third question was: "Have you used AI to generate texts or images for your content?" According to the respondents, 86% of respondents find AI technologies beneficial in the media industry and indicated that they have used text generators.

The fourth question was: "Are you satisfied with the results created by a text-based neural network?" Answering this question, 67% of the interviewed journalists expressed satisfaction with the generated results.

The fifth question was: "Do you think the implementation of AI will increase productivity in the media industry?" According to 58% of the respondents, integrating AI into media will enhance their efficiency. However, 14% of journalists highlighted the need to improve AI technologies, addressing the issue of further training

AI systems and the users of these technologies. It is noteworthy that the Government of the Russian Federation is actively supporting the development of AI technologies. On February 15, 2024, the President of Russia signed a decree updating the "National Strategy for the Development of Artificial Intelligence until 2030" (Presidential Executive Office of Russia 2019). This strategy outlines the main areas of focus, including the advancement of scientific research in AI, personnel training and education, the creation and development of innovation infrastructure, the application of AI in the economy, and a range of issues related to state management and the security of AI implementation and usage.

The conducted research within the professional journalistic community demonstrates that the public is interested in understanding the principles of AI tools and their potential benefits.

5 Conclusion

Based on the conducted research and the analytical report "2023 Index of Intellectual Maturity of Economic Sectors, Social Spheres, and Government Administration System of the Russian Federation, National Center for Research and Innovation under the Government of the Russian Federation," the authors conclude that the Russian economy is ready to implement AI. The adoption of AI is progressing at a significant pace. Currently, the average level of AI integration in the key sectors of the Russian Federation stands at 31.5%, with the financial sector, healthcare, and information and communication technologies reaching an AI penetration of 49.5% (Presidential Executive Office of Russia 2019). Compared to 2021, the average level of AI utilization in the country has increased by one and a half times. However, despite the achieved results, the primary obstacles to implementing and developing AI remain limited financial resources, a shortage of qualified personnel, insufficient necessary data, and a low level of awareness among employees and leaders regarding the capabilities of AI.

AI technologies represent a powerful catalyst for the sustainable development of Russia's economy. Their implementation contributes to the optimization of production processes, the enhancement of efficiency, and the competitiveness of various industries.

References

AGORA. 2023. *Digitalization of retail 2023–2025: Trends and current solutions*. August 17. https://www.agora.ru/blog/tsifrovizatsiya-riteyla-2023-2025/. Accessed 2 Nov 2024.

FederalPress. 2023. *Machines treat people: How neural networks are used in Russian medicine*. August 9. https://fedpress.ru/article/3259662. Accessed 2 Nov 2024.

Government of the Russian Federation. 2017. *National program "Digital Economy of the Russian Federation"* (approved by Order of July 28, 2017 No. 1632-r). Moscow, Russia. http://

static.government.ru/media/files/9gFM4FHj4PsB79I5v7yLVuPgu4bvR7M0.pdf. Accessed 2 Nov 2024.

Gusev, A. V., and D. E. Sharova. 2023. Ethical problems in the development of artificial intelligence technologies in healthcare. *Public Health* 3 (1): 42–50. https://doi.org/10.21045/2782-1676-2023-3-1-42-50.

Kaurova, O. V., A. N. Maloletko, and A. V. Tkach. 2020a. Regional cooperation in the formation of food resources in the digital economy. *Fundamental and Applied Research Studies of the Economics Cooperative Sector* 4:13–32.

Kaurova, O. V., A. N. Maloletko, L. V. Matraeva, and N. A. Korolkova. 2020b. Determining the composition of indicators assessment of the level of digital economy development in the region (regional digital environment). *Fundamental and Applied Research Studies of the Economics Cooperative Sector* 1:138–149.

Kryukova, E. M. 2021. Theoretical Understanding of social networks as a modern digital marketing tool for the hotel and tourism business. *Social Policy and Sociology* 20 (2): 24–31.

Makarov, M. Yu. 2020. The impact of artificial intelligence on productivity. *Economics and Management* 26 (5): 479–486. https://doi.org/10.35854/1998-1627-2020-5-479-486.

Pavlenko, O. A. 2023. Innovative approaches to improving production efficiency in mechanical engineering: From automation to the use of artificial intelligence. In *Generation of the future: The view of young scientists-2023: Collection of scientific articles of the 12th international youth scientific conference, in 4 volumes*, ed. A. A. Gorokhov, vol. 4, 130–133. Kursk, Russia: University Book.

Polennikov, A. M. 2024. The use of artificial intelligence technologies to optimize technological processes in production. *Bakery of Russia* 68 (2): 88–99. https://scinetwork.ru/issues/1103. Accessed 2 Nov 2024.

Presidential Executive Office of Russia. 2019. *National strategy for the development of artificial intelligence until 2030* (Approved by Executive Order of October 10, 2019 No. 490). Moscow, Russia: Kremlin. http://www.kremlin.ru/acts/bank/44731. Accessed 2 Nov 2024.

Shevchenko, D. A., E. M. Kryukova, V. V. Zelenov, and V. V. Galstyan. 2024. Harnessing the power of artificial intelligence in advertising. *Practical Marketing* 1 (319): 60–64. https://doi.org/10.24412/2071-3762-2024-1319-60-64.

Tochka Prodazh. 2020. Cooperation moves to a digital platform. *Tochka Prodazh*, December 16. https://tpmag.ru/news/potrebkooperacziya/kooperacziya-perexodit na czifrovuyu-platformu. Accessed 2 Nov 2024.

Zubarev, Yu. N., D. S. Fomin, A. N. Chashchin, and M. V. Zabolotnova. 2019. Use of uncleaned aircraft in agriculture. *Perm Federal Research Centre Journal* 2:47–51. https://doi.org/10.7242/2658-705X/2019.2.5.

Problems and Prospects for Applying Artificial Intelligence Technologies in the Field of Technological Leadership Policy

Svetlana N. Kuznetsova, Elena P. Kozlova, Victor P. Kuznetsov, Natalia S. Andryashina, and Elena V. Romanovskaya

Abstract Technological leadership can be ensured using artificial intelligence (AI). The drivers of strengthening technological sovereignty are innovative platforms, such as industrial parks and technology parks. The policy of technological leadership is associated with a high degree of risk. Thus, the state allocated about 1.2 billion rubles to support developments associated with AI. The research aims to create a model for the development of digital transformation processes in industrial parks and technology parks. A model for the development of territorial infrastructure to support the processes of developing and introducing AI technologies can improve financial indicators on the use of business models that contribute to an increase in the adaptability of business processes to changing conditions. The research emphasized problems and analyzed the prospects for using AI in the field of technological leadership. AI technologies are concentrated in the field of technological leadership policy. AI increases production efficiency. Therefore, to analyze large volumes of information and automate and accelerate work processes, it is necessary to use AI tools. The use of AI technologies aims to promote domestic developments to international markets, which ensures steady growth and global technological leadership. Economic growth points are created by supporting technology parks. Thus, the state forms a favorable environment for developing residents working in industrial and technology parks.

Keywords Industrial parks • Technologies • Artificial intelligence • Technological leadership • Industry 4.0

JEL Codes L5 • N6 • O1

S. N. Kuznetsova (✉) · E. P. Kozlova · V. P. Kuznetsov · N. S. Andryashina · E. V. Romanovskaya
Minin Nizhny Novgorod State Pedagogical University, Nizhny Novgorod, Russia

A. Karbekova (ed.), *Ethics of the AI Economy: A System View from the Positions of the Theory of Stakeholders*, Ethical Economy 73,
https://doi.org/10.1007/978-3-032-23423-0_30

1 Introduction

In 2020, the global average level of implementation of artificial intelligence (AI) decisions was 54%. The Russian indicator in 2021 was 21%. AI is expected to be the most promising technology. The percentage of implementation of AI technology was 20% in 2023 and 50% in 2024. The introduction of AI will add 11.2 trillion rubles to Russia by 2030. Therefore, it is necessary to form a single system of national regulation of large-scale and safe use of AI (Association of Industrial Parks of Russia n.d.).

Developments in the field of AI are currently moving into the new phase of practical application, while issues of the applied value of the created solutions are raised. In the field of technological leadership policies, AI technologies are in demand, which reduce time costs and save the resources used or increase profits. AI significantly increases the effectiveness of production and business processes. AI is an instrument for developing new products and markets, as well as reducing business costs.

The research outlines the issues affecting the implementation of technology in the realm of technological leadership policy. It identifies the shortage of skilled professionals as the primary risk to the technological development of the Russian Federation. Additionally, the study highlights concerns including cyberosis and cyber-attacks, the impact of political and economic sanctions, an energy crisis with limited resources, as well as environmental challenges and climatic changes (Bylyeva 2023).

Technological and industrial parks are the subjects of technological partnership. The coordination of the strategy and tactics of the integration processes is the global goal of technological partnership. It is necessary to create an economic and legal framework to develop technological partnerships and ensure the transition to technological leadership. It is projected that Russia's GDP will increase by 288 trillion rubles by 2030. This increase is possible to ensure by creating a technological platform on which it is important to synchronize complex projects in the field of economically reasonable import substitution. It is important to apply experimental legal regimes by removal from general regulation and for technology development.

The presented strategic goals and lines of technological modernization by the authors are characterized as part of the main challenges. For research and development, the scientific and technological potential of technological and industrial parks is evaluated.

Interested parties are committed to fostering scientific collaboration by identifying potential consortia and establishing research priorities. Strengthening the scientific infrastructure requires the development of educational programs, along with evaluating the principles for setting standards and implementing a certification system for financing key areas.

A plan is being developed to establish priorities and exchange the results of research on the creation of an organizational structure to develop a roadmap and determine partnership tools. The roadmap provides a portfolio of projects to achieve total sovereignty. Complex support for various fields, including science, education, and culture, is needed to attain technological cooperation, subordinate to strategic goals, and consider resource restrictions.

Technological cooperation is manifested through the partnership of industrial sites within the framework of a unified production and technological chain. There is a need to integrate Russian industry into international cooperative relations.

This research aims to identify and evaluate the readiness for using AI technologies to ensure its accelerated and productive penetration into various industries. It is necessary to connect state support with the active use of AI to stimulate industrial parks and technology parks to increase efficiency. The authors propose introducing a model for the development of the territorial infrastructure of parks to support the processes of introducing and developing technology in the field of technological leadership policy (Fig. 1). The economic effect of the implementation of AI in industries and public administration currently exceeds one trillion rubles.

The proposed model provides a positive effect from the introduction of AI technologies: increasing the margin of sale of products and a decrease in the duration of downtime of equipment and unscheduled costs. The introduction of AI technologies reduces transaction costs, making it possible to replace the missing competencies of staff, improve the quality of solutions, and ensure effective risk management. For example, regional industrial technology parks in the field of electronic industry will receive subsidies that are aimed at creating and developing sustainable development technologies. The authors propose an industrial data platform that provides technological leadership through the introduction of advanced digital technologies. The authors note that AI can increase the speed, safety, quality, and personalization of production.

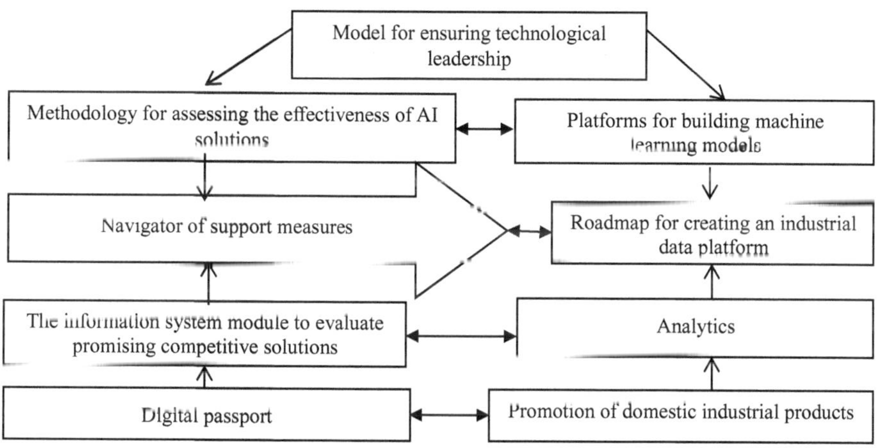

Fig. 1 A model for the development of territorial infrastructure to support the processes of developing and introducing AI technologies. Source: Developed by the authors

2 Literature Review

In the field of technological leadership policy, the problems and prospects for the application of technology are considered in the works of Russian and foreign authors.

L. O. Izilyaeva, Ya. K. Vasiliev, K. S. Mirokiyants, and A. I. Yasaviev (2024) determined that a wide range of opportunities and challenges represent the prospects for the development of the application of AI in politics.

L. M. Gokhberg, Yu. V. Turovets, K. O. Vishnevsky, and others showed that AI is an instrument of innovative transformation of socio-economic systems (Gokhberg et al. 2025).

N. A. Karaseva and T. D. Klimacheva (2024) considered the prospects for using intellectual systems based on neural networks and ML by managers in the industry. S. L. Katanandov and A. A. Kovalev (2023) considered the role of AI in public administration. S. N. Kuznetsova and others considered the role of digital technologies and AI in innovative transformations of the economy and business (Kuznetsova 2024; Kuznetsova and Kutepov 2024; Kuznetsova and Kutepova 2024; Kuznetsova and Lapaev 2024a, b).

A. V. Romanova (2022) notes that AI has great potential and is a breakthrough technology. N. V. Sedykh and I. P. Fokanov (2022) identified ways to solve the problems and prospects for the formation of technology.

3 Materials and Methods

The research used regulatory documents and statistical materials from the Association of Industrial Parks.

Industrial parks and technology parks that introduce AI technologies provide a 5% increase in profitability. The introduction of AI technologies ensures the growth of the country's GDP by 1% by 2025. In the field of AI development and data storage, it is necessary to build a solid foundation in the form of its own technologies, the creation of which is a strategic task of the state to ensure domestic digital sovereignty. Although the use of AI increased 1.5 times since 2021, it remains low at the regional and municipal levels. This is mainly due to the lack of the necessary infrastructure and data, as well as the personnel deficiency. Complex measures are needed to train promising personnel. For this purpose, it is necessary to build the interaction of universities and business.

AI technologies are central to the strategy for achieving technological leadership. The authors argue that an economic breakthrough across various industries, as well as advancements in the security sector, can be realized through the implementation of AI. In Russia, AI is viewed as a key driver for strengthening the nation's technological sovereignty. Efforts are underway to stimulate the adoption of AI technologies and to advance fundamental research in this area. Additionally, the government is introducing new support measures, including a certification system for AI technologies. In the electronics sector, specific regions (e.g., the Republic of Bashkortostan, the Vladimir Region, the Nizhny Novgorod Region, and the Republic of Tatarstan) will receive federal subsidies to develop industrial technology parks and enhance their infrastructure.

The infrastructure established in industrial and technology parks fosters the production of innovative electronic products. Automated robotic systems for contactless data collection and parking monitoring within these parks are under development, which is expected to boost the production of electronic auto components. Moreover, efforts are underway to develop and industrialize technologies for creating digital electronics and system software, as well as power and radio electronics.

It is necessary to create a platform of industrial data on the provision of technological leadership, as presented in Fig. 2.

The authors outline several industrial tasks that can benefit from the proposed platform using AI. Examples include predictive analysis for detecting equipment failures and computer vision systems to monitor the proper use of personal protective equipment. They identify video analysis and predictive analytics as the primary areas where AI is in high demand within production. AI technologies also play a significant role in optimizing logistics routes, managing supply chains, and controlling loading operations. As a result, the authors propose introducing recommendation systems and digital assistants in industrial and technology parks. Additionally, promising AI applications include leveraging generative neural networks for production planning and enhancing the robotization of production lines (Morozova et al. 2024).

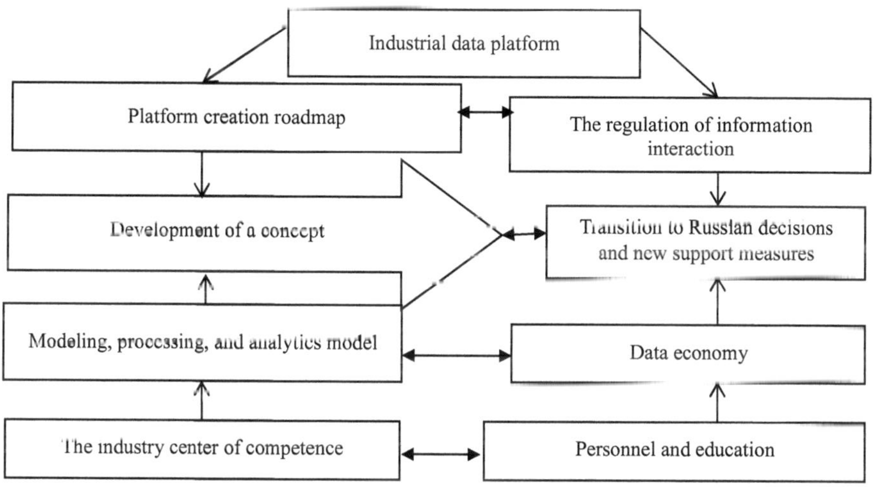

Fig. 2 Industrial data on the provision of technological leadership. Source: Developed by the authors

4 Results

The authors argue that advancing technology from research to practical implementation is crucial for boosting R&D investments and enhancing patent activities. They emphasize the need to nationalize AI research while fostering international collaboration through joint projects with friendly nations. Investment in AI is projected to grow significantly, from $154 billion in 2023 to $300 billion by 2026. It is estimated that AI technologies will contribute over $15 trillion by 2030. Table 1 details the forecasted investment volumes in AI from 2024 to 2030.

The current stage of digitalization in industrial and technological parks is characterized by the need for AI. The introduction of AI-based decisions aims to increase the accuracy of managerial decisions, which is determined by the minimization of the influence of the human factor. Table 2 presents the indicators of the AI roadmap.

The use of AI in the industrial sector covers the following key areas:

- Automation of warehouses and optimization of logistics: AI develops optimal routes considering time and costs;
- Forecasting and making decisions: AI provides forecasting volumes and process optimization;
- Control and quality: Based on AI, a computed vision reveals a deviation from the norm with significant accuracy;
- Safety: Automated monitoring systems are used to conduct preventive maintenance of equipment. Prevention of emergencies is ensured by virtual models of real systems, such as digital doubles;
- Resource management: AI can predict the wear of the main production funds, prevent downtime, and optimize depreciation costs. It is necessary to use AI to

Table 1 Investments in AI in 2024–2030

Sources of investment	The amount of investment, billion rubles
Federal budget	33.3
Sberbank	99.73
Russian Direct Investment Fund (RDIF)	5.6
The remaining extrabudgetary sources	7.22

Source: Developed by the authors

Table 2 Target indicators of the AI roadmap

Target indicator	2021	2022	2023	2024	2025	2030
The volume of investments in the AI of industrial and technology parks, billion rubles	11.63	21.63	32.13	42.63	53.13	105.63
Including Sberbank, billion rubles	9.73	19.73	29.73	39.73	49.73	99.73
Including the RDIF, as well as partners, million rubles	1.9	1.9	2.4	2.9	3.4	5.9

Source: Developed by the authors

analyze the market situation and prepare optimal production schedules, minimizing the costs and risk of deficit or excess products.

Significant problems of industrial and technological parks, including the following, characterize the development of technology:

- In industrial and technological parks, there are no ready-made solutions when creating a universal intellectual system. The development of an individual approach to implementing the model of business processes of industrial sites is characterized by unique functions of the implementation of AI;
- The data in industrial and technological parks are not digitized, which complicates the implementation of AI. The presence of confidential information requires the depersonalization of the data provided. To detect deviations used by the system as a result of the absence of data, it is necessary to expose the volume of reference data;
- The development of AI solutions that accelerate the specialization process includes the process of marking data and interpretation of information. Difficulties in the implementation of AI technologies are eliminated as a result of the implementation and development of AI in industrial and technological parks;
- There is a problem of reducing the use of personnel with the advent of advanced technologies. The technology is expected to optimize the work of about 800 million people in industry by 2030 (Smirnova et al. 2024).

5 Conclusion

In the near future, 33% of domestic industrial parks and technology parks intend to introduce AI into production processes. The authors predicted the multiple acceleration of the implementation of AI in the sectors in 2025. The volume of investments in the implementation of AI will total 33.3–145.85 billion rubles by 2030, including 112.6 billion rubles from the federal budget. The effect of the implementation of the AI technology strategy will be 11.2 trillion rubles. The application of AI technologies can boost profitability by 5% and reduce costs across various stages of production. The authors highlight that AI holds significant potential for industrial and technology parks, particularly in sectors such as engineering, metallurgy, chemicals, and oil industries.

The concept of technological partnership is the basis of the ionic-technological sovereignty, which ensures the following:

- Activation of the transfer of the results of R&D;
- Increased competencies of innovative management in the field of transfer, implementation, and development of R&D results;
- The creation of an effective technology transference and the formation of a coordinated system for supporting techno and industrial parks using the results of R&D.

Therefore, it is essential to form a model of innovative ecosystems. Based on technological and industrial parks, the authors propose integrating the center of technology transfer. It is also important to carry out national production cooperation and corporate R&D, which simplifies commercialization procedures, solves economic problems, and leads to the achievement of state sovereignty in the technological sphere. Investments in venture projects in 2025–2030 will amount to 50 billion rubles. The mechanism of technological partnership proposed by the author opens the opportunity to reduce technological dependence and switch to more reasonable economic relations. To implement the mechanism, corporations need to transfer part of the tasks for outsourcing to techno and industrial parks.

The implementation of technology solutions under the policy of technological leadership has led to increased additional revenue. The annual revenue of industrial and technology parks is distributed as follows:

- 8% generate less than one trillion rubles;
- 10% generate between 400 and 900 billion rubles;
- 15% generate more than ten billion rubles;
- 31% generate between 100 and 400 billion rubles;
- 36% generate between 10 and 100 billion rubles.

Moreover, the introduction of AI in these parks has resulted in an extra 60 billion rubles, including more than 27 billion rubles in additional income and over 32 billion rubles in savings (Yashina et al. 2024).

About 50 billion rubles are planned for the implementation of technological leadership. The forecast for 2025–2030 anticipates significant investments to boost technological leadership in the manufacturing industry. By 2030, the gross added value and production index are expected to increase by 40% compared to 2022. This progress will be achieved through elevated investments in techno and industrial parks, aiming to raise the internal costs allocated to R&D to 2% of GDP. Furthermore, domestic high-tech products—produced through internal development channels—are projected to account for 1.5 times the consumption volume observed in 2023, while the revenue of technological and industrial parks is expected to grow sevenfold.

References

Association of Industrial Parks of Russia. n.d. *Official website*. https://indparks.ru/. Accessed 12 Jan 2025.

Bylyeva, D. S. 2023. Collective and artificial intelligence. *Vestnik of Minin University* 11 (2): 13. https://doi.org/10.26795/2307-1281-2023-11-2-13.

Gokhberg, L. M., Yu. V. Turovets, and K. O. Vishnevsky. 2025. *Artificial intelligence in Russia: Technology and markets*. Moscow, Russia: HSE University.

Izilyaeva, L. O., Ya. K. Vasiliev, K. S. Mironiyants, and A. I. Yasaviev. 2024. The possibilities and risks of using artificial intelligence in the field of political relations of the Russian

Federation. *Economics and Management: Scientific and Practical Journal* 1:136–139. https://doi.org/10.34773/EU.2024.1.24.

Karasev, N. A., and T. D. Klimachev. 2024. Theoretical aspects of studying problems and prospects of artificial intelligence in the management of Russian companies. *Creative Economics* 18 (2): 337–356. https://doi.org/10.18334/CE.18.2.120490.

Katanandov, S. L., and A. A. Kovalev. 2023. Technological development of modern states: Artificial intelligence in public administration. *State and Municipal Management. Scholar Notes* 1 (1): 174–182. https://doi.org/10.22394/2079-1690-2023-1-1-174-182.

Kuznetsova, S. N. 2024. The economic efficiency of industrial parks as a factor in overcoming technological backwardness and import dependence. *Actual Problems of Modern Transport* 3 (17): 34–42.

Kuznetsova, S. N., and M. M. Kutepov. 2024. Localization as a tool for forming a cluster economy. *Moscow Economic Journal* 9 (10): 45–57. https://doi.org/10.55186/2413046X_2024_9_10_397.

Kuznetsova, S. N., and L. I. Kutepova. 2024. Implementation of the idea of cross-sectoral cooperation of industrial parks. *Moscow Economic Journal* 9 (9): 218–228. https://doi.org/10.55186/2413046X_2024_9_9_382.

Kuznetsova, S. N., and D. N. Lapaev. 2024a. Comprehensive economic security of technological and industrial parks. *Economic Security* 7 (4): 951–966.

Kuznetsova, S. N., and D. N. Lapaev. 2024b. Integration of controlling into the management system of techno and industrial park. *Controlling* 2 (92): 2–9.

Morozova, G. A., I. E. Mizikovsky, E. V. Kornilova, E. Y. Trifonova, and S. N. Kuznetsova. 2024. Formation and development of digital marketing in a business environment. *International Journal of Economic Policy in Emerging Economies* 19 (3–4): 248–258. https://doi.org/10.1504/IJEPEE.2024.139086.

Romanova, A. V. 2022. National strategy for the development of artificial intelligence: Legal analysis, problems and prospects. *Young Scientist* 46 (441): 319–322. https://moluch.ru/archive/441/96548/. Accessed 20 Jan 2025.

Sedykh, N. V., and I. P. Fokanov. 2022. Problems and prospects of artificial intelligence technology development. *The Journal of Natural and Humanitarian Research* 44 (6): 266–267.

Smirnova, Z. V., M. V. Mochalina, S. N. KuznetSova, E. P. Kozlova, and E. P. Garina. 2024. Trends in the development of e-commerce in enterprises. In *Ecological footprint of the modern economy and the ways to reduce it*, ed. B. S. Sergi, E. G. Popkova, A. A. Ostrovskaya, A. A. Chursin, and Y. V. Ragulina, 197–200. Cham, Switzerland: Springer. https://doi.org/10.1007/978-3-031-49711-7_34.

Yashina, N. I., S. N. KuznetSova, E. P. Kozlova, E. P. Garina, and E. Y. Denisov. 2024. Methodological aspects of budgetary monitoring of the implementation of national projects in the regions of Russia. In *Ecological footprint of the modern economy and the ways to reduce it*, ed. B. S. Sergi, E. G. Popkova, A. A. Ostrovskaya, A. A. Chursin, and Y. V. Ragulina, 419–424. Cham, Switzerland: Springer. https://doi.org/10.1007/978-3-031-49711-7_69.

Economic Development of Leading Industries in the Kyrgyz Republic by Disseminating Artificial Intelligence and the Evaluation of This Development

Venera A. Musaeva, Svetlana V. Zatravina, Gulmira Sh. Artykbaeva, Roza A. Sekieva, and Alymbek Erdolatov

Abstract The research aims to develop a scientific and practical approach to the economic development of the leading industries in the Kyrgyz Republic through the dissemination of artificial intelligence (AI), intended to fully unlock the potential of this growth. To this end, the authors conducted an empirical study based on statistics from the Kyrgyz Republic for 2010–2022. The authors employed trend analysis to examine the dynamics of the economic development of the country's leading industries during 2010–2022. Using regression analysis, the authors developed a model to assess the impact of the spread of AI technologies on the economic development of these key industries in the Kyrgyz Republic. The main conclusion is that the industrial economy of the Kyrgyz Republic is experiencing a recession due to a reduction in the share of the mechanical engineering, high-tech, and textile sectors within the overall industrial structure. Additionally, AI plays a countercyclical role in the country's industrial economy by accelerating the development of the food, high-tech, and textile industries. Ultimately, a novel mesoeconomic methodological approach to industrial automation based on AI is proposed, with the advantage of considering the sector-specific characteristics of the Kyrgyz Republic's industrial growth. The authors demonstrated future economic development prospects of the country's leading industries through further dissemination of AI up to 2030. This is supported by an original forecast which suggests that, provided a complete transition to "smart" production by 2030, the Kyrgyz Republic will achieve a significant increase in the share of the high-tech and textile sectors within its industrial structure.

V. A. Musaeva · R. A. Sekieva · A. Erdolatov
Kyrgyz National University named after Jusup Balasagyn, Bishkek, Kyrgyzstan

S. V. Zatravina (✉) · G. S. Artykbaeva
Scientific Research University «Kyrgyz Economic University named after M. Ryskulbekov», Bishkek, Kyrgyzstan

A. Karbekova (ed.), *Ethics of the AI Economy: A System View from the Positions of the Theory of Stakeholders*, Ethical Economy 73,
https://doi.org/10.1007/978-3-032-23423-0_31

Keywords Economic development • Leading sectors • Industrial economy • Kyrgyz Republic • Spread of artificial intelligence

JEL Codes L16 • L52

1 Introduction

The Fifth Industrial Revolution has brought significant changes to the global economic order. In recent years, industry has become the new arena for worldwide competitive struggles. In today's world, the pace of economic growth is important, as well as its sources, with industry being the most preferred. Consequently, service economies that recently underwent post-industrialization with a reorientation towards service-based business operations are now rapidly embracing Neo-Industrialization 5.0, increasing industrial production by leveraging frontier technologies of Industry 5.0.

The Kyrgyz Republic is no exception; alongside other countries affected by scientific and technological progress, it has initiated and is currently experiencing dynamic industrial economic development, which accelerates and underpins its growth. The industrial vector of economic growth and development in the Kyrgyz Republic is recognized as a strategic priority at the national level and is enshrined in the relevant regulatory framework (UNIDO and IIASA 2018). Selecting the right technological landscape is crucial for successfully implementing this approved vector.

Artificial intelligence (AI) is at the core of the technological landscape of the Kyrgyz Republic's digitalizing economy. This is evidenced by the government processes that, at the beginning of 2025, intensified efforts to legally enshrine the priorities of an AI-driven economy in the Kyrgyz Republic (Administration of the President of the Kyrgyz Republic 2025). Nevertheless, a significant problem impeding the alignment of the regulatory acts mentioned (Administration of the President of the Kyrgyz Republic 2025; UNIDO and IIASA 2018) is the vague understanding of the impact of artificial intelligence on the industrial growth of the Kyrgyz economy.

It is worth noting that accumulated international experience demonstrates the contradictory nature of this impact, which varies among countries. In some cases (in some countries and certain industrial sectors), AI is in high demand. It enables establishing smart productions that are high-performance and possess outstanding global digital competitiveness. However, in other cases (in specific examples of countries and industrial sectors), AI does not provide evident advantages either due to its lower demand compared to other automation tools (e.g., robots) or because of inadequate infrastructural support and production complexes.

Thus, the Kyrgyz Republic requires a robust scientific rationale for implementing AI in specific industrial sectors. In view of this, it is pertinent to develop a new, industry-specific (i.e., a mesoeconomic) approach to industrial automation based on

AI, which will allow for targeted technological transformations in the industrial economy and achieve greater efficiency from Neo-Industrialization 5.0 than the existing macroeconomic approach that does not consider the specific features of industrial sectors.

It is advisable to focus primarily on the leading industrial sectors to reap the greatest benefits for the industrial growth of the Kyrgyz economy. Based on the arguments presented above, this research aims to develop a scientific and practical approach to the economic development of the leading industrial sectors in the Kyrgyz Republic through the widespread adoption of AI, intended to fully unlock the potential of this development.

2 Literature Review

This research is based on the scientific concept of industrial economy as presented in the works of Bogoviz and Ragulina (2020). The fundamental premise of the macroeconomic methodological approach to industrial automation using AI, developed within this concept, is the assumption that the diffusion of this smart technology uniformly accelerates the development of all industrial sectors (Litvinova 2020).

A review of the literature has led to the identification of the following industrial sectors, which are considered to be the leading ones in today's economic environment:

- The chemical industry (Mf_1) (Burkhanov et al. 2022);
- The food industry (Mf_2) (Kazambayeva et al. 2023);
- The mechanical engineering industry (Mf_3) (Khayitov and Ulugbek 2023);
- The high tech industry (Mf_4) (Mkrtchyan et al. 2024);
- The textile industry (Mf_5) (Yalmaev et al. 2020).

A notable gap in the existing scientific knowledge is that, despite several publications on the spread of AI in the economy of the Kyrgyz Republic, particularly the work of Popkova et al. (2024), the consequences of smart automation for the sectoral development of the industrial economy in the studied country are not explained. In an effort to address this literary gap, this research poses the research question (RQ): "How does the proliferation of AI impact the economic development of the leading industrial sectors in the Kyrgyz Republic?".

3 Materials and Methods

The empirical study presented in this research is based on statistical data for the Kyrgyz Republic from 2010 to 2022 (Table 1). In the initial phase of the research, a trend analysis is used to dynamically assess the state of the leading industrial sectors in the Kyrgyz Republic: chemical (World Bank 2025a), food (World Bank 2025b),

Table 1 Economic state of leading industries and the spread of AI in the Kyrgyz Republic

	Share of leading industries, % of value added in manufacturing					
	Chemicals	Food, beverages and tobacco	Machinery and transport equipment	Medium and high-tech manufacturing	Textiles and clothing	Industry activity index, score
	Mf_1	Mf_2	Mf_3	Mf_4	Mf_5	IA_{AI}
2010	0.208	13.579	1.165	3.446	3.89	0.5
2011	0.081	14.143	0.84	3.715	4.556	0.7
2012	0.15	21.022	1.341	6.743	6.928	0.6
2013	0.091	15.718	1.056	6.606	4.56	0.6
2014	0.124	14.936	0.723	4.134	3.839	0.6
2015	0.101	13.985	0.588	2.957	3.713	0.6
2016	0.134	12.722	0.803	2.71	3.783	0.6
2017	0.189	17.716	1.044	2.778	2.764	0.6
2018	0.145	18.491	1.01	2.373	3.944	0.5
2019	0.169	13.977	1.167	2.239	3.937	0.4
2020	0.362	15.191	0.783	2.121	2.676	0.4
2021	0.305	17.406	0.877	2.267	2.664	0.5
2022	0.305	17.406	0.877	2.268	2.664	0.5

Source: Developed by the authors based on UNCTAD (2023) and World Bank (2025a, b, c, d, e)

mechanical engineering (World Bank 2025c), high-tech (World Bank 2025d), and textile (World Bank 2025e).

In the second phase of the research, the authors used regression analysis to determine the impact of the diffusion of AI technologies [measured by the "Industry Activity Index" (IA_{AI}) as part of the "Frontier Technology Readiness Index" calculated by UNCTAD (2023)] on the share of the leading industrial sectors (Mf_{1-5}) within the overall industrial structure.

The third phase evaluates the prospects and develops an original forecast for the future economic development of the leading industrial sectors in the Kyrgyz Republic, extending to 2030 through further adoption of artificial intelligence and a complete transition to smart production.

4 Results

As a result of the first stage of the conducted research, devoted to the assessment of economic development of the leading industries of the Kyrgyz Republic, a comprehensive view of this development in 2010–2022 was formed (Fig. 1).

Figure 1 reveals the following trends in the economic development of the leading industrial sectors in the Kyrgyz Republic:

- The share of the chemical industry in the industrial structure increased by 46.635% (from 0.208% in 2010 to 0.305% in 2022);

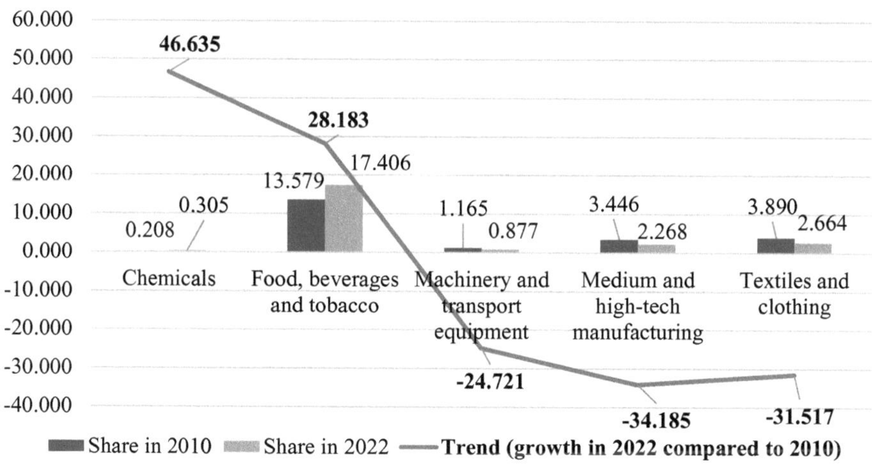

Fig. 1 Trend analysis of economic development of the leading industries of the Kyrgyz Republic in 2010–2022. Source: Developed by the authors

- The food industry's share rose by 28.183% (from 13.579% in 2010 to 17.406% in 2022);
- The mechanical engineering sector declined by 24.721% (from 1.165% in 2010 to 0.877% in 2022);
- The high-tech industry's share diminished by 34.185% (from 3.446% in 2010 to 2.268% in 2022);
- The textile industry's share decreased by 31.517% (from 3.890% in 2010 to 2.664% in 2022).

These trends indicate an economic downturn in most of the leading industrial sectors in the Kyrgyz Republic. As a result of the second phase of this research, the following model has been developed to assess the impact of the diffusion of AI technologies on the economic development of the leading industrial sectors in the Kyrgyz Republic:

$$\begin{aligned} Mf_1 &= 0.5789 - 0.727 * IA_{AI}, \\ Mf_2 &= 15.865 + 0.057 * IA_{AI}, \\ Mf_3 &= 1.1689 - 0.4116 * IA_{AI}, \\ Mf_4 &= -1.6322 + 9.236 IA_{AI}, \\ Mf_5 &= 0.8537 + 5.4675 IA_{AI}. \end{aligned} \quad (1)$$

Model (1) indicates that for every one-point increase in the diffusion of AI technologies, the composition of the leading industrial sectors shifts as follows: the chemical industry's share decreases by 0.727%, the food industry's share increases by 0.057%, the mechanical engineering sector's share decreases by 0.4116%, the

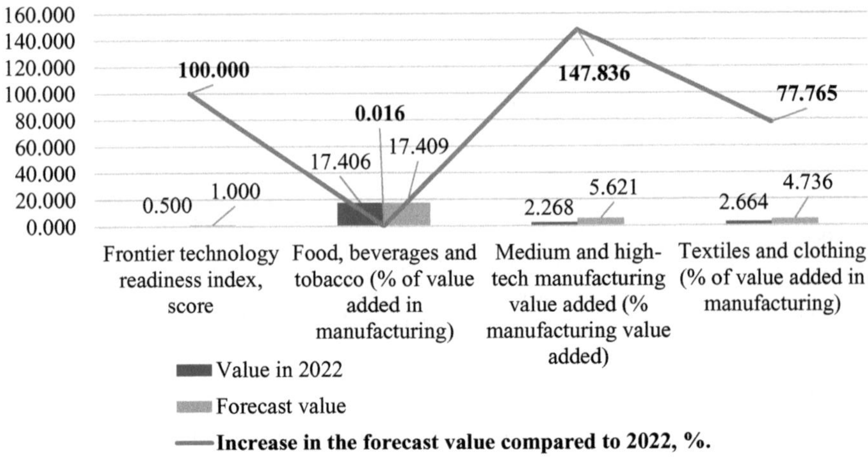

Fig. 2 Forecast of the increase in the share of leading industries in the Kyrgyz Republic under the full transition to smart industries. Source: Developed by the authors

high-tech industry's share increases by 9.236%, and the textile industry's share rises by 5.4675%. Consequently, smart automation contributes to the economic development of only three leading sectors in the Kyrgyz Republic: the food, high-tech, and textile industries.

As a result of the third phase of this research, a forecast for the future economic development of the leading industrial sectors in the Kyrgyz Republic up to 2030 has been identified through the further diffusion of AI. This forecast is reflected in an original projection of increased shares for the three selected sectors, assuming their complete transition to smart production (Fig. 2).

As shown in Fig. 2, when the diffusion of AI technologies reaches the maximum possible score of 1, the forecast for the composition of the leading industrial sectors by 2030 is as follows:

- The food industry's share will increase by 0.016% (from 17.406% in 2022 to 17.422%);
- The high-tech industry's share will rise by 147.836% (from 2.268% in 2022 to 5.621%);
- The textile industry's share will grow by 77.765% (from 2.664% in 2022 to 4.736%).

Thus, smart automation will significantly accelerate the economic development of only two of the selected leading sectors in the Kyrgyz Republic: the high-tech and textile industries.

Table 2 Comparison of alternative methodological approaches to industrial automation based on artificial intelligence

Leading industry	Disclosure in the literature within the macro-economic approach	Identified the impact of AI on the industry (regression) within a meso-economic approach
Chemical	Burkhanov et al. (2022)	Negative (−0.727)
Food	Kazambayeva et al. (2023)	Weak positive (0.057), near zero
Machine-building	Khayitov and Ulugbek (2023)	Negative (0.4116)
High-tech	Mkrtchyan et al. (2024)	Strongly positive (9.236)
Textile	Yalmaev et al. (2020)	Strongly positive (5.4675)

Source: Developed by the authors

5 Discussion

The obtained results complement the scientific concept of industrial economy and continue the studies of Bogoviz and Ragulina (2020), Litvinova (2020), and Popkova et al. (2024), revealing the differences in the consequences of the spread of AI technologies among the leading industries in the Kyrgyz Republic. The achieved results formed the evidence base for the transition to a new, meso-economic methodological approach to industrial automation based on AI, the difference between which and the existing macroeconomic approach is shown in Table 2.

As shown in Table 2, it has been determined that the diffusion of AI exerts a negative impact on the economic development of the chemical (−0.727) [contrary to Burkhanov et al. (2022)] and mechanical engineering (0.4116) [contrary to Khayitov and Ulugbek (2023)] industries in the Kyrgyz Republic.

In contrast to Kazambayeva et al. (2023), it was found that AI-based automation has a slight positive (0.057), essentially negligible, effect on the economic development of the food industry in the Kyrgyz Republic.

It has also been demonstrated that the implementation of AI in the Kyrgyz Republic provides a strong positive impact on the economic development of the high-tech (9.236) [confirming Mkrtchyan et al. (2024)] and textile (5.4675) [confirming Yalmaev et al. (2020)] industries.

6 Conclusion

In conclusion, the main scientific findings of this research and the innovative, original conclusions based on them are summarized as follows. First, the analysis of the dynamics of economic development in the leading industrial sectors of the Kyrgyz Republic from 2010 to 2022 has revealed a recession in the country's industrial economy, evidenced by a decline in the share of the mechanical engineering, high-tech, and textile industries in the overall industrial structure.

Second, the developed model of the impact of the diffusion of AI technologies on the economic development of the leading industrial sectors in the Kyrgyz Republic indicates that as the level of AI diffusion increases in the country, the shares of the food, high-tech, and textile industries within the industrial structure also grow.

Third, a forecast for the future economic development of the leading industrial sectors in the Kyrgyz Republic through further adoption of artificial intelligence (extending to 2030) has been established. This projection suggests that, provided a complete transition to smart production, there will be a marked increase in the shares of the high-tech and textile industries within the industrial structure.

The theoretical significance of this research lies in the proposed new mesoeconomic methodological approach to industrial automation based on AI, which has the advantage of considering the sector-specific characteristics of the industrial growth of the Kyrgyz Republic's economic system. Its practical significance is underscored by the original forecast, which enables the joint implementation of Neo-Industrialization 5.0 (UNIDO and IIASA 2018) and AI-based industrial automation (Administration of the President of the Kyrgyz Republic 2025) in the Kyrgyz Republic up to 2030.

References

Administration of the President of the Kyrgyz Republic. 2025. *On the development of the strategy for the development of artificial intelligence in Kyrgyzstan.* January 31. https://www.gov.kg/index.php/ru/post/s/24937-adylbek-kasymaliev-bizdin-maksat-globaldyk-texnologiyalyk-kun-tartiptegi-zasalma-intellektti-mamlekettik-processterge-sistemaluu-zana-masstabduu-kirgizuu. Accessed 28 Feb 2025.

Bogoviz, A. V., and Y. V. Ragulina, ed. 2020. Industry competitiveness in the new economy [Editorial]. In *Industry competitiveness: Digitalization, management, and integration*, vol. 1, v–vi. Cham, Switzerland: Springer. https://doi.org/10.1007/978-3-030-40749-0

Burkhanov, A. U., B. Tursunov, K. Uktamov, and B. Usmonov. 2022. Econometric analysis of factors affecting economic stability of chemical industry enterprises in digital era: In case of Uzbekistan. In *Proceedings of ICFNDS '22: The 6th international conference on future networks & distributed systems*, 484–490. New York, NY: Association for Computing Machinery. https://doi.org/10.1145/3584202.3584274.

Kazambayeva, A. M., M. K. Begeyeva, K. U. Nursapina, and R. Rakhmetova. 2023. Systematic approach to sustainable development in agricultural and food systems—Example of Republic of Sakha (Yakutia) and the Arctic Zone. *Problemy Ekorozwoju [Problems of Sustainable Development]* 18 (1): 226–234. https://doi.org/10.35784/pe.2023.1.24.

Khayitov, S., and K. Ulugbek. 2023. The Role of IT on Transportation, logistics and the economic growth among Central Asian countries. In *Internet of things, smart spaces, and next generation networks and systems*, ed. Y. Koucheryavy and A. Aziz, 649–655. Cham, Switzerland: Springer. https://doi.org/10.1007/978-3-031-30258-9_58.

Litvinova, T. N. 2020. Managing the development of infrastructural provision of AIC 4.0 on the basis of artificial intelligence: Case study in the agricultural machinery market. In *Digital economy: Complexity and variety vs. rationality*, ed. E. Popkova and B. Sergi, 317–323. Cham, Switzerland: Springer. https://doi.org/10.1007/978-3-030-29586-8_37.

Mkrtchyan, T. M., A. B. Karbekova, D. S. Zakharov, and O. K. Pakhomova. 2024. AI and machine learning in inclusive development to personalize user experience and increase digital literacy. In *Digital inclusiveness: Bridging the divide in the digital economy*, ed. E. G. Popkova, 25–35. Singapore: World Scientific Publishing. https://doi.org/10.1142/9789811270826_0003.

Popkova, E. G., S. T. Ergasheva, N. K. Savelyeva, and M. A. Troyanskaya. 2024. Change management for the sustainable development of the agrarian economy of artificial intelligence. *Global Journal of Flexible Systems Management* 25:79–90. https://doi.org/10.1007/s40171-024-00383-2.

UNCTAD. 2023. *Frontier technology readiness index, annual*. https://unctadstat.unctad.org/datacentre/dataviewer/US.FTRI. Accessed 28 Feb 2025.

UNIDO and IIASA. 2018. *Regional development, regional integration, and economic development: Strategic elements of industrial development in Kyrgyzstan*. Vienna, Austria: UNIDO. https://www.unido.org/sites/default/files/files/2018-12/Справочный_документ_к_Стратегии_Промышленного_Развития_Киргизстана.pdf?_token=2005708218. Accessed 28 Feb 2025.

World Bank. 2025a. *Chemicals (% of value added in manufacturing)*. https://data.worldbank.org/indicator/NV.MNF.CHEM.ZS.UN?view=chart. Accessed 28 Feb 2025.

World Bank. 2025b. *Food, beverages and tobacco (% of value added in manufacturing)*. https://data.worldbank.org/indicator/NV.MNF.FBTO.ZS.UN?view=chart. Accessed 28 Feb 2025.

World Bank. 2025c. *Machinery and transport equipment (% of value added in manufacturing)*. https://data.worldbank.org/indicator/NV.MNF.MTRN.ZS.UN?view=chart. Accessed 28 Feb 2025.

World Bank. 2025d. *Medium and high-tech manufacturing value added (% manufacturing value added)*. https://data.worldbank.org/indicator/NV.MNF.TECH.ZS.UN?view=chart. Accessed 28 Feb 2025

World Bank. 2025e. *Textiles and clothing (% of value added in manufacturing)*. https://data.worldbank.org/indicator/NV.MNF.TXTL.ZS.UN?view=chart. Accessed 28 Feb 2025.

Yalmaev, R. A., V. A. Shalaev, A. T. Giyazov, and G. K. Tashkulova. 2020. The perspectives of provision of new quality of growth of economic systems in the digital economy. In *Digital economy: Complexity and variety vs. rationality*, ed. E. Popkova and B. Sergi, 30–38. Cham, Switzerland: Springer. https://doi.org/10.1007/978-3-030-29586-8_4.

Artificial Intelligence as a Key Avenue for the Sustainable Economic Development of the Kyrgyz Republic's Industrial Sector

Svetlana V. Zatravina, Aizhamal Bekturganova, Guras D. Zhaparov, Raiza Zhuma kyzy, and Aizat A. Bigali

Abstract The research aims to determine the role of artificial intelligence (AI) among the main directions for the sustainable economic development of industry in Central Asia and identify opportunities for optimizing these directions in the Kyrgyz Republic as a country in Central Asia. The authors conducted a trend analysis of the economic development of the industrial sector in the Kyrgyz Republic from 1990 to 2023, alongside a factor analysis of this development in Central Asia for 2025. Additionally, the authors identified a Central Asian model of sustainable industrial development. This model reveals the logic behind state regulation of the industrial economy in the countries of Central Asia, which constitutes its theoretical contribution. Based on the model, the authors conclude that AI plays a significant role among the main avenues for sustainable industrial development, with prospects for state regulation in Central Asia that also include expanding industrial credit financing, increasing national electricity production, and developing a low-carbon industry. The authors developed practical recommendations to enhance state regulation of the industrial economy in the Kyrgyz Republic in its selected key areas. Implementing these recommendations will ensure a fuller realization of the potential for sustainable industrial development in the Kyrgyz Republic in the coming years.

Keywords Industry of the Kyrgyz Republic • Innovations in industry • Green economy • Sustainable economic development • Industrial development of the Kyrgyz Republic • Artificial intelligence

JEL Codes L51 • L52

S. V. Zatravina (✉) · G. D. Zhaparov · A. A. Bigali
Scientific Research University «Kyrgyz Economic University named after M. Ryskulbekov», Bishkek, Kyrgyzstan

A. Bekturganova
Kyrgyz State Technical University named after I. Razzakov, Bishkek, Kyrgyzstan

A. Karbekova (ed.), *Ethics of the AI Economy: A System View from the Positions of the Theory of Stakeholders*, Ethical Economy 73,
https://doi.org/10.1007/978-3-032-23423-0_32

1 Introduction

Sustainable manufacturing stands out as one of the most promising vectors for the economic development of countries for two main reasons. The first reason is that the rapidly growing global demand for goods is met within the manufacturing sector. Consequently, the capacity and productivity of a nation's industrial base directly determine the economy's ability to meet domestic demand for goods, achieve success in import substitution, and maintain a favorable balance of trade.

Additionally, despite ongoing and intensive automation, the manufacturing sector remains highly labor-intensive in its production and distribution processes—a condition that will continue for the foreseeable future. As the sector expands and its production capacities are increasingly utilized, the number of jobs created will grow, positively impacting employment and stabilizing the labor market.

Furthermore, industrial development defines a country's standing in the global economy, which is now undergoing the Fifth Industrial Revolution. Advances in manufacturing open up access for countries to global markets as exporters of high-tech products. The rapid growth of the manufacturing sector has underpinned the economic miracles of recent decades. Nowadays, this industrial resurgence enables nations to achieve high levels of global digital competitiveness and make their economies more attractive to foreign investors.

The second reason is that only a resilient industrial sector can truly serve the interests of society, which is the primary beneficiary of economic development. In this context, resilience is understood as a multifaceted attribute of the manufacturing sector, reflecting, first, the stability of industrial economic growth. An economy mired in crisis is, by nature, unstable. Second, the reliability of infrastructure and resource bases, which are essential for industrial growth, is critical because their absence poses a significant risk of crippling manufacturing activities.

Third, environmental sustainability, a core component of sustainable development as defined by the United Nations, is essential. Sustainable development in manufacturing implies increased energy efficiency in production and distribution, a shift toward renewable energy sources, improved environmental characteristics of products, a commitment to green sales, and safe disposal and recycling practices. Without such environmental measures, an industrial economy cannot be deemed sustainable today.

A pressing issue is that, although economic theory and practice have developed a fairly clear concept of sustainable industrial development, there remains uncertainty about how this development is achieved across different economic systems. Special attention should be given to artificial intelligence (AI) as a potential driver of industrial economic growth amid the Fifth Industrial Revolution.

R. Zhuma kyzy
Academy of Public Administration under the President of the Kyrgyz Republic named after Zh. Abdrahmanov, Bishkek, Kyrgyzstan

Moreover, the experiences of developing countries, particularly those in Central Asia, require independent and in-depth study. Recognizing the significance of this challenge and the need for its resolution, this research aims to define the role of AI among the main directions of sustainable industrial development in Central Asia and identify prospects for optimizing these directions in the Kyrgyz Republic as a Central Asian country.

2 Literature Review

This research is based on the theoretical framework of the industrial economy, in which a key indicator of industrial development is the increasing share of value added by manufacturing in the country's GDP (Karbekova et al. 2023). The existing literature related to this concept identifies the following main directions of state regulation for the industrial economy to support and stimulate sustainable industrial development:

- The development of an e-government system based on AI to enhance access to digital public services for all industrial sectors and automate state monitoring, control, and management (D_1) (Sukhodolov et al. 2018);
- The establishment and protection of industrial design rights for innovative manufacturing products as a form of intellectual property, strengthening their technological competitive advantages (D_2) (Mukhomorova et al. 2020);
- Improving access to financial resources for industrial enterprises through the advancement of the national credit system (D_3) (Eshov et al. 2024);
- Industrial diversification through antitrust regulation of the industrial economy and by encouraging manufacturers to expand their product range (D_4) (Yuldashev et al. 2021);
- The expansion of national electricity production, a crucial production resource in the industrial economy that determines manufacturing capacity utilization, cost efficiency, price competitiveness of industrial goods, and the potential for industrial automation (D_5) (Bogoviz et al. 2018);
- The development of logistics to improve the accessibility and quality of transport and logistics services, which are critical for establishing supply chains and sales channels in the industry, as well as for optimizing manufacturing operations (D_6) (Menglikulov et al. 2023);
- Reducing the energy intensity of GDP by transitioning to energy-saving technologies in the industry, thereby decreasing the demand for fuel and energy resources by manufacturers (D_7) (Bogoviz et al. 2017);
- Promoting low-carbon industry by reorienting the industrial economy toward clean energy derived from renewable sources (D_8) (Gulnora 2022).

A comprehensive review of these measures has revealed a gap in the current scholarly literature: it remains unclear which of these state regulatory directions for the industrial economy truly ensures sustainable industrial development in specific industrial economies, particularly in Central Asia.

Moreover, the role of AI remains undefined. Given this gap in the literature, this research poses the research question (RQ): "What contribution does the development of an AI-based e-government system, along with the implementation of the other key state regulatory directions for the industrial economy, make to the sustainable industrial development in Central Asia?"

3 Materials and Methods

This research is based on an econometric methodology and is conducted in the following order. The first step of this research is to determine the sustainability of the development of industrial economic in the Kyrgyz Republic. To do this, the authors performed a trend analysis to examine the dynamics of the share of value added by manufacturing (MNFsed) in the country's GDP from 1990 to 2023.

The second step is to assess the impact of state regulation of the industrial economy on sustainable industrial development in Central Asia. For this purpose, a factor analysis is conducted. Using regression analysis, the dependence of MNFsed on implementing the key directions of state regulation of the industrial economy (D_{1-8}) is determined based on the data presented in Table 1.

Based on the results of the second step, the most effective state regulation directions (those with positive regression coefficients) are selected. In the third step, the prospects for sustainable industrial development in the Kyrgyz Republic are determined by increasing the implementation of these selected regulatory measures. For this purpose, the maximum values from the sample for the selected measures are substituted into the regression equation to forecast the growth of the corresponding indicators in the Kyrgyz Republic.

4 Results

In the first step of this research, the authors evaluated the sustainability of industrial economic development in the Kyrgyz Republic. The results of the trend analysis are presented in Fig. 1.

According to Fig. 1, the share of value added by manufacturing in the Kyrgyz Republic's GDP in 1990 was 26.41%. It peaked in 1992 at 32.14% during the reviewed period, then experienced a sharp decline, reaching a low of 7.90% in 1996. Subsequently, dynamic fluctuations ensued; by 2023, the share had fallen to 12.60%.

The downward trend—amounting to a 52.27% decrease in 2023 compared to 1990—indicates unstable industrial economic development in the Kyrgyz Republic. To uncover the causes of this phenomenon, the second step of the study involved a factor analysis using the data from Table 1. This analysis established the effects of state regulation of the industrial economy on sustainable industrial development in Central Asia, resulting in the formulation of the following model:

Table 1 Main directions of sustainable economic development of industry in Central Asia in 2025

Country	Government AI readiness index, score 0–100	Industrial designs by origin/billion PPP$ GDP	Domestic credit to private sector, % GDP	Domestic industry diversification	Electricity output, GWh/million pop.	Logistics performance, score 0–100	GDP/unit of energy use, per thousand 2015 PPP$ GDP	Low-carbon energy use, %	Manufacturing, value-added, % of GDP)
	D_1	D_2	D_3	D_4	D_5	D_5	D_7	D_8	MNFsed
Afghanistan	16.92	0.0	0.0	0.0	0.0	0.0	0.0	0.0	7.61
China	72.01	25.7	185.4	97.8	6282.6	72.7	6.9	18.3	26.18
India	62.81	1.6	50.4	94.9	1259.9	59.1	10.0	11.2	12.93
Iran	43.88	5.0	60.3	83.7	3914.3	9.1	4.4	1.2	19.41
Kazakhstan	51.41	0.2	25.0	61.2	6056.5	27.3	6.9	4.0	12.25
Kyrgyzstan	36.55	0.2	21.9	26.1	2035.9	9.1	7.6	50.6	12.60
Mongolia	42.36	21.8	41.0	38.8	2219.2	18.2	5.8	2.5	6.30
Pakistan	40.47	0.3	14.8	87.3	673.4	0.0	10.1	16.4	13.60
Russia	64.72	1.2	54.4	91.6	0.0	22.7	4.7	13.6	12.45
Tajikistan	36.72	0.0	10.6	67.8	2125.1	18.2	10.4	63.7	15.14
Turkmenistan	32.64	0.0	0.0	0.0	0.0	0.0	0.0	0.0	20.46
Uzbekistan	53.45	0.7	36.7	37.8	2043.8	22.7	5.8	2.4	18.88

Source: Developed by the authors based on the materials from Oxford Insights (2024), WIPO (2024), and World Bank (2025)

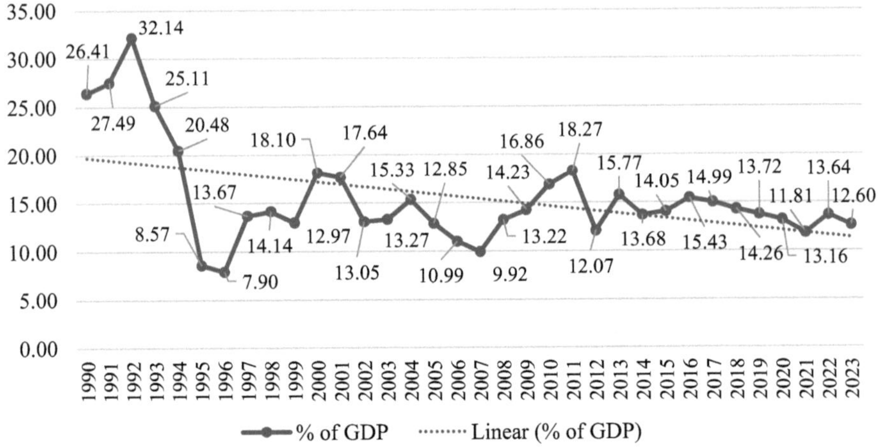

Fig. 1 Trend analysis of economic development of industry in the Kyrgyz Republic in 1990–2023, % of GDP. Source: Developed by the authors based on the World Bank materials (World Bank 2025)

$$\begin{aligned} \text{MNFsed} = 12.594 + 0.004D_1 - 0.419D_2 + 0.142D_3 - 0.001D_4 + \\ + 0.0005D_5 - 0.073D_6 - 0.290D_7 + 0.026D_8, R^2 = 0.7607 \end{aligned} \tag{1}$$

Model (1) implies that in Central Asia, 76.07% of the sustainability of industrial economic development in 2025 is determined by implementing key state regulatory measures. Among these, only four measures (D_1, D_3, D_5, and D_8) positively affect the sustainability of industrial development.

Specifically, a one-point increase in the development of an AI-based e-government system in Central Asia leads to a 0.004% rise in the share of value added by manufacturing in GDP. Similarly, a 1% increase in private sector lending boosts this share by 0.142%. Furthermore, a 1 GWh/million population increase in electricity production results in a 0.0005% rise; a 1% increase in the share of low-carbon energy in total energy consumption contributes an additional 0.026%.

The third step of this research assessed the prospects for sustainable industrial economic development in the Kyrgyz Republic by intensifying the implementation of these selected regulatory measures. For this purpose, the maximum values from Table 1 for D_1, D_3, D_5, and D_8 were substituted into model (1). The forecasted growth of the corresponding indicators in the Kyrgyz Republic is presented in Fig. 2.

Figure 2 illustrates that intensifying state regulation in the selected key areas of the industrial economy in the Kyrgyz Republic, raising them to the maximum levels achieved by Central Asian countries by 2025, could boost the share of value added by manufacturing in the nation's GDP by 316.45%, from 12.60% in 2025 to 52.47%.

To achieve this, the following recommendations are proposed for enhancing state regulation of the industrial economy in these targeted areas:

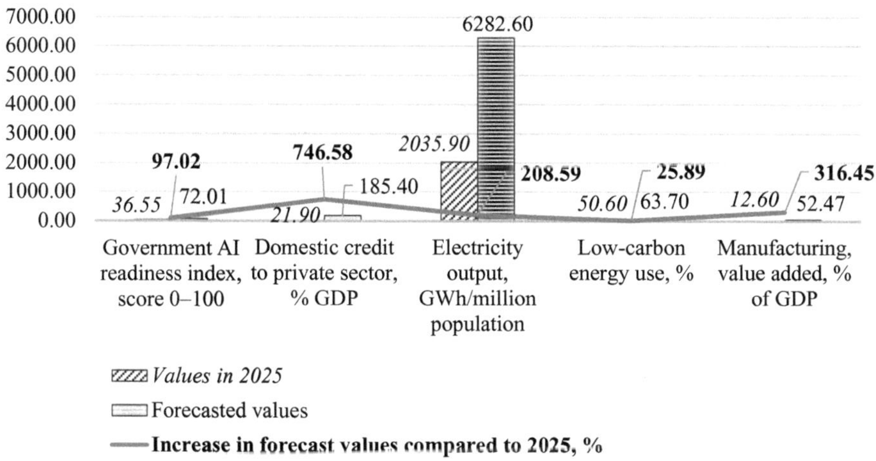

Fig. 2 Forecast of sustainable economic development of industry in the Kyrgyz Republic under the activation of state regulation. Source: Developed by the authors

- Increase the development of the AI-based e-government system by 97.02%, from 36.55 points in 2025 to 97.02 points;
- Expand private sector lending by 746.58%, from 21.90% of GDP in 2025 to 185.40% of GDP;
- Raise electricity production by 208.59%, from 2035.90 GWh/mn pop. in 2025 to 62,852.60 GWh/million population;
- Boost the share of low-carbon energy in total energy consumption by 25.89%, from 50.60% in 2025 to 63.70%.

5 Discussion

This research has expanded the theoretical framework of the industrial economy and contributed to the literature by Karbekova et al. (2023), unveiling a fresh perspective on the key directions for the sustainable industrial development of the Kyrgyz Republic (Table 2).

Table 1 shows that sustainable industrial development in Central Asia is supported by the implementation of state regulatory measures, including the development of an AI-based e-government system [confirming the findings of Sukhodolov et al. (2018)], enhanced access to financial resources for industrial activities [as noted by Eshov et al. (2024)], expansion of national electricity production [confirming the findings of Bogoviz et al. (2018)], and the advancement of low-carbon industry [as observed by Gulnora (2022)].

Conversely, sustainable industrial development in Central Asia is undermined by measures such as establishing industrial design rights as intellectual property

Table 2 Alternative views on the main directions of sustainable economic development of the industry of the Kyrgyz Republic

Main directions of state regulation of the industrial economy	Disclosure of trends in the existing literature	Consequences of direction realization for industry in Central Asia (regression)
Development of an e-government system based on AI	Sukhodolov et al. (2018)	Sustainable development (0.004)
Registration of rights to industrial design as an intellectual property object	Mukhomorova et al. (2020)	Sustainability breach (−0.419)
Increasing the availability of financial support for industrial operations	Eshov et al. (2024)	Sustainable development (0.142)
Diversification of industry	Yuldashev et al. (2021)	Sustainability breach (−0.001)
Increase in national electricity production	Bogoviz et al. (2018)	Sustainable development (0.0005)
Logistics development	Menglikulov et al. (2023)	Sustainability breach (−0.073)
Reduction of energy intensity of GDP	Bogoviz et al. (2017)	Sustainability breach (−0.290)
Development of a low-carbon industry	Gulnora (2022)	Sustainable development (0.026)

Source: Developed by the authors

[contrary to the findings of Mukhomorova et al. (2020)], industrial diversification [contrary to the findings of Yuldashev et al. (2021)], the development of logistics [contrary to the findings of Menglikulov et al. (2023)], and reducing GDP energy intensity [contrary to the findings of Bogoviz et al. (2017)].

6 Conclusion

The conclusion of this research is that AI plays a significant role among the key directions for sustainable industrial development, with its potential for state regulation in Central Asia also linked to the expansion of industrial credit, increased national electricity production, and the advancement of low-carbon industry.

The developed Central Asian model of sustainable industrial development holds theoretical significance because it explains the logic behind state regulation of the industrial economy in Central Asian countries. Moreover, the recommendations for enhancing state regulation of the industrial economy in the Kyrgyz Republic in these targeted areas have practical significance because they will make it possible to realize the potential for sustainable industrial development in the Kyrgyz Republic in the coming years.

References

Bogoviz, A. V., S. V. Lobova, Y. V. Ragulina, and A. N. Alekseev. 2017. A comprehensive analysis of energy security in the member states of the Eurasian economic union, 2000–2014. *International Journal of Energy Economics and Policy* 7 (5): 93–101. https://econjournals.com/index.php/ijeep/article/view/5447. Accessed 3 Mar 2025.

Bogoviz, A. V., S. V. Lobova, Y. V. Ragulina, and A. N. Alekseev. 2018. A critical review of Russia's energy efficiency policies in agriculture. *International Journal of Energy Economics and Policy* 8 (3): 67–75. https://econjournals.com/index.php/ijeep/article/view/6331. Accessed 3 March 2025.

Eshov, M. P., G. K. Abdurakhmanova, A. U. Burkhanov, N. B. Abdusalomova, and S. T. Ergasheva. 2024. Perspective on adapting international financial reporting standards (IFRS) to the latest trends in international business development: Conclusion. In *Development of international entrepreneurship based on corporate accounting and reporting according to IFRS*, 235–236. Leeds, UK: Emerald Publishing Limited. https://doi.org/10.1108/S1877-63612024000033B029.

Gulnora, A. 2022. Financial development and renewable energy consumption. In *Economic growth and wellbeing: Evidence from the Belt and Road Initiative countries*, ed. R. Salahodjaev, 35–53. Hauppauge, NY: Nova Science Publishers.

Karbekova, A. B., S. G. Makhkamova, N. A. Inkova, and O. K. Pakhomova. 2023. Automation based on datasets and AI of corporate accounting and sustainability reporting in quality management in Industry 4.0. *Proceedings on Engineering Sciences* 5 (S2): 265–278. https://doi.org/10.24874/PES.SI.02.007.

Menglikulov, B., S. Umarov, A. Safarov, T. Zhyemuratov, N. Alieva, and A. Durmanov. 2023. Ways to increase the efficiency of transport logistics—Communication services in Uzbekistan. *E3S Web of Conferences* 389:05036. https://doi.org/10.1051/e3sconf/202338905036.

Mukhomorova, I. V., A. Giyazov, G. K. Tashkulova, and N. K. Atabekova. 2020. Priority of intellectual resources for development of digital entrepreneurship. In *The 21st century from the positions of modern science: Intellectual, digital and innovative aspects*, ed. E. Popkova and B. Sergi, 415–421. Cham, Switzerland: Springer. https://doi.org/10.1007/978-3-030-32015-7_46.

Oxford Insights. 2024. *2024 Government AI Readiness Index*. Great Malvern, UK: Oxford Insights. https://staging2.oxfordinsights.com/ai-readiness/ai-readiness-index/#download-reports. Accessed 3 Mar 2025.

Sukhodolov, A. P., E. G. Popkova, and T. N. Litvinova. 2018. Basic characteristics of information economy. In *Models of modern information economy: Conceptual contradictions and practical examples*, 17–24. Leeds, UK: Emerald Publishing Limited. https://doi.org/10.1108/978-1-78756-287-520181003.

WIPO. 2024. *Global innovation index 2024: Unlocking the promise of social entrepreneurship*. 17th ed. Geneva, Switzerland: WIPO. https://www.wipo.int/web-publications/global-innovation-index-2024/assets/67729/2000%20Global%20Innovation%20Index%202024_WEB3lite.pdf. Accessed 3 Mar 2025.

World Bank. 2025. *Manufacturing, value added (% of GDP)*. https://data.worldbank.org/indicator/NV.IND.MANF.ZS?view=chart. Accessed 3 Mar 2025.

Yuldashev, N. K., V. I. Nabokov, K. V. Nekrasov, and B. O. Tursunov. 2021. Innovative and export potential of the agro-industrial complex of Uzbekistan. *E3S Web of Conferences* 282:06004. https://doi.org/10.1051/e3sconf/202128206004.

Artificial Intelligence as an Innovative Trend in the Digital Transformation of Business Processes in Enterprises

Ekaterina V. Kuzmina, Svetlana A. Shevchenko, Mariya I. Kuzmina, Tamara I. Tchechet, and Valentina A. Dorzhdeeva

Abstract In the context of global changes, digitalization has become a driving force for economic development, making the issues of digital transformation and the application of artificial intelligence (AI) in enterprises and all areas of business extremely relevant. This research analyzes existing interpretations of AI and provides an overview of the basic tools and promising technological trends in AI, including machine learning, computer vision, transformers, and AI agents. The authors formulate and propose conceptual guidelines for implementing AI technologies in enterprises undergoing digital transformation to enhance innovation and financial performance. The research demonstrates the effectiveness of adopting AI as an informational solution that fully contributes to the sustainable development of an enterprise and the achievement of its primary goals. Managing a company's digital transformation is possible only by creating methodological concepts that integrate AI into business processes at the strategic, tactical, and operational levels. Optimizing business processes based on AI services refines production, generates additional value, increases labor productivity and product quality, and manages supply chains. The research proposes a methodological approach centered on developing a mechanism for optimizing an enterprise's business processes through the application of AI technologies in the context of ensuring its sustainable development.

Keywords Digital transformation • Digital maturity • Artificial intelligence • Business processes • Manufacturing enterprises • Transformers • AI agents • Machine learning • Robotization

JEL Codes O14 • O31 • O32 • O33 • M21 • R11 • R12

E. V. Kuzmina (✉) · S. A. Shevchenko · M. I. Kuzmina · T. I. Tchechet · V. A. Dorzhdeeva
Volgograd State Technical University, Volgograd, Russia

A. Karbekova (ed.), *Ethics of the AI Economy: A System View from the Positions of the Theory of Stakeholders*, Ethical Economy 73,
https://doi.org/10.1007/978-3-032-23423-0_33

1 Introduction

In the context of global competition, the growth of the global economy directly depends on the development of high-tech sectors and industrial enterprises, whose effective use of innovation and production potential is determined by advanced information processing technologies, the implementation of digital technologies, and the availability of digital capacities. Digital transformation plays a crucial role in enhancing the innovative activity of enterprises and business sectors that are strategically important to the economy.

Artificial intelligence (AI) provides innovative tools and technological solutions for making management decisions aimed at the sustainable development of an enterprise, taking into account a high degree of uncertainty and rapidly changing market conditions. AI services optimize business processes, reduce production costs, and increase labor productivity through real-time monitoring and analysis of technological cycles.

The scientific novelty lies in the development of a mechanism for optimizing an enterprise's business processes through the application of AI technologies in the context of ensuring its sustainable development.

2 Literature Review

AI can collect and accumulate metrics, analyze large datasets, and monitor processes, thereby driving enterprise development and achieving high financial and economic performance. AI models process and analyze information quickly, efficiently, and without error, eliminating human bias and enabling the formulation and adoption of effective management decisions. This is why AI is currently a key factor in the digital transformation and innovative development of enterprises.

According to Rai et al. (2019), AI is a set of methods that endows machines with the capacity to perform cognitive functions such as perception, learning, and reasoning. Chalmers et al. (2020) assert that employing AI in enterprises opens up extensive opportunities for enhancing economic and financial outcomes. Sena and Nocker (2021) concluded that innovative business models allow companies to coordinate their activities to achieve planned results, ensuring consistency in management decisions.

Mussel (2021) defines AI as a scientific discipline that develops the theoretical foundations and practical methodologies for creating technologies that perform functions based on human intelligence—specifically, analysis, learning, and making informed decisions.

According to Vislova (2020), AI is an element of the digital economy that involves the collection and analysis of vast amounts of data, the automation of decision-making processes, and the establishment of algorithm-driven intelligent services across various business sectors.

Khisamova et al. view AI as a combination of information services and digital technologies that achieve the intellectual automation of data collection, analysis, and processing—tasks traditionally performed by humans while adhering to ethical principles (Khisamova and Begishev 2020).

In the authors' view, AI encompasses digital technologies such as machine learning, computer vision, and expert systems for automating complex tasks, capable of engaging in intellectual activities like self-learning based on established rules and knowledge bases, drawing logical conclusions, and adjusting management decisions.

3 Materials and Method

An innovative avenue for developing industrial enterprises in the realm of digital solutions is AI, which makes it possible to coordinate and control all business processes in a virtual environment by creating a unified information field. To achieve sustainable enterprise development, it is essential to digitize all business processes, including quality management, production organization, logistics, innovation activities, and marketing management. Integrating AI algorithms, with their limitless capabilities and extensive functionality, into production and management processes accelerates decision-making while significantly enhancing its quality and effectiveness (Arkhipova 2020; Buravlev and Vetoshkin 2024; Gorodnova 2021).

AI is a top investment priority for more than one-third of global companies and serves as a driving force for global GDP growth (Alizada and Muradli 2020; Gorodnova 2021; Shollo et al. 2022). Consulting firm Bain & Company has reported that by 2027, the global market for AI technologies will reach $990 billion (TSSonline 2024). Furthermore, over 40% of enterprises are implementing AI algorithms and services. Consequently, the market for algorithm-driven solutions and innovative products will continue to expand, and the demand for AI technologies will steadily grow.

In developing the sequence of stages for enterprise digitalization and establishing conceptual guidelines for applying AI technologies to enhance innovative and financial performance, empirical, theoretical, and general-logical methods of scientific inquiry were employed. Graphical techniques and organizational-structural systematization were used as the research tools.

4 Results

4.1 *Artificial Intelligence as an Innovative Trend in the Development of Manufacturing Enterprises*

The application of AI tools creates additional competitive advantages for manufacturing enterprises, such as the optimization of supply chains, improvement of technological and economic indicators, introduction of innovative products, significant reduction in product and service design and development time, and increased flexibility and responsiveness of business processes to external and internal conditions. AI undoubtedly stands among breakthrough digital solutions because its technical and functional capabilities are employed across all industries and areas of activity, transforming the very principles of business organization and management.

AI technologies are classified into two groups—basic services and applied tools. Basic AI services involve the collection of empirical data and the identification of recurring patterns in similar situations. This category of digital solutions includes machine learning, deep learning, expert systems, and knowledge systems. Applied AI tools encompass groups of algorithms united by recurring tasks and functions, such as motion detection, object recognition, and image generation.

Promising technological trends for AI systems in enterprises include the following:

1. Transformers are architectural neural networks and data fusion models (including NLP), as well as generative adversarial networks (GANs) that describe trillions of parameters and offer functionality for a wide range of tasks, such as ViT, GPT, RAG, and BERT;
2. Democratization of AI provides users with convenient and efficient platforms by creating machine learning tools and models (Low-code/No-code). Automated machine learning (AutoML) allows for the use of large models to collect, analyze, and interpret data without human intervention. Few-shot learning methods enable AI to learn from a small number of examples; one-shot learning trains a model using a single example, while zero-shot learning allows the model to learn immediately without examples;
3. AI agents are collections of autonomous information-analytical elements that can interact with external environmental factors, execute operations without human intervention, and learn from their own experiences.

Undeniable advantages of integrating AI into enterprise management and production functions include the following:

1. Optimization of work processes because AI services accelerate development and testing phases, thereby reducing design costs and actively fostering innovation;
2. Improvement in efficiency and productivity by automating technological processes, reducing the likelihood of errors, and shortening production cycles;
3. Planning of equipment maintenance and repair—sensor data is transmitted to AI service software in real-time, enabling timely prediction of component wear and malfunctions of key assets, which helps prevent downtime and operational disruptions;
4. Management of logistics flows and supply chains—AI systems collect and analyze data on resource availability and finished products, forecast raw material and supply consumption, and plan market demand for product categories;
5. Enhancement of product quality based on AI services that monitor production processes, analyze energy consumption and physical parameters of finished products, and promptly prevent defects and deviations from standards.

Despite these advantages, implementing AI also entails certain limitations and risks. One major challenge lies in development and operation. The development of AI software requires extremely high standards because even a minor error or malfunction can lead to significant losses that exceed those caused by human error. In this context, the digitalization of business processes must consider the specifics of the production process, technological features, and the degree of innovation within the company.

The primary goal of enterprise digitalization is to enhance and optimize all of its business processes (Fig. 1). Achieving this objective begins with assessing the company's digital maturity. Additionally, it is essential to develop a mechanism that establishes a phased sequence of interactions among all components, restructures the hierarchical relationships between all participants, and determines the order in which production, management, and logistics processes are transformed.

During the digital transformation, enterprises must integrate cyber-physical AI systems to automate production systems and optimize repetitive cycles. It is crucial to digitize information and organize data collection, record-keeping, and storage on

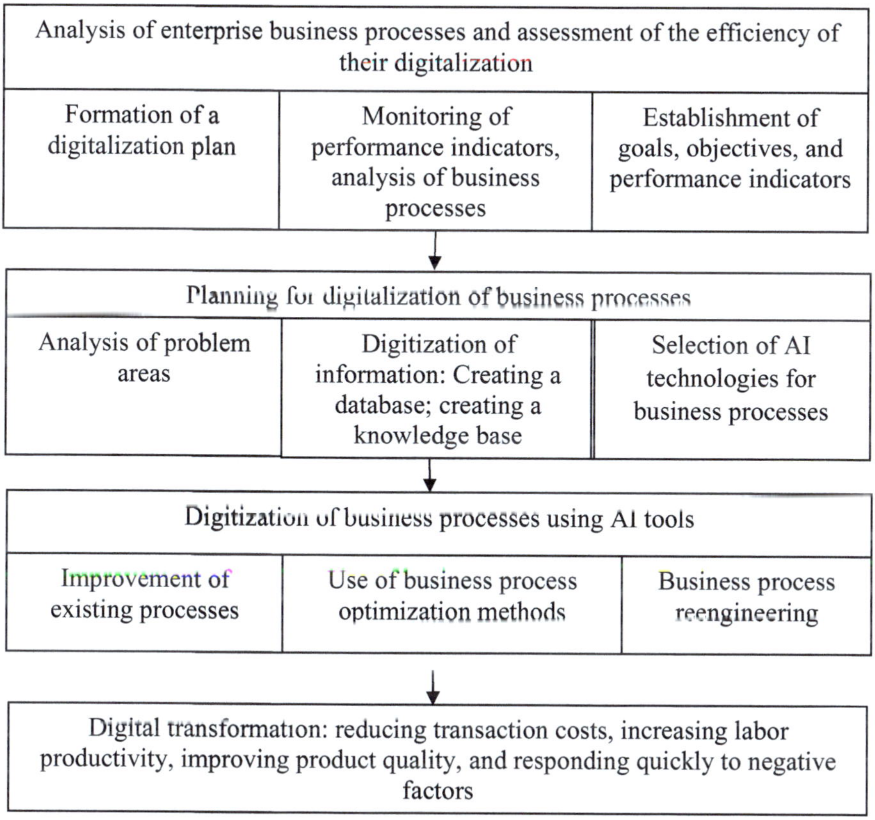

Fig. 1 Algorithm for digital transformation of the enterprise. Source: Developed by the authors

computer media. Informatization involves converting all data into an electronic format, thereby enhancing the efficiency of information exchange in a unified format.

Digitizing business processes makes it possible to ensure the interconnectedness of processes and data within the established information system. This objective can be achieved using technologies such as Computer Aided Logistics Systems—a service providing continuous informational support throughout the product lifecycle; Material Requirements Planning—a service for the automated planning of raw materials and supplies; and Computerized Maintenance Management Systems—a service for managing equipment maintenance and repair. Business process reengineering focuses on modifying enterprise processes to boost operational efficiency.

The effectiveness of AI-based digital transformation is reflected in cost reduction, increased profits, and improved financial condition. Within the structure of a manufacturing enterprise's management, AI creates a digital infrastructure and an innovative environment, refining business processes and reshaping hierarchical relationships.

4.2 *Mechanism for Enhancing Business Processes of a Manufacturing Enterprise Based on AI Technologies*

The use of AI in optimizing business processes ensures the innovative development of an enterprise, establishes a foundation for producing high-tech products, and enhances its competitive advantages. AI technologies automate and optimize routine processes and perform functions such as production management, design and oversight of technological chains, and predictive analytics (Chalmers et al. 2020). Clearly, the AI-generated information space constitutes an infrastructural system that accumulates vast amounts of data by integrating equipment, technologies, and software within a single environment, thereby enabling the execution of a wide range of tasks.

Optimizing business processes through the application of AI requires their decomposition using formalization and a detailed description of the management system (Fig. 2). This decomposition classifies the enterprise's processes into three categories: management, production or core activities, and support. Production business processes involve the sequence of actions required to create a product, including production management, dispatching, and the analysis of labor productivity and quality. Management business processes comprise a series of actions to achieve set objectives, including financial management, marketing, human resources, inventory control, and strategic management. The third category, support processes, does not directly participate in the production cycle but is essential for the effective execution of core activities.

Application software and operational components of AI services execute, analyze, and control business processes. One key advantage of AI is the ability to swiftly access specific data segments, thereby increasing added value, managing logistics flows, reducing production costs, and enhancing product quality. Data is

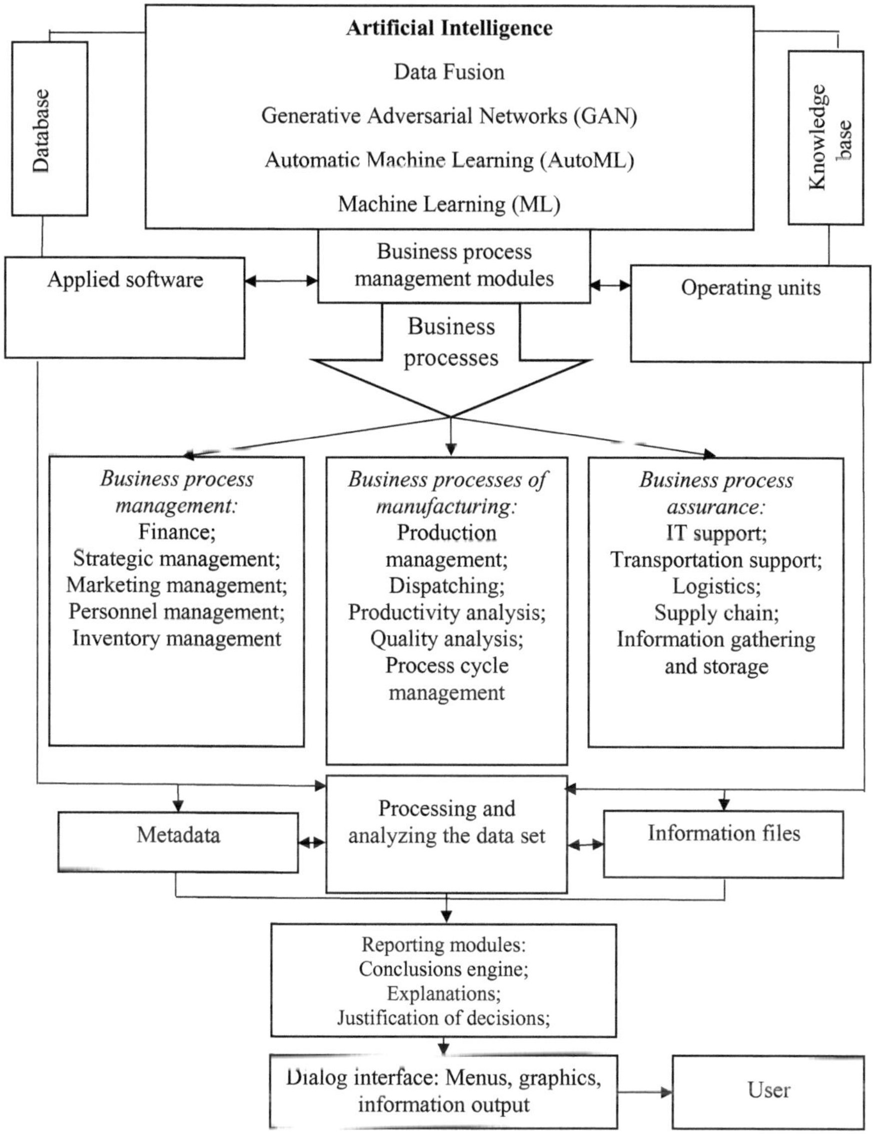

Fig. 2 Mechanism of optimization of business processes of the enterprise based on the application of AI technologies. Source: Developed by the authors

generated at the sensor level, with processing and analysis carried out through comprehensive evaluation, statistical control, and agile analytics.

During the reporting module stage, metadata is integrated via an information output mechanism, facilitating the formulation of well-founded decisions. A conversational interface automates formatting and visualizes reports for end users and stakeholders.

5 Conclusion

Intensifying competition and expanding market opportunities dictate the need for refined corporate management, where AI emerges as the key factor in optimizing business models. AI technologies hold limitless potential for developing enterprises and all areas of business. Integrating AI into business processes will reduce transactional costs, increase profits, and create conditions for generating technological, innovative, and informational resources for manufacturing enterprises.

The authors define AI as digital technologies encompassing machine learning, computer vision, and expert systems designed to automate complex tasks. These systems can engage in intellectual activities such as self-learning based on established rules and knowledge bases, drawing logical conclusions, and refining management decisions.

The research presents a mechanism for optimizing an enterprise's business processes through the application of digital technologies in the context of ensuring sustainable development. A distinguishing feature of this mechanism is the use of AI technologies and tools to improve business processes in management, production, and support functions.

Thus, under contemporary conditions, AI and optimized business processes foster the growth of manufacturing enterprises and many other sectors, serving as drivers of innovative activity, generating additional value-added factors, and enhancing financial and economic performance.

References

Alizada, A. V., and V. A. Muradli. 2020. Information and artificial intelligence. *Bulatov Readings* 1:37–38.

Arkhipova, L. I. 2020. Big data and artificial intelligence in business: Development and regulation. *Big Data and Advanced Analytics* 6 (3): 122–127. https://libeldoc.bsuir.by/bitstream/123456789/39061/1/Arkhipova_Bolshiye.pdf. Accessed 15 Feb 2025.

Buravlev, A. I., and V. M. Vetoshkin. 2024. Artificial intelligence: Essence, principles of operation, areas of application. *Armament and Economics* 2 (68): 33–42. https://viek.ru/68/vie_24_2(68)-033-042.pdf. Accessed 15 Feb 2025.

Chalmers, D., N. G. MacKenzie, and S. Carter. 2020. Artificial intelligence and entrepreneurship: Implications for venture creation in the fourth industrial revolution. *Entrepreneurship Theory and Practice* 45 (5): 1028–1053. https://doi.org/10.1177/1042258720934581.

Gorodnova, N. V. 2021. Artificial intelligence in economic diplomacy and international trade. *Russian Journal of Innovation Economics* 11 (2): 565–580. https://doi.org/10.18334/vinec.11.2.112214.

Khisamova, Z. I., and I. R. Begishev. 2020. The nature of artificial intelligence and the problem of legal personality determination. *Bulletin of the Moscow State Regional University. Series: Jurisprudence* 2:96–106.

Mussel, L. V. 2021. Modern stage of Artificial Intelligence (AI) development and application of AI methods and systems in power engineering. *Informational and Mathematical Technologies in Science and Management* 4 (24): 5–20. https://doi.org/10.38028/ESI.2021.24.4.001.

Rai, A., P. Constantinides, and S. Sarker. 2019. Next-generation digital platforms: Toward human-AI hybrids. *MIS Quarterly* 43 (1): 3–9.

Sena, V., and M. Nocker. 2021. AI and business models: The good, the bad and the ugly. *Foundations and Trends in Technology Information and Operations Management* 14 (4): 324–397. https://doi.org/10.1561/0200000100.

Shollo, A., K. Hopf, T. Thiess, and O. Müller. 2022. Shifting ML value creation mechanisms: A process model of ML value creation. *The Journal of Strategic Information Systems* 31 (3): 1–20. https://doi.org/10.1016/j.jsis.2022.101734.

TSSonline. 2024. The global AI market will grow to nearly $1 trillion by 2027. *TSSonline*, October 2. https://www.tssonline.ru/news/mirovoy-rinok-ii-k-2027g.-virastet-pochti-do-1-trln-dollarov. Accessed 15 Feb 2025.

Vislova, A. D. 2020. Current trends in the development of artificial intelligence. *Proceedings of the Kabardino-Balkarian Scientific Center of the Russian Academy of Sciences* 2 (94): 14–30. https://doi.org/10.35330/1991-6639-2020-2-94-14-30.

Comparative Analysis and Application of Digital Governance Potential in the Republic of Armenia

Bakur V. Martirosyan, Zaven R. Haroyan, Liana A. Fidanyan, and Ruzanna V. Gevorgyan

Abstract This research examines the development of digital governance in the Republic of Armenia within the context of various indexes of electronic governance. The research aims to examine the position of Armenia in the digital governance process and identify the strengths and weaknesses of e-governance through quantitative and qualitative analyses. The main issues considered in this research are the ranking of Armenia and its trends in main electronic government indexes, the multidimensional classification of countries by digitalization indicators, and the e-participation case of Armenia. The research subject is a comparative analysis of the development of digital governance in the Republic of Armenia. Initially, the authors introduced the role and importance of digital governance. Next, the authors conducted a comparative analysis to understand Aremina's position and documented tendencies in digital governance. Various comparisons were made to understand the course of implementation of digital governance process in Armenia according to different indexes. To classify economies with varying levels of digitalization, the authors conducted a cluster analysis using the SPSS software package. The analysis was based on three indicators: the E-Government Development Index (EGDI), the Corruption Perceptions Index (CPI), and the Global Innovation Index (GII). The practical manifestation of the development of digital governance was presented in the context of participatory governance. The authors analyzed the existing problems and obstacles of participatory governance in the Republic of

B. V. Martirosyan (✉)
Armenian State University of Economics, Yerevan, Armenia

Eurasia International University, Yerevan, Armenia

Z. R. Haroyan
Eurasia International University, Yerevan, Armenia

French University in Armenia, Yerevan, Armenia

L. A. Fidanyan · R. V. Gevorgyan
Armenian State University of Economics, Yerevan, Armenia

A. Karbekova (ed.), *Ethics of the AI Economy: A System View from the Positions of the Theory of Stakeholders*, Ethical Economy 73,
https://doi.org/10.1007/978-3-032-23423-0_34

Armenia according to the components of electronic participation and made proposals to improve the level of electronic participation.

Keywords Digital economy • E-government • Cybersecurity • Comparative analysis • Cluster analysis • E-participation

JEL Codes H11 • H83 • O38 • O57

1 Introduction

The development of digital technologies impacts many areas of social activity, bringing changes not only to science and business but also to the implementation of effective public administration systems (Alekseeva and Filimonova 2024).

The digitalization of public administration can be seen as a natural progression, aligning with the general logic of governance in modern democratic countries. It supports the strengthening of democratic principles and increases the efficiency of public administration. Such development processes strengthen democratic principles, create favorable conditions for economic growth, enhance national welfare, and contribute to the formation of a more civilized society. They also reduce operational costs and provide a stable environment for business, thereby stimulating domestic and foreign investment (Avetisyan 2024). According to studies by the World Bank, the effective application of digital technologies can boost a country's economy by up to 1–2% and increase tax revenues by up to 15%.

As already mentioned, the application of digital technologies in a country's governance system includes different sectors. For example, it contributes to the accessibility and quality improvement of the services in the healthcare and education systems. In the field of transport and infrastructure, it contributes to the design of the optimal transport routes and the development and implementation of smart cities programs, thanks to the correct location of infrastructures. Thus, technological interchange of the public administration system is at the focus of scientific interest. Comparative analysis may be of research interest as it can support adopting the best international practices in Armenia.

2 Methods

During the research, the authors used some quantitative and qualitative methods, providing relevant results. They are as follows:

1. Descriptive statistics: Calculating mean, growth rates, and rankings for indices. The results are as follows:

    - Armenia's EGDI grew from 0.52 (2016) to 0.84 (2024);

- Average growth rate for Armenia in e-participation: 12.65%;
- The comparison of Armenia's ranking improvement across years.

2. Index-based analysis: Examination of various digital governance-related indices. These indices involve statistical computations based on various parameters such as online service availability, telecommunication infrastructure, human capital, etc. The results are as follows:

   - Armenia ranked 48th in EGDI (2024), showing an improvement from previous years;
   - In e-participation, Armenia ranked 27th, with a significant annual growth rate of 12.65%;
   - CPI score for Armenia: 47 (indicating moderate corruption);
   - Armenia's GII rank: 63rd, showing strong innovation potential but weaker investment in resources.

3. Cluster analysis: K-means clustering to classify countries based on EGDI, CPI, and GII scores. The results are the identification of the following three clusters:

   - High-performing countries (e.g., Denmark, South Korea, and Estonia);
   - Moderate performers (e.g., Armenia, Georgia, and China);
   - Low-performing countries (e.g., former CIS countries with low digitalization scores).

4. Time series analysis: Examination of trends of Armenia's digital governance progress from 2012 to 2024 using historical data. The results are as follows:

   - Armenia's EGDI improved from 0.52 (2016) to 0.84 (2024);
   - E-participation index showed remarkable growth: from rank 103 in 2018 to 27 in 2024.

5. Comparative analysis: The comparison of Armenia's digital governance strategies with best practices from Estonia, Singapore, the UK, and the UAE. The results are as follows:

   - Identified gaps in Armenia's cybersecurity and institutional readiness;
   - Suggested policy recommendations, such as creating a centralized digital governance body.

3 Results

Nowadays, the interest of advanced countries and the international community towards digital solutions for public administration is increasing. Currently, various international organizations employ indices and indicators calculated with different methodologies to evaluate the degree of digitalization of public administration. The following indices are included in the research.

3.1 E-Government Indexes

The E-Government Development Index (EGDI) was developed by the UN Department of Economic and Social Affairs (UNDESA) (UN E-Government Knowledgebase n.d.-a). This index aims to estimate the level of e-government development of countries. The following three factors are considered in the methodology of calculating this index:

- The accessibility of digital services provided by governments (Online Services Index);
- The accessibility of the Internet, mobile, and fixed line services (Telecommunication Infrastructure Index);
- The level of education and digital skills (Human Capital Index).

The e-Participation Index (EPI), which was developed by the United Nations, evaluates citizens' engagement in governance processes through digital technologies (UN E-Government Knowledgebase n.d.-c).

Digital Quality of Life Index (DQL), which is developed by Surfshark company (Surfshark 2024), evaluates the digital quality of life of people in different countries.

There are other indexes as well, like Digital Readiness Index (DRI) (Cisco n.d.), Index of Multiple Deprivation (IMD) (Consumer Data Research Center n.d.), Digital Intelligence Index (DII) (Digital Planet n.d.), Digital Economy and Society Index (DESI) (European Commission n.d.), World Digital Competitiveness Ranking (IMD n.d.), Global Cybersecurity Index (GCI) (ITU n.d.), Open Data Barometer (ODB) (Open Data Barometer n.d.), and Global Innovation Index (GII) (World Intellectual Property Organization 2024a).

It should be noted that Armenia is included in most of the indexes mentioned. The examination of Armenia's position in various indices shows that it has mostly below-average or average positions. It is noticeable that Armenia ranks lowest in the index systems, where cybersecurity and institutional readiness are considered. These fields can be considered mainly vulnerable for the Republic of Armenia. Therefore, implementing more targeted and systemic measures is important in these fields.

Thus, it is necessary to cover some indices characterizing the level of digitalization of public administration and conduct a comparative analysis of countries according to these indicators.

3.1.1 E-Government Development Index (EGDI)

EGDI is a composite indicator that measures a country's preparedness to provide and employ e-government services. EGDI is the weighted average of three component indexes, which are the Online Service Index, the Telecommunication Infrastructure Index, and the Human Capital Component (UN E-Government Knowledgebase n.d.-b).

The average value of EGDI for Armenia has improved in 2024, reaching 0.6382 points instead of 0.6102 points in 2022. The data describing the distribution of the EGDI value by continents in 2024 (UN E-Government Knowledgebase n.d.-d) indicates that the index of Europe is significantly higher than the world average level, but Asia and America slightly exceed it.

According to the E-Government Development Index, there have been significant changes in the rankings of countries from 2003 to 2024. The UN E-Government Knowledgebase presents data on the top ten countries in the world according to the EGDI value (UN E-Government Knowledgebase n.d.-a).

According to the 2024 UN classification, Armenia ranks 48th out of 193 countries in the E-Government Development Index (EGDI), with a score of 0.8422 (Table 1) (UN E-Government Knowledgebase n.d.-d).

In the region (Armenia, Georgia, Azerbaijan, Iran, and Turkey), Turkey leads according to the 2024 EGDI index. Compared to 2022, Turkey significantly improved its score, rising 21 positions to rank 27th out of 193 countries. Armenia follows next in the region, having also made notable progress—advancing 16 places from 64th in 2022 to 48th in 2024 (UN E-Government Knowledgebase 2024).

3.1.2 Corruption Perception Index

According to the Corruption Perception Index published in 2024 by Transparency International Anticorruption Centre, the global level of corruption remains disturbingly high, while efforts to combat it are increasingly ineffective. According to the Corruption Perceptions Index (CPI), more than two-thirds of countries score below

Table 1 EGDI and E-Participation ranking, index values, and growth rates, 2016–2024

EGDI	**2024**	**2022**	**2020**	**2018**	**2016**
Rank for Armenia	*48*	*64*	*68*	*87*	*87*
Index value of Armenia	0.84	0.74	0.71	0.59	0.52
Annual growth rate of Armenia (%)	13.51	4.23	20.34	13.46	−11.86
Average growth rate of Armenia (%)	7.93				
World average index value	0.63	0.61	0.59	0.54	0.49
World annual growth rate (%)	3.28	3.39	9.26	10.2	4.2
World average growth rate (%)	6.07				
E-Participation	**2024**	**2022**	**2020**	**2018**	**2016**
Rank for Armenia	27	64	57	103	84
Index value of Armenia	0.85	0.58	0.75	0.57	0.52
Annual growth rate of Armenia (%)	46.56	−22.73	32.18	7.99	−0.75
Average growth rate of Armenia (%)	12.65				
World average index values	0.49	0.44	0.57	0.56	0.46
World annual growth rate (%)	11.36	−22.81	1.79	21.74	17.95
World average growth rate (%)	6.0				

Source: Compiled by the authors based on UN E-Government Knowledgebase (n.d.-b, c)

50 on a scale from 0 (highly corrupt) to 100 (very clean). The global average score remains unchanged at 43, underscoring the urgent need for stronger anticorruption measures worldwide.

The index shows the following (Transparency International Anticorruption Center 2025):

- Approximately 6.8 billion people live in the countries where CPI value is lower than 50, which is equivalent to 85% of the world's population of eight billion;
- For the seventh year in a row, Denmark leads the list (90 points), followed by Finland with almost equal results (88 points) and Singapore (84 points).

A country's CPI score is calculated as the arithmetic mean of the scores from all sources used in the assessment. In Armenia's case, the 2024 CPI score of 47 is the average of six different source scores used to determine the final value (Transparency International Anticorruption Center 2024).

The dynamics of Armenia's CPI score from 2012 to 2024 indicate overall improvement. Between 2012 and 2018, Armenia maintained a stable trend. From 2019 to 2024, the country achieved a significant increase in its index. In 2024, Armenia reached 47 points, sharing the 63rd–64th positions with Croatia (Transparency International Anticorruption Center 2025).

In the countries of the region, the leader in this index is Georgia with 53 points (53rd place). Armenia is in the second place (UN E-Government Knowledgebase 2024).

3.1.3 Global Innovation Index (GII)

Global Innovation Index provides a comprehensive analysis of the current state of global innovation. Global Innovation Index (GII) includes around 80 indicators, which are grouped into two sub-indicators: innovation resources (input) and innovation output (World Intellectual Property Organization n.d.).

These two sub-indices represent innovation capacity and performance of a country. The overall GII score is the average of the input and output sub-indices; countries are ranked based on their combined scores.

In the Global Innovation Index 2024 published by the World Intellectual Property Organization (WIPO), Armenia ranks 63rd globally, marking an improvement of 9 positions compared to the previous year. As an upper-middle-income country, Armenia holds 15th place among 34 countries in its income group. In terms of innovation output, Armenia ranks 55th. For innovation input (resources), it ranks 79th, indicating a high level of efficiency in converting available resources into tangible innovation outcomes (World Intellectual Property Organization 2024a; World Intellectual Property Organization 2024b).

According to Fig. 1, over the past 5 years, Armenia has made progress in the rankings of the Information and Communication Technologies (ICT) sub-index, rising 17 positions to reach 61st place in 2024 compared to 2019 (World Intellectual Property Organization 2024a).

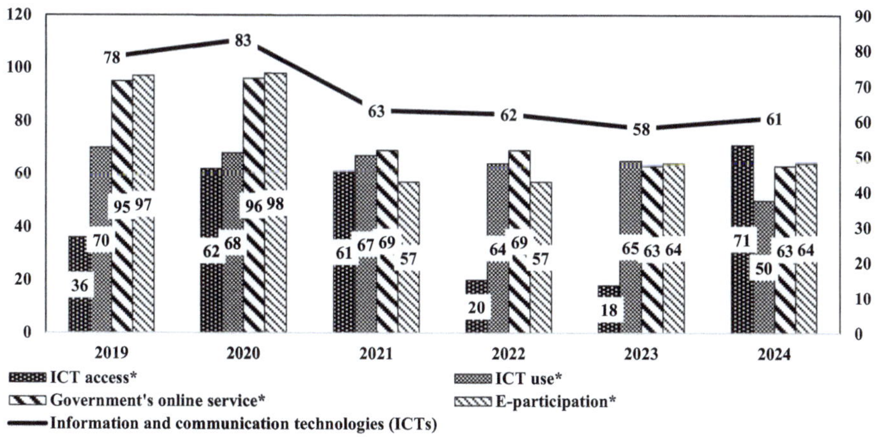

Fig. 1 Armenia's ranking points according to the information and communication technology (ICT) sub-index indicators for 2019–2024. Source: Compiled by the authors based on World Intellectual Property Organization (2024a)

3.2 *Multidimensional Classification of the Countries by Digitalization Indexes*

For a multidimensional classification of countries with different levels of digitalization, it is necessary to conduct a cluster analysis according to the E-Government development index (EGDI), Corruption Perceptions Index (CPI), and Global Innovation Index (GII).

According to clustering, 39 countries of the world were distributed into three clusters. The first and the second clusters include 14 countries each. The third one includes 11 countries.

According to the mentioned indices, the "best" performing group is Cluster 2, which has the highest average scores among the three clusters. This cluster includes leading countries such as Denmark, Estonia, South Korea, Japan, Norway, the USA, and several other European nations.

The third cluster is considered to be the "worst" in terms of its indicators, which mainly includes former CIS countries with below-average positions in the rankings.

The first cluster holds an intermediate position, with its indicators falling between those of the second and third clusters. This cluster includes such countries as Armenia, Georgia, China, Moldova, Lithuania, Latvia, and others.

In recent years, Armenia has generally shown positive progress in major international digitalization indices. This improvement can be attributed to several factors. Notably, the Armenian government's growing emphasis on digital development is reflected in the institutional launch of the reorganized Ministry of High-Tech Industry in 2019 (Ministry of High-Technological Industry of the Republic of Armenia n.d.). Another important step in the field was that Armenia joined the "Open Government Partnership" initiative in 2011 (Government of the Republic of

Armenia 2011) to improve the governance system by promoting transparency. As a result of these efforts, Armenia was recognized as the champion of the Asia-Pacific region in 2015 for its initiative to create and implement a municipal management information system. Additionally, the Centre for Strategic Initiatives developed a draft strategic document titled Armenia's Digital Agenda 2030 (Government of the Republic of Armenia 2017).

3.3 E-Participation

On a practical level, to observe and analyze the participatory governance toolkit and its implementation for Armenia, a classification must be done. Various organizations (OECD 2001; UNDESA 2014) and scholars classify the depth of interaction between the state and society into four main categories, which can be broadly summarized as: e-informing, e-consulting, e-involving (collaboration), and e-empowering (Al-Dalou and Abu-Shanab 2013).

The primary tool of e-informing is e-gov.am website. However, the crucial flaw of this website is that platforms that provide electronic services are not fully represented.

One example of an e-consulting tool is the website e-draft.am, which allows users to review draft legal acts submitted by various departments of the Republic of Armenia. Users can search for specific drafts, track their progress, view submitted proposals, and, if registered, submit their suggestions. The platform also provides access to summaries of submitted feedback, indicating which proposals were accepted or offering justifications for rejections. According to the website, it has 157,800 registered users and receives 10,000–15,000 daily visitors. However, there is a risk that some potential beneficiaries may not be able to participate due to a lack of awareness or access to information.

E-involving (collaboration) is facilitated through several platforms, some of which are fully operational, while others are either underperforming or still in development. The most effective platform is e-request.am, which enables users to submit online applications, inquiries, and complaints to government bodies. The site handles nearly 1000 submissions per day, with applications accounting for 62% of all messages. Additionally, all of Armenia's enlarged municipalities operate interactive websites based on the Municipal Management Information System (MMIS), enhancing local-level digital engagement.

A similar website operates for the city of Yerevan (activecitizen.yerevan.am). Nevertheless, its toolkit is quite weak. The website e-petition.am was launched in 2020 as a tool for e-democracy and public participation, allowing users to submit individual and collective petitions as part of the decision-making process. However, according to the site's statistics, the number of petitions submitted in 2024 did not exceed 100. A relatively more active platform is azdararir.am, which enables citizens to report incidents containing elements of a crime—either anonymously or by providing personal information. In 2024, the platform received an average of about one report per day. Unfortunately, Armenia currently lacks a functional e-empowering platform that would enable activities such as e-voting or crowdsourcing ideas for policymaking.

In summary, the spontaneous implementation style of e-government (particularly, e-participation) is noticed. Existing platforms do not provide the opportunity to propose functional improvements through electronic tools.

4 Conclusions

The index analysis, based on three key indicators that best reflect the development of digital government, shows that Armenia has made significant progress in recent years. As highlighted by the cluster analysis, Armenia falls within the "middle-position" cluster. Additionally, the evaluation of the country's e-participation level also indicates positive developments.

A more thorough observation of the digital governance of Armenia gave an opportunity to reveal the main existing problems and gaps in the field. Several suggestions were made on how these various problems could be addressed.

Existing problems require complex solutions for the Republic of Armenia, which relate to legislation, including the creation of a legislative system that is more protected from cyberattacks, and the provision of additional technical resources (e.g., in terms of creating a complex and comprehensive platform of integrated data).

There are several government agencies responsible for e-government. The management of this process should be done from a single center, which will exclude evasion of responsibility and slow down the process.

Although the state has already implemented a basic set of e-participation tools, the full development of a comprehensive e-participation system requires the inclusion of key functions, such as facilitating public discussions, expert evaluations, and the involvement of professionals in relevant fields. These elements would enable citizens and the professional community to participate more meaningfully and improve the quality of their proposals. By establishing institutional mechanisms for in-depth expert dialogue, it would become possible to better assess the feasibility, justification, and credibility of proposals submitted to the state or municipal authorities.

In general, new developments further emphasize the necessity to consider the improvement of digital governance in Armenia as a strategic direction for the country's development.

Data Availability

- Data on the E-Government Development Index (EGDI) by continents in 2024 is available at https://figshare.com/ with the identifier https://doi.org/10.6084/m9.figshare.28800890.

- Data on the top ten countries in the world by ECDI index in 2024 is available at https://figshare.com/ with the identifier https://doi.org/10.6084/m9.figshare.28785122.v1.
- Data on the EGDI index in the region in 2024 is available at https://figshare.com/ with the identifier https://doi.org/10.6084/m9.figshare.28779329.
- Data on the Corruption Perceptions Index of Armenia in 2012–2024 is available at https://figshare.com/ with the identifier https://doi.org/10.6084/m9.figshare.28783970.
- Data on the Corruption Perception Index in the region is available at https://figshare.com/ with the identifier https://doi.org/10.6084/m9.figshare.28784936.
- Data on the top countries in the world by Corruption Perception Index is available at https://figshare.com/ with the identifier https://doi.org/10.6084/m9.figshare.28785347.
- Data on the top ten countries by Global Innovation Index in 2024 is available at https://figshare.com/ with the identifier https://doi.org/10.6084/m9.figshare.28784957.
- Data on the countries' Cluster Membership is available at https://figshare.com/ with the identifier https://doi.org/10.6084/m9.figshare.28784984.
- Data on the Final Cluster Centers is available at https://figshare.com/ with the identifier https://doi.org/10.6084/m9.figshare.28785194.

References

Al-Dalou, R., and E. Abu-Shanab. 2013. E-participation levels and technologies. In *Proceedings of ICIT 2013: The 6th international conference on information technology*, 4–5. Amman, Jordan. https://tinyurl.com/6rwcek9y. Accessed 28 Feb 2025.

Alekseeva, M. V., and E. A. Filimonova. 2024. Theoretical and historical legal sciences. *Legal Order and Legal Values* 2 (2): 14–21. https://doi.org/10.23947/2949-1843-2024-2-2-14-21.

Avetisyan, L. 2024. *E-government survey-member states questionnaire*. https://publicadministration.un.org/egovkb/Portals/egovkb/MSQ2024/Armenia%20-%20MSQ2024%20.pdf. Accessed 28 Feb 2025.

Cisco. n.d. *Cisco digital readiness index*. https://www.cisco.com/c/en/us/about/csr/research-resources/digital-readiness.html. Accessed 28 Feb 2025.

Consumer Data Research Center. n.d. *Index of multiple deprivation (IMD)*. https://data.cdrc.ac.uk/dataset/index-multiple-deprivation-imd. Accessed 28 Feb 2025.

Digital Planet. n.d. *Digital intelligence index*. https://digitalintelligence.fletcher.tufts.edu/trajectory. Accessed 11 Feb 2025.

European Commission. n.d. *The digital economy and society index (DESI)*. https://digital-strategy.ec.europa.eu/en/policies/desi. Accessed 28 Feb 2025.

Government of the Republic of Armenia. 2011. *"Open government partnership" initiative*. https://www.gov.am/en/open-government/. Accessed 28 Feb 2025.

Government of the Republic of Armenia. 2017. *Armenia digital agenda—2030 long-term strategy presented*. November 29. https://www.gov.am/en/news/item/9211/. Accessed 28 Feb 2025.

IMD. n.d. *World digital competitiveness ranking*. https://www.imd.org/centers/wcc/world-competitiveness-center/rankings/world-digital-competitiveness-ranking/. Accessed 28 Feb 2025.

ITU. n.d. *Global cybersecurity index.* https://www.itu.int/en/ITU-D/Cybersecurity/pages/global-cybersecurity-index.aspx. Accessed 11 Feb 2025.

Ministry of High-Technological Industry of the Republic of Armenia. n.d. *About the ministry.* https://hightech.gov.am/en/ministry/about. Accessed 28 Feb 2025.

OECD. 2001. *Citizens as partners: Information, consultation and public participation in policy-making*. Paris, France: OECD Publishing. https://doi.org/10.1787/9789264195561-en.

Open Data Barometer. n.d. *The open data barometer.* https://opendatabarometer.org/. Accessed 28 Feb 2025.

Surfshark. 2024. *2024 digital quality of life index.* https://surfshark.com/research/dql. Accessed 28 Feb 2025.

Transparency International Anticorruption Center. 2024. *Armenia 2024: Corruption perception index in Armenia.* https://transparency.am/assets/documents/1739216454-11687-302.pdf. Accessed 22 Feb 2025.

Transparency International Anticorruption Center. 2025. *CPI 2024 results of Armenia and other countries*. February 11. https://transparency.am/en/media/news/article/5251. Accessed 28 Feb 2025.

UN E-Government Knowledgebase. 2024. *Compare countries.* https://publicadministration.un.org/egovkb/en-us/Data/Compare-Countries. Accessed 28 Feb 2025.

UN E-Government Knowledgebase. n.d.-a. *About.* https://publicadministration.un.org/egovkb/en-us/About. Accessed 28 Feb 2025.

UN E-Government Knowledgebase. n.d.-b. *E-government development index (EGDI).* https://publicadministration.un.org/egovkb/en-us/About/Overview/-E-Government-Development-Index. Accessed 28 Feb 2025.

UN E-Government Knowledgebase. n.d.-c. *E-participation index.* https://publicadministration.un.org/egovkb/en-us/About/Overview/E-Participation-Index. Accessed 28 Feb 2025.

UN E-Government Knowledgebase. n.d.-d. *Data center.* https://publicadministration.un.org/egovkb/en-us/data-center. Accessed 28 Feb 2025.

UNDESA. 2014. *UN E-government survey 2014: E-government for the future we want.* New York, NY: UNDESA. https://publicadministration.un.org/egovkb/portals/egovkb/documents/un/2014-survey/e-gov_complete_survey-2014.pdf. Accessed 28 Feb 2025.

World Intellectual Property Organization. n.d. *Global innovation index.* https://www.wipo.int/en/web/global-innovation-index. Accessed 28 Feb 2025.

World Intellectual Property Organization. 2024a. *Global innovation index 2024: Economy profile—Armenia.* https://www.wipo.int/gii-ranking/en/armenia/section/economy-profile. Accessed 28 Feb 2025.

World Intellectual Property Organization. 2024b. *Global innovation index 2024 ranks.* https://www.wipo.int/gii-ranking/en/rank. Accessed 28 Feb 2025.

Personalization of Customer Service in Retail Banking by Using Artificial Intelligence

Davit A. Sahakyan, Ruzan A. Sahakyan, Hayk A. Sargsyan, Hasmik A. Torosyan, and Gayane E. Sargsyan

Abstract The rapid evolution of artificial intelligence (AI) has revolutionized retail banking, shifting service delivery from traditional standardized models to intelligent, hyper-personalized experiences. AI-driven solutions powered by machine learning (ML), natural language processing (NLP), and predictive analytics are redefining customer engagement, satisfaction, and operational efficiency. This research aims to assess the impact of AI-driven personalization on banking performance and customer retention while addressing challenges related to AI governance and ethical considerations. The research employs qualitative research methods, provides a historical analysis of market trends, presents practical examples, and offers forecasts to assess the role of AI in enhancing customer interactions, generating recommendations for financial products, and detecting fraud. Additionally, it examines the pace of AI adoption, analyzes industry statistics, and evaluates the regulatory framework shaping AI-driven banking services. In addition to advantages, this research also examines key challenges associated with AI-driven service personalization in banking and finds out how global regulations impose strict AI governance measures. As a result, financial institutions must prioritize explainable AI (XAI) frameworks, ethical personalization strategies, and bias mitigation techniques. By analyzing these factors and balancing the benefits of AI adoption with the need to minimize associated risks in retail banking, this research proposes a comprehensive roadmap for the transparent, trustworthy, and regulatory-compliant implementation of AI. This roadmap aims to ensure fairness, customer-centricity, and alignment with ethical and legal standards.

Keywords Artificial intelligence • Customer service • Digital banking • Personalization • Retail banking

D. A. Sahakyan (✉)
French University in Armenia, Yerevan, Armenia
e-mail: davit.sahakyan@pers.ufar.am

R. A. Sahakyan · H. A. Sargsyan · H. A. Torosyan · G. E. Sargsyan
Armenian State University of Economics, Yerevan, Armenia

A. Karbekova (ed.), *Ethics of the AI Economy: A System View from the Positions of the Theory of Stakeholders*, Ethical Economy 73,
https://doi.org/10.1007/978-3-032-23423-0_35

JEL Codes C89 • G21 • G40

1 Introduction

Recent reports indicate that over 60% of retail banks globally invest in AI-driven personalization strategies, with an expected market growth of $138 billion by 2030 (Kovalenko and Komenchuk 2024). By leveraging recent market trends and real-world case studies, this research highlights how AI-powered chatbots, virtual assistants, and real-time predictive models are optimizing banking services, significantly improving customer retention and conversion rates. With AI adoption in banking projected to grow at 30–40% CAGR by 2027 (Statista 2025), financial institutions are integrating automated decision-making and behavioral analytics to enhance customer experience. Furthermore, predictive models estimate that over 80% of banking interactions will be AI-assisted by 2030, with AI-driven personalization reducing customer churn by 25–35% (McKinsey and Company 2024).

This research aims to examine the role of AI in personalizing customer service in retail banking, focusing on the following aspects:

- Analyzing AI-driven personalization techniques;
- Evaluating the impact of AI on customer satisfaction and operational efficiency;
- Assessing market statistics and future predictions for AI adoption in banking;
- Exploring the ethical, regulatory, and privacy concerns associated with AI-driven personalization;
- Development of a roadmap for AI implementation in compliance with contemporary international regulations.

2 Methodology

This research employs a qualitative approach to provide a comprehensive understanding of the implementation of AI in retail banking, particularly in providing personalized services to customers.

The following data sources are used for the research:

- Academic literature: Various types of algorithms and their concepts are examined; their implementation in retail banking is analyzed. Challenges, risks, and ethical concerns are also analyzed;
- Industry publications: These reports are used to analyze the evolution and future trends of digitalization and AI implementation in retail banking and its use cases and success stories.

3 Results

3.1 Evolution of Retail Banking and Customer Service

The historical evolution of retail banking has transitioned from traditional branch services to AI-powered digital experiences, reshaping customer interactions and operational models.

The customer service evolution in general and retail banking has also moved from in-person interactions to digital-first, AI-powered engagement models.

By 2025, AI-driven hyper-personalization will be the core of general and retail banking customer service.

In the evolving financial landscape, a customer-centric approach has become a fundamental strategy for banks aiming to enhance customer satisfaction, drive engagement, and maintain competitive advantage. This approach prioritizes the needs, preferences, and behaviors of customers, ensuring that banking products and services are tailored to provide a seamless and personalized experience.

Research by PwC indicates that 73% of customers consider their overall experience with a bank to be a critical factor in their financial decisions (PwC 2018). Furthermore, personalization has been shown to drive revenue growth in the banking sector. According to McKinsey, banks that implement AI-driven personalization in their services can increase their revenue by 10–15% (Manoharan 2024).

A customer-focused approach also serves as a key differentiator in an increasingly digital banking environment. With Accenture projecting that digital banking usage will reach 90% by 2025, banks must continuously innovate to meet evolving consumer expectations (Accenture 2024; PwC 2025). This includes enhancing mobile banking platforms, integrating AI-powered chatbots, and offering seamless omnichannel banking experiences (Figs. 1 and 2).

The data highlights the rapid evolution of digital banking, driven by increasing online and mobile banking adoption and the growing integration of AI in financial services.

Retail banking has transitioned from in-person branch interactions to digital-first AI-powered engagement models. A survey by Zendesk revealed that 72% of

Fig. 1 Global digital banking adoption. Source: Developed by the authors based on the materials of Smith and Abbott (2024)

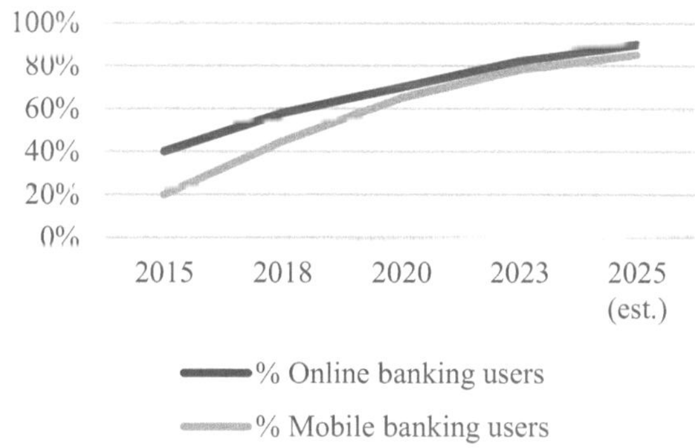

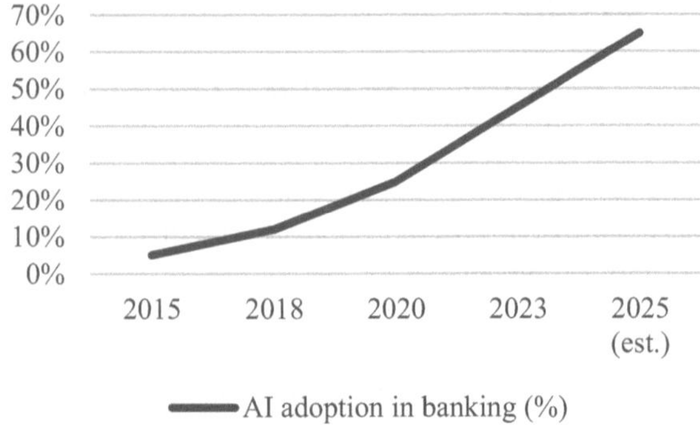

Fig. 2 AI adoption in banking (%). Source: Developed by the authors based on the materials of Smith and Abbott (2024)

customers consider personalization as "highly important"; 77% of banking leaders acknowledged that personalization leads to increased customer retention (Allocca 2024).

A study by Accenture suggests that banks can achieve up to a 6% increase in revenue within 3 years by integrating AI with human interactions, emphasizing the financial benefits of AI-driven personalization (Abbott 2024).

3.2 *AI-Based Models in Retail Banking*

There is a wide range of AI algorithms that are currently used in business, particularly in banking, which increases the efficiency of decision-making processes and customer relationship management. Let us explore the implementation of some of these algorithms in retail banking.

Linear regression is a statistical method used to predict continuous variables, making it particularly valuable in the banking sector for tasks such as loan pricing and market trend analysis (Provost and Fawcett 2013). Wells Fargo has successfully implemented an AI-driven linear regression model to predict fluctuations in loan interest rates. This approach has led to a 22% increase in loan pricing accuracy, subsequently improving approval rates (Filipsson 2025).

Logistic regression is a widely used statistical method for binary classification, making it particularly valuable in the banking sector for risk assessment and fraud detection. JPMorgan Chase has successfully implemented logistic regression-based risk prediction models to enhance credit risk assessment. This approach has led to a 20% reduction in default rates, thereby improving the accuracy of credit scoring (Rose 2025).

Decision trees are a widely used ML technique in banking for classification tasks, such as risk assessment and customer segmentation. Random forest, an ensemble learning method that enhances prediction accuracy by combining multiple decision trees, is particularly effective in improving fraud detection and customer segmentation. For example, Barclays has successfully implemented random forest models to detect credit card fraud in real-time, significantly reducing fraud-related losses and saving the bank approximately $3.5 billion annually (Barclays 2024).

K-Means clustering is an unsupervised ML algorithm widely utilized in banking for customer segmentation based on spending behavior. By analyzing customer data, HSBC identified distinct segments within their customer base and tailored their marketing strategies accordingly. This initiative led to a significant increase in personalized offer conversion rates of 150%, transforming passive clicks into genuinely engaged visitors (Novatiq 2025).

Transformer-based models (e.g., BERT, GPT, and T5) are advanced natural language processing (NLP) systems that excel in understanding and generating human-like text. These models have significantly transformed the banking sector by enhancing customer service and sentiment analysis. Bank of America's virtual assistant, Erica, leverages advanced AI to respond instantly to customer inquiries, thereby reducing the workload on call centers. Since its launch in 2018, Erica has surpassed two billion interactions, assisting over 42 million clients and handling approximately two million interactions daily (Newsroom 2024).

Market basket analysis (MBA) identifies customer purchasing patterns by determining products or services that are frequently bought together. By analyzing customer purchasing behaviors, American Express managed to identify product pairings that resonate with their clientele, leading to a significant increase in cross-sell revenue. This data-driven approach has resulted in a 35% boost in cross-sell revenue, demonstrating the efficacy of an MBA in financial services (Pardo 2024).

3.3 *Challenges and Ethical Considerations*

AI-driven personalization in banking relies on vast amounts of customer data to enhance financial services. However, this raises significant concerns regarding data security, unauthorized access, and privacy violations. Ensuring compliance with regulatory frameworks and implementing robust mitigation strategies are crucial to maintaining customer trust. Financial institutions are mandated to comply with data protection regulations such as the General Data Protection Regulation (GDPR) and the Payment Services Directive 2 (PSD2) in the European Union, and the California Consumer Privacy Act (CCPA) in California. These regulations are designed to safeguard user data and ensure transparent processing practices.

AI models in banking have the potential to improve efficiency and decision-making. Nevertheless, they can also inherit biases from historical data, leading to unfair treatment in areas such as loan approvals, credit scoring, and investment recommendations. If not properly managed, these biases can reinforce existing inequalities and expose financial institutions to legal and ethical challenges. For example, Wells Fargo faced a lawsuit alleging that its AI-driven mortgage underwriting system disproportionately denied applications from Black, Hispanic, and Asian borrowers or offered them less favorable terms than white applicants (Viancourt 2024).

While AI enhances efficiency and personalization in banking, many customers remain skeptical about AI-driven financial decisions due to concerns over transparency and lack of human oversight. Ensuring explainability and customer confidence is crucial for widespread AI adoption in the financial sector. A 2023 global study revealed that 61% of individuals are wary about trusting AI systems, and 67% report low to moderate acceptance of AI in banking (KPMG 2024). Customers expect explainability, human oversight, and clear reasoning behind AI-driven financial decisions, particularly in high-stakes areas such as loan approvals and investment recommendations.

As AI adoption in banking expands, regulators are strengthening AI governance policies to prevent unethical data usage, bias, and unfair financial practices. Compliance with evolving regulations is essential for banks to maintain transparency and ethical AI implementation. EU AI Act (2023) classifies AI-driven banking decisions as high-risk, mandating extensive compliance audits to ensure fairness and accountability in financial decision-making (European Parliament 2023).

3.4 Future Trends

It is expected that AI in the banking market will grow from $26 billion in 2024 to $138 billion by 2030 (Kovalenko and Komenchuk 2024).

As AI continues to reshape the banking sector, its future will be defined by hyper-personalization, emotional intelligence, blockchain integration, and enhanced AI-human collaboration. These advancements will drive efficiency, improve security, and create more personalized financial experiences for customers.

The next phase of AI in retail banking will focus on real-time, hyper-personalized financial services powered by advanced predictive models. AI will dynamically adjust loan rates, credit limits, and investment advice based on real-time behavioral data, ensuring tailored financial solutions.

Future AI models will incorporate emotional intelligence to improve customer interactions and financial decision-making. AI will analyze voice, text, and facial expressions to understand customer emotions, enabling more empathetic service. AI-powered virtual assistants will provide emotional support during financial crises, such as debt management and loan restructuring, ensuring a more human-like banking experience.

The fusion of AI and blockchain will enhance security, transparency, and reliability in financial transactions. AI-powered blockchain solutions will create secure and tamper-proof customer profiles, reducing fraud and unauthorized access.

Rather than replacing human advisors, AI will act as an intelligent co-pilot, providing insights while human experts make the final decisions. AI will assist financial advisors by analyzing real-time market trends, customer data, and risk factors, improving investment and lending decisions.

Despite the rapid adoption of AI in banking, several critical areas remain underexplored. Addressing these gaps will be essential for ensuring ethical, transparent, and customer-centric AI-driven financial services.

Ensuring fairness and transparency in AI-driven banking decisions remains a major challenge. Future research should focus on developing bias detection frameworks, explainable AI (XAI), and regulatory strategies to prevent algorithmic discrimination.

Understanding how customers emotionally react to AI-driven financial recommendations is crucial for building trust and improving adoption rates. Future studies should explore customer sentiment analysis, behavioral economics, and AI-human interaction dynamics in banking.

Many underserved populations lack access to essential financial knowledge. Research should investigate how AI-powered educational tools, chatbots, and virtual financial advisors can bridge the gap and improve financial literacy, particularly in low-income and emerging markets.

4 Conclusion

This research examined how AI-driven personalization is transforming customer satisfaction, operational efficiency, and financial product customization in retail banking, focusing on key AI technologies such as ML, NLP-based chatbots, predictive analytics, and recommendation engines.

The key takeaways are as follows:

- AI-based models significantly improve customer engagement and retention, as well as financial inclusion;
- Predictive analytics reduces customer churn, while AI-driven recommendation engines increase financial product conversion rates;
- AI-powered fraud detection systems prevent billions in financial losses annually by leveraging real-time transaction monitoring and anomaly detection;
- Despite its benefits, AI in banking faces critical challenges such as data privacy risks, algorithmic bias, and stringent regulatory compliance requirements.

4.1 Implications for Banks and Policymakers

The increasing adoption of AI-driven personalization in banking presents opportunities and challenges. To maximize benefits while mitigating risks, banks and policymakers must take proactive measures to ensure responsible AI implementation.

Banks must prioritize explainable AI (XAI) models that provide clear and interpretable financial recommendations. AI systems should be designed to reduce bias, enhance customer trust, and improve financial inclusion. Banks must implement robust encryption, strict access controls, and ethical AI governance to protect customer data.

Regulatory bodies must establish clear, enforceable AI policies, ensuring compliance with GDPR, CCPA, and PSD2 regulations. Policymakers should mandate periodic AI audits to assess model fairness, accuracy, and adherence to ethical standards.

4.2 Recommendations for AI-Driven Banking

To fully harness AI's potential while addressing ethical, regulatory, and operational risks, financial institutions should adopt a strategic approach to AI-driven banking. The following recommendations outline key areas for improvement:

- Banks should integrate AI automation with human oversight to enhance decision-making;
- Financial institutions must implement bias audits, explainable AI (XAI), and AI fairness frameworks to ensure ethical and unbiased decision-making;
- AI-driven tools like chatbots, virtual assistants, and recommendation engines should be leveraged to improve financial literacy among underserved and low-income populations.

4.3 Final Thoughts on the Future of AI in Retail Banking

As AI continues to evolve, the future of retail banking will be characterized by hyper-personalization, predictive analytics, and a customer-centric approach. It will set new standards for digital banking.

The next decade will be defined by AI-driven automation, enhanced personalization, and ethical AI governance. By prioritizing transparency, fairness, and customer empowerment, banks can ensure a seamless, secure, and customer-centric financial ecosystem, driving innovation while maintaining trust in AI-powered financial services.

References

Abbott, M. 2024. *Banking on AI banking top 10 trends for 2024*. https://www.accenture.com/content/dam/accenture/final/industry/banking/document/Accenture-Banking-Top-10-Trends-2024.pdf. Accessed 30 Jan 2025.

Accenture. 2024. *Banking: The future is back: Trends shaping the industry in 2025 and beyond*. https://www.accenture.com/content/dam/accenture/final/industry/banking/document/Accenture-Banking-Top-10-Trends-2025-Report.pdf#zoom=40. Accessed 30 Jan 2025.

Allocca, S. 2024. 4 ways personalization is evolving at top banks. *The Financial Brand*, February 4. https://thefinancialbrand.com/news/personalization/4-ways-personalization-is-evolving-at-top-banks-174569. Accessed 23 Jan 2025.

Barclays. 2024. *Annual report 2023*. https://home.barclays/content/dam/home-barclays/documents/investor-relations/reports-and-events/annual-reports/2023/Barclays-PLC-Annual-Report-2023.pdf. Accessed 30 Jan 2025.

European Parliament. 2023. *EU AI Act: First regulation on artificial intelligence*. https://www.europarl.europa.eu/topics/en/article/20230601STO93804/eu-ai-act-first-regulation-on-artificial-intelligence. Accessed 25 Jan 2025.

Filipsson, F. 2025. *AI case study: AI-powered trading algorithms at Goldman Sachs*. Redress Compliance. February 12. https://redresscompliance.com/ai-case-study-ai-powered-trading-algorithms-at-goldman-sachs/. Accessed 13 Feb 2025.

Kovalenko, D., and O. Komenchuk. 2024. *Top 15 AI trends in banking for 2025*. Uptech. December 6. https://www.uptech.team/blog/ai-trends-in-banking. Accessed 29 Jan 2025.

KPMG. 2024. *Trust in artificial intelligence: 2023 global study on the shifting public perceptions of AI*. https://kpmg.com/xx/en/our-insights/ai-and-technology/trust-in-artificial-intelligence.html. Accessed 28 Jan 2025.

Manoharan, G. 2024. Optimizing customer experience through AI-powered personalization in banking: Data engineering perspectives. *International Research Journal of Engineering and Technology* 11 (5): 1874–1888. https://www.irjet.net/archives/V11/i5/IRJET-V11I5257.pdf. Accessed 29 Jan 2025.

McKinsey & Company. 2024. *The state of AI in early 2024: Gen AI adoption spikes and starts to generate value*. Washington, DC: McKinsey Global Institute. May 30. https://www.mckinsey.com/~/media/mckinsey/business%20functions/quantumblack/our%20insights/the%20state%20of%20ai/2024/the-state-of-ai-in-early-2024-final.pdf. Accessed 30 Jan 2025.

Newsroom. 2024. *BofA's erica surpasses 2 billion interactions, helping 42 million clients since launch*. April 8. https://newsroom.bankofamerica.com/content/newsroom/press-releases/2024/04/bofa-s-erica-surpasses-2-billion-interactions%2D%2Dhelping-42-millio.html. Accessed 28 Jan 2025.

Novatiq. 2025. *150% uplift in conversion rates for HSBC*. https://www.novatiq.com/casestudy/marketer-success-story-150-uplift-in-conversion-rates-for-hsbc/. Accessed 28 Jan 2025.

Pardo, E. 2024. *A look inside American Express's cross-sell strategies*. May 8. https://welcome.comperemedia.com/insights/financial-services/a-look-inside-american-expresss-cross-sell-strategies. Accessed 17 Jan 2025.

Provost, F., and T. Fawcett. 2013. *Data science for business: What you need to know about data mining and data-analytic thinking*. 1st ed. Sebastopol, CA: O'Reilly Media.

PwC. 2018. *Experience is everything: Here's how to get it right*. https://www.pwc.de/de/consulting/pwc-consumer-intelligence-series-customer-experience.pdf. Accessed 15 Jan 2025.

PwC. 2025. *2025 AI business predictions*. https://www.pwc.com/us/en/tech-effect/ai-analytics/ai-predictions.html. Accessed 21 Jan 2025.

Rose, C. 2025. *AI: Driving smarter, faster credit risk decisions for banks*. January 13. https://www.cedar-rose.com/blog/ai-driving-smarter-faster-credit-risk-decisions-for-banks. Accessed 24 Jan 2025.

Smith, K., and M. Abbott. 2024. *Banking in the age of generative AI*. Accenture. February 28. https://www.accenture.com/us-en/insights/banking/generative-ai-banking. Accessed 30 Jan 2025.

Statista. 2025. *Estimated value of the banking sector's artificial intelligence (AI) and generative artificial intelligence (gen AI) spending in the Americas in 2024, with forecasts until 2028*. February 6. https://www.statista.com/statistics/1557315/americas-banking-sector-ai-spending-forecast/. Accessed 30 Jan 2025.

Viancourt, P. 2024. *AI is already costing financial institutions millions: Here's how to manage the risks*. May 30. https://www.ncontracts.com/nsight-blog/ai-is-costing-financial-institutions-millions. Accessed 21 Jan 2025.

Exploring Patterns in E-Government Development: A Multivariate Approach

Armen M. Ktoyan and Ani S. Khachatryan

Abstract Recent achievements in digital technologies have caused significant changes in the global economy. Digital technologies have resulted in ongoing innovation in almost all sectors of the economy, leading to changes in the essence and structure of products and services. Digital technologies have also affected public service delivery, known as e-government, where citizens are actively involved. To monitor the performance of countries and evaluate the progress on the scope and quality of e-service deliveries, the benchmark on e-government is required. It will allow revealing the readiness of countries for digitalization, identify main areas where extra efforts are required for improvement, adjust priorities and enhance the effectiveness of public services, and foster the active use of digital technologies to deliver government services. During this research, the authors aim to provide insight into patterns of digital government development and identify the level of digital readiness maturity. For this purpose, the authors used cluster and factor analyses based on the components of e-government, e-participation, and digital readiness indices for 143 countries. The analysis explores three groups of countries: "Emerging e-governments," "Digital governance adopters," and "Champions." Moreover, the authors conducted a factor analysis to measure the progress of countries on the "Digital Governance Driven" factor. The findings are vital for benchmarking e-government progress and revealing digital governance gaps, providing guidance on the improvement of e-services, enhancing digital readiness, and encouraging e-involvement.

Keywords E-government · Digital technology · Cluster analysis · Digitalization · Factor analysis

JEL Codes H11 · L86 · O33

A. M. Ktoyan (✉) · A. S. Khachatryan
Armenian State University of Economics, Yerevan, Armenia

A. Karbekova (ed.), *Ethics of the AI Economy: A System View from the Positions of the Theory of Stakeholders*, Ethical Economy 73,
https://doi.org/10.1007/978-3-032-23423-0_36

1 Introduction

The impact of the digital technology on global economic development is undeniable. The development of ICTs inevitably penetrates different segments, including government. In literature, the diffusion of technology in the delivery of government services is known as "e-government." Economists use different terms, such as "digital government" and "mobile government," to refer to the usage of digital technologies in the government sector that enhances the communication between the government, public, and business sectors (Huda et al. 2022). The integration of digital technologies into governance structures helps reduce administrative costs, modernize public administration, foster accountability, encourage public participation, and increase efficiency and the quality of online services (Kawabata and Camargo 2023). However, the pace of adoption and diffusion of digital technologies in government sectors is different in various countries due to information and communication infrastructures, the level of innovation and digital readiness, human capital, and socio-economic development. Therefore, the authors assessed the level of digital government, applying cluster and factor analysis based on a wide range of indicators that describe the country's digital governance capabilities: e-government, e-participation, and digital readiness. The research aims to highlight the benchmark of e-governments, evaluate their performance and progress, reveal gaps, identify similarities and disparities among different groups of countries, and unveil patterns of digital governance that are crucial in decision-making for reviewing targets, adjusting priorities, and implementing more effective governance frameworks.

2 Materials and Methods

The literature widely accepts that digital technology is the engine of economic development through improving the quality and efficiency of economic structure, enhancing the level of total factor productivity (Antonelli 2003), upgrading industrial structure, and forming a way to the high-quality and sustainable development of the economy (Sledziewska and Włoch 2021; Su et al. 2021). High-quality economic development can be achieved by improving decision-making, increasing the efficiency of allocating resources, and enhancing production efficiency by transforming technological achievements into productive forces with new technologies. The digitalization of the economic structure can help leap the "middle-income trap" and overcome the problems regarding low-value production activities and scarcity of functional upgrades, as well as move from low-value to high-value activities in global production networks, which will cause the transformation of economic growth from "quantitative change" to "qualitative change" (Qi and Chu 2022). The digital economy provides effective new development ideas to find solutions to essential economic issues and boosts wealth. It is a key driver of economic growth that paves the path to common prosperity (Li and Ma 2023).

The scope of national digital economy strategies includes national strategies regarding ICTs, e-government, and cybersecurity strategies that used to co-exist with other complementary strategies, such as national innovation strategies or development strategies. Particularly, the following significant pillars of national digital economy strategies can be distinguished:

- Develop telecommunications infrastructure and provide access to the Internet;
- Promote the ICT sector;
- Strengthen e-government services that will provide access to public sector information and data;
- Strengthen trust, including digital identities, privacy, and security.

In this context, an important component of national digital economy strategies is the continuous effort to provide e-governance (OECD 2015). E-governance is perceived as the application of electronic means, firstly in government-citizen and government-business interactions. Moreover, it involves the application of electronic means in internal government operations to improve governance (Backus 2001). R. Heeks illustrates e-governance as the application of ICTs to enhance public sector processes and service delivery. He highlights three main positive impacts of e-governance: the improvement of government administrative operations, the connection of citizens, and the fostering of external transactions (Heeks 2001). According to the UN E-Government Survey, e-governance is a driver of sustainable development that improves people's access to public services. Digital technologies play a pivotal role in supporting the provision of public services and fundamental services in health, education, safety, and security. E-governance is the milestone for evolving efficient, resilient, accountable, and inclusive institutions enabling the provision of public online services that are important for sustainable development (United Nations 2022).

S. Basu outlined the importance of e-governance as "more than just a government website on the Internet." According to the author, its objective is to support better management of government, citizens, and businesses. In other words, it aims to ensure effective governance of social and economic resources in the country to benefit its citizens. Providing government services that meet people's primary needs makes governments more transparent, responsive, and accountable when struggling with corruption, which is typical for developing countries. He affirmed that e-governance helps bridge "the digital divide" (the gap between the educated elite and uneducated poor) and enhances the standard of living (Basu 2004).

H. Margetts, P. Dunleavy, S. Bastow, and J. Tinkler studied the impact of e-government and affirmed that the use of ICTs by government agencies may reduce transaction costs in the development of policy innovations based on technology innovation (Heeks 2001; Margetts et al. 2003).

In the literature, numerous studies have been conducted on the observation and assessment of the outputs of e-government based on the descriptive indicators that evaluate the performance of e-government. Heeks recommended the model for assessing the success and failure of e-government based on the seven dimensions: information, technology, processes, objectives and values, staffing and skills, management systems and structures, and other resources (time and money). Based on these dimensions, the design-reality gap is estimated, which reveals mismatches between e-government project design and reality, focusing on reducing the gap and mitigating the risk of e-government failure through ongoing monitoring and actions Heeks (2003).

Based on the previous 18 selected studies, Huda, Kurniasari, and Ruroh suggest a pyramid model for the evaluation of the quality of e-government holistically based on the following three main dimensions:

- User satisfaction including reliability and efficiency, compatibility, perceived benefit, trust, responsiveness, and overall satisfaction;
- Site quality, including information quality, system quality, service quality, perceived usefulness, ease of use, accessibility, security and privacy, effectiveness design, and content;
- Facilitating conditions, including IT infrastructure (Huda et al. 2022).

Chen and Aklikokou applied a two-step cluster analysis based on cross-national secondary data for 191 countries to measure how the development of e-government is related to the government's effectiveness and control of corruption. The results affirmed the positive relationship between e-governments' development and government effectiveness and control of corruption (Chen and Aklikokou 2019). Using descriptive statistics, correlation, and cluster analysis, Machova and Lnenicka (2016) grouped countries and examined the specific challenges, trends, and the progress of e-government in 2008–2014 in the European Union countries to uncover similarities and define areas that were affected by the European recession in 2007 and the European debt crisis since the end of 2009. Choudhari, Banwet, and Gupta (2010) conducted cluster analysis on risk and performance variables and identified three subgroups: low, medium, and high-risk e-government projects. They evolved a risk evaluation model in India. Páez, Parra Fonseca, and Rios Incio (2024) applied factor analysis distinguishing three factors (e-administration, e-services, and e-democracy) and analyzed the importance of each factor to measure e-governance.

As a result of the literature review, the authors chose cluster and factor analysis for e-government performance assessments. The analyses were conducted using SPSS package for 143 countries based on the indicators of e-governance, e-participation and digital readiness (Table 1).

During the research, the authors applied cluster analysis to classify countries based on the wide range of indicators describing the quality and digitalization status of public service delivery. The necessity of the usage of cluster analysis in this research is mostly related to the fact that it allows for discovering the interconnections of the objects and implementing scientifically justified classification (Jain and Dubes 1988). First, the authors carried out hierarchical clustering to find the optimal number of clusters. According to the results of clustering, the optimal number of clusters is equal to the subtraction of the number of observations (i.e., 143) and the number of steps (i.e., 140), after which the coefficient of squared Euclidean distance dramatically changes. Thus, the optimal number of clusters is 3. Then, the k-means method was applied to diversify clusters and conduct variance analysis (ANOVA) (Orlova 2009). Based on the number of clusters, the final cluster centers are calculated to interpret cluster profiles and identify the characteristics of e-government for

Table 1 The indicators and sources

Components	Description	Indicators	Source
E-Government Development Index (EGDI)	Evaluates the development of e-government	• Online Service Index • Human Capital Index • Telecommunication Infrastructure Index	UNeGovKB
E-Participation Index (EPI)	Assesses citizen involvement in decision-making through digital platforms	• E-Information • E-Consultation • E-Decision-making	UNeGovKB
Digital Readiness Index (DRI)	Measures the country's ability to adopt and leverage digital technologies	• Basic Needs • Ease of Doing Business • Start-up environment • Technology Infrastructure • Business and Government Investment • Human Capital • Technology Adoption	CISCO

Source: Developed by the authors based on EGDI, EPI (UN EGOVKB n.d.) and DRI (CISCO 2021)

each group of countries. As a result, the countries with the same digital governance development status will appear in the same group.

The authors also used the method of factor analysis that helps reduce dimensionality and identify latent variables that contribute to e-government.

First, several tests are required to determine the strength of the correlation between the variables (Yong and Pearce 2013). The Kaiser-Meyer-Olkin (KMO) test was carried out, which gave a result of 0.909, which affirms that the dataset is adequate for factor analysis.

Bartlett's Test of Sphericity was also applied. The null hypothesis of this test is that the variables are orthogonal (not correlated). The result of the p-value was 0.000, confirming that the variables are significantly correlated to justify factor analysis. The results of both tests affirm that the data is suitable and factor analysis can proceed.

Factor analysis was performed by applying the Principal Component Analysis (PCA) extraction method. Once factors were extracted, Varimax rotation was used as an orthogonal rotation method to perform the factor loadings that represent the correlation between the variables and factors (Harman 1976). The results of factor analysis contribute to revealing the main factor of the digitalization of public services, unveiling the main issues, redefining targets, and reordering priorities.

3 Results

To reveal the quality of public service delivery and the extent of digitalization, the authors implemented a cluster analysis using the components of the e-governance index, e-participation index, and digital readiness index. The results help to group 143 countries based on their similarities and distinguish those groups considering their characteristics. It will help to unveil hidden patterns of digitalization for different groups of countries and consider each group and unique model of e-government.

As a result, three clusters are distinguished. The vast majority of countries are included in Cluster 2. Cluster 3 is the smallest, containing only 26 countries. Cluster 1 includes 48 countries. The results of ANOVA show that all indicators are statistically significant in the classification. The analysis of final cluster centers allows for defining the identity of each cluster by revealing their distinguished features (Table 2). Thus, Cluster 3 has the highest mean values for all indicators and is considered a target for others. Therefore, it is named as "Champions". Countries involved in this group are outstanding in innovation, progressive, and leading in e-government.

Cluster 1 is described as having the lowest final centers. These countries face challenges regarding the interaction between citizens and government and the availability of participatory services available on government websites. Therefore, it is necessary to take active measures to overcome these issues, make progress in the digitalization of public service deliveries through increasing the quality of online services and developing telecommunication infrastructure and human capital, and enhance the facilities deployed by the government to encourage the citizens' engagement in significant governmental activities. Therefore, this cluster is named as "Emerging e-governments."

As far as countries in Cluster 2 are concerned, they have succeeded in e-government readiness to some extent, demonstrating a high level of ICT-based service deliveries, a wide scope of online services, and broader public involvement in digital government services. However, those accomplishments are insufficient for becoming leaders. The underperformance in technology adoption, technology infrastructure, and fostering a business environment to promote investments impede the achievement of higher adoption and diffusion of digitalization. Therefore, this cluster was named "Digital governance adopters."

Table 2 Final cluster centers

	Cluster		
	1	2	3
EPI	0.28198	0.63886	0.86880
Online_Service	0.38449	0.72518	0.90367
HCI	0.42494	0.75616	0.91731
Telecommun_infrastr.	0.40956	0.85452	0.95797
Basic_needs	−1.16417	0.50072	0.87038
Business,Gov. Invest	−0.72146	−0.15507	1.74654
Ease_of_doing_business	−1.01583	0.21797	1.24346
Start_up_environment	−0.56688	−0.20101	1.46000
Technology_adoption	−1.05646	0.20478	1.30308
Technology_infrastr.	−1.04625	0.16986	1.48962

Source: Calculated and developed by the authors based on EGDI, EPI (UN EGOVKB n.d.), and DRI (CISCO 2021)

Based on the results, a comparative analysis can be conducted. Thus, cluster membership shows that countries with the highest level of economic development and progressive innovation systems are mostly included in Cluster 3. This group of countries includes Switzerland, Sweden, Austria, the USA, the United Kingdom, Denmark, Canada, and others. These countries stand out among others with advanced services, developed infrastructures, strong citizen involvement, and institutional support.

Cluster 1 consists of least-developed African countries such as Bolivia, Congo, Benin, and Chad. These countries performed with limited facilities and ICTs used by the government, less developed public sector infrastructure, and lower engagement of citizens in online platforms. Hence, large-scale reforms are needed in these countries to realize their full potential in the improvement of efficiency and quality of public service delivery through digital technologies.

Cluster 2 mostly includes developing (including EAEU) countries such as Russia, Armenia, Belarus, Kazakhstan, Kyrgyzstan, Georgia, Argentina, Belarus, and Bulgaria. These countries initiated reforms to achieve the digitalization of public services and improve the interaction between the government and citizens. It contains countries with efficient public services but limited citizen engagement and growing e-services but strong public involvement.

This approach helps to point out the main weaknesses that should be in the scope of attention, redefine targets, adjust priorities, and implement more effective policies to achieve those targets and boost the adoption and diffusion of digital technologies in public services.

Behind cluster analysis, the authors applied factor analysis to obtain a broader perception of digitalization models prevailing in various countries.

According to the results, 75.8% of the variation across e-government, e-participation, and digital readiness indicators is explained by only one factor. Therefore, only this factor is enough to account for most of the variability. In other words, only one composite variable is sufficient to represent the key information about the digitalization of public services.

Observing this factor and revealing its main descriptive parameters (e.g., factor loadings), valuable conclusions can be made regarding the contribution of original indicators to Factor 1. Thus, Factor 1 has the strongest statistical relationship with the variables of technology infrastructure, technology adoption, and human capital, whereas it is less correlated with start-up environment and business and government investment indicators. In other words, strong ICT and advanced digital technologies mostly contribute to the first principal component. Therefore, Factor 1 can be interpreted as a "Digital governance driven" factor, as a measure of the digitalization of public service delivery. Table 3 shows that Singapore, Iceland, the USA, Denmark, Sweden, and other developed countries demonstrate the strongest performance in e-government, e-participation, and digital readiness. The experience of these countries can be perceived as the best practices of improvement for low-factor value countries that have weak digital governance, lower public engagement in online services, and less developed infrastructure (Table 3).

Table 3 Factor values by countries. "Digital governance driven" factor

Singapore	1.992	Estonia	1.508	Norway	1.413
Iceland	1.861	the UK	1.503	Australia	1.395
the USA	1.820	Netherlands	1.503	Germany	1.357
Denmark	1.764	New Zealand	1.493	Japan	1.354
Sweden	1.626	Finland	1.472	UAE	1.255
Luxembourg	1.619	Switzerland	1.413	Canada	1.229
South Korea	1.613	Ireland	1.413		

Source: Calculated and developed by the authors based on EGDI, EPI (UN EGOVKB n.d.) and DRI (CISCO 2021)

4 Conclusion

During the research, the authors analyzed e-governance, e-participation, and digital readiness in 143 countries for 2024. First, using cluster analysis, the authors classified countries based on a wide range of indicators describing digital governance. This approach helped discover the similarities within the cluster and differences among clustered countries in terms of the autonomy of public services, e-participation, and digital readiness. Each cluster was observed as a unique development pattern towards digital public service delivery. The authors distinguished three clusters: "Emerging e-governments," "Digital governance adopters," and "Champions." Developed countries with a progressive digital public service, developed ICTs, and active engagement of citizens are included in the cluster of "Champions." In turn, the least developed countries with less developed technological infrastructure, less technological adoption, limited e-governance, and low e-participation are grouped in the cluster "Emerging e-governments," revealing the necessity of reforms. Most developing countries, including EAEU countries, are involved in the "Digital governance adopters" cluster. These countries have initiated some efforts towards e-governance. However, the results confirm that those measures were not sufficient enough to reach the cluster of "Champions."

The factor analysis makes it possible to reveal the "Digital governance driven" factor and its priorities. The factor is highly associated with digitalization and sophisticated public service delivery with the usage of digital technologies. Combining cluster and factor analysis, it stemmed that the countries with higher factor value of "Digital governance driven" factor are grouped in the "Champions" cluster, which stands out among others with the highest level of performance in digital governance, strong citizen participation, advances public services, and developed telecommunication infrastructure. The least developed countries have lower factor scores because of underdeveloped e-government, limited technological capacities, outdated telecommunication infrastructure, and low public engagement in e-services. This approach of cluster and factor analyses are essential techniques that enable policymakers to evaluate and benchmark the e-government performance, outline the main challenges that impede the implementation of e-government initiatives, identify areas of improvement of e-services, review targets, redefine priorities, and contribute to the enhancement of the scope and quality of digital public services.

References

Antonelli, C. 2003. The digital divide: Understanding the economics of new information and communication technology in the global economy. *Information Economics and Policy* 15 (2): 173–199. https://doi.org/10.1016/S0167-6245(02)00093-8.

Backus, M. 2001. *E-governance and developing countries: Introduction and examples* (Research Report No. 3). Hague, Netherlands: International Institute for Communication and Development (IICD). https://bibalex.org/baifa/Attachment/Documents/119334.pdf. Accessed 4 Apr 2025.

Basu, S. 2004. E-government and developing countries: An overview. *International Review of Law, Computers & Technology* 18 (1): 109–132. https://doi.org/10.1080/13600860410001674779.

Chen, L., and A. K. Aklikokou. 2019. Relating e-government development to government effectiveness and control of corruption: A cluster analysis. *Journal of Chinese Governance* 6 (1): 155–173. https://doi.org/10.1080/23812346.2019.1698693.

Choudhari, R. D., D. K. Banwet, and M. P. Gupta. 2010. Assessment of risk in e-governance projects: An application of product moment correlation and cluster analysis techniques. *Electronic Government, an International Journal* 8 (1): 85–102. https://doi.org/10.1504/EG.2011.037699.

CISCO. 2021. *Digital readiness index 2021*. https://www.cisco.com/c/m/en_us/about/corporate-social-responsibility/research-resources/digital-readiness-index.html#/. Accessed 4 Apr 2025.

Harman, H. H. 1976. *Modern factor analysis*. 3rd ed. Chicago, IL: University of Chicago Press.

Heeks, R. 2001. *Understanding e-governance for development*. Manchester, UK: Institute for Development Policy and Management. https://doi.org/10.13140/RG.2.2.14715.46882.

Heeks, R. 2003. *Most eGovernment-for-development projects fail: How can risks be reduced?* Manchester, UK: Institute for Development Policy and Management. https://hummedia.manchester.ac.uk/institutes/gdi/publications/workingpapers/igov/igov_wp14.pdf. Accessed 4 Apr 2025.

Huda, M. N., E. N. Kurniasari, and S. M. Ruroh. 2022. A systematic literature review of e-government evaluation. *Journal of Local Government Issues [LOGOS Journal]* 5 (1): 32–48. https://doi.org/10.22219/logos.v5i1.19784.

Jain, A. K., and R. C. Dubes. 1988. *Algorithms for clustering data*. Upper Saddle River, NJ: Prentice-Hall.

Kawabata, M. K., and A. S. Camargo Jr. 2023. E-government innovation initiatives in public administration: A systematic literature review and a research agenda. *Administration & Society* 55 (9): 1873–1904. https://doi.org/10.1177/00953997231185847.

Li, N., and Z. Ma. 2023. The digital economy is an important path to boosting common prosperity. *Applied Mathematics and Nonlinear Sciences* 9 (1): 169–180. https://doi.org/10.2478/amns.2023.2.00169.

Machova, R., and M. Lnenicka. 2016. Modelling e-government development through the years using cluster analysis. *JeDEM—eJournal of eDemocracy and Open Government* 8 (1): 62–83. https://doi.org/10.29379/jedem.v8i1.412.

Margetts, H., P. Dunleavy, S. Bastow, and J. Tinkler. 2003. Leaders and followers: E-government, policy innovation and policy transfer in the European Union. In *EUSA conference*. Nashville, TN: EUSA. https://aei.pitt.edu/6549/1/000437_1.PDF. Accessed 4 Apr 2025.

OECD. 2015. *OECD digital economy outlook 2015*. Paris, France: OECD Publishing. https://doi.org/10.1787/9789264232440-en.

Orlova, I. V., ed. 2009. *Multidimensional statistic analyze in economic problems: Computer modelling in SPSS: Textbook*. Moscow, Russia: University Textbook.

Páez, Á. E. P., C. P. Fonseca, and F. R. Rios Incio. 2024. Design and validation of an instrument to measure e-governance through factor analysis. *Data and Metadata* 3:332–332. https://doi.org/10.20944/preprints202405.0017.v1.

Qi, Y., and X. Chu. 2022. Development of the digital economy, transformation of the economic structure and leaping of the middle-income trap. *China Political Economy* 5 (1): 14–39. https://doi.org/10.1108/CPE-09-2022-0012.

Sledziewska, K., and R. Włoch. 2021. The foundations of the digital economy. In *The economics of digital transformation: The disruption of markets, production, consumption, and work*, ed. K. Sledziewska and R. Włoch, 1–17. London, UK: Routledge. https://doi.org/10.4324/9781003144359-1.

Su, J., K. Su, and S. Wang. 2021. Does the digital economy promote industrial structural upgrading? A test of mediating effects based on heterogeneous technological innovation. *Sustainability* 13 (18): 10105. https://doi.org/10.3390/su131810105.

UN EGOVKB. n.d. *E-Government Development Index (EGDI).* https://publicadministration.un.org/egovkb/en-us/About/Overview/-E-Government-Development-Index? Accessed 4 Apr 2025.

United Nations. 2022. *United Nations e-government survey 2022: The future of digital government*. New York, NY: UNDESA. https://ifap.ru/library/book652.pdf. Accessed 4 Apr 2025.

Yong, A. G., and S. Pearce. 2013. A beginner's guide to factor analysis: Focusing on exploratory factor analysis. *Tutorials in Quantitative Methods for Psychology* 9 (2): 79–94. https://doi.org/10.20982/tqmp.09.2.p079.

Conclusion: Aggravation of Ethical Contradictions of the AI Economy in the Conditions of the Fifth Industrial Revolution and Ways to Resolve Them

Aziza B. Karbekova

The primary conclusion of this book is that ethics is the cornerstone for the development of the AI economy. Collectively, the chapters of this book illuminate and describe an ethical path for the AI economy—one that offers it a powerful impulse toward sustainable development, making it less contradictory, more humane, and more environmentally conscious. The key findings of the book can be summarized as follows, along with the author's specific conclusions drawn from them:

- The use of neural networks is accompanied by numerous cyber threats (e.g., cyber fraud, cyber extremism, and cybercrime), which present serious ethical challenges to the AI economy. These threats diminish quality of life, undermine sustainability, and hinder growth. To uphold ethics more fully in the AI economy, a targeted, active, and systemic response is required. This includes implementing an ethical model for organizing smart cities, ensuring balanced consideration of stakeholder interests during the introduction of smart innovations, and promoting ethical human resource management in smart industries;
- For the AI economy to develop sustainably, its ethical dimensions of social adaptation and human communication must be thoroughly addressed. This calls for the humanization of smart marketing, careful analysis and incorporation of public opinion in the information society, state support for institutions that uphold social identity in the digital age, and a broader humanization of digital civilization;
- The ethics of machine learning within the AI economy should be governed by stakeholder theory. This requires integrating ethical business and regulatory practices into various communication channels: human-machine (involving neural networks, chatbots, and voice assistants), machine-to-machine (based on

A. B. Karbekova
Jalal-Abad State University named after B. Osmonov, Jalal-Abad, Kyrgyzstan
e-mail: aziza-karbekova@mail.ru

A. Karbekova (ed.), *Ethics of the AI Economy: A System View from the Positions of the Theory of Stakeholders*, Ethical Economy 73,
https://doi.org/10.1007/978-3-032-23423-0

the Internet of Things), and AI-mediated human communication (such as voice-to-text input, machine translation, and automated proofreading for errors and typos);
- The ethical boundaries of smart automation in the state regulation of the AI economy extend through industrial automation, which requires humanization, and through the development of e-government systems, which demand increased social orientation.

Thus, the book provides a critical reassessment—a "reverse view" of the AI economy—revealing the hidden side behind its high productivity, digital competitiveness, and technological leadership. Beneath the surface lies a range of ethical inconsistencies that provoke criticism from all stakeholder groups.

The methodology proposed in this book, along with its suite of practical tools and governance measures, has scientific and applied value. It enables comprehensive monitoring, thorough consideration, and enforcement of stakeholder interests in state regulation and corporate governance of AI economy development. The introduced ethical approach to smart automation makes crisis management possible, enhances the AI economy's attractiveness and viability for all stakeholders, and helps soften its contradictions and rough edges. This is the principal advantage of the author's approach.

Additionally, although this book outlines the ethical trajectory of AI economy development in the present day, the model continues to evolve, suggesting a high likelihood of new ethical challenges emerging in the future. Based on the findings of this research, we can conclude that the AI economy remains insufficiently ethical even at this early stage of smart automation. This leads to the reasonable expectation that ethical contradictions may intensify in the coming years under the conditions of the Fifth Industrial Revolution.

This book has revealed several key risks for the AI economy of the future. Among them is the risk of entire economic and geographic areas becoming depopulated, as both workers and residents are displaced. There is also the risk of transitioning from intelligent support for human resource management (HRM) to its total smart automation. From the standpoint of economic ethics, special attention must be paid to the socio-psychological adaptation of digital workers to being managed by AI systems.

Moreover, it is crucial to consider the risk of exponential increases in AI functionality and its expansion into new sectors of economic activity—areas where fundamentally new ethical conflicts may arise. Of particular concern is the risk associated with processing large volumes of personal data within the AI economy, including the potential for leaks and breaches of confidential information.

These anticipated risks of escalating ethical contradictions in the AI economy, especially in the context of the Fifth Industrial Revolution, and potential ways of resolving them, require further academic investigation—an endeavor proposed for future volumes.

MIX
Papier aus verantwortungsvollen Quellen
Paper from responsible sources
FSC® C105338
FSC
www.fsc.org

If you have any concerns about our products,
you can contact us on
ProductSafety@springernature.com

In case Publisher is established outside the EU,
the EU authorized representative is:
Springer Nature Customer Service Center GmbH
Europaplatz 3, 69115 Heidelberg, Germany

Printed by Libri Plureos GmbH
in Hamburg, Germany